Love,
to Dorothy (Merka)
White -

Pauline Ruffin

The Other One

This is a collection of memories and events as recalled by the author. No claim is made or implied that this work is factually verified or can stand any legal scrutiny. The reader may accept the accounts or not, with no recourse.

The cabin painting on the cover is by Jackie Clark.

ISBN-13: 978-1492190462
ISBN-10: 1492190462

This is a self-published book.

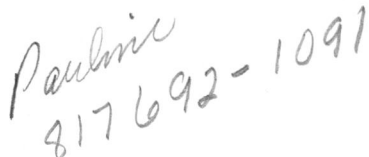

Pauline
817 692-1091

Thanks to:

Phil, my son, spent many hours helping get the book together, published, and printed. I could never have done it without his expertise.

Jackie Clark, a great artistic friend who painted the log cabin on the front cover of "The Other One"

Thom, my son, who wrote in my book and always had faith in me

Dr. Kallal and the people who work for him, who have taken care of my physical condition and are all great friends

Friends who had faith in me and encouraged me from the start, including many from First Baptist Church Watauga and Broadview Baptist.

Forward

You will be blessed to see the perspective and wisdom that my friend Pauline Ruffin shares in these pages of her memories. Pauline had three sisters, one was the pretty one, another was the smart one, and another was the sweet one. Pauline was the "other sister". She never lacked in these areas, but she combined them with style and grace that would light up the office when she entered. Every encounter would begin and end with a smile and a hug for all in her path. Her virtue would warm our day. She overcame grief and pain with a smile and memories of her friends and family. My hope was to be able to relieve her challenges in her body so she had a chance to keep singing and sharing with friends she visited regularly.

Kevin J. Kallal, Md

your friend,

Kevin Kallal MD

About the book

Mark Twain said about his own autobiography that a book that enumerates only the big things is no proper picture of the writer's life at all; that life itself consists of the writer's feelings and interests with an incident here and there to hang the feelings on. That being our primary guide, my brother and I encouraged (pushed?) our mother to begin writing simply by writing anything at all. She wrote as she speaks, with thoughts of the moment and memories of long ago falling upon the page as they deign to do so. We have edited the result, certainly, but the construction remains much as a conversation with a close friend: activities of the day, memories of other times, and explanations of how things have come about.

If you're looking for scandalous secrets from the past, this is not your book. I found some surprises here that deal with her feelings, but nothing astounding. I was a bit surprised at some of the frank statements, but not much. Is it chronological? No, neither is it topical. Family and close friends are the focus here, with the overarching imperative of God's love and purpose.

The last chapter contains thoughts and memories from a variety of people who know her, but as editor, I reserve the right to place mine at the front of the book.

My mother loves unconditionally. She will fight for those she cares about, and do her best to ensure their success. She is perhaps the most optimistic person I know (a characteristic I have largely inherited), and loves a challenge.

Growing up with her as my guide, my hardest lesson has been that logic cannot always win over feelings. To put the statement in her head, it would become: "Logic (or, perhaps, my son) doesn't always make sense."

Introduction

I have decided to name my book "the other one", because it is an autobiography. I am the youngest of five sisters, four of us raised together. All of them are half-sisters, except for Margaret. She and I are the only two children of Mama and Daddy. The other three, Leona, Ruby, and Addie, and our brother Louie are all siblings from Daddy and his first wife Laura. We didn't know Addie until 1988. This situation is explained later.

Mama's children, Richard, Louis, and Robert, were siblings from Mama and Nick Shiro. Now back to my title.

Leona was known as the smart one, because she was a small, but energetic girl, who liked to work, especially out in the fields with Daddy. She also liked to hear people talk about it, how smart she was, and how small. She really was a hard worker, in the fields or in the house. She was first named Leon, and Mama re-named her Leona.

Ruby was the sweet one, and she really was. She was cute, very pretty with her red hair; she was kind and sweet to everyone. She was always there to run to, for Margaret and me, for sympathy and understanding.

Margaret was the pretty one with her medium brown hair and her blue eyes. Her complexion was clear and light. She really was a pretty girl.

And I, Pauline, was the other one.

Chapter 1

I used to tell people we had running water, because someone was always saying, "Pauline, run to the well, and get a bucket of water".

I was about three years old when our family moved from Madison Street, Okmulgee, Oklahoma to McCurtain County, 9 miles from Valliant, situated on Highway 70 in the southeastern corner of the state. Daddy and Louie had gone before and checked out the country. They bought an 80-acre plot of ground, part bottomland and partly sandy, with a spring close to the house (not yet built), and Pine Creek about 1/4 mile, Little River 3 miles or so from our place. I don't know what Daddy paid for the place, but I think he had a car which was part of the deal. He brought a team of mules, Blue and Rhody, a part of our lives for many years.

On our way from Okmulgee, as Daddy and Louie went to make the deal for the place, Mama brought all the girls, Leona, Ruby, Margaret, and me to Uncle Leslie's house in Texarkana, Texas. Uncle Leslie's wife, Lelia Knoblock had recently committed suicide—shooting herself in the temple. She was found in an outhouse of some kind, on their place. I was so small I was vaguely aware of what went on, but learned much later there was some question about the situation, and if she was actually the one who did it.

Their three children, Leslie Junior, Jim, and Lucille, were left, as well as Uncle Leslie. It was a bad time for all of them, but they had a nice, large home and we enjoyed being there. Uncle Leslie sort of hibernated in the living room with his radio; this was 1932 and there was no TV, and we were always told to be quiet and not do anything to disturb him because of his "nerves".

My birthplace, 1929

But it was always a thrill two or three times a year, when they drove from Texarkana to spend a few days with us. He always brought Jim, Leslie Junior, and Lucille with him. Sometimes Lucille would stay with us a few weeks, and once, Leona went home with them, and stayed a while in Texarkana, Ruby went once. Mama went a few times and took Margaret and me when she went.

I remember once when we were there, Margaret and I were invited to sing at the church where they went. It was the Red Cut Baptist Church. I don't remember what we sang, but the two songs we liked to sing at that time were "If I Could Hear My Mother Pray Again" and "Beautiful Isle of Somewhere". I think it was the latter. We were small, about six and eight years, and had learned by ourselves to sing harmony.

Once there was a funeral at Rufe about 3 miles from our school, and someone came after us to sing there. The singing with harmonies continued throughout our lives and was a very large part of it. We learned to play the guitar and mandolin, and used to play for parties and dances (against Daddy's wishes). Daddy liked our music but was afraid we'd get in with the wrong crowd at dances.

Mom's other brother, Jim Knoblock lived in New York. He was a very brilliant man and inventor of several things—an air conditioning system, and a certain gas mask. Those were the days he and many others worked for Thomas A. Edison, who got the credit for things invented by his employees. But Uncle Jim was a genius in his own right.

We loved Uncle Jim. We didn't see him often, but many times a year he would send large boxes of clothes, drapes, rugs, etc. for the house he had designed. We knew when he wrote to Mama he enclosed a check, which helped the family a lot. It was the time of The Great Depression and we were living very frugally.

Daddy worked hard farming and raising crops, and Mama always worked hard in the garden and canned lots of food. We raised potatoes, yams, corn, peas, beans, etc., and all of those helped. Mama did a lot of canning, and taught us to preserve lots of food during the winter months.

Then the "money crop" was peanuts, usually paying for the last year's debts and buying enough seed to plant another crop. The money from Uncle Jim helped, and the clothes he sent were put to good use. Mama was an expert seamstress. She taught us girls to sew, cook, can, and of course help on the farm. Louie was good help on the farm, and Robert worked some; just wasn't at all interested in farming. He was a great cartoonist, and as time passed, he was an electrical and electronics expert. Ironically, we had no electricity on the farm in those days, no gas or any running water. We burned wood, and had a well for water. I used to tell people we had running water, because someone was always saying, "Pauline, run to the well, and get a bucket of water".

Richard worked in a telegraph office all his life and Lewis drove a truck. Louie was a farmer and later worked for the railroad till he retired. Richard then lived in Lubbock, later in Fort Worth. Robert moved around. Meantime I was the youngest and used to have a reputation of being spoiled, a title I heartily disagreed with. As a matter of fact I dare anyone raised in a family like ours, on the farm in depression times, with no spending money, food that was raised by our own hands, everybody working and struggling to get by, to refer to the littlest one as spoiled.

But don't misunderstand me; I had food, clothing and shelter, and our family was close, not having trouble with each other, but all considered one family, and everybody got along. I don't know why I was considered spoiled, but it didn't matter. I was never made to work very hard, or undergo any kind of unkindness. I was very close to Ruby. She was about six or eight years older than I, and was always ready to hold me, sing to me, and comfort me and Margaret whenever we needed her.

Leona, three years older than Ruby, was okay, but not loving with us the way Ruby was. Louie was a big brother, not bad, but not close to me, until we grew up more, but was special after we got older. Robert has always been a very sweet brother. He and Ruby were the same age and very close to each other.

Richard and Lewis lived in Fort Worth and normally just visited us occasionally.

Richard's oldest son, Dan Richard was my age. I was three weeks older than he, and he and I were good friends growing up and afterward. Richard was Mama's oldest, and was married to Juanita. They married about the same time Mama and Daddy did, in Okmulgee. Juanita said she was part Indian, but she herself was very light-complexioned. Richard was always quiet, talkative sometimes, but I guess he didn't get much chance with Mama and Juanita. Their dad, Nick Shiro, was Greek and a very quiet man. Richard and Robert had a lot of his qualities, but Lewis was more talkative and joked a lot, and I guess was more like Mama. He was a lot of fun. I loved him because he always kidded me, and he was a great guy to be around.

Isn't it strange? I guess we have to grow up to realize how much some of our family means to us. I was so fortunate to have four wonderful brothers and three sisters in my life. But there was another sister I never met until I was nearly 60 years old. She was Addie Fagan and was the oldest child of Daddy and Laura. When she was somewhere between the ages of two and four, she had spinal meningitis and then polio, and the results of these devastating diseases left her slightly retarded and crippled with some facial paralysis and crossed eyes. She was about twelve when Laura left the family for another man. Leona was five, Ruby three, and Louie about ten. Daddy had to find a job, and couldn't care for Addie and all the rest, so he had to put her in what was called a state school in Enid, Oklahoma. He took Louie with him, wherever he worked, and Leona and Ruby were with relatives for a while, until he moved to Okmulgee, Oklahoma, and met Mama's family.

Eventually, the older kids at home all married and moved away. Richard and Juanita lived in Lubbock, Texas. They had three children: Dan, Morris, and Rose Ann. Dan was my age, Morris a few years younger, and Rose Ann still younger. Lewis had never lived long in our house but spent most of his time in Fort Worth where his dad lived. Robert lived at home, but left periodically to work in Fort Worth, Denver, and a few other places. He used to hop a freight train to go from one place to another, but spent a lot of time at home. Richard and his family moved to Fort Worth in the early 40s.

Louie farmed at home; Daddy gave him enough land to farm a little and build a house. He married Lennie Lebow and built them a house a short distance from ours, but they lived for a while at our house while building theirs.

Leona married Baustin Jacobs and then moved to Arizona where they lived for a while. Baustin had a twin brother, Austin, who also lived in Arizona. He and Austin worked together, sometimes in the copper mines in Miami and Globe, Arizona. For a short time, Louie and Lennie went to Arizona and worked in the copper mines. They came home once, and had bought an old Model A Ford; it had a rumble seat and an engine you sometimes had to crank to get started. They eventually had a girl named Evelyn, followed by 2 boys. The boys were Ronnie and Glenn. Glenn was born after they had moved to Fort Worth, in 1949.

Ruby married Lennie's brother, Vernon, and they lived with the Lebows, Vernon's and Lennie's parents, for a while before building a little house of their own, after their first baby girl, LaVerne was born. Later, they had Alice, and last was Janice, also in 1949.

About the same time LaVerne was born, Leona's daughter, Carolyn was born. Also about this time, Mama, Daddy, Margaret and I lived by ourselves in our house. Margaret and I were about nine and seven, respectively. One day while we were staying at Louie and Lennie's house for some reason—I'm not sure; maybe it was when they had gone with Ruby and Vernon to Kansas City to work for a while. But when we came home from school, Daddy told us that he and Mama had gone with the Henry Smythes to Idabel (our county seat) in their old car. Mama was sitting on the outside seat of the car, and there were no doors on the car. The car lost its brakes and started rolling downhill. Daddy told Mama to jump out; he was afraid she'd fall out otherwise, and when she did, she fell in a sitting position on a lot of rocks. She was badly hurt, her pelvis broken many times, and also her back, as they discovered later.

They got the doctor from Valliant, and then called Uncle Leslie in Texarkana. He came after her, and took her to the St. Michael Hospital in Texarkana. When they told us about it, he had serious doubts that she would live, but if she did live the doctor there said she would certainly never walk again. So life without Mama began. Margaret and I would be keeping house, cooking, and all the other things Mama had been doing all this time with not much help from the two of us. Daddy was so good to us, as I think about it now; I realize he was hurting so bad, but always the best dad in the world. Margaret and I were really young for such responsibility, but even though we were still in school and a little careless about the work we did (and didn't do), we had some help. Leona came home from Arizona with the five-month-old baby. We were so glad to see and help take care of a baby, and have Leona help us do the work. We were happy to turn a lot of the work over to her. Lucille also had a baby girl, Melba Jean, who stayed with us some.

By this time we were back in a house which now had six rooms, no air-conditioning in those days, also no electricity. Mama improved over time. She was in a full body cast, then one half that size. She would come home for a while, and have to go back to Texarkana. I am now, more than ever, so thankful for Uncle Leslie and the way he took care of Mama. I know some people in those days who broke bones and spent the rest of their lives in bed, and they had never had the medical help Mama had. Except for Uncle Leslie, she would have probably done the same, but gradually, she threw down her crutches and walked.

Mama improved over time. Our house was built of rough lumber in the early 1930s. We had a great fireplace in the living room, and wood-burning kitchen stove. For some reason, Daddy never built a flue, but the stove pipe section reached from the kitchen stove up through the upstairs bedroom—it must've kept the whole upstairs warm. Mama used to complain to Daddy about it, but he never seemed to have time to do anything about it. Eventually a section must've come off at the top in the upper section, just a short way up over the wooden roof, so sparks would fly out, and several times, had come through. We had no fire protection out in the country. There was our well to draw water from, but somehow the house survived many years. There were always other families living with us: Lucille and her daughter Melba, her husband Buck sometimes, Leona and Baustin and Carolyn, the Roy Wilsons, Juandell and Beverly and sometimes Roy, and others. Mama was still in her wheelchair on this particular day, and Robert and I were doing the washing. We had the wash pot boiling the clothes and the three types of wash and rinse water. We were just about finished, but the water was dirty and still in the tubs, and someone yelled that the house was on fire.

We, Margaret and I, got Mama and her chair out the back door when we ran upstairs and could see the flames. Robert grabbed a bucket of water from the tubs and started to go up the ladder that was leaning against the house; as he started to go up the first rung of the ladder, it broke. Robert was not very fast to say the least, but he finally made it to the top of the house. He was carrying two buckets of water. He dumped the first bucket full down just as Lennie looked up and caught the bucket of water in her face. She innocently looked down a couple of seconds, and a bucketful fell on the back of her head and neck. Robert had grabbed the first tub he came to (the dirty one the clothes had been washed in) rather than the rinse tub. Altogether it was a comedy of errors, but the fire was finally put out!

It was a couple of years later. I was 12 years old and getting ready to start to school as a freshman in the ninth grade when the house completely burned down. I had spent the night at Ruby's, and in the morning Vernon went to Rufe, about 2 miles away. He came back and told me our house had burned down. I just couldn't believe it at first, but he finally convinced me, and I'll never forget how I felt as I walked home. I figured everything was gone, and there would be no high school for me after all that. I got home, and was surprised at all that had taken place! Someone had taken down the cabinet that Daddy had built, a wall cabinet, and someone had fixed up a kitchen under the old tree in the front yard.

I found out many years later that when the house had caught fire that last time, and burned down this time, while I was spending the night at Ruby's, Margaret, Juandell, and Beverly had been playing some game upstairs. When they heard someone yell that the house was on fire, they didn't pay any attention, and kept their game going a while, until they realized it was for real and they rushed downstairs to help. There were many things saved.

Someone had cleaned up the large chicken house. It still had a dirt floor, but the walls had been scrubbed. Three beds had been set up in there, a tarp attached to it, and a bed was set up under it. Amazing, but quite a lot of furniture had been saved. I'm not sure who all was there at the time of the fire, but I understood Margaret had saved several things, including cooking utensils, etc. Not many clothes were saved, but we were thankful for what was. The only thing standing was the clay fireplace and chimney. One thing that was saved, ironically, was the culprit, the cook stove. It was nice too, with the warmer reservoir at the top over the burners. Also the singer sewing machine that had been in the family for years, had been saved. Among the lost somewhere were many family pictures, sorely missed by others later, as we spent hours taking inventory of the lost and saved items. We were always thankful no one was injured. In a short time we moved into a little four-room house close to the Ruffin family, about a mile away. I decided to go ahead and start school, the grade Margaret was going to. She was a little more excited than I was, but she was two years older than I, but we did okay. I dropped out after a three or four months, started back, but never finished. Later, after I had a family, I got my GED. We only stayed a few weeks in the little house. We moved into the house Louie and Lennie had been living in, and Daddy built a nice little log house for us. It was three rooms, with a large front and back porch. He screened in the back porch.

The back porch was a pleasant part of the house, serving as a bedroom in the summertime. The year was 1940. Uncle Tobe and Aunt Lizzie moved close to us. Lizzie was Daddy's sister, a tiny little woman who never weighed over 100 pounds except when she was pregnant. She had given birth to eight kids that I knew of, helping to sharecrop. Floyd was their oldest, married to Elsie. Frankie, the oldest girl, married Herschel and had a house full of kids: 12. Then Harmon, who didn't marry until much later and had four kids. Omia, who married my brother Robert, and Faye and Waylon, about my age. Last were the twins, Ruby and Robert. The family had been living in Celeste, Texas, but traveled around quite a lot. We, Margaret and I, were glad to have folks nearby. Fay and Waylon went to school with us before Margaret and I started to High School, and so did Ruby and Robert, the twins. Not long after that, Daddy's brother, Uncle Clem and Aunt Ophelia moved close to us with their two sons, Jewell and Marvin. They were close to my and Margaret's ages. Uncle Clem had one son who was in the Army. His name was TC, and he had gone into the service with Audie Murphy, a real hero in World War II. TC was a real hero himself.

I remember when Pearl Harbor was bombed at the beginning of World War II, now actually the beginning of the US being in the war. The rest of the world had already been involved since the late 30s. I was at Aunt Lizzie's and they had heard about it on the radio. I'd been hearing a lot about the war all over the world, except President Roosevelt hadn't yet let us get into it, but now he did, and the whole world was engaged in the war. I was 12 at the time, and had been worried for years about the war going on, and wondering when we were going to get into it. I remember praying every night for the Lord's protection, and hearing about the hardships in other nations. I had a horror of air raids, bombing, etc. Now the bombing of Pearl Harbor brought the war closer to home and reality for us in the United States, and the nation changed overnight.

All efforts were made to collect metal—different kinds of materials such as rubber, some medical supplies, etc. No more quinine capsules or rubber sole shoes could be found, and even some food such as sugar was rationed. You could not buy tires, cars were no longer produced, gas and many other things were rationed, much donated to help soldiers. Nylon and other synthetics were not invented yet. Silk stockings were not available; the silk was saved to make parachutes. Complaints were seldom heard, as it would have been unpatriotic—a word not commonly used these days! All young men had to register with the U.S. Army when their 18th birthday came. They would be eligible for the draft after that. My brothers were all older and didn't have to go, but my future husband, Sherman, volunteered, as well as many others from our neighborhood and the rest of the USA. Of course, some were rejected because of medical reasons. We knew a man who took enough aspirin to make him have heart trouble; others were conscientious objectors, not believing in fighting wars, who didn't have to go into the service.

We had many young men who were drafted or chose to enlist, and many were heroes, some being killed or maimed. Robert, my brother, Sherman, Uncle Leslie's sons, Jim and Leslie Junior all served several years. Robert came home and went hunting, fell from a tree, and had to be medically discharged. Sherman served two years, went to France and Italy and came home, divorced from Viola, his wife of a couple of years, and he and I were married in 1946. Leslie Junior was a crack pilot, and flew under Gen. Curtis LeMay. He made many successful raids and retired as a colonel. Jim, I don't know much about how he fared. I know he married a couple of times when he got out, and had a son Darren. Leslie had two sons and married Peggy. Both Leslie Junior and Jim are now dead, and so is Lucille, their older sister. Uncle Leslie married a second time to Virginia Carr, a widow with two boys. She was a sweet lady, and we had several visits from her after the death of Uncle Leslie.

I went back to Arizona with my sister Leona when I was 15. Margaret had been there with her, a few months before I went. Leona lived in Miami, Arizona with her daughter, Carolyn. Baustin's' work sent him away to work a lot, but he was there part of the time. Baustin was always a favorite of mine; he had a great personality and I never saw him unpleasant or mad at anybody. His brother, Austin, who also was in Miami with his wife, Hazel and their twins, Lee and

Lora, were sweet to me and sometimes let me sit with the twins when they went out. They were cute kids about Carolyn's age. While I was there in Arizona, I went to the jewelry store and bought myself a guitar. It was a pretty good guitar, I guess, or so it seemed to me. I paid for it with money I made babysitting mostly with the twins, but I know Leona helped some too. Arizona was an interesting place. Leona and Baustin lived in a small but well-kept house in Miami. There was a series of hills, so to get from the house to the street, you had to go down a flight of steps. The small downtown area was really down, it seemed to me. A flight of steps, a few streets, and it was fun just to walk around. I usually took Carolyn with me, she was 3 to 3 1/2 years old, and we enjoyed the sights.

I came home alone on the bus by myself. It took nearly 3 days, maybe less, but I didn't do well on a bus in those days, except remember, I was 15. I sat by a very nice soldier and we talked and visited, and his name was Don Dunlop. Once I woke up and my head was nestled on his shoulder. I used to wonder why he never wrote to me. I came to Fort Worth, visited my brother Richard, his wife Juanita, and kids Dan, Morris and Rose Ann. I stayed a few days with them before I came home; also visited my other brother, Lewis and his wife, Murrell. They didn't have any kids at that time. After a few days in Fort Worth, I rode the bus home. Buses were the real mode of travel in those days. There were two main ones: Continental Trailways and Greyhound.

Many years later, my son Phil worked for Greyhound. He worked for a while for them in Dallas and in Cincinnati, then came home and worked for a while for a hospital system in Dallas. He soon left there, and is now working in Allen, Texas, still in Communications.

Margaret and I learned we could give each other home permanents. They came in a box with the wave solution and neutralizers, cost less than two dollars, and were the first cold waves to come out. Normally, at the beauty shop, we were hooked up to a contraption that applied heat to the hair to make it curl. If it got too hot in spots, which it always did, the operator would fan it to cool it, but sometimes too much heat was applied and it would singe some of the curls. But the Tonys, as they were called (brand name), were successful, and great time, money, and hair saving.

My hair has always been so fine and very dark and with my dark brown eyes that I looked Indian, but if I didn't keep my hair fixed, I was not good-looking to say the least. But just as a footnote, I really am 3/16 Indian, a fact few of us knew until recently. I'm the only one of the Fagan girls who shows the Indian blood. My brother, Louie used to tease me about being a little Choctaw and sometimes looking Mexican because of my dark hair and eyes and dark complexion. My Daddy was dark, too, but his brothers, Uncle Clem and Uncle Monroe, were not. Aunt Lizzie, his sister, was light, but their family was Indian. Their grandmother, my great-grandmother, was full-blooded Choctaw, and my great-grandfather was one-half Cherokee, as explained later.

Daddy was born in Amity, Arkansas. I'm not sure where the others were born, but probably the same place. They all had moved to Texas, around Wolf City. I never met my dad's mother and dad; her name was Lara Elizabeth, and his was Bradford Chapel Fagan. He died before my birth, and she died when I was about six or seven. I don't remember him, but I vaguely remember seeing her once.

Until I was eight years old, my mother's mother, Sarah Elizabeth Nobles Knoblock lived with us. She died when I was eight, and she was somewhere around her early 80s. I was so used to her being with us, it hurt pretty badly when she was gone. She was a sweet grandmother, and helped raise us kids. She was a smart lady, and was quite a poetess. I still have several of her poems, well written. They've since been typed, and some of them framed, on our walls. She died in 1937 after being sick for several days. The doctor said she had uremic poison.

Later, I remember that a doctor from Paris, Texas came to the house one day to do hemorrhoid surgery on Daddy. I was scared for him and was surprised when I never heard a sound from the other room. Daddy had suffered a long time from the illness, and I often saw blood on his clothes, so it was certainly a big relief from that when it was taken care of.

A lot of people had surgery for appendicitis, and the doctors would go to their homes to do the procedure. I thought at the time it must been something of a trend to have an appendectomy, as several of our neighbors had this done, normally to younger women. So life went on changing from one day to another, but I guess when you're a kid growing up, it seems the same. War became a way of life to me. I always prayed that we would win victory over the Nazis, who were the "bad guys". My mother was about half German. Her dad, Lewis Casuth Knoblock was full-blooded, but I didn't think of him being bad. I never met him, and I knew very little about him, but I couldn't believe he was a bad guy just because he was German.

Meantime, we were also at war with other countries, Japan for one, and we referred to them as "Japs", not a nice way to refer to them; we dropped that term after it was all over. At the time we saw them as a totally heartless race of people, with no thought or mercy on our allies. Many of the Japanese residents had been resettled in California and lived in compounds, I guess a little like prisons. It's a fact, and not a very nice commentary on our own country. I can't explain it, but it was thought to be the right thing at the time. They were returned at the end of the war to live free, as we all were. During this time, Aunt Lizzie's daughter, Ruby, died with what seemed to be strep throat. She was 12.

The war was over in 1945 when the US dropped atomic bombs on Japan and just about devastated the two large cities, Nagasaki, and Hiroshima. Nothing else worked, and the emperor there kept holding out. Germany had surrendered after Adolf Hitler had committed suicide and nearly all of Germany was wiped out. Germany was ill-prepared for war in the first place, and it was the nations the Nazis had practically beaten into submission that kept them going. But the atomic bombs caused the Japanese to give up finally. It was a great day when peace finally arrived all over the world.

I know there are many people, including Americans, who think we were merciless and heartless people for killing and maiming so many of the innocent Japanese people, but it was a fact of life that we had to take desperate measures for the sake of all people. It was a great day and a day of thankfulness for us to know the war was finally over, and our brave troops were on their way home.

I guess I fell in love with Sherman when I was little. The Ruffins lived about a mile from us and Ruby and Sherman went together a lot. Sherman was always sweet to little kids, and he used to tease me. When we all came home from church, I'd complain about having to walk, so he carried me. He was a good friend to Robert, too, and was at our house a lot. He and Ruby broke up when they were teenagers, and he left to join the CCC camp—they were young boys who learned to build roads, bridges, parks, etc. There was also the NYA—I don't know which came first, but we didn't see him much after that.

Ruby eventually started going with Vernon Lebow, Lennie's brother. Lennie was Louie's girl. They got married: Louie and Lennie, and Ruby and Vernon.

I never dated much. I think because we had strict parents and didn't dare indulge in some of the activities the other girls did, we had the name of being stuck-up or something. I was also a little shy (at that time only), but dating was done early in those days and usually consisted of a boy walking a girl home. Remember, there were no phones, and it was wartime, so the older boys were off to war, and the boys we knew at school had no money or cars. Besides, where would we go???

I took my guitar to a party one night at the Henry Weavers'. Henry had several kids. One was Son and the other was Gene. Most of the kids learned to play guitars, and we'd have a better time when we had them at parties: just guitars and mandolin, and once in a while someone with a fiddle. We usually had to persuade Daddy to let us go, but he said okay if we had someone go with us. We depended on our friend, Irma Harrell, who usually went. She had two sisters, Olive and Helen, about our ages, and she always looked after us. Sometimes Vernon would be there to play the fiddle, but we couldn't depend on him because he drank with the rest of them.

That Saturday night I was twelve, too young to date, but a boy named Maskell Blackwood walked me home. He was an orphan boy and he and his sister Odell lived with a family there: the Honeywells. That was my first date, so I guess I got excited and got home before I realized I'd left my guitar at the Weavers. But I figured, oh well, what can happen? I'd go back and get it tomorrow.

I walked to church at Rufe the next morning. It was a deserted country road, but I saw someone who stopped and talked to me. I don't remember who it was, but I was told that Son had been playing my guitar after I left, and Henry his dad, took the guitar away from him and broke it to pieces on the iron bed. Thus, the end of the $4.45 guitar from a mail-order catalog. I was so upset I went after it after I came home from church, and Son apologized for it, but I brought it home. It couldn't be fixed. I was told Henry said that he would pay for it, but he never did.

Henry had two daughters: Geraldine and Maxine Weaver. They were good friends of mine. A tragic accident happened a few years later. Son and Gene were playing with a truck, of all things, and Gene ran over Son and killed him. It was an accident, but very sad.

In 1945, late in the year, there was a party at our house. I answered the knock at the door, and there stood Sherman, home from the war, and so handsome I could hardly believe my eyes! He had on a leather jacket and civilian clothes. I was on cloud nine for the rest of the evening! He was in the process of getting a divorce from his wife of about two years, Viola; seems she couldn't leave the other men alone while he was overseas. He was 9 1/2 years older than I, but it didn't seem to matter. I was crazy about him. I had him on my mind all the time, and he seemed to feel the same way at times. Then I wouldn't see him for a while, and he seemed to stay away, but I was careful not to chase him. "Good" girls just didn't do that, in those days.

One night I had a date with Don from Ohio, and we went to a movie. Don was visiting Robert Musset, his buddy during the war, a very nice guy. We stopped at a party at Mary Moran's, and while I was there, another fellow, Tom, convinced me I needed to have a date with him. He was home from the war, and (I found out later) a drunk and a flirt. I feel stupid even writing about it now, but finally I told him he could go to church with me on Friday night at the school. It was close to my home; he could pick me up and we'd walk to church. He had wrecked a number of cars, and I wouldn't ride in the car with him. He said okay, and I hoped he'd forget it.

Don took me home. I didn't tell him about Tom. Somehow I think he knew. I worried about it though. In all honesty, I really didn't know Don any more than I did Tom. But he seemed to be fine.

The next evening I got ready, hoping Tom wouldn't come and that Don would. Earlier that afternoon, Calvin Caldwell, a Choctaw Indian and neighbor, came over and spent a long time talking to Daddy in the living room. I got ready to go and watched the road to see what would happen next. I saw two people coming down the road to the house. Of course it was Tom, but I didn't know why Leo Caldwell, another Indian, was coming with him with a tow sack full of something he was carrying. It was beer, of course, in cans. Just as they got to the house, Don drove up in his car. I went to Don and explained to him that I promised Tom he could go to church with me. He understood, and drove off.

The rest of the evening would have been a nightmare, except for the ending. We walked to the church, Leo coming along with his sack of beer, and Tom and me arguing all the way. He tried to get sympathy from me, but I had finally realized what a loser he was. I told him to straighten up and absolutely not to embarrass me. We went in with Tom holding onto my hand for dear life. I wrenched my hand away—the preacher was singing a gospel song and playing the guitar, and Tom sang out, "AAH-HA, San Antone!!!" I went and sat by Sherman's sister-in-law and tried to ignore him. After a while he went on outside, and the preacher planned to talk to him later.

Church was over and I dreaded to go out, but who should I see when I walked out the door? Sherman! He came up to me and asked if he could take me home. I've never been so glad! I hadn't seen him for ages. He and his brother James had told Tom to go away—he didn't need to be with a "nice girl" like me—so Tom left, looking for a girl who had quite a reputation.

So Sherman walked me home, and we talked until late in the night. I asked him why I hadn't seen him in so long, and he said he didn't know, just trying to think things out in his mind. But he decided he wanted to be with me, and he couldn't have made me any happier. So we were together again. He asked me if I'd go with him on Sunday afternoon to the low-water bridge to take some pictures, and of course, I said yes. We planned to go after I'd gone to the church at Slim.

The church in Slim was a church that had no preacher, except once a year a preacher came to conduct a revival and baptisms. I had become a member of the church a couple of years before and sometimes went to services on Sunday. No preaching, no Sunday school, not much of a service, but we did get to sing. I had become a member of this church, but knew nothing about the beliefs and practices until my good friend in Fort Worth explained these things to me, and helped me to find a church in which I really belonged, and will always.

On Sunday morning I started to church. I walked the 2 miles, and just as I got about halfway, a car came by and stopped. Tom got out and asked if he could walk with me. I was cool, and said, "Sure, it's a free road, but don't get the idea we're going together." He said okay, he didn't blame me, but wanted us to go somewhere after church. I told him no, I had a date, and anyhow, I wouldn't go with him. We continued to argue, but finally we got to the church. I went in, and he walked away.

I never saw him after that until just before our wedding, Sherman's and mine. But I was anxious to see Sherman that afternoon. He picked me up early and we went out to the low-water bridge. It was a favorite place for couples to go and we enjoyed it. I believe Sherman had helped build the bridge. I remember he kissed me. I could tell he was getting serious, and so was I.

In a few nights he took me to a movie. The lights went out on his old 1929 Chevy, but the night was light, and there was no traffic anyway. After we got home, he kissed me and told me he was falling in love with me. I told him I loved him too.

What I didn't tell him was what had happened before, when he was staying at home for those weeks, and before he and I made any commitments to each other. I had gone to a movie with Jerry Barnett. I'd carried a torch for him a long time, but by now had forgotten anyone except Sherman. Jerry had asked me to be his girl, and said he was crazy about me. He kissed me and got very emotional. I told him I loved Sherman and could never care about anyone else.

I had also gone with Don, the ex-soldier from Ohio. He asked me to go to Ohio with him, and I said no, I couldn't go anywhere with someone I wasn't married to. So he asked me to marry him. I refused, thanked him, and told him I was in love with Sherman. I didn't know if I'd be with Sherman again, but I didn't care for anyone else. I learned later that Don just wanted me on the rebound. He was in love with Mary Fleming, who was in love with Robert Musset.

Then Sherman and I were back together again and everything was fine. He got the divorce and it was final. So we planned to get married in August of 1946 after my birthday. I was seventeen the 22nd, and we planned our wedding for the 31st.

I got this far in my book when my emotions got the best of me, and I haven't written another word until tonight, a week later. When I got this far I was upset just writing about our relationship and remembering how happy we were, getting ready to share our lives. I had known the Ruffins since I was three years old, but now things were different. Sherman's mother, Agnes, was a sweet lady and a great neighbor. She was the one neighbors depended on if they were bad sick. She was a midwife, and delivered many babies, including her daughter Bea's twin girls. She had sat with my grandma, Mama's mother, for several days until she died in her 80s.

But this was a new situation. I was surprised to see enlarged pictures of Sherman and his divorced wife, Viola, hanging on the wall, and she showed me more snapshots of Viola. I mentioned it to Sherman, but he wouldn't say anything to his mother about it. After we married, this never changed. Later, I would remember the pictures when I saw them coming between us.

But for now, I was convinced they didn't mean anything. I was trying to forget them, even though they were not moved, year after year; the same ones kept their place on the walls of their home.

I was so happy as we got ready for the big day. Uncle Jim sent me some money to help out, and I was so glad to get the help. I went to Idabel and got a new dress; it was lime green, soutache around the sweetheart neck. It was right after the war was over, and we lived very modestly. Also the large weddings were out, not that I could have had a large wedding anyhow, nor did I want one.

Sherman was just out of the Army and was drawing a check for $20 a week, so he was saving up for us to go to Fort Worth. And I had spent my $20 on my dress and less than $7 for a pair of brown heels. My hose were not nylons, but semi-sheer cotton. Juanita had given me a pair of rayon ones, but they were too red and shiny.

I was happy. I had a new gown, and I made myself a great robe out of (of all things) a pair of drapes from Uncle Jim in New York (just call me Scarlet O'Hara).

The day came, and I got ready. Sherman was to be there at 8 AM, but I got ready and waited—and waited. About 8:45 my eight-year-old cousin, Alice Fay came. Alice was staying with her grandparents, my Uncle Clem and Aunt Ophelia. She was such a beautiful girl, with waist-length, brown, curly hair and the great brown eyes of the Fagans.

She told me Sherman, living 1/4 mile from Uncle Clem, asked her to come and explain to me that he was trying to get the car started. As I found out later, Sherman and Mabel, Earl's wife, about six or seven months pregnant, had been pushing the car all over the place trying to get it started. No luck, until Sherman went to the neighbors and borrowed a coil, installed it on the car, and finally got it started. So about 10 AM, he drove up to the house. Mama and I got in the car and he kept it running. Meanwhile he was afraid if he let it die, he'd never get it started again, but by the time we had stopped and got back to the road, it died again. Someone came by in a wagon, and Sherman had him help get it started again. This time they hooked up the horses (or mules; I've forgotten which), and succeeded.

So we got to Idabel, to the courthouse, where the blind preacher who ran the concession stand in the entrance of the courthouse married us. I was so happy. I had married the handsomest and the sweetest man in the world, and I knew that God had ordained our marriage. I still think that; I wouldn't have ever wanted to marry anyone else, and I wish he knew now how much I loved him and still do.

Couples are bound to forget this at times, and get careless about caring and mess things up as we did, but I've never regretted that day in Idabel. I don't know about him; he never seemed to open up too much, but most of the time in the 54 1/2 years we were together, we loved each other. Sherman sometimes would seem to be miles away, and not talk much. He could close up completely, and then eventually come around and open up a little.

Some people say you never can forget your first love. Sherman was my first love, but he had been married before. Somehow I wouldn't let myself believe he was still in love with Viola, and he didn't seem to ever think of her. He was a good husband—good to me and the three kids, and worked very hard all his life to take care of us.

What he didn't tell me for many years was that he was an alcoholic. He used to drink sometimes at home. We didn't go out, and he never drank with the fellows he worked with. But when Leona & Baustin came, they'd bring a bottle of whiskey with them, and he'd drink with them. He started buying a little whiskey now and then, and later decided to quit. That's when I realized he liked it a little too well.

Because he didn't want to be a bad influence on the kids, and he knew it wasn't right, he quit, but seldom had a glass of wine, and we used to have a margarita at El Fenix restaurant. But when Paulette and Bill were playing in town, we would go to hear them and he got started again. This was many years later. He never drank as long as the kids were still at home.

For the most part, we got along pretty well. He always wanted me to stay home, and not work out. But it became necessary for me to work and help at home as expenses increased.

Sherman was raised in a home where there was seldom any talk about personal feelings or Christianity. I know his mother was a Christian; you just knew by the way she lived. She seldom talked about it, if ever, so being married and having a Christian family was a new experience for Sherman. I used to talk to him a lot, and while we were dating and engaged we used to go to the school for church service on Sundays. Sherman had a great voice, and sometimes directed the music. He could sing lead, tenor or bass. But he still denied any beliefs about Jesus. I prayed for him and felt that he would come to understand the plan of salvation and accept the Lord. After we married, I was still a member of the church in Oklahoma, my good friend, Brother Charles Russell led me to accept the Baptist faith. Sherman and I were married seven years when he was saved and joined the Broadview Baptist Church where Mama and I belonged. I had become a Baptist in 1950 right after Daddy's death.

Our family was finally all together there at Broadview. The three kids were all baptized later; Thom at six years old, Phil at eight, and Paulette at six. What a blessing Broadview was to us all through the years! I would have no idea how to raise a family without leading them to serve the Lord. Sherman was faithful to go regularly to church services, and did everything he could to lead the family in worship and living the Christian life. He eventually taught some classes, brought devotionals, and worked with the men keeping the church grounds nice, and worked on the building and grounds when it was needed.

Sherman was a great friend to Charles Russell as Charles was with us all through the years. Charles and Ora moved to Oklahoma after Daddy's funeral. We hated to see them go. They are now living, retired, in Mineral Wells, Texas, and we have been good friends all the time. I'm still in touch with them. Sherman became a Christian when Brother Garrison was pastor. The Garrisons were also very good friends, but he retired in 1956, because he was 65 and had some medical problems. They both died soon afterward.

We had several pastors at Broadview after that. Southwestern Seminary was downtown, and there were always preachers and music ministers attending and looking for a church in which to serve. We had many people coming and going. The church was also close to the air base.

I worked with people of all ages, from the nursery to beginners, primaries,' juniors, and seniors, also young adults. Later, at Azle Avenue and First Baptist Church, Watauga, where I go now, I teach older adults. Church has always been a large part of all of our lives. Broadview Baptist, where our family went for many years, meant so much to all of us. We were friends with the entire congregation, which was not large, but we were all seemingly involved in everything. We had many social activities, and so many young people, there was always something going on. Also, this was right after the war was over, and people were hungry for church and fellowship with other believers. We had Training Union, WMU, regular study courses, RAs and GAs. We had bible drills, pizza parties, picnics, and ball games. And everyone got involved. Many years later, when our family went to Azle Avenue, there were no young people, a not-so-good music program, and we were a city church. It was so different.

Sherman had bought a little model A after we moved out to Sansom Park. It was okay. We thought it would be handy for me to drive, but I tried it, and decided I'd rather not. So Sherman gave me the other one; he drove it for a little while, but finally gave up and sold it.

Thom was little when I started to Broadview, and he rebelled. He used to have a fit when we started to go in, but I took him in anyway, and he got used to it quickly. He used to go up and stand with me in the choir when we sang. Consequently, he learned to sing alto as I did, and as he grew older, he could sing all the parts: he, Phil, and later, Paulette. They were all very good at singing any part. We used to sing all four parts as a quartet. Music has always been important to us all. Sherman had a good voice, too, and could sing any part, but he didn't sing much. He finally let smoking mess up his voice. He gave up smoking when he was about 36; he later thought that quitting smoking was responsible for prolonging his life until he was 81.

A short time after I became a member of Broadview, I was driving one day, and I had quite a conversation with the Lord. I was so happy that I'd become a

Baptist, and was learning so much about the Christian life, I was thinking about all my brothers and sisters and their families who didn't seem to know the Lord. I didn't know of any of them who attended church. I did know Richard's wife, Juanita was Catholic, though I felt she was not very serious about it. But I knew Vernon, Ruby's husband was an alcoholic. Ruby had been baptized but never went to church. Anyway the Lord himself spoke to me and said, "Now this is your job, to witness and try to bring all your brothers and sisters and families to me." I objected a little—I was the youngest one of our family. How could anyone put any confidence in me? And what would I say? He said, "I'll be with you and tell you what to say—just have faith in me." It occurred to me that he was telling me this was my task, and I wouldn't have to do it by myself. What a Savior we worship! I never had a doubt about it. I knew what he was telling me to do, so I said, "Okay, Lord, I'll do it, but please, never leave me, and speak to each one as I do." And what He accomplished after that is spectacular! Don't ever doubt the Lord; He'll do what he says.

After this episode and we talked that day, I know each one accepted Him. Today, Robert and I are the only two of our siblings still living, but we know all the rest are gone to be with Jesus. I'll enumerate each one and their eventual conversions. Just as He promised, He was with me all the way.

Margaret started going to church at Broadview where we went, and was saved and baptized. She was having a bad time throughout those years, and changed jobs several times. She was a good worker, but she had some social issues. Margaret was smart, knew how to find a job, and was an expert seamstress. She always excelled in sewing. She was hard of hearing, which caused some problems with paranoia; she was a sales clerk at Leonard's for some time, but her home life was not good. Her husband Jack gave up his job, a fairly good job at Container Corporation, and never could find another one. The only thing he could do, or did do, was drive a bus or taxi. He was not a very strong person in a physical way, and was not trained to do much. He had a nice personality, but was self-conscious because his eyes were crossed.

Margaret contacted an eye doctor, and arranged for him to have eye surgery. It corrected his eyes, but he never could see very well, although he did drive and did okay. In later years he had a rider beat him up and rob him, and after that, he had seizures and was unable to drive. He was always antisocial, and died with pneumonia when he was about mid-70s in age. They had separated and divorced. Margaret married again, a man named Otis Ogden.

They lived in a large house on Daggett Street in Fort Worth, so Jack was on his own, but they had him move in the house with them later. I have analyzed their lives (as if I could do such a thing) and decided that when two people get married, one of them needs to be a leader and the other one a follower. Obviously, they can't both lead. Now wait a minute. I'm not advocating one being the boss and the other one obedient. But people with personalities like Margaret and Jack don't need to be together. They are like two kids, with no leadership.

I remember when Sherman and I married, I was so young, and really depended on him a lot, but he was up to the task. He wasn't bossy, but he was very helpful in guiding me, and we made decisions together as much as possible. But we both grew and mostly together; especially in the years as our children were growing up. When Sherman and I married, I look back now, and I realize we lived in a completely different world. The war was over, and we hadn't realized how life was changed for everybody. It wasn't so strange to us, that Sherman was so adamant about my not working outside the home. Many of our close friends felt the same way. But we were country, and thought the way our folks did, that women should be home with the kids.

But, as time went on, and I could see how wages were fairly low according to prices, I began to see where we surely could use some extra money. While the children were growing up to school age, I knew they needed me at home. But the week after I had Paulette, the baby, in school, I went to the cleaners, and James was ready to put me to work. That was fine with Sherman, too. I was familiar with the sewing part of it, and it only took me a few days to learn the rest. It was just part-time, and I didn't work if the kids were home unless Mama was there to look after them. Once I learned the cleaning business it wasn't easy to stay at home. Sometimes, when I was laid off (this did happen—it was a very unsteady type of work), I would go and look for something else. I always found someone who would hire me. Just as often, I'd decide I didn't want the job.

I didn't take some of the jobs I found, because they paid practically nothing, and I felt that they weren't worth leaving home for. I worked for Bobby's Cleaners, TCU Cleaners, 7th Street Cleaners, and another one I think. I was looking for something else when our good friend, A. E. Stephens asked me to help him start an A&P School. It was 1966.

Chapter 2

"I laughed all the way to the bank."

Margaret and Jack's only son, Jacky, was born a year after our son, Thom was born. Jack was out of a job, and Margaret was making drapes for living. She worked for several years and several companies, and learned a lot about the drapery business. Sherman and I kept Jacky Junior and Jack's mother kept him a lot too. We offered to take him and raise him, but Margaret and Jack said no. So we just helped, and Mama kept him a lot. He was allergic to milk, so she fed him mulsoy, a soybean product that had been refined and fed to babies who couldn't drink milk. In those days they obviously hadn't started putting nutrients in the mulsoy. Jacky was a little, skinny boy, pitiful because he was seemingly unhealthy. I felt he wasn't cared for properly, so all of us pitched in and did what we could. For a time, Margaret was in her own business, making draperies at her home. When I wasn't working elsewhere, I helped her some. She was very good at it, but it wasn't for me.

Robert and Omia lived in Oklahoma part of the time. Robert was a TV technician. Part of the time they lived close to us in Fort Worth, Robert worked at a TV shop in White Settlement. They had Betty Jean &, Kenneth, who were older than our kids. But later, they had a baby while living close to us. The baby was mongoloid, a big blow to the family. This was about 1953, when Paulette was a baby. They told us he probably wouldn't live long, as his heart was very weak, and they said those babies seldom lived over 14 years. This was many years ago, and they have made a lot of strides in this field since then. But obviously, this baby's heart was just too weak to make it more than 8 months.

Dr. Mal Rumph, a doctor here in Fort Worth, called Robert in to talk to him, and I went with him. We all knew there was something wrong, but none of us had seen the baby yet, not even Omia. It was so sad to sit there and watch Robert, as the doctor told us very bluntly about the baby's condition, and explained what to expect.

As it turned out, David Paul (which they named him) only lived to be eight months old, most of that time spent in the hospital with other sick babies. When they'd bring him home, he'd have seizures and they'd have to rush him back to the hospital. When he died, he weighed the same as at birth. Later, they had two other boys, Mark and Roy. They were healthy children, just as Betty and Kenneth had been.

Lewis Shiro lived in Fort Worth and drove trucks. He married Murrell Gentry, and was married to her many years. They had Jimmie Louis, Laurine, Tina, and Nicky (after Mr. Shiro). Their story is a long one, and rather sordid at times. Finally after the last child was married, they divorced. Murrell was killed in a car wreck later, and Lewis married a Mexican lady with kids. She was not in love with him, and was not good to him, so they divorced, and Lewis lived alone, and developed Alzheimer's disease. He was a good man, was treated rather badly. He died after having dementia for some time. But his last years were spent living close to Laurine, who cared for him and took care of him the best she could. I had loved him so much, and always remembered the way he called me Pobum, a word Margaret had called me when we were little. He called Margaret Martita, which I called her, trying to say Margaret.

Richard, Mama's oldest son, was married to Juanita Ackley in Okmulgee. Their son, Danny was born three weeks after I was. Richard worked as a telegraph operator, a job that does not even exist anymore. But they had Dan, then

Morris, and then a girl, Rose Ann. They lived in Lubbock for a while, then moved to Fort Worth. We used to enjoy their coming to see us in Oklahoma. Dan and I were buddies, and Margaret and Morris played together. We came to Fort Worth occasionally, Mama, Margaret, and me, and we loved visiting all Richard's and Lewis' families.

Mama's health got worse. She still had a lot of trouble with the bones she had broken, and she eventually had to use a walker at times. But I remember when Richard died. He had been sick for a while and although she tried not to show it, Mama was a little partial to Richard, her firstborn. She walked into the viewing room to see him in the casket. I think it was one of the saddest times of my life to see her go over to look at him.

Mama was gone by the time we lost Lewis. She had fallen and broken her leg again two years before, and hadn't walked since. She was in a nursing home in White Settlement. Thom, Phil, Paulette, and I were with her when she went into a coma. Alice, Ruby's middle daughter, was in the Harris Hospital downtown, dying with cancer at the same time. Mama had named Alice, and they were very fond of each other. They died about two hours apart. Alice went first—we got a call while we were there with Mama. This was in 1987. Mama was 96, Alice 45.

The funerals were a day apart. After Alice's funeral and burial close to their home in Cleburne, Mama was taken to the Moran Cemetery at home in Oklahoma and buried beside Daddy. He had been buried there January 1, 1950, and this was 1987. Mama used to say you never feel old until your mother dies, and I guess she was right. I missed her so much, and Alice too. Lennie was sick quite a bit, and only lived about another year or so before dying of cancer.

My A&P School was going along well in Arlington, and was now FAA and VA approved. I was working hard and loving it. But expenses were climbing and it wasn't always easy to keep the bills paid. Somehow we managed.

But our personal lives, mine and Sherman's, were also having ups and downs. Mostly downs. Sherman had started drinking, and I was ignoring it, busy with my own life which consisted mainly of whatever was going on at the school. I was thinking about maybe selling, if anyone wanted to buy. I hated to have to turn the school over to anyone else, but I was also thinking about expanding, and I knew it would take a lot more money. I hated the thought of borrowing.

Sherman called me one day, and told me he had bought a new truck. It was a brand-new Ford. Then a few weeks later, he called me and told me he had retired. He was 65. Always, he had put his life into being the best of marble masons and took so much pride in the beautiful work he had done. But he had finally let the drinking get the best of him. I had ignored his drinking, and he always denied that he was drinking. He thought as long as he drank vodka, no one could tell.

My friend, Ray Williams, who had been a good business friend for years and helped me several times, asked me about buying the school. He and another man that worked for Dalfort, that had replaced Braniff, came to see me. We went to lunch and talked about it. I had already talked to another man, a real estate salesman who wanted to buy me out. He had forfeited on the deal a year before, so I told Ray and Hugh (the other man), I would wait for them, and decide what I wanted for the place. It all looked good, so I was waiting for our next meeting. I had put a price on it of $750,000.00.

Time passed, and finally in a few weeks, I called Ray Williams and asked him how the negotiations were coming along. He said they were definitely considering the situation, and it seemed favorable. So I waited again, but felt pretty good.

Sure enough, Ray and the other guy, Hugh Crull, came out again, and we decided to close the deal. I was to work as school director, employed by Dalfort, and to be paid by them for three years. The school would be under my direction, and I would be working under the school president. Hugh was the vice-president over me. This meant my driving to Dallas Love Field to receive a pretty good salary. Although it wouldn't cover the $750,000 I'd asked for, I would be retired in three years, and I agreed to refrain from having another school for three years. Also, I was getting a nice down payment of $250,000, my own office, and the same company benefits as the other employees.

We were in agreement, and we set the date for the final transfer of the school. I was accompanied to the president's office at Dalfort by Paulette, Thom, my CPA, Mike Seale, and my attorney, Gaylen Groce. On my way home the day before our signing the deal, I went by the Hulen Mall and bought myself a new dress and a nice blue coat.

So the deal was made. In a way it was good. I still taught my IA and my A&P refresher courses. I already knew many of the employees, and they were all very nice to me. Dalfort had built a nice school upstairs over the maintenance area, and I was still doing some recruiting.

Hugh Crull turned out to be a real horse's backend! I found out the following. He had been a director over the flight training, and drew the same salary I was now drawing. He got mad and demanded a better position, so they made him a VP. But he was only getting $10,000 more a year than I, so he resented me all the time I was there, and he took it out on me. He stopped me doing my refresher courses, both A&P and IA, and told me I should be sitting in my office and writing memos.

In several ways, I was cheated out of money and generally having hassles, but after a year, I was released from my contract and was paid off for the other two years remaining. Great! I laughed all the way to the bank.

Meantime, Paulette and Bill had divorced, and she moved in with me in my apartment in Benbrook. I had a two-bedroom, two-bath apartment close to them, and it was also close to Phil and Sherry. It was a nice place; I bought a new washing machine and dryer and some of the other things I needed. So I had plenty of room, and I was glad for them to be there, but Matt, about 3 1/2 years old, was very unhappy and cried for his daddy. Finally Paulette went back to Bill, and later she left again and moved in with me.

I filed for divorce, and it became final in a little while. I called Bobby, my nephew's wife, about a duplex. Bobby had just started her real estate career. My duplex was her only sale before she quit. She immediately found one for me in North Richland Hills. It was an unbelievable deal; I took it and paid cash for it. My nephew's son, Will, and his friend, both policemen, moved into one side, and Paulette, Matt, and I took the other. It was nice. Each side had three bedrooms, two baths, a double garage, a laundry room and wood-burning fireplace. All this took place while we were still working for Dalfort, the three of us, Paulette, Bill, and me.

Paulette got a divorce from Bill, and before long she quit her job and got one as a secretary downtown. Bill still worked for Dalfort, and he got married to Becca soon after their divorce. Paulette was dating Jeff Agnew, a steel guitarist who plays at the Grapevine Opry.

After I left Dalfort, I bought a dry-cleaning pickup station from Jeanne. Thom had bought it for her after their divorce. Paulette got the news that she had contracted cancer of the breast, and would undergo chemo and radiation. She was fired from her job—a sorry deal—but she managed to keep up her insurance payments.

She and I ran the cleaners; we soon started selling clothes, too, and bought a new sewing machine and serger. I did some sewing, and even taught a few A&P and IA courses. Paulette was still singing at the Johnny High Country Music Revue, and soon became a singer at several funeral homes: Greenwood, Mt. Olivet, and Biggers. A good friend, Sylvia White, whose voice was a lot like Paulette's, got Paulette started at the funerals. Paulette also worked at Johnny's office in Grapevine. Jeanne had named her cleaners Ruffins Classic Cleaners, but when we started selling ladies clothes, it became Paulette's Sassy Fashions also. The cleaners business was very slow, and we finally dropped it, but moved the fashions store down to a log cabin building down the highway. We later moved the store to Davis Boulevard, close to where I live.

My good friend, Dr. T. L. Childs, who had been my doctor since we came to Fort Worth and delivered all my children, and took care of all of us, had left town, so it was time for me to find a new doctor. I had been to a couple—one I went to had forgotten I was there, and left me in a waiting room; everyone had gone, and finally someone found me. Such an experience discouraged me from going back to the same one, so I found a Dr. Reed, who took my blood pressure a time or two, and retired. When I went back to him, needing my BP taken again, he was gone, and the office was taken by a young man named Kevin Kallal. He has been exactly what I've needed for all these years since 1990. He wouldn't let me go that first day without looking into my condition, finding what I did need, and in the process, maybe saving my life. He has been "my" doctor ever since.

Sherman and I went back together in May, 1990, and bought a house in Watauga. Paulette married Jeff soon after, and they bought a house in Grapevine. Her cancer had been in remission for a year, and we hoped it was gone for good, but it wasn't to be. She died in December, 1993 after having a stem cell transplant, spending two months in Baylor Hospital in Dallas. She was 40 years old. Her son, Matt was only seven.

After writing here a few days ago, I became so blue remembering all this, I put this away for several days, but life goes on. I'm not normally a solemn person, but losing a child is about the worst thing imaginable. Sherman was deeper in depression than he had ever been and never seemed to overcome her death. It's hard to remember many times when he wasn't depressed, but this was far worse.

As I've been for a long time, I lived my life, not over the grief, but trying to keep on living. A few days after Paulette's funeral, I got a call from Ray Williams, my friend from Dalfort. He asked me if I'd be interested in teaching A&P classes at E-Systems in Greenville, Texas, about 85 miles from home. It was a great thing for me to be able to drive the distance to Greenville and come home by supper time. Sherman cooked for us, and had supper ready when I got home, around 7:30. I would get there to start classes about 3 PM. I used to play Paulette's tapes while I drove.

Meantime, we were still going to church at Azle Avenue. Or rather, I was. Sherman was going when he was able, but he was having more problems with his heart and had five bad discs in his back and had to take a lot of pain medicine. There were countless trips to the ERs, and I never knew if it would be the last, as his condition became worse all the time. The last work he had done was right after we moved into our house on Lyndale Drive. He worked a few days on the mausoleum at Greenwood Cemetery, but couldn't keep it up and had to quit trying. He had done a lot of work on our place, but he had to stop that, too. He eventually stopped watching TV or reading, and just sat in his chair, not talking or doing anything but seeming to brood.

When I talked to him about it, he said there was nothing wrong—he had bought hearing aids but wouldn't wear them. He was a little more cheerful when anyone came over, but otherwise he never anything much to say.

As I think about it now, I realize how different we were, and how I had always gone places without him. I tried to enjoy life, regardless of the way he had never wanted to go anywhere or have anything in common with me. So I guess I'd let the rift grow wider, and let us grow apart more than ever.

A man I met was an electronics instructor, Boni Fraustro, and we decided to start a school together. It was a fast decision, and I will always remember that I failed to call on the Lord about this, or failed to listen to him about it. We started our school in Meacham Field in a suite downstairs. I was doing instruction in A&P, and he did FCC. We made it a partnership, but it didn't last but a few months in 1994 & 1995. We closed it down. I was still teaching occasionally at home, and he the FCC in his home, but we closed our school and don't work together any more.

Our church was in a downtown area—north side. We started, as a lot of churches were doing, sharing it with the Spanish-speaking congregations. I was driving alone to church, and having to leave Sherman at home. He needed me here, but I kept going until his death in 2001. He had a lot of surgeries, and was doing so bad, eventually I couldn't leave him.

Paulette's mother-in-law, MM died about two years after Paulette died. Jeff married again to Pam, one and one half years after Paulette's death. His father, Neil lived alone in Memphis for several years, and then moved to a Grapevine apartment where he lived for a time before he died.

Sherman died at home in 2001. Hospice had come in and cared for him for a few days. I looked at a couple of nursing homes for him—he had spent a couple of weeks at Westside Care Center, but came back home. He hated nursing homes, as most people did at that time, and was ready to come back home. I went to Manor Care on Skyline Drive, where I now am a volunteer, but decided against it. He had been in Manor Care on Glenview Drive, but didn't stay very long. But hospice took such good care of him at home.

One of my former students used to volunteer for hospice and played a musical instrument for the patients. Sherman loved it. He died at about 2 AM one morning, and the hospice nurse was with him. A few days before, the whole family was with him and we all told him our goodbyes. I don't know how much of that he heard, but he seemed better after that.

We had been married 54 1/2 years, not counting the nine months we've been divorced. For a few days after the funeral, I just sat around at home, all alone, thinking about all the years we had together and knowing he was free of pain and with the Lord, and with Paulette, and many more of our families.

In a couple of weeks I got a call from Johnny Hooper. Several months before, I had visited Irene, my good friend I'd met when we moved to Sansom Park in 1947. She was in Fireside Lodge on White Settlement Road. She had broken her hip and had lost her husband and son, who were both buried at Greenwood.

She had two brothers, Howard and Johnny. I had known them both briefly, and had seen them and their families once in a while. Johnny's wife, Esther had died a couple of years before. He came to see Irene while I was there. We talked, he told me he had an aneurysm in his aorta, and could die any time, but he was okay, and visited Irene several times while I was there. We went to the cemetery, taking Irene to see her son, Terry's grave. She had never seen it. He was buried there, and so was her husband, Ed. Johnny's son, Jim drove her in the truck, and I rode with Johnny. Afterwards, I went with Johnny and Jim to have lunch. Johnny called after Sherman's death and asked if I would go to lunch with him. He said, "I know your husband died a little while ago, but you still need lunch," so I said okay. He got lost, and it was about two hours before he got to my house, but he finally made it and we went to lunch.

Johnny began to come nearly every day, and we'd go to lunch or go anywhere. He would be willing to take me shopping or wherever I wanted to go. A sweet man, he also went with me to find a church. Azle Avenue had been given to the Spanish-speaking people, so we went to a church that was by the fire hall in Sansom Park. We saw some we knew there, but it was too far from me. We went to the First Baptist Church of Watauga where we were immediately impressed, and the Sunday School we were invited to had such great people. We were ready to join about the second or third time we went. So every Sunday, Johnny would come out to my house to take me to church.

Every once in a while, I'd go after Matt, and he would spend the day with me. One day he wanted me to take him to the animal control center to look at the dogs. His dog, Biscuit had been given away and he missed her, and of course he missed his mother. He said, "Grandmother I promise not to get one, I know my dad won't let me have it, but I just want to see them." So we went to see the dogs.

I reminded him I couldn't keep one either. My yard was small, and I didn't want a dog in the house. But we went to see them in the pound. And of course, we found the sweetest large black and white Border Collie and Springer Spaniel mix who immediately fell in love with us, as we did him. We visited him a couple of times and signed the papers. I agreed to take him home with me until Matt convinced Bill that he would take care of him, if he would let him bring him home, but he never could.

He was a great dog. We named him Elvis. He was smart and loving, but not housebroken, so he was an outdoor dog. Johnny loved him, too. Elvis would sit out on the back porch on the marble table and watch for us to come home. He could see in the living room from there, and never missed seeing us come in. Johnny always went out to pet him as soon as we got in. Elvis loved Matt, and Matt loved him, but he could never take him home.

We took him to get his shots. We bought him a house. He had many birds come up and play with him, eat his food, and drink his water. He was always good-natured, never barked, and loved every body. He never was bothered by the birds.

I began to have a lot of trouble with my back. I had surgery on my spine, an upper disk, and had recovered. But this got bad, and I finally spent time having to take some heavy medicine and eventually have two more surgeries. During these months of illness and recuperating, I was having trouble taking care of Elvis. A saleslady at Albertson's grocery store talked to me one day, and it seemed to be providential. I told her I would have to find another owner for Elvis, because I was getting unable to care for him. She and her husband came to see him, and of course fell in love with him, and came after him the next Saturday. Johnny was here and we were very upset to see him go. I believe Elvis was actually crying as he looked out the car window. I'd had to trick him to get him in the back of their car. They drove away; later I called the lady and she assured me he was fine. He had another collie to play with, and I could hear them barking together. He had never barked before when I had him here. I was glad he was happy and well, and had even lost some weight.

I got better, after recovering and spending several weeks of therapy and staying at Phil and Sherry's. Then, after having a light stroke, I gradually got well. Johnny was with me through it all.

As soon as I could get over the stroke, I came home and was able to take care of myself. It's not called a stroke, but a TIA. I guess it's lighter than a real stroke, but I did have to learn to walk—it took me a few days.

During this time, my sister in Arkansas, Leona Jacobs died. She is buried in Van Buren beside her husband Baustin, who died several years before. Her daughter, Carolyn lives close by with her husband, Dale. Their daughter, Julia and her husband live next door on the mountain in Rudy.

But Johnny, always concerned about me and the family, and I his, has had physical problems, too. In May of 2004 he had to have his aneurysm surgery. He came through it fine, but the doctors had almost waited too long. It had gotten so large they had to do the radical surgery, so it took a long time to recover. Just about the time he was on his feet again, he walked out on the wet street to talk to a truck driver and was hit and knocked down; his hip was broken, and after having a doctor mess it up further, had to have corrective surgery. He's been unable to walk since. He has broken his other hip, and other breaks. Right now in 2008, he is a patient at Manor Care on Skyline Drive in River Oaks. He is in a wheelchair, and will probably never walk again, except two or three steps at a time. But we are still very close, and love each other. His daughters and son are taking care of him. He is 92.

When I finally had to retire, I had a hard time. Retirement doesn't mean you quit working and sit in the sunshine, or by a fire, depending on the weather. I'm still working, still teaching at home when I have students. I walk frequently, and I found a great job as volunteer at Manor Care, two hours on Tuesday and Thursday afternoons, 2-4 PM.

I've grown to love many of the patients (Mama used to call them inmates), and I'm grateful for the Lord's leadership. I readily accepted when Betty at Manor Care asked me to do this. I find myself doing all sorts of things like leading music, conducting games I never did before, and sometimes just visiting and counseling.

More than ever, I find myself in charge of the activities, as Betty has other duties to attend to. But I don't mind; it's a real challenge and I'm learning a lot. I spend what time I can with Johnny, and I go and see him an extra day or two at Avalon, where his folks moved him. I do a little extra visiting too. Some of the patients ask me to help them in different ways, but I am limited in what I can do for them. They hate to see me leave, and when I'm not there, I really miss them.

Sometimes I feel really lonely at home alone. I remember when Mama used to live alone, and she'd tell me she hadn't seen another person in days. I went to see her, but not as often as I should have. When a woman works out, it's easier to neglect some who depend on you. And I realize that more and more, as time goes by, friends are working, and you feel isolated. But that shouldn't last long. I seldom let it get me down. It's best to stay busy; there are many things to take my mind off myself. So much of the time in the evening, I get a call from Thom, which always gives me a lift. He is such a thoughtful son. A lot of the time I cook something, desserts most of the time, but occasionally something I can freeze and have later. I gave away my freezer—it was causing my electric bill to be so high, and I have a very large refrigerator and a side-by-side freezer together. As I write, in this in 2010, it's getting close to Christmas.

When I went to Manor Care on Thursday evening (yesterday), Johnny was very ill, and not talking coherently or hearing well. They have trouble keeping him dressed, but they're giving him so much strong medicine like morphine, he can't think or talk straight. I'm worried about him. We had a Christmas "store" yesterday, and I was so worn out, but I went to a Rack Room shoe store, and bought a pair of shoes. I was wearing a pair so worn out, my feet were hurting bad. But I went on to Ginger Brown's and stayed until 9:30 PM. I took three songs I'd written down for Karen and Jeff to learn, hopefully.

Karen, my friend Nicole, and I had planned to make candy today, but Karen made other plans and Nicole and I decided to wait until Monday. She was babysitting today. I spent a lot of the day trying to select some of Paulette's recordings to put on a new CD for Alan Cook. Phil would make the CD for me out of tapes. But they were so mixed up, I decided to take him the CD I had already made. When Phil came by, he still took some tapes with him because he plans to make more CDs.

Thom called and talked to me a long time. He was tired and stressed because of the economy, etc. He told me Michael, Suzanne's son, is hospitalized with what they think is Crohn's disease. It sounds bad, but I don't know much about it. Thom said Michael is 6' 3" and real slim. I guess the reason could be the Crohn's, if he has that.

It had been a year since I had met Don and Jane Laughenhauser when they'd been kind enough to come after me to go to Alan's party. I was a little surprised to see that Don had remembered where I live, but he did. Janet was sick, and I was going with Don. Alan had sent them an invitation like he had sent me. They answered and asked if they could bring anything to the party. He answered back saying, "Yes, Pauline." So Don picked me up, and we drove to Alan's in Dallas. Don was a perfect gentleman, and very thoughtful.

There were a lot of people there for the party. He had a lot of food and everything to drink. We talked, sang some Christmas songs, and had a good time. Most of these people were Episcopalians and I knew from his old church and probably some from his new one. Alan's brother, Warren was there from Nebraska, a nice guy, a lot like Alan. Alan has several brothers. A while later, Warren died. He had the same type cancer Alan had been fighting.

Don and I got back here by about 9:30 PM. He had asked me for one of Paulette's tapes, and I was glad to give him one. I gave Alan the new CD Phil had recorded for me. But I worked two days trying to find certain songs she had done, so Phil could make a better CD, but never had found the ones—all of them—that I wanted. I explained this to Alan, but he said it was okay.

I got up today, hurting as usual, didn't sleep too good last night, and a little concerned about whether to go to church or to the hospital. I felt sure my arm was broken at the wrist.

When I started to get out of the bathtub, I instinctively leaned on my left arm and WOW! I nearly went into orbit, it hurt so badly. So I decided it was the hospital, no question now. I called Sherry, and she insisted I needed to let Phil come after me and take me to HEB hospital. He was about to take Kyle to church, and would come after me and take me on to HEB. So I got ready, and soon he got here after taking Kyle.

I was taken care of well. I had x-rays made, and sure enough, there was a fracture in my wrist. They put a fiberglass splint on it, and I'm to go see Dr. Kallal to see about seeing an orthopedic doctor or a plastic surgeon. So Phil went after Kyle, and came back after me. Afterward, I took them to lunch at Spring Creek Barbecue on Airport Freeway, and after that, we went to

Walmart, where I picked up a few things I could cook easily. I was so tired when I finally got home.

I got a call from Kim Ballog, my deacon. He stopped by the drugstore to pick up my prescription they had, but they were closed, so I'll get it tomorrow. But he bought me an ice bag, which I needed, and brought it; he wouldn't even let me pay him. What a super friend he always is. I gave him the rest of the candy.

Nita called me and offered to help me however I needed her. I told her I was going to try to drive tomorrow, but I'm not sure I can. I told her I would count the bodies lying in the street behind me, and judge whether I should be driving.

I drove myself and managed fine. No casualties left in my path. I saw physician's assistant Rick, who had helped me before. He said he had been in San Antonio for a few years. He had Sharon in the office to make an appointment for me at a hand doctor at North Hills. Nita called me, and I told her I could drive myself, and if I needed to, I'd let her know and she could come get me.

After Morris and I started Love Aviation Training Center, I knew we'd have to get approved by the FAA, the TEA, and whoever else had to check us out. We hadn't been in operation long until Steve, my ex-boss, sent an Arabic friend of his to check us out. He saw all over our place, and I explained it all to him as I led him through. I knew he had been back at Steve's for several months, and I knew Steve had sent him. Sure enough, Steve called me the next day, and I told him I knew he'd sent his friend to check up on me. He planned to inform the TEA, hoping they'd shut us down.

I had done the work to get Steve's school TEA approved, including getting the catalog ready and implementing the records and rules concerning the continued approval. He assured me he hadn't turned me in, but I knew he had. "It doesn't matter, Steve," I told him. "I've already started the process, and I'm getting my stuff ready".

And sure enough, I got word from the TEA, the Texas Education Agency. They were coming to visit me. The man came right on time; he was very cooperative with me, and gave me enough time to get all my schedules, records, and lesson plans ready. Also, he said they'd give me a break, and only charge me half price for approval; only $500.00 instead of the regular $1,000.00.

After that, I got us approved by the FAA, the TEA, and approval of the county for help with some of the students' tuition. Later, we had NATTS approval, but it was taken away when the school was sold to Dalfort.

During this process, Steve came to see me, this time on good terms. He had wrecked his airplane, flying at night with no airport lights, and had broken his neck. He was wearing a brace to hold his head erect. Someone brought him, I forgot who, and left, so Steve stayed the rest of the evening. I took him home after dark. He closed down his school; he had lost his designated mechanics examiners license because of letting examinees cheat, as many others had, and he was still pretty ill with his broken neck. He told me he was proud of me, and hoped there were no ill feelings. I replied that there were none, that I appreciated all he had taught me, and was glad I'd made him proud. I really meant it. I realized then, and I do now, that my accomplishments were not easy to come by. I couldn't have done them at all without his help. He was keeping it secret, he thought, that the Basket Case had been with him when he'd had the crash. The woman we referred to as Basket Case was the latest woman he was having an affair with. The nickname fit her, and she may have lost it altogether by the time Steve died.

He told me he was sick, and would never be well again. He developed cancer and lived a couple of months or so. After his death, his wife and I had a good talk, and made up sort of, after all the lies he had told her about me. I guess we never were the same friends we've been once, but we were friends the rest of her life. She died a few years later of high blood pressure and a bad stroke, which left her unable to talk.

I see some of their kids once in a while. We have always been good friends, nearly like family.

I hear from my old friend Beverly Wilson sometimes. He's been taking chemo for his non-Hodgkin's lymphoma, and he told me today that he has one more chemo treatment to go, and there's no more cancer now. Great news—I always pray for him and we enjoy telephone conversations occasionally.

I went to my oncologist last week, and she gave me a three-month supply of Femora. It's the cancer medicine I'm supposed to take every day for five years and she'll give me more. She also gave me a list of contacts that may help me pay for some; I'll call them and find out. I've given up on buying it, as it would cause me from $350 a month to $500. I thought it would be only about 5% effective but she said it was 50%, so I'll be glad to get the medicine. I did get some help from a company who paid for it.

I drove by the church yesterday and picked out the picture of me for the new church directory. I also ordered one picture each for Thom and Phil; they'll make a nice Christmas present.

Things have become slow at Ginger Brown's, along with the rest of the economy, so Jeff and Karen won't be playing there weekly as they've been for years. So I won't be going on Thursday nights, the way I've done for so long. I miss going and all the friends there, etc. Some of us are planning to go just to get together one night.

Phil is working in Cincinnati, Ohio, where the company is sending him for a year. His family is still here, and he comes home some, and Sherry goes there occasionally. He got a nice camper trailer, and has just moved into it. It's a bit larger than what he'd expected to buy, which is a good thing.

November is over; today is December 1, 2009. I can't believe time passes so fast—it will soon be 2010. I can remember Daddy and Mama talking so many years ago, wondering how many of the family would live to see the year 2000. Not many of us did; Robert and I are the only ones left. Laurine and I are leaving Thursday to go and see Robert and Omia in the nursing home at Idabel. We'll come back on Friday, and spend the night at the Microtel Motel. Roy told me he might not be there, so we won't see any of our folks probably. Mark isn't living with his family any more so we'll probably just go to the cemetery; I hope the weather doesn't get too bad. It's supposed to rain and maybe even snow a little here.

I am having a couple of students sometimes. I don't keep them on a regular schedule; they come when they can. I'm here most of the time when I know they're coming.

Thom is working with Phil, and they're planning to help me get all my debts paid off before January, so I'll be free of debt. They take care of my savings, and I'm so glad to have them do it.

January, 1948

After Tommy was born January 23, Mama stayed a while with us. The day we came home from the hospital, Daddy had been staying in an apartment downtown. Aunt Mary, Mama's ex-sister-in-law, had an apartment building off East Belknap on Samuels Avenue. It was one room. Daddy was staying in the apartment and Mama moved in with him. In about four or five days we went to see them. Mama came home with us and spent a week or so to help take care of me and the baby. Daddy would come out, on a bus that came down Jacksboro Highway, and walk the five or six blocks to our house. His blood pressure had become very high, and he'd had some mini-strokes. Instead of seeing a doctor, he took garlic, which was thought to be a good treatment for blood pressure at that time. You could smell the garlic a good way off.

Sherman and I began to talk to Mama and Daddy about moving them in with us. Mama was willing and ready, but it took us a little longer to convince Daddy. Finally we did, and we went after them in a few weeks. Tommy was nine months old, active and bright and talking early. He loved the attention he got from both his grandparents. We visited Sherman's parents, the Ruffins, and they visited us. His mother, Agnes, was busy with kids and grandkids all her life, and was a great babysitter. She was a large lady, and that great body of hers was a nice, soft place for a crying or colicky baby. I enjoyed discussing world affairs with Sherman's dad, Johnny. We always loved to visit with them, and so did my parents.

Daddy lost no time starting to help us fix up our place, finishing a bathroom we had started, and building of a new kitchen, bedroom, and paying for most of it. He bought a new refrigerator, and we got rid of the old icebox we had been using. We had two bedrooms. He paid for a lot of the materials. He and Sherman both worked on the project. We built onto the house later, had a large den, another bedroom, and bath. Sadly, Daddy didn't live long enough to enjoy all the improvements. He had a violent stroke at age 61, December, 1949. We took him back home to be buried at the Moran cemetery. His funeral was January 1, 1950.

Janice, Ruby's third daughter, was born on December 28, the same day Daddy died. We went to see her when we got to Oklahoma. Her face seemed to be a little paralyzed, and her eyes were crossed. Tommy, 21 months old now, was asleep while the funeral service was going on, but woke up as we started to leave, and started to cry and reach out for the gravesite. Mama asked us to take him back and show him Daddy in the casket, so we did. He stopped crying and said "bye" and waved to Daddy. He seemed to understand everything, and I think he did.

Later we were at the old Leonard's Department Store, and he saw someone walking ahead of us. He started running after him, saying "Tom-Daddy", his name for his granddaddy. I felt like crying myself, as I picked him up and explained that it wasn't Tom-Daddy, just a man who looked like him.

Mama stayed with us for some time, later moving into a home. We helped her get a house on Buchanan Street. She never married again, although she still looked good and didn't show her age until just before she died. But she worked all those years babysitting for neighbors, and for me and Margaret. Margaret worked to support her family all her life. Mama was only 57 when Daddy died, and lived until she was 96 ½. A couple or three years later we made another trip to Oklahoma, this time to bring Ruby and Vernon back to Fort Worth with us. Vernon got a job with the Santa Fe railroad, and they moved up on the north side on 24th St. off Azle Avenue. The two girls, Laverne and Alice, entered school at Lake Worth.

Janice grew up, a very bright little girl. Ruby was a sweet mother, and an ideal one for all of the girls, especially Janice who was very self-conscious and had to deal with remarks and stares of thoughtless people. We all wondered why they hadn't seen doctors about her facial condition and her eyes; she couldn't see well. But she was a very determined and brave girl; when she graduated from high school she went to work at a large department store, and has worked ever since. She went, herself, to the doctor who performed two or three radical surgeries to her face and eyes. He released the pulled muscles in her face, and her eyes are now straight, although her side vision is limited and she wears glasses. But she took care of her parents. Vernon's job didn't last long; he did a little painting, but never stopped the drinking until much later. When he died.

Janice inherited her mother's kind, sweet ways. She learned early to be independent and take care of herself, as well as being there for the rest of the family. She's never dated, never had a social life, except with family.

Vernon died in his bed, in the house Janice had bought for the three of them. A few years later, Alice came to live some of her last weeks before dying in 1987. She died from cancer two hours before Mama did at Westside Care Center, close to Ridgmar Mall; Alice was at the Harris Hospital downtown.

Alice was buried in Cleburne, and Mama in Oklahoma at Moran cemetery. Lewie and Lennie are both at the Rufe Cemetery, and Mama, Daddy, Jack, Margaret, Grandma Knoblock, and Addie are all buried at Moran along with Sherman's folks. Ruby is buried at Ash Greek in Azle, where Ronnie Griggs is also buried. Ronnie was killed in his front yard, and the case has never been completely settled to the satisfaction of the family.

Chapter 3

"Loose Lips Sink Ships"

I sold a set of A&P books this morning to a young man getting ready to go over to Iraq for four months. He hopes to be ready to test when he comes back in April. It's Kevin; his wife is the granddaughter of Randall and Dee. They are secretly married, but they're having another wedding in April. I promised not to tell. Only her mother knows, and now me.

I talked to Carolyn this evening. We always have fun talking, but we are both very concerned about the war situation. Israel has sent ground troops to Gaza, and is still bombing. Just like the Bible predicts. It looks bad, and people are blaming Israel for taking up for themselves. But the Palestinians are still sending rockets into Israel. It's strange, how people never see what's causing the Israelites to fight. Just like prophecy.

I washed and rolled my hair for church tomorrow. I finally got my e-mail working on Gmail, thanks to Phil and Sherry. Also I got a new cartridge for my printer, thanks to Phil who ordered it. But several of my e-mail friends don't have my new address. I'm still a little green about it so will take me a few days. A few days later I'm still learning and calling Phil regularly. But today was choir rehearsal for our seniors, and I was asked to be director. Ginger was to have her pacemaker installed at 10 AM, and Jaye was there at the hospital with her. But there was no one there except Carlene and me, so I came on home and got ready to go to Manor Care.

I'm afraid Johnny has just about lost it. He is so mixed up. I helped John, another volunteer, deliver some magazines and small gifts to some of the patients, and then when I went back to see Johnny, he had gone back to bed and didn't seem to be thinking straight at all. He couldn't hear. I got up to leave, and he got upset with me because I talked too loud. Last night, as I was fixing my supper I got a call from Matt. I was so happy to hear from him; he came over and ate supper with me. I had fixed salmon patties and some vegetables, and I fried some potatoes.

He stayed a while with me and later went to Phil and Sherry's, and got his Christmas present I had left there. I had told him it was a coat. Today was a nice day—a lot warmer than yesterday. It got colder by tonight, but I think the rest of the week will be warmer—at least until the weekend.

On Saturday, I went to a wedding for my friends, Roxie and Johnny Davis. It was a little strange, right outside the exchange building at the stockyards, but Johnny and Roxie seemed to be happy,

Roxie was in a white, western-style dress with lots of petticoats and her oversize straw hat, and Johnny Davis with fancy cowboy clothes, his big black hat, cowboy boots, and an overcoat. The ring bearer was his dog—it looked like a corgi—and rings were tied to the coat he wore. So when it was time, Johnny whistled, and the dog trotted over and stopped while Johnny untied the string holding the rings.

I went alone, but the parade from the stock show was just over and there were people all over the place. All the men there for the wedding were dressed like cowboys, and the women wore dresses that look like the old West movies.

When I got home, I started to go to Phil's. I bought two chickens already cooked, and wanted to take one to Phil's. The phone rang, and it was Beverly, my good friend from Aransas Pass. He told me Juandell had died last Tuesday. I had been thinking about Juandell all week and felt like he was worse or gone, and sure enough, he was. I'm so sorry. I liked Juandell a lot. We were never as close as Beverly and me, but he was an old friend and I was very sad; we grew up together so long ago.

I called Pete Mitchell this afternoon and told him about Juandell.

I went to church tonight. We had cakes and drinks later, and I'm to direct the Sweet Spirit Singers on Tuesday. We are going to North Point Nursing Home to sing for them.

In December 1994, Thom sent for Sherman and me to come to Washington DC to spend a few days with them. Thom and a woman he was engaged to had just broken up. He and Debby were seeing each other again, but hadn't made any definite plans yet. In fact, Debby was a little resentful about the relationship, Thom's and Diane's, and was hesitating about getting back together with Thom.

Thom had a high-rise apartment downtown and was a great homemaker, also a great host for dinner parties. He had made reservations for him, Debby, and another couple at the Ford Theater to see "A Christmas Carol," but she had refused to go with him. He took us, and it was wonderful. We saw the exact spot where Abraham Lincoln was shot. He also took us to see George Washington's old home and grounds, and since it was George Washington's birthday, we got to go on inside the house and up on the third floor. We saw his office and all the whole estate. He took us downtown and we rode the bus all around the city with the driver explaining everything to us about the statues, buildings, etc. I remember the driver had some reindeer horns he was wearing for the Christmas season.

Meantime, Thom was trying to win Debby back. He took us to Williamsburg where Lesley and Ben were living, and he brought Debby a beautiful new watch. I guess it did the trick. They became engaged soon after that. Sherman and I got home in time to have Christmas at home.

One of the most memorable times we had was a visit to the Ruffin plantation. We had to pay admission, even though we were kinfolk. It was the old home of Edmund Ruffin, a rebel from the South in the Civil War. He was too old to fight, but fired the first shot in the Civil War. He was quite a smart man; he wrote several books and had made a lot of strides in his fight for the South. I have some pamphlets as well as books he wrote, and he and Sherman look nearly alike in the picture, except Edmond's hair was long, shoulder length. But their facial features are nearly exactly alike.

The plantation was beautiful. Some of the Civil War was fought in the backyard of the place right near the water of the James River, but it sure is beautiful. Thom and Debby talked to the man there about having their wedding there, but it was decided to have the wedding at the historic home of Robert E. Lee.

We visited them the next year or two, and they had a three-story townhouse. Debby's oldest daughter, Wendy lived with them. We enjoyed this visit, too. Thom took me to the capitol, the archives, and also to the museums. The Holocaust museum was a once-in-a-lifetime event, but a very sad occasion—

sights that are hard to get out of your mind. We saw pictures of so many innocent people, most of whom were prisoners at the death camps, the bins of shoes removed as the prisoners went into the gas chambers, even the pitiful plates and spoons they used. We saw the hard beds, the rags that had been clothes, etc. There were recordings of prisoners' voices, telling about their experience. There were body bins, a couple of them from the death chamber.

After that we went to the Aircraft Museum which, by that time, I was so emotionally worn out I didn't appreciate it nearly so much as I did when we went to the new Aircraft Museum in 2008.

After a second visit to my back doctor and that many more x-rays, I'm going in the morning to have an epidural injection with cortisone into the pinched nerve. Dr. Elders said it may completely remove the pain. At any rate, I'm glad to do that. I went Friday for pre-op. Randall, my good friend, volunteered to take me for the procedure at Baylor in Trophy Club on Highway 114. After I get home, Sandra Evans is coming, bringing our lunch and a movie. I heard this newsflash: Congress has just passed a bill, the House and Senate, no one has even read it, but it's supposed to solve the problems with the economy, the brainstorm of our US president Obama and his henchmen. Gov. Huckabee has renamed the bill passed which is self-explanatory—C for Congress, R for Relief, A for Action, and P for Package.

No one has read all of it, but it's going to cost over a trillion dollars to spend, because we're in so much debt???? Obama has had less than 3 weeks in office. He promised "change", but has neglected to explain the term. Nobody seems to question his politics, his opinions, or his personal life, but our great nation's economy is in the tank, and still going down. Who knows what will happen next?

So I got ready to go for the epidural procedure on Monday. I set my alarm for 4:30. The nurse at Trophy Club Baylor had informed me my appointment had been changed to 7:50 so I needed to get there by 6:45 AM. I called Randall to make sure he didn't mind getting up so early, and he assured me he was planning on it. What a guy! I've never had a friend like him. My alarm was set wrong, and Randall called me and woke me up at five. I got up, and got ready and he was there in about 30 or 40 min. He was in Dee's car; it didn't take long to get there. The procedure went well, and when we got back home, Randall stayed long enough to hear the two songs I had written with Bill, sung by Paulette, I had failed to send them to him—I didn't have his correct e-mail address. He liked them, he said.

He left and I called Sandra Evans who was going to Chic-Fil-A to get our lunch. She brought it and stayed a while. She is another great friend.

Several days have passed, and I know I easily forget a lot. I'm so much better. I'm to go see Dr. Elders next Wednesday for a follow-up visit. I'm better as time goes on—today is Saturday, February 28, the last day of February. I spent a lot of today at Laverne's. Carolyn and Dale are there till Monday. We enjoyed visiting, and there's been a new development in Laverne's life is. She's broken off her romance with Kearney, and is planning to marry Jim. He has been staying at her place for a while, and has a mobile home parked on her place. He's from Ronnie's family and has been a good friend of hers for a long time. I have been keeping a secret for several days. Karen told me she and Jeff were going back to Nashville, Tennessee again. They went several years ago and did some shows, and Jeff won some contests, but didn't get any big breaks, so they came home. Actually they never went this time, after all, as I later found out.

I fixed supper for Randall and Dee last Wednesday. It had been so long since I cooked for anyone, I was anxious about whether I could. But it was okay, not great. We enjoyed it, and they were very gracious about it.

My computer finally died; I spent 12 hours trying to revive it, but it was terminal. So Phil ordered another one; it is to be here next Tuesday. It's coming with the new keyboard and a larger monitor than I have now. He's going to get it all hooked up at his house, and then bring it here. I really miss it, but have been kind of keeping up with my e-mails on Phil's computer. I'll be glad to get mine back. It turns out, Phil and Jonathan ordered new parts, and Phil built me a whole new computer.

I talked to Thom on Thursday; he was in San Francisco. He said his office is to be moved from Warrenton, Virginia to Bethesda, Maryland. I don't know how far it is from their house, but always places in Virginia, Maryland and Pennsylvania are close together, or seem so to me. Thom drives a lot, but doesn't seem to mind, and so does Debby.

I spent nearly all Saturday and Sunday of last week, February 28 and March 1, at LaVerne's. Carolyn and Dale were there. Also, the man I'd met before who played the guitar the last time was there again. This time, LaVerne told me they planned to get married. This was Jim. She told Kearney, she said, she'd never been in love with him in the first place; she couldn't escape the fact that he was Alice's husband. But she hadn't told Kearney that she and Jim were engaged to be married yet...she knew he'd be hurt.

My voice is messed up with sinus trouble, but I sang two of my songs, "Dreaming" and "Hard Luck Reverie", a cappella.

Carolyn and Janice were sitting on the couch, and when I finished singing my songs, Carolyn said, "Pauline, you sound great—we decided you sound sultry and sexy!"

"Thanks", I said, "but I'm just in my older flirties."

We did some oldies; I sang "The Old Apple Tree in the Orchard" and "Ain't We Crazy!" Carolyn wants the words to both songs and I promised to send them to her.

I was supposed to go and see Dr. Elders for a follow-up visit after the procedure last week, but I called and begged off because we were to go to Manor Care and sing on Tuesday when my appointment was due. They set me up for the next Tuesday, so I'll miss choir practice, and I hate to miss choir. We went on Tuesday, and I was glad. There were about ten of us, and we got Johnny's wheelchair up in our group so he could sing with us. I stayed with him and sang, and afterward, he told me it was the first time he'd ever heard me sing and loved it. His hearing is so bad that he was elated to be able to hear me.

I went with Jann, Dan Shiro's daughter, to El Paseo to eat lunch. We got back to Manor Care; it was my regular day to have a game with the residents. Today it was a Bible quiz, which I love to do. I had two books with questions and answers to choose from. We didn't have many to participate—about five of us all together—and we had a great discussion.

After that, I went and visited Johnny a while, and did some more visiting. It's amazing so many of the residents expect me to be a nurse or nurse's aide, and asked me to do stuff I can't possibly do, just being a volunteer. Life at Manor Care has some funny moments. Last week, my good friend Pauline Wasser wanted me to help her get to the bathroom. I explained to her that I wasn't allowed to do that, and I couldn't even do it, since I'm neither a nurse nor an aide. I stood in the door and watched for a nurse, and asked her for help. Pauline asked if I would come back to see about her, and I promised I would. But I went on to do my thing as a volunteer, and I forgot until too late. I figured she'd forgotten about it anyway. But she hadn't, and yesterday she asked me to move so she could get back in bed by herself, and again I told her I'd get a nurse to help her. Once again, she asked me to come back to see about her, and I promised to. She reminded me that I hadn't come back like I promised before, said she had been awake and had her door open and waited for me.

We had a really good spelling bee in the dining room. Jann, Janet, and Jack were there, and Johnny. There were about six or seven residents and they enjoyed it and were, surprisingly, great spellers. Afterwards I went back to see Pauline. She was being fed her supper. I kissed her forehead and said, "See, I told you I'd be back to see you," and she said, "Yes, but you didn't say it would be six months before you got here." I laughed and teased her and she said she loved me. It was Thursday, and I went and spent the rest of the time with Johnny, until 5:45 PM. I went on to Ginger Brown's. Johnny was getting worse. They said later that he had gone out of the building and tried to get into a red truck that belonged to one of the staff, so they decided to put an alarm on his arm. We talked a long time about it, and they promised to do a blood test and a kidney analysis and see if he had an infection that would cause him to do that. But I can finally see that he was getting a lot worse and his memory was about gone. The day after that, he had forgotten all about it; it seemed he never did believe he did it anyway.

I went on the Ginger Brown's, and had a great time. My friends, Sandra and Jay Evans came with their daughter, Rachel, Johnny Davis, and Roxie, and a large part of Karen's mother's church were there. They had their music director, Edward with them. What a nice guy! He and I sang a John Denver song together, and then Edelweiss. We loved singing together. He's going back to Montana, his home, for a few days, but he promised he'd be back. We agreed we sang well together, as did most everyone else. Randall complemented me and I kept the song going in my mind. I've loved it ever since the kids sang it in the school choir. I haven't heard any more about Jeff and Karen leaving for Nashville; I'm keeping my fingers crossed. Sandra came by and had coffee with me this morning.

It has rained for several days, fortunately, but is supposed to be clear and nice tomorrow afternoon.

I called Thom; he was just coming home from Chicago. It's March 14, 2009, Sherman's birthday. He was born in 1920, 89 years ago today. He was 81 when he died in April, 2001. I'm still lonely without him, and feel I could have handled life differently, but I try not to brood.

I called Robert and Omia today. No answer. I called Mark's cell phone. No answer there either. I called Roy's home number but had to leave a message, and then I called Kenneth and talked to Mary. She talked to me for about an hour. Robert was in the hospital, and Omia had been taken to Mena, Arkansas to Betty's. Mary gave me Roy's cell number, so I called him. He had taken Omia to Betty's. He told me Robert was very low on potassium, and couldn't come home for a while. He had a potassium drip and seemed better today. But he has a lot of dementia, and they both need to be in a nursing home. I know it won't be easy to get Robert to go.

Laurine and I plan to go see Robert in Idabel. I learned that Mark and Bonnie are divorced. She lives in their house two doors from Robert, at home with her two boys. Mark is living somewhere else with a woman. I also found out Greg Shiro is a flight attendant for Southwest Airlines. He has his private pilot rating, but wants someday to get more flight ratings.

It's St. Patrick's Day, and my friend and former student for 30 years came today for his IA renewal. He came to me 30 years ago, and was feeling bad because he had failed his A&P written exam. He is dyslexic and I promised to keep working with him till he got through all of it. He did extra well, and I could see he was an extremely intelligent man. He got finished, and three years later he came to me to help him get his IA. So he got that, and has been coming to me every year for his IA renewal. His name is Jimmy Collier.

I love him and his wife, who came with him today. He works on aircraft and race cars in his own business in Jefferson, Texas, in spite of being partially blind. Today I realized all over again how very intelligent he is, and he is amazing. We went to Joe's and had lunch, and I made his diploma with the computer, first time I've been able to do this, thanks to Phil.

I got a call from a new student. He is coming out tomorrow, an A&P, and I got a call from Manda and Jacky, and he told me she was going to nurses' school and would finish soon. She is very excited and happy and already has her CPR rating. Jacky said they finally removed his gallbladder and he is going to get $600 a month from SSI. He said he's going to Valera, a service station, and work 24 hours a week, but will go back to Whataburger later. I have another IA renewal on Saturday.

I got more good news. Jimmy Collier had come earlier last week, and I got a call from Chris Beams, who came today and will finish on Friday. Kenneth's wife, Mary called me. She said they had told Roy that Robert is having mini-strokes and not Alzheimer's. He does have dementia, but maybe if he has mini-strokes it's possible he'll get better. But he won't be able to go home, and neither will she. I think the hospital is helping Roy to get them into a nursing home. He's trying to get Medicaid for them. Robert thinks he's in Paris, Texas, so is still pretty disoriented. I talked to Janice, and she told me Ruby had some spells that sounded like mini-strokes.

I went to Manor Care as usual on Thursday. I was surprised to know that we had lost not just Janie Mitchell, one of our patients, but also Trudy, a sweet lady who also was a favorite, always had a smile, and said she felt fine even when we knew better. Later of course, after staying with Johnny until he ate his supper, I went on to Ginger Brown's. Johnny Davis and Roxie were there, and it was a good night. The remarks Karen had made about the going to Nashville seem to have gone away. They have several weeks booked, Randall told them, and it all seems to be planned. Randall told me Dee was having a bad ear infection and was very ill with it. Today, Friday, I called and asked about her. She's taking antibiotics that haven't seemed to help.

It's been quite a week so far. I discovered I have a large lump in my left breast. I had a lumpectomy there many years ago. Dr. Mary Brian did the surgery, and said there was very little chance, maybe 5% it would ever return. I'm having a mammogram on Friday and will see Dr. Brian on the second. I'm a little uneasy and hope it's nothing, but will be OK. I had three IA renewal students on Saturday. These were two I see every year for this, and one new fellow from Egypt. We had a great time. The Egyptian's wife came and went to lunch with us at Joe's. James Collier had come earlier last week, and I got a call from Chris Beams, who came today and will finish on Friday.

I heard from Kenneth, and he said they had taken Robert home and that Omia had gone home too. They'll arrange for Nick to stay with them during the day. Omia adamantly refused to go to a nursing home. Kenneth told me when Robert was in the hospital, he asked a 19-year-old nurse to run away with him. When she told him no, he got embarrassed, but forgot it in a few minutes.

I got a new A&P student this week. He's a Mexican and a really nice guy. He plans to come Monday, Tuesday, and Wednesday.

I went to Manor Care yesterday and Johnny was ill, has a really bad cold and was about half conscious, but he got up and went to the dining room with me.

I called Janet this morning and she said he fell on Monday. He has a bad kidney infection and they're giving him some strong antibiotics.

Laverne called me today. She and Jim got married on Saturday. She says they're very happy, and she had told Kearney about it before they had married. I know he was pretty hurt. I started to call him, but decided against it for now. I plan to host a party for them and the family later when they get back from a honeymoon trip. Laverne called this morning and said they're coming home soon.

I went to Baylor last Friday and had a mammogram. I have a very small lump in my left breast, the same one that Dr. Mary Brian did a lumpectomy on about 10 years ago. Today, Monday, I had a biopsy that was a bit painful but a little complicated. They put clips in my breast to mark where the tissue was removed, and the mammogram didn't show where it was, so I had to have a second one. It was successful, but I was curious about clips and I asked Dr.

Gregory what they meant by these clips. He had been watching world war two movies and heard the motto, "Loose lips sink ships." Misunderstanding what I said, he said they sink ships.

A little surprised, I said, "And you put those things in me?" He kept apologizing, but later I couldn't stop laughing. Carolyn called to see how I was and we laughed so hard!

Mary called me this afternoon and told me Robert and Omia were going to go to a nursing home in Idabel, and will be in the same room. My student came this afternoon. I like him, we get to talking and I have to tear myself away. We enjoy each other, he is such a nice guy and very intelligent, very personable. The next day I was on my way to Manor Care, and Dr. Matt Jeffries called me to tell me the results of the biopsy. It was definitely cancer, not the worst kind, but not the best either. He was gentle as possible, and broke the news as gently as he could. I didn't cry. I wanted to, but kept my self-control and my emotions as well as I could. I told him, "Well, you made a place for yourself in my book." I told him the episode about the loose lips. We laughed and he told me to please call them, to come and see him and the two nurses who work with him, and to be sure to ask any questions I had, and to let them know how I got along. I went on to Manor Care. I told Betty and Gaye and Jann I was fine. Somehow, I knew I'd be okay whatever happened.

My dear friend, Sandra took me to see Dr. Mary Brian. Things moved very fast. I was set up for surgery at HEB on April 14, at 11:15 AM. I called Dr. Kallal, my family physician for 20 years, to get some Xanax to help me sleep. I never cried, neither was I upset, just couldn't sleep well, so I guess I was a little nervous. The doctor told me to come in at 7 AM the next day. He was very upset about me—he's always been so careful about my having breast cancer because of the lumpectomy I'd had, and Paulette's condition. I had called him when I first found the lump, and he warned me to see Dr. Brian as soon as possible, but now he seemed to regret not being the first doctor I had seen. Later he filled out the papers to admit me to the hospital.

Thom's company was sending him to Dallas on the 13th and 14th; he meant to spend the night at home here, or I'd come to Dallas to be with him. But he came to my house on the 13th, and took me to the hospital on the 14th, and we met Phil and Sherry there. The company postponed his meeting in Dallas, so he stayed at the hospital with me.

People, some from the church, and others began to gather. I counted 16 who were in the waiting room for my surgery. Jeanette brought Johnny in his wheelchair. She brought him to my room; he was so sweet and so glad to see me. My surgery was over, and I began to wake up. I was not in pain and never had that pain medicine after waking at all.

Late in the evening the next day, the 15th, Thom brought me home. I was okay. I took some Tylenol as usual, and we kept the bulb drained as needed. Thom is so good to me, and takes care of me so well. The next morning, Sandra came over and had coffee and snacks with us. Thom is going to write a story for The Senior Gazette and send it there about my being in Alexandria, Virginia and going to the mall there. The taxi never came for me, and a strange lady gave me a ride home. It was a funny story, and funnier when Thom told it.

Later, a sweet lady from the church, Judy Stillwell called and came by, and brought us all sandwiches and cookies and little bowls of fruit. It was great; we had a nice visit. Thom had to leave for the airport and home at 4 PM, but he'll be back next week. His postponed meeting will be held in Dallas.

I'm doing okay, have had many e-mails and phone calls. The most important call was from Dr. Brian, telling me all my tests were negative—I needed no chemo or radiation, and no more cancer. I made many calls and e-mails and messages on Facebook telling the good news to everyone including the girls and Dr. Jeffries at Baylor Breast Cancer Center.

When Thom first came, we had dinner at the Olive Garden and saw Matt. I told him about the breast cancer and he cried. He looks good and was doing fine, but I was upset to see him upset, but he assured me he was fine.

Today, Matt called me. I let him know I was fine. He just wanted to tell me he loved me and didn't mean to be so busy, but was working on the album he was doing. I assured him I understood it and was happy about his music going well, and always knew he loved me.

I got a message from Terry Thompson yesterday that Denise, Donna's sister had died. I called Donna, and we had a nice visit on the phone. Denise's funeral is to be this afternoon. Donna was so sweet, and said she wants to go to church with me. She promised to go with me as soon as I'm able to go. I go see Dr. Brian next Thursday, and after that I should be ready to drive and pretty much resume a normal life.

Kathy called me from Johnny's today, and took her phone and let me talk to Johnnie on the speakerphone. He could hear me well for a change. They fixed his room up and it looks homier. Randall called me and told me he had taken Dee to Waffle House; she didn't eat much, but that made me hungry. I decided to make pecan pancakes for supper, which were really good. I've got too much appetite.

Several days have passed. I'm about well, but still in some pain. Last Thursday when I went to see Dr. Brian (Janet took me), she said I was still having too much drainage, and should use the drain until it hurts a lot less. After we left there, we went to eat at IHOP, and then went to visit Johnny at Avalon. He was so glad to see me. He'd been calling me two or three times a day, but couldn't hear me but very little.

Randall's wife is doing well now, just takes a few days. I've talked to them regularly. She had a pacemaker installed, and finally got her heartbeat back in rhythm.

Dr. Brian told me I could drive now, but not to go far, just in my own community, but I went to Ginger Brown's the other night. Roxie came after me, and brought me home. We were a little later arriving than usual, and Randall called me while we were on our way. He said my fans all wanted to know when I'd be there. It was a good night. Joyce gave me a nice gift. It was Jeff's birthday and we had a party for him.

Thom came to see me again and we went to the Olive Garden. We didn't see Matt, it was his night off, but we had a good time and a good supper. Thom spent the night with me. I talked to him today and he said he's coming back Tuesday and will come here. We're to go eat about 8 PM. I'm having a class start, so will probably have students on Tuesday 'til nine.

Also in the paper yesterday, Saturday, there was to be a static air show, it was a war bird display. Nearly all were WW2 planes but some modern ones and helicopters. I called Jim and Donna, and asked if they wanted to go. They did, and took me. After visiting the show about two hours or so and, wow! We walked all that time. We went to the Colonial and ate, had a great lunch. I was so tired when I got home, but rested a while and went to the store.

I went to church this morning, enjoying all the attention, and after eating lunch at home, I went to see Johnny. We had a good visit and saw Howard and his friends, Sam and Gina. Later, Janet and Jack and Randy came in. Randy brought his recordings and played them for us. He has sent Randall a couple, and Randall was really impressed. They were pretty good.

Jim Ed came to see his dad. Before that, one of the ladies there who was about as daft as Johnny, began to show me how to direct music. She was very intellectual, and knew what she was doing. She said she was going to test me when I came back, to see if I remembered what she told me.

We had a nice visit, but I had to leave and get home. I need to rest a lot these days, to get over the effects of the surgery.

Chapter 4

"Don't ever kiss me like that unless you mean it."

I called Pauline Rice and we went to Joe's diner to eat. Afterward, we went to Walmart to buy groceries. As I was going down the last aisle between two other frozen food counters, I watched as a young man stand there with the door open. He had on a little a large black coat, (it was a warm day, 67°) and he was putting items inside his coat. I stood still and watched him and he turned around and smiled at me, and spoke pleasantly, half smiling. I returned the remark, but looked into his eyes; no smile, and I guess I looked stern and fierce as Jonathan once said about his school teacher. I just wanted him to know I saw him and what he was doing. But it never fazed him. He was still standing there filling his inner pockets of the coat while Pauline and I had our groceries checked and went out. I told the cashier who checked us out what was going on, and she told some more who worked there. I don't know if anyone confronted him or not, but I found out after we left that Pauline, unsuspecting what the young man was doing, asked him if he knew where the frozen pie crusts were. He indicated other freezers beyond that one, and we laughed about it later. I still wonder if he got stopped by the time he got out.

When we got home I saw my neighbor, Karen and asked her to come over and have dessert with us. She did, and after she left I showed Pauline the pictures Phil had posted on my Facebook, then I took her home.

Sherry, my daughter-in-law, called me and we went out and ate at Chili's Sunday night, February 28, 2010. Happy birthday, Bill Hartmann! Tomorrow is March 1. Thom has been planning on being here in the evening, but the weather has been so bad twice since before Christmas his flight has been canceled. He's supposed to be here Monday evening, and I hope he does, but bad weather is being predicted, so we'll see.

We had good services at church this morning. Pauline Rice and I went to Joe's for lunch. We had a sandwich, and after I took her home I went to see Johnny. As always he was glad to see me. He seemed to be a little better today. I didn't stay long, I was feeling pretty bad with arthritis and came home early. I looked at the paper, took a short nap, and went to church tonight. I fixed a small grilled cheese sandwich and some fruit. Monday, March 1—I'd been expecting Thom and sure enough he called me early and said he'd be here. He got here early, about 4:30 to 5 PM. I called and found out Matt was going to be working, so he made reservations for us at his section at PF Chang's. I finally got to get Thom's Christmas and birthday presents, and we got to look at some of the e-mail pictures of my birthday party on my Facebook.

We went on to Grapevine, and Matt was happy to see us. We had a very expensive meal. I think the manager gave us a one-half price break, which was nice. He also gave Thom some dessert coupons for when he went to Las Vegas later.

Thom, after he brought me home and we talked a while, had to drive to Dallas where he had a hotel room; he had lots of meetings tomorrow. But we had a good visit.

This morning, I was glad to see a beautiful day; sunshine and the temperature in the low 50s. It's election day for the state primaries, and I voted at the Watauga Community Center.

I fixed my lunch and went to Manor Care. I went by the bank and cashed a check first, and left for Manor Care about 1 PM. Betty, the lady I work with, had us down for target practice, but I took some dominoes and we played until time was up. I came on home at 4 PM, fixed my supper, and got ready to see the election results beginning at 7 PM. Rick Perry won the GOP primary for governor. Other than that, I didn't know any of the candidates well enough to care much. There is so much mudslinging, it's confusing as heck.

I did some washing this morning, and after lunch I went to a funeral. It was at Shannon, Rufe Snow, for our friend Louise Elliott's mother. Louise and her husband, Jerry had been taking care of her for a few months. The service was nice. The pastor, Dennis, brought the message, and Jaye Biles sang a medley of old hymns; about 25 attended.

I got a call from Ahmed, an IA; he was here last year to get a renewal. He is coming next Tuesday for renewal again. I'm waiting to hear from Art Befort about him and Mark and Mac Rogers, but it will need to be sometime this month.

I got up late this morning, and it's a bad idea. If I don't get up early around six, I hurt so bad with arthritis, it takes longer be up and going. I have to sit a few minutes before I can make coffee and get breakfast. This morning I was thinking, "How can I go to the nursing home twice a week?" But I was okay in a little while and changed my mind. I got going, rolled my hair, dried it, and went on to Manor Care. It was a good day. There were three tables of dominoes going, and then I played Millionaire with about six ladies.

When I left there, I went to Avalon to see Johnny. He was already in the dining room when I got there. He was happy to see me, and I stayed and ate supper with him.

Before we ate, I went to his room to use his bathroom, and on the way back to the dining room I saw David, Howard's grandson. He wanted me to go in and see Howard, so I did. Howard is very close to death, and didn't seem to be conscious at all. Hospice is staying with him. David said he hadn't been eating, which was not surprising.

After Johnny and I ate, he started trying to find money to pay for supper. He always does, and doesn't understand when I tell him it's been taken care of. Once, he said he needs to quit going out because he didn't have money to pay. Also he's beginning to be really messy with his food.

I drove home about 6 PM; it's Thursday night, and I missed being at Ginger Brown's with all of our friends.

One of the men from Manor Care came by and reminded me who he was. I'd seen him before; we knew we knew each other and it finally dawned on him. He used to sing with Jeff some at Ginger Brown's. He was at Manor Care for rehab after knee replacement, he said. His name is Jerry Pierce and I knew him well, but I'd forgotten his name as he had mine, so we got reacquainted. I think he sings with Jeff at Tater Junction or somewhere. To backtrack, I had gone by IHOP on the way to Manor Care and had lunch. Morris and Bobby were there. We visited for a while; Morris had had some surgery on his hand and wrist from arthritis. Guess we've all got it.

On Friday I woke up feeling much better; so much better, in fact, that I decided to go to the mall. I called Pauline, but she was expecting a man to do her yard and trim her hedges. She wanted to go, but she said that this man was already an hour late and she hadn't heard from him.

I went to North Hills Mall, and walked through to Macy's. On the way, at the food court, I saw several other friends who were always there. I stayed for a few minutes visiting, and went on to Macy's. Got some new makeup, and then went to Dillard's, looked a little, and then back to Penny's where I'd parked. I was amazed! I had worn the SAS shoes I bought years ago when I had foot surgery. I couldn't believe it; they hadn't hurt all the time I was out and walking all over the mall. I'm going tomorrow to get some new ones in black or brown. These are blue, so comfortable when I got home I went to Walmart for a few things. After I'd rested, I fixed my supper. Thom called me and talked a while. He was listening to a book about Ted Kennedy who had died a few weeks ago and somebody had written a book about his life. Lesley gave the book to him for Christmas or his birthday.

I called Kearney this evening. He hadn't called me for some time, and he was waiting to see if I'd call him. It's been a beautiful day today; I think it's been about 70° bright and sunny, just a little breeze.

I've done just about nothing as far as housecleaning. I'm promising myself that tomorrow, Saturday, I'm cleaning my house.

But it turned out I didn't. I was under the weather for a few days. Johnny's brother, Howard died, and I was unable to go to the funeral. Johnny did not go because he was also unable, and when I saw him a few days later, he asked me where Howard was and I told him. The administrator came in, and seeing Johnny was upset, she read me the riot act, but it didn't matter. I'm sure he's already forgotten it by now. I feel the same way his family does, that he has the right to know. I'd want to know if I were in his place. I'm sure he forgot it in a couple of hours.

Phil came home last week for a vacation. Carolyn and Dale came to Texas, and parked their beautiful new fifth wheel near Jacksboro, Texas. Carolyn is feeling better, but still not real well. I went with Laverne, Jim, and Janice to see them all Friday. Laverne and Janice fixed lunch and took it so Carolyn didn't have to cook.

Then on Monday, yesterday, Phil, Sherry, and I went to Laverne and Jim's. Carolyn and I were there, and Robert, Rhonda, and Marvin. Jim played his keyboard, Rhonda and Marvin played guitar and bass, and we all sang. I think we were all thrilled and surprised all over again by the way Phil sang such a great tenor. His voice just blows me away all over again. But we all sounded good, and we sang all afternoon and evening. We left between 8 and 9 PM.

I had taken a large quantity of rolls made that morning, and Laverne cooked an excellent roast with gravy and potatoes. Phil and Sherry brought a coconut pie, and there was a cake. It was such a great meal. Phil took pictures while we were singing "Mansion Over the Hilltop," and then he put it on YouTube. I was a little shocked at first, but finally decided it wasn't so bad, but our singing was a hundred percent better when his camera battery was low and he sang with us. He's been home this weekend and is here for next weekend.

Randall called and told me Johnny High had died. He was our good friend and mentor to so many musicians, including Paulette. Johnnie was my age; had been in the music business for many years, and was a much beloved man in the industry. He's been having a lot of heart trouble for years, but has kept on doing the show until about a month ago. His funeral is tomorrow, Saturday, at the country music theater. Visitation will be tonight, 6-8 PM. I decided to go to visitation and not the funeral, as the theater will be running over and I may not have a place to sit. Anyway I've already made plans to go to Denton with the Broadview "kids" to meet Ken Norris tomorrow. Ken was our music and youth director at Broadview for many years.

Nicole brought her new baby girl, picked me up, and we went to run a couple of errands—mine to the office supply and hers to Walmart. Then I took us to Cotton Patch for lunch. It's my first time to see Larissa Joy. What a beautiful little girl! We had a good time.

I have a doctor's appointment with Dr. Kallal on Monday morning. My feet are swollen, mainly the left foot and ankle.

Then Tuesday at noon, Art and Mac will be here for their IA renewal course. Others should come before this month is up. Ahmed Hassan, a man from Egypt came last week.

I went to Johnny High's visitation at the Arlington Theatre. Tents were set up outdoors, and several of them for the overflow crowd expected tomorrow. We lined up, signed the guest books, and filed into the theater. Johnnie High was in the casket, in state, in front of the stage. There were several large wreaths and flower arrangements, one large blue guitar, and his casket arrangement was all yellow roses. Johnnie looked awfully poor, he had lost weight so badly, but he was still handsome. Several people greeted me and suggested I sit down and watch the pictures being shown on the giant screen. These were all slides of Johnny and others. I saw a great one of Johnny and Paulette. It was beautiful. He was still healthy and good-looking and Paulette was so happy, and her eyes fairly shone. I watched the whole lot several times to keep seeing that picture. I saw Kevin Bailey, his wife, Patsy, Johnny and Christy Struble, Bill and Randy Brooks, Mike (the wild man), and several others, including Jeff and Pam, Maurice Anderson, and his wife.

The family was waiting at the end of the line: Wanda, Lou Ann and her husband Johnny, and Ashley and her husband. Ashley is expecting her baby the 20th-25th. I came on home and will be ready to go to Denton tomorrow. My ankle is badly swollen.

On Saturday, Kerry came after me as she had promised to do. The weather was cold, raining and snowing lightly. There were patches of snow all over, but it didn't turn very cold until later in the day. We drove to the Walmart parking lot where we met the others, June Tyndall Moreland, Kevin Blue, Billy Kent, David Childress, and Carol Deramus, and we left. Kerry and I rode with Kevin and Billy. Kevin drove his minivan, and we got to Pancho's along with the others in about 30 to 40 min. We were seated at three tables put together, and visited until Ken Norris got there. Ken is 68 years old, but doesn't look it. He was at Broadview Baptist, music and youth director in the mid-1970s. We went through the serving line to get our food, and spent the whole rest of the day there. Several took pictures, and they are all on my Facebook, along with some messages.

Ken told us he had a case of Hodgkin's disease a few years ago. He had been having treatments and was okay now. He's teaching school in Paris, Texas. We stayed until 5 PM; it was snowing some when we drove home. We were a little concerned about Ken—he had to drive a lot farther than we did, and in the direction of worse weather.

Johnny High's funeral was today, and I found out later that Bill Brooks officiated at the funeral. I understand there was a lot of music.

Sunday was a lot better, considerably warmer but very windy. After church I went with Ginger and her daughter with her son and a friend to Joe's diner. Ginger bought our lunch and I will reciprocate soon.

Afterward, I went home and got ready to go to see Johnny. I stayed about an hour with him, and when I got home I rested a while and went on to church. My left foot and ankle were badly swollen, but I have an appointment to see Dr. Kallal in the morning.

I had an appointment at 9 AM at the doctor's office. I got there a few minutes early. The day has been nice, much warmer. Spring, finally. Dr. Kallal's son, Mike was with him. I was glad to meet him; I'd met Kevin's family many years ago when Michael was small. He was nice looking and very friendly. Dr. Kallal wanted me to get an x-ray of my foot and ankle. I didn't need to have an appointment. I came back by the Omega and had lunch, then came home.

Randall said he said he had talked Karen Griggs. They still don't know what's wrong but are sure it's not leukemia. That's a relief! I fixed my supper and watched Humphrey Bogart and Lauren Bacall in The Big Sleep. Sherman and I saw it many years ago. It was made the year we married, 1946.

I got a call from Art Befort—he and Mac are coming in the morning instead of the afternoon. The IA refresher will take eight hours. I happily consented. He and Mac stopped and got doughnuts, and I made another pot of coffee. These guys come every year, and I enjoy them so much. We went to Joe's for lunch. I got a call tonight from James Collier. He'll be here Thursday for his IA renewal so I'll have to beg off at Manor Care again. Maybe I can make it up the next week.

It's been a busy week! Everyone is finished with their IA renewals, except Chris Beams will have another half day on Monday.

Today I went to the funeral of a great guy and good friend, Dr. Hospers. He has owned the museum in Meacham airport since 1995, starting with the B-17, a beautiful airplane used in World War II so many years ago. He built the museum with more World War II aircraft and many items collected over the years. Dr. and Col. Bill Hospers and his wife Chuckie had been married many years, and he had named the B-17 Chuckie after her. This was done to woo her into the field of aviation, which he loved, and it obviously did the job. She involved herself in all he did, and took care of him when he became dependent and in a wheelchair.

He had been my student when I had my school in Arlington. He was a dear man, had a great sense of humor, and I'll always remember an incident at Love Aviation when he was going to school. He always asked for a snack, so we went in the kitchen and found something to eat. He was an osteopath, and I asked him about a stitch in my side. He said, "I'll take care of it, lie down on the floor on your stomach," so I did, and he began to feel my spine. "That's it," I said, as he touched the spot that hurt so bad. He put a knee in my back, and I yelled. It felt like he'd put all his weight on my back. Bill Hartman walked in. Bill's dry humor took over as he said, "Would you like for me to come back later?" The stitch was gone, and we all had a good laugh. The Hospers used to go wherever Paulette and Bill played, and he used to have Paulette sing at the osteopathic doctors' meetings. Later, he got injured and became wheelchair-bound, but he remained active in his museum and the activities he still sponsored. He had a big dance every year in the hangar, with dinner and a World War II theme. All of aviation will miss him greatly.

Soon after the funeral I came home, ate some lunch, and called Pauline Rice to see if she wanted to go to Stein Mart with me for a big sale they were having. She did, and we went. She got a couple of tops and I got a got a skirt; a little disappointing but we enjoyed seeing Dee and met her new manager, Steve. Randall had told me about him. When we left, we had sandwiches and cake and I took her home. She's better, but I worry about her because she's not well.

I have stopped taking the Femora. I think it's making my foot and ankle swell, and it really seems to be making my arthritis worse. I took it last about four days ago or so, a little early to tell for sure if I'm better. I intend to call Dr. Krekow Monday and ask her about it. She may want to give me something else.

I had four men all together for their IA renewals. I reported my records to Donald Green, the FAA man in California who is over this course. Surprisingly, he e-mailed me back immediately with a very nice message, thanking me and saying he hoped I'd keep on doing this course for several more years. I was glad to get his kind words.

On Easter Sunday I went to church. At noon, we took the rolls I'd made on Saturday at home, and drove to Laverne's. I was the first one there for some time. Later, Janice and Betty Graham came in. We had ham, mashed potatoes, and vegetables, a great lunch. The rolls were perfect—I'd made them yesterday. I left them to cool about 15 min. and sealed them up in plastic bags.

Then we took them out, put them on a flat pan and covered them with foil, and heated them up at 350 degrees for 10 minutes. They were fresh like they were fresh baked.

After a while, Jeff and Karen came. Also Dustin, his wife and baby, Karen's sister and her boyfriend, Carly, Sam, and Karen's parents came. We all had a great time, and I was one of the first to finally leave. It was after 9 PM when I got home.

Several days ago I restarted the cancer medicine, Femora. I figured it wasn't having any effect on my arthritis.

A few days ago I had my neighbor on my mind. She is Sonia Pullen about 35 or so, and has two children: a girl, five, and a boy, three. She is married to Eric and is unhappy because her husband is gone from home a lot, but she is disabled. She had breast cancer and a stroke, which left her crippled and epileptic. She called one day and asked me if I could take her to the dollar store. I could, and did so that afternoon. We talked, and she told me she was bored when she went to church. We talked more, and I felt that she really needed the Lord in her life. I thought about it for a while, and the next day I called our pastor, Dennis Hester, and got an appointment with him at 1:45 PM. We had a long talk. I explained to him that my car was small, the car seat was huge, and I'm getting too old to take the responsibility for transportation of another family. As I write this, I feel so selfish for the way I felt when I explained the situation to him. Also, I said some man should talk to her husband. Dennis suggested I go ahead and bring her and the kids to church a few times and someone would help me.

I came home, feeling better about it and the talk the preacher and I had, also a prayer together. I knew this was right, and then later that evening the little girl, Ariel, asked me if I could talk to her mother. I did, and we had a really good talk. She had accepted the Lord as her Savior years ago and didn't realize she was still saved. I explained to her about God's love being forever, and she hadn't known that, or didn't seem to. Plans were made—they'll go to Waco over the Easter weekend. The next week she and the kids are going to church with me. I'm excited! It's wonderful for Him to tell me what to do and then pave the way for me. What a Savior! She went for a while, and has since stopped or is going somewhere else, but we're still friends. Sonia and her family are black. She is pretty much unable to use her left side. Since then, she has had her right breast removed, and reconstruction done on both breasts.

Jack Steppick, Janet's husband died. I met Kathy at Avalon, where Johnny was. We had just found out that Jeanette's husband, Jack had passed away. Johnny was glad to see us. We arrived at the same time and told him about Jack. He was sorry of course, but we knew he wouldn't remember it for very long. We visited him for a while and left. I went to church Sunday night and was worn out later. I'm beginning to realize what getting old—dare I say it—does to people. Ginger laughed when I told her I felt like I'd been "rode hard and put up wet". Jack's funeral will be next Thursday, a graveside service at 2 PM at Mount Olivet Cemetery.

The next day I went to Manor Care. To my surprise, our game turned out to be Dominos, and to my further surprise, some of the residents I'd expect to play least of all turned out to play, and really enjoy it. Several played and played well.

I put on a small pork roast in the crock pot and it took several hours. When I got home from the nursing home it was perfect. I fixed mashed potatoes and green beans. I cleaned up the kitchen and took out the trash to be picked up in the morning. As I took it out to the curb, a couple of cars drove up across the street at the Pullen's. Someone yelled, "Pauline!" and they waved at me, three of them. It was Marianne and Sam, her husband, and Paul Michael, to see Sonia and Eric. I walked over there and talked with them. They stayed quite a while, talking to all of us. Marianne and I talked and went over to my house. I showed her my yellow rose bush, blooming beautifully, and my marble porch and entry and the rest of the house. They left soon—I was so glad they visited the Pullen's and talked to all of us. Marianne is quite a girl! I'm impressed with her work on so many projects.

I have had quite a case of pneumonia, plus several days with laryngitis. I've been taking a prescription for antibiotics, and for several days I took a prescription for cough syrup. It made me sleep all the time, so I stopped taking the cough medicine two days ago but I'm still feeling bad. I'm going to leave off the antibiotics tomorrow.

I missed church last week. It was raining, so our picnic was rained out. I guess we'll have to have it later. I've missed seeing Johnny, but will see him tomorrow. Hope he'll understand when I tell them why I haven't been to see him.

Thom called me and told me what he and the girls are planning for me about the last part of June. I'll go to Fairfax to see him and Debby. Then he'll take me to Williamsburg to Ben and Lesley's, and she'll take me to Amy and Jeremy's in Franklin, Tennessee. I'll fly home from there.

A man gave me an estimate for cleaning up the damage on the tree in back, and should be out next week or the next and a do a lot of work for me, trimming the trees and hauling off the brush.

Thom and Debby came yesterday about 4:30 PM; they stayed all night with me. Sherry and I had fixed supper for them, Kyle, Jonathan, and Jamie. Sherry fixed a ham and vegetables, and I made hot rolls and two coconut pies. Thom, Debby, and I went to breakfast at Joe's before they left town.

We were going to watch the UFO movie but my DVD wouldn't work, so Thom went out and bought me a new one. He also bought several movies and we watched one last night. It was "An Affair to Remember," a great old movie. I don't think I've ever seen it before.

After we ate at Joe's, and Thom and Debby left, they were going to Mansfield to an 80th birthday celebration for their friend, Ralph.

Thom and Debby have made plans for me to visit them in Virginia before Thanksgiving. I'll be there six days. I have my ticket and schedule—will leave November 24 and come home on the 30th.

Matt was supposed to come and eat with us last night. He got busy and forgot, and was very upset about it. Jonathan called him, and then he talked to me. I assured him it was okay, and not to worry. He was tired and had a bad day. I'm worried about him.

Johnny has been so very ill. He is better but still has some pneumonia. I go and see him as much as possible but still don't know if he'll be okay.

Sherry, my daughter-in-law and I got back from Idabel about four this afternoon. I had gotten the news on Facebook that my brother Robert was in the hospital with pneumonia, so Sherry and I left yesterday and drove, stopping at Valliant for a cup of coffee (me) and Sherri had a soft drink. We went to a small café, and while we were there a woman about 77 came over and talked to us. She said she was from Powderly, Texas, and because her whole family had moved away, she was lonely and going to stay at a motel in Valliant, next to the café, for five years. I told her my Daddy had help build the school in Powderly, and at the same time, had cooked at a friends' restaurant. His specialty was making pancakes and he used to make them at home after that. This was in the 1940s, and I was about 10 or 11. I remember, after that, he always explained to us how pancakes were to be made and cooked. He knew it all. We laughed at him and usually turned the job over to him.

We left and drove on to the Microtel motel, and stayed in the same room where Laurine, her daughter Jennifer, and I had stayed the last time we went to see Robert and Omia. We visited Robert in the hospital, then went on to the nursing home and saw Omia a little while. I got a call from Thom while we were there in Robert's room, and he told me we'd have a Thanksgiving meal Thursday, and we were going to Waxahachie for supper the next week. I talked to Roy, and he said he'd meet us at the Catfish Café in a little while. He came to Robert's room, and we all drove to eat. As usual, we had a good supper, and Sherry and I went back to the motel. We were a little tired, but decided to go to Walmart and buy a pair of pillows.

We got up about 7 AM today, had a Coke and coffee and orange juice for both of us. We went back, saw Omia a few minutes, and went on to the hospital. Stopping at the gift shop, we saw people I knew and that Robert had known.

We got him a couple of books—he still likes to read, a little bird vase with yellow roses, and some candy and gum. We saw him for a few minutes, and he was hoping to go home in a little while. He doesn't realize they live at the nursing home.

We found out later that he did get to go back to the nursing home, so I know Omia was happy. She's been really worried about him. We came home. It rained all the way. I went immediately to vote. It's Election Day, and I'm watching the results as I write this.

I'm sitting in my recliner watching "Magambo", made in 1953, starring Clark Gable, Ava Gardner, and Grace Kelly, plus a large part of Africa's population. It's been a busy afternoon. Dee and Randall were going to come with me and eat lunch at Joe's, but he was trying to make arrangements for Dee to have some surgery on Monday and there were complications. Finally he had Dee set up for a pre-op about noon, so our lunch was postponed for tomorrow. I ate some leftover pizza, and went to Joe Smith's funeral. He had been at Manor Care a couple of weeks, and I could tell he was bad. He tried to talk to me, but couldn't, except to say, "Hello, Pauline." Joe had been a deacon at Broadview years ago before they moved to Lake Worth Baptist, and his wife, Doris had died a few months ago. He was a Deacon at our church, Broadview, several years.

I was a little late getting to Manor Care, and did some visiting first. We had several certificates made out for the veterans. Later, I passed them out and expressed appreciation to the ones receiving them. Among them was Rose Jones, who had been in the Coast Guard years ago.

We played a game, finishing at 4 PM, and I went to see Johnny. I had supper with him, and didn't stay long afterward, but came home alone. It was getting dark by the time I got home. Time is passing fast and I'm not making much progress on my book. I've been getting ready to go to Virginia, but am lagging on that. I leave on Wednesday, and my good friend, Randall is taking me to the airport. He has advised me to be ready to get to the airport two hours early, as it's supposed to be the busiest day to travel in the whole year. They just started some extreme security checks for all passengers, so I'll have to deal with that. He also said I needed to have a wheelchair to wait so I won't have to stand in line. I called Thom, and he agreed and is arranging it.

I went to Avalon this afternoon to see Johnny. He was very upset, thinking it was three in the morning, and that I was running around with other men. It was 3 PM and I finally convinced him, but I doubt he'll ever quit thinking I'm going with somebody.

I was at the hospital Monday morning with Randall; Dee was having hernia surgery. Their daughter-in-law was also there. The surgery was successful, and Randall brought her home in a couple of days. He told me this evening she was doing okay.

We still don't know where Phil is going to work. He had a lead about a job in Dallas that he hasn't heard yet. It would be so good if he can come back home to stay. Sherry is going to spend Thanksgiving with him.

I went to Janet's house yesterday. Laurine's daughter, Janet was there, and so was Cindy, my nephew Ken's daughter. We had a nice time, and looked at a lot of pictures. Cindy put some of them on Facebook today.

For five months around 1970 (between years at Steve's school) I worked for Dick Hartman's Real Estate in River Oaks. I did some rentals, rental inspections, management for rental places. I drove a little Volkswagen beetle—it belonged to Mr. Hartman. It had many leaks and no heater, as I recall, and this was during a very cold winter with snow and ice everywhere— unusual for this area. But I didn't mind. I enjoyed my work learning about real estate and making new friends. But it didn't last long. Jack Shafer called me one day, and asked me to come and work with him at the school. Steve had sold it to Braniff. I had been encouraged to get my real estate license, but I wasn't interested. Aviation had gotten to me, I guess, and I was happy when Jack called me.

Jack and I had worked hard to get Stephens' school certified by the FAA. But when Braniff moved the school to Dallas, they had no one to operate the office, records etc., as I had done before. So I resigned the real estate management, and happily began the trip to Dallas and back home every day. I worked a few miles from the school, keeping records and whatever I could do, a long way from the school. I was not allowed to go there to get things I needed, as the man in charge wouldn't allow me to see the students. I was told the students didn't need a "den mother". I managed to persuade this man that it was necessary that I go and talk to the students and get the records I needed to report to the FAA and other government offices, so he agreed reluctantly and said, "Okay, Pauline, I'm going let you go this one time and get back here as fast as you can! I have work for you to do".

"Really?" I asked, "What work?" because I knew better than anyone else what there was to do. His answer was a vague. "I'll let you know later. Just hurry back." Meantime, the younger woman who worked with me was about forty years old and pregnant. I went on to the school, enjoyed visiting with everybody, and took a lot of pictures. I got back late—no one ever knew the difference.

They hired me for about a year, and decided that one of the two of us girls had to go, so it was me. I was sorry, and they had paid me well, but I was confident I'd be okay.

Charlie Stephens and another man (they both worked at the Braniff school as instructors) started classes at a place on North Main in Fort Worth. Steve wasn't having classes any more, but he had a small building on his place where he was doing some inspections, etc. Charlie asked me to work for him and the other man, to help recruit students for the A&P refresher. So I did, and after a few days, they both were called to work elsewhere. They left, leaving the school to me.

I was unprepared to have a school, in both preparation and finances. I got a student through later, my first teaching experience. This was after Alan left. Alan Cook came to my school. He was on one of the last planes leaving Vietnam; a friend of Bill Taylor, a young man who also had come from Vietnam. Alan was to become a good friend, too, and was there when Charlie and "The Killer" left. Alan finished his course and got his license, and I had him to help get another student or two through. But I ran out of money, and he had to go and find himself a job. He was from Nebraska, and I took for granted he'd go back there where his mother still lives.

I closed the school and looked for work. I got a job for a few days for a used car place. Then I went to Denton, Texas, and worked for Denton Piper Sales selling aircraft parts. I lasted a few months and was called back to—guess where? Steve's! So after I got back to Steve's, it was the class I had in 1977. I taught every day after that, and sometimes in the evening, and locations away from the school, as explained earlier. After so many people had come from the Middle East, and had been cheating on the tests, we were watched closely by the FAA. Steve had been certified to give written exams as well as the oral and practical. I was helping to administer the written exams (called a proctor), but was stopped later, as more students were found cheating—some in our school. A new student, Morris Dixon, and I began to talk about having our own school after things got so bad. Steve lost his DEA for both written and practical exams; students were coming, but rarely. Morris and I got more excited about our school. We decided to get away from the scandal in Fort Worth, and planned to go to Dallas, at Love Field. I waited until the last minute to tell Steve of our plans. I knew he would be upset with me, but I figured it would be well to be as far away as Love Field, where we would have no competition problems with Fort Worth.

In 1981, Morris Dixon, a student from one of my first classes, and I began to talk about setting up our own school. Many foreign students coming from the Middle East had been cheating on the tests, and Steve had lost his DME, so we had to send the students elsewhere to take their tests. This was the written and practical exams, so attendance fell off and was nearly nil when we took the big step and started Love A&P Learning Center at Love Field, Dallas Texas. Morris Dixon and I opened the school on September 1, 1981, in the north concourse, immediately opposite the Braniff terminal. The Braniff Company closed the day before, sadly for the third and final time, but Love A&P opened for business. We had 501 square feet: one large classroom, two small classrooms, and one break room.

I got a small loan from the bank; my son Thom was the president. Opening the new school the same time the Braniff Airlines Company closed may not have been the best idea we could do, but we were both confident and excited, counting every dollar carefully. We got enough large tables and folding chairs to furnish the classrooms. A friend gave us a refrigerator for our break room where we kept cold drinks and some sandwich stuff. Water fountains and restrooms were in the hallway. For a few days, very few people came in, which gave us a chance to scout around for supplies, books, and all materials. Slowly but surely, people began to take interest. We had classes mornings, and evenings, and sometimes in the afternoons, taking care of students whenever they could come.

I knew what was close. We would have to be approved by the TEA, as Stephens Aircraft had. But I was not really worried, as I had handled the approval of that school, so I was ready to start making up the paperwork and catalogs for Love A&P. One day I realized that the man coming in was from the TEA. In a few days, we got our certificate of approval, and not long later, we got approval for some financial assistance for students. By this time, we were teaching classes in both A&P and Inspection Authorization. Due to a promise made to us by a friend in the FAA (he was unable to carry it out), we made the move from Dallas to Arlington, to a building that had been a very nice, large church building. The church had moved a couple of blocks down the street.

All the time we had the school in Arlington, we were working on getting FAA certification, and it happened about 1984. This meant we could teach all the FAA subjects in a 1900 hour course, and students needed no previous experience. We still taught the refresher courses, and also inspection authorization courses. This was more complicated and could cause more battles with the powers that be, but we won them and came out victorious. The short courses did not need to be approved, because they were not regulated by the FAA.

Meanwhile, my whole home life was falling apart, and although Sherman had resented the school from the start, he hated it now, and began to drink heavily. We were estranged, in the same house, and both of us unhappy, only I was excited about the school. I was never prone to being unhappy, but he was the opposite, and drank to avoid reality. Actually, Sherman had been unhappy, and finally I realized—he had been an alcoholic since his time in the Army, but had not drunk because of the family. He started back when I started the school, and we used to go to hear Paulette and Bill when they appeared in the motels and clubs in Fort Worth. He couldn't take one drink and quit, but would drink all the time we were there.

Paulette and Bill were a big hit in many places around Fort Worth, such as The Pecan Plantation, The Cuckoo's Nest in Granbury, and a couple of other places on the west side of Fort Worth.

Sherman had said flatly that I couldn't start my own school. It was a new beginning for my school, and near the end of my marriage, but I was happy, and felt that we would be okay. Of course I was a little apprehensive as we began to make definite plans. We planned to open our school at the Love Field terminal on September 1, 1981, in the north concourse, 501 sq. ft., immediately opposite the Braniff terminal. The Braniff Company closed the day before, sadly, for the third and final time. But Love A&P opened for business. I got a small loan from the bank, where my son, Thom was the president.

We advertised in some of the aircraft publications, some of them being sent overseas. So we got several foreigners, and I was working with some with the immigration services and some other organizers for financial help for students. After a year, the school was moved to Arlington, Texas, where we stayed several years until I sold it to Dalfort in 1989. We had a nice building in Arlington, with part of another building for practical work. We modified part of the main one, and had my good friend Dennis Arrick to build some partitions to separate classrooms. Also it was nearer to home than Love Field was.

Paulette and Bill moved home the Monday we moved the school to Arlington and Paulette went to work for me. In a few days, Bill also went to work with us, and we began to work to build up the school using computers, and before long, to start working on FAA certification.

Memories come back to us as we grow older and somehow pieces of the puzzles begin the fit together as we meditate on events and people in the past. As I grew up in the Plainview community during World War II years, there were people in my life that I remember, that I guess helped shape my life. I never dated much as a young girl—boys my ages were not interested much, and the ones who would have been were in the military. There's something—or was then—about a man in a military uniform that is very attractive, but I was in love with Sherman. There were others, but he was foremost in my mind.

After Sherman came home, a divorced man now, my love for him and his for me became evident to everyone, although I was only 16 years of age. It was all secretive on my part at first. I had dated a couple of times with a man named Taylor, a handsome fellow, and about the same age as Sherman, 26. Although I liked him, I was not very interested. Our time together was short, and mutually not great.

And there was Don Robison. Don and I double dated with Leonard and Joyce, a couple who later married. Don was visiting a friend named Robert. They were in the Army together. Robert was engaged to marry a friend of Margaret and me. Margaret had had a date or two with Don, but then he and I started dating. It was all very casual. Don was 26, Sherman's age, a gentleman, I liked him. We, the four of us, rode in Leonard's car, a one-seated car, so I had to ride on Don's lap when we went to Idabel to a movie. Finally, one night when we were alone, Don asked me if I would go back to Ohio with him. I was a little shocked. Times were different then, and such a thing was unheard of, by me at least.

My brother, Louie warned me, and I think he told Daddy I may be dating a married man. Who knew if Don was a respectable person? And how many wives did he have already? I promised Louie I'd be careful.

So I was only 16, I couldn't go away. My parents wouldn't let me, and anyway I couldn't go with someone I didn't know well and wasn't married to. So he suggested vaguely that we would be married. I told him I wouldn't, and that I was in love with Sherman. I didn't see Sherman much but I was still crazy about him. So Don and I parted good friends, no one heartbroken, and I found out later he was really in love with Mary, Robert's girl. He went back to Ohio, alone. Mary and Robert Musset married.

Then there was Jerry. I'd known Jerry nearly all my life—he was a neighbor. He had two sisters, Pauline and Kathleen, and a brother, Tom. Tom was in the Army, but Jerry wasn't. When I was a teenager, I had a crush on Jerry. He was a great friend of my brother Robert, he and Tom. They used to go camping together, and I'm sure, did some drinking together. But we were good friends, and once Jerry and I went camping with Robert and Omia on the river. It was fun. Jerry and I used to go to church at the schoolhouse on Sunday mornings. We were in the same Sunday school class and sometimes we attended one of the parties we used to have during the war years. Margaret and I used to play at parties and he liked to sing with us sometimes. Later, as we grew a little older, Jerry and I dated briefly. One day I was in Valliant, and I saw him. He asked me if I would go with him that night to a movie, and I said yes.

So he came and picked me up in his truck. It was a Saturday night and had been raining. We got to Valliant, to the movie (which we never got around to seeing) and he went and got us a cup of coffee, which we had as we sat in his truck to talk. He got romantic, and asked me to be his girl. I had dreamed of this several times, but now this feeling for him was about over. I told him I appreciated him, but I was in love with someone else. He kissed me, and it was not a casual kiss, and I responded, feeling a bit guilty for some reason.

He said "Don't ever kiss me like that unless you mean it", and he actually cried, and told me he loved me, and wished I'd change my mind about Sherman. Finally, he took me home. I talked to him once again, just before we were married, and he wished us happiness.

Many years after that, Sherman and I used to go to the Labor Day reunion at Rufe, Oklahoma. Once I went alone, with Margaret one year. We saw Jerry and visited. Jerry had been married two or three times, and today his wife was out of town. I never met her. When the festivities were about over, Jerry took Margaret and me to his house. He and his wife lived in a trailer house on the old Rice place. He got a gun, a large pistol, and we went to do some target shooting. We went to a spot near the lake. Our farms had been sold for building the new lake, and the three of us shot a few times. It was enjoyable to renew old acquaintances, and Jerry talked about his son, who is a singer, as well as my daughter Paulette. Once, as we were driving and had stopped for something, Jerry suddenly put his arm around me and kissed me. It was a short but sweet kiss, and there was no apology or explanation. I don't even know if Margaret saw us, she never indicated she did.

Another time we were in Oklahoma, and drove past Jerry's trailer home. I stopped and talked to him. He was not well, was having some stomach trouble. Sometime after that I heard that he was in the hospital in Dallas. I was in the office at my school, then in Arlington. I called him, and we talked a while. He told me he was going to die; he had cancer, and was in the last stages. I told him I was so sorry, and would pray for him. That was our last time to talk. He died soon after.

In 1980 I was instructing at Stephens Aircraft School at Meacham field. Then two men started one day, to get their A&P ratings at the school. They were airman from the air base, very good friends, Ken Elliott and Art Brown. We became very good friends, the three of us. They were, I thought, about to retire from the Air Force soon after getting their license and I hadn't heard from them again. I knew they had formed a trucking service, and I wondered about them. Students come and go, and at a school like this sometimes you might keep in touch, but rarely do you see them, unless they come back for Inspection Authorization ratings. I had wondered about them, and where they were living, if they were still in aviation, and I had decided these were two I would never see again.

Chapter 5

"If you're interested I'd like to buy your passport if you'll sell it."

I was feeling a little restless. Johnny had died the last of December, 2010. I was spending a lot of time visiting shut-ins and going to the nursing homes. I went to Manor Care twice a week, and on Thursdays our Sweet Spirit Singers met at the church. I'm feeling good, my arthritis seems to be under control, and I am doing some walking, I just have to rest a lot. I enjoy going to Manor Care

This started out to be a fairly rotten week. I made an orange slice cake, and forgot to put enough flour in it, so it went immediately into the trash. Wednesday I made another one—a very costly recipe—and didn't cook it long enough in spite of the 1 3/4 hours called for, and it too went into the trash.

Unfortunately, I agreed to have a salesman come out to talk about a so-called government rebate on attic insulation. I lost my temper, and that didn't go well. Then I got a call from the exterminators, **and they're to come out on Tuesday. It went badly, too.** I went to see Pauline Rice, and we went out, spent the whole afternoon, and the day went fine. We visited Artie Taylor and stayed with her a little while. Her son and daughter-in-law who stay with her needed to go on an errand. Pauline is feeling better. She fell in love with some new **tiny kittens in Artie's yard. Later, we went to get her medicine, and then went** to Golden Corral and ate supper.

On Wednesday evening I went to church for Awanas. We are having a banquet next Wednesday, and then we stop meeting until after school starts.

Phil e-mailed me and said they're going to Mayfest with Jonathan and Jamie on Friday, so we won't be watching Benson DVDs the way we normally do. Thursday I got ready and went to our choir meeting, Sweet Spirit Singers. We met, nine of us, and decided to go to Ashwood Assisted Living where Beth lives, to sing this month. Also, we're going on the 19th. Some will be gone on the last Thursday. We enjoyed our session. I came home and decided to go to Braum's and have lunch before I went to Manor Care.

I got to Manor Care before one today. I saw on the calendar that we were having two parties today, one for the staff and one for the residents. I did some stuff for Betty; she's still not well, but still working hard. I did some visiting and ate a couple of tacos. Then she and I were working in her office, and she told me someone was coming to sing to entertain the residents. She'd told him we couldn't pay people for that any more, but he said it was okay, he'd do it for free. This is very unusual. Most of the time they don't come without pay, except choirs don't charge.

When Art and Ken had obtained their A&P ratings in 1980 and had gone, I wondered about them, if they had retired from the U.S. Air Force and then left the area, but never heard anything more about them. I was completely caught off guard. Betty met the man standing there, talked briefly with him, and had to go, forgetting to introduce him to me. But something about him held my attention. He looked familiar, but I didn't place him until I told him my name and he said his name was Ken Elliott. I repeated after him "Ken Elliott." "I know a Ken Elliott from Carswell," and he said, "That's who I am." I said, "There used to be another one...." "Art Brown," he supplied, and I realized he was really the Ken Elliott I knew. I hugged him, and I guess he thought I was one of the patients there, and a little off my rocker. I finally explained to him who I was. He remembered, and we were both so thrilled to see each other we were in a state of shock. He had his guitar with him, but didn't bring any other of the sound equipment. We visited, and he sang the old songs I knew. We both sang together, almost all of the songs. I sang alto, because he was playing in the lower keys and I could reach the notes.

The patients, quite a few of them, came in, and they really enjoyed hearing us and wanted him to come back. He promised he would. We all knew, he, myself, and Betty, that this seemed to be not a coincidence, but a providential thing. He'd just started playing and singing, but appeared at a lot of nursing homes and some restaurants. We promised to get together at IHOP close to Manor Care with Art, who lived at Haslet. He told me he's a Baptist. His wife had died in 2009. Ken told me he lives now, as he always has, on Ranch House Road, in Willow Park, It's the same street that my son, Thom and Jeanne used to live on.

I'm still excited. It's always good to see old friends again, but Ken has always been special to me, he and Art too. I'm anxious to get together with them. I called Pauline Rice as soon as I got home, and she was happy for me. While we were talking, my doorbell rang. I got off the phone, and the truck was driving away. There was a large box on the porch. It was from Thom and Debby: two dozen beautiful roses and a green vase to put them in. A great Mother's Day gift. Later, I talked to Thom to thank him. They were having dinner with Debby's girls, and they all said for Thom to wish me a happy Mother's Day from them. I have a great family! And it is a great Mother's Day.

On Friday, after seeing Ken Elliott on Thursday, he called me and asked me if I would meet him and Art Brown Saturday morning at 7 AM at IHOP. I agreed. When I asked where, he told me it was off loop 820, at the Jacksboro Highway. So I set my alarm. I knew I'd have to get up early, since it was quite a distance. I arrived just before seven and both men met me in the parking lot. Ken had told Art they were meeting with an old friend, but didn't say who. Art was completely surprised, and didn't immediately recognize me, so Ken told him who I was. He was glad to see me, and gave me a big hug. We went in, and the place was nearly empty for a few minutes. People began to come in then, and there were many waiting to be seated. We had so much catching up to do, it took us about four hours to finally decide to leave. They determined it had been 31 years since they'd finished the A&P School in 1980. I was teaching at Steve's school; I hadn't started my school yet. I took my camera and we took some pictures. Ken said he'd call me; he wants to take me somewhere to hear a band that he was familiar with. I don't know where or when until he calls. Ken told me he wanted me to sing with him sometimes in the nursing homes. I was very happy to agree to that.

I was impressed with Ken's guitar playing, and the way he sang. He seemed to be not the least bit shy, and belted out the words, so that it was inspiring. I was so surprised; I never knew he sang. I remembered he had told me some of his folks, an uncle and a cousin, were into some singing and song writing, and he was surprised that I remembered. He said he had just started his singing after his wife died and he found himself at loose ends. So a cousin told him to get "off his can" and get busy with something

Yesterday after church, I came home and picked up two pies I had made, and went on to the Sullivans where we had lunch. Phil and Sherry gave me a new camera for Mother's Day. It's digital, but seems to be simple to operate. I finished the pictures in my disposable camera, and took them to be developed this morning.

I went to visit a little while with Pauline Rice, and we went and ate lunch at Wendy's. She needs to get out more, and it's frustrating that she is unable to drive yet. We came back by the house here for a while before I took her home.

The pictures turned out great. I was so proud of them, especially the ones we had taken at IHOP. Ken is such a handsome man, and Art is, too. I took the pictures we had taken to Manor Care on Tuesday and showed them off. I haven't heard from Ken yet, but expect to soon. While I was at Manor Care, I saw my friend Dorothy Glover. She told me J.B. was there—he has diabetes and had lost some toes. I went to see him and visited with him a few minutes. He's had a rough time but still plans to do a concert at Manor Care. He has been a singer for so many years. But time seems to have taken a toll on him and Dorothy. But he'll never stop singing. He has a marvelous voice.

I went to our choir practice at church yesterday. I'm not sure I'll be able to keep going. We have to get there at 8:30 AM on Sunday, and that's awfully early for Sunday morning.

I love to sing, but my voice needs practice or something.

On Friday I walked over to Sonya's. She said her order for her bra and prosthesis from Hangers was ready to be picked up, but she didn't have a way to get downtown to get them. I said I'd take her as soon as Ariya came back from school, so we left a little after 2 PM and I drove downtown. It was a bad time, the traffic was terrible, but we made it. When I returned home, I found a small note in my door; it was printed in block letters and said, "If you're interested I'd like to buy your passport if you'll sell it." There was one name and a phone number added.

I talked to Phil; he and Sherry came over and they had Kyle with them. They picked me up, and we went out to eat. I showed them the note, and we decided I should show the note to the police the next day. We watched a couple of DVDs of Benson and they left.

I had acquired a passport years ago when I thought I might go to Egypt to teach some classes. I didn't use it; it was long expired and was in a lockbox at the bank. I wondered who in the world would want an old passport and how did this person know I had one? I called a couple of neighbors, to see if they'd received similar notes on their doors, but apparently mine was the only one.

On Saturday morning, I went to the police department, and after much waiting, finally roused a policeman. I handed him the note along with an explanation about the passport, and he took the note into his office while I waited. He came back in looking rather amused, and said, "Aren't you the lady who has a Passport parked in your driveway?" I suddenly realized my neighbors had been using my driveway to park their son's Honda Passport until he could take it to school. He's starting to college. We had a good laugh, the policeman and me, and I explained to him that I hadn't paid much attention to the car in the driveway, but it was definitely a Passport. I told Sherry Stein the story, and we have had many laughs over it.

Ken and I had a date last Saturday, but he had to call it off; he's going to come and see me this week. We plan to sing at the picnic our church is having next

Sunday evening, and we'll be practicing a couple times this week. I'm happy about it, but maybe a little nervous and excited, being the ham that I continue to be.

It's been a busy week. Ken and I spent Monday afternoon talking and singing, but more visiting and catching up. We will spend tomorrow morning getting ready to sing at the church picnic at Northfield Park—just a few songs—about a 30 or 40 minute program. I went to choir early, after picking Doris Wynn up. We went over to the Ashwood Assisted Living and Nursing Home on Glenview Drive. There were ten of us, and it was a great session. C.L. was back from a mission trip he'd taken with some other fellows from the church. A crowd of residents was waiting for us, and sang with us. It was great; we all enjoyed it, and they want us back, so we need to make some arrangements about singing in the nursing homes.

Ken will be here in the morning, and we'll wrap up the plans to sing at the picnic.

The decision to sing there was a good one. We practiced two times, and we were ready. Our church group was impressed with Ken's personality; he fits right in, and he liked our people. Phil and Sherry were there. They took a video of our complete program lasting about 30 to 40 min. He put our first one, "Take Me Back To Tulsa," on my Facebook.

Matt and his band have finished their first CD, and will release it on June 10 at a bar in Denton. I plan to go. Matt wrote most of the songs on the CD.

Richard and Chere Bradford had supper with me tonight. I have cooked such a little lately, I was determined to make a good meal for us, as I love these people dearly. I got barbecued ribs at Spring Creek; I've made some company potatoes and hot rolls. I went to Dr. Kallal's this morning for a physical and blood work. I seem to be okay; will hear from the blood test in a week or so. I had to go back and redo the blood test, and was told the next day that everything turned out fine; there is nothing wrong.

It's been a great Memorial Day weekend. I picked Pauline Rice up and we went to Greenwood Cemetery. The florist was closed, and I hadn't bought any flowers to put on the graves, but may take some later. We went from there to find a museum Phil had told us about, but it was closed. We'll go back later. We came back to the café on 199. It had been William's Steakhouse for many years. It was near our house on Buchanan Street and is now a family style café. We had lunch and came on home. Then this morning, I received a phone call from my friend, Alan Cook. He is recovering from a very serious surgery and is doing well. The cancer is gone, and he'll be going home soon from the VA hospital where he has been for a week or so. The surgery and prognosis is nothing short of miraculous.

Ken Elliott, my friend from 1980, is leaving to go to New Hampshire tomorrow for a couple weeks. He'll call me before he leaves, and when he comes back, I'll be going with him some to sing. He was a big hit with my friends at church, and my kids and me, of course. He's always been special to me, but the more I see him, the more impressed I am. He's really a great guy.

Matt and his band, The Forgeries are releasing their new CD, Cupids Handgun next Saturday night, June 10 at a place in Denton, Texas about 40 miles from here. It's their first CD to be published, and Matt wrote most of the music. They are appearing at a place called Andy's. I'm not sure, but hope to go and hear them.

Later I decided not to go to the bar where Matt's band was playing, but apparently it went well. He'd contacted me and told me it was a bar, not a restaurant, so he advised me not to come.

My friend Alan Cook has had his surgery, and is doing well. I got an e-mail today from him. My next door neighbor Sandy is very ill; she has cancer and is now in the oncology ward at Peter Smith Hospital. She's not to have that many more treatments, and will be sent home soon, and hospice will be caring for her. So her son and brother aren't having any hope left.

A friend from Broadview, Ken Blue died a couple of days ago. I met with friends and family for visitation last night. I saw lots of my friends I taught so many years ago in Sunday school, training union, GAs, etc. We are planning to have a party at my house soon, to visit. I've heard from several today on my Facebook.

I was at Manor Care today. I visited quite a bit, saw Rose Jones a while, and visited with JB Glover and others. Then we had a Bible quiz with 5 residents.

Thom sent me an itinerary today for my trip to Virginia in November. I'll spend a week with him and Debby, and a week with Lesley. I'll be gone from November 22 to December 11.

I've been pretty busy with Sherry's family, visiting the Sullivans. On Saturday Phil, Sherry, her cousin Dorian, Robin, Adam and I all went to the Frontiers of Flight Museum in Dallas, at Love Field. It's nice, with several older aircraft— some of them really classic. It was fun; we took several pictures.

After the museum, Phil drove us to a place that sold Thunderbirds. The only ones in the showroom were models from 1955 to 1957. They were beautiful, restored, and didn't have prices listed. They had a sign on the door—open by appointment only—so we called, and the owner was there and opened the place for us. We also went into the warehouse where there were many cars, most of them covered, some getting ready for the showroom. There were other model cars, but not many.

After the Thunderbird place, we went to Red Hot & Blue for barbecue and had supper. Sherry's relatives all have gone back to Tennessee. My brother Robert's wife, Omia fell and broke her hip, and had to be taken to Texarkana for surgery. She's doing okay now, and has gone back to the nursing home in Idabel, Oklahoma. My friend Alan is doing well too.

Sunday is Father's Day. I'm going to Johnny's grave with Jeanette. I couldn't find it if I tried. He is buried by Esther, his wife, in a back part of that large cemetery. I miss Johnny. It's been nearly 6 months since his death, but when I see a picture of him I still miss him, and what a good man he was.

An ex-student just called me tonight, and is looking for work. He got his license years ago, and immediately had a stroke, and is still unable to use his left hand. Finding a job in aviation with only one hand is not easy. He has a job now, but is looking for a better one. I gave him some leads, but don't have much to offer.

My sister-in-law Omia is okay and back in the nursing home at Idabel, along with my brother Robert. They are 90 and 86 now, and stay in bed most of the time.

I'm going back to Manor Care both Tuesday and Thursday now, while Betty, the activities director, is still having some health problems. Our choir, the Sweet Spirit Singers, is still meeting. Numbers are down, but we're hoping, as we're getting better, and plan to keep going to the two nursing homes where we've been: Ashwood and Green Valley.

Ken came home and we are planning to visit two nursing homes close by here where we will sing, and one to hear Ken's friend Brian perform.

A couple weeks ago, I was at Manor Care and realized my friend J.B. Glover was there. I knew him from Azle Ave. Baptist Church. I was a member there for many years, until after Sherman's death in 2001, when Johnnie and I went to First Baptist Church in Watauga. He is a great singer, and has been a music director for many years. J.B. is married to Dorothy, another good friend of mine from Azle Avenue church. They married in 1993, just before Paulette's death.

J.B. had surgery today; amputation of his left leg above the ankle. He is diabetic. He is still a music director at a church north of town, but may have to resign now. So I visited with him yesterday, and we recalled singing together.

I'm getting e-mails about Alan, and now from J.B., and he's doing well. I'm so thankful. I went with Jeanette on Sunday to Johnny's grave in Mount Olivet. I took some pictures of his, but they aren't developed yet.

Yesterday, Monday, I had a call from my friend, Dorothy Glover. J.B. had been sent to HealthSouth; after his surgery he got worse, and they took him back to the hospital downtown. She needed me to take her to the hospital to see him. He had been taken to HealthSouth too quickly, and had quit breathing and had no heartbeat for a time, so they rushed him back to the hospital. I took her, and we spent the day until about 5:30 PM with him in the cardiac intensive care unit. He's just a bit better today; his heartbeat was way fast and has come down some. The doctor thinks he's had a heart attack. I called Dorothy and she said his brother would be with him today.

I'd been intending to go hear Ken and his friend, Brian yesterday at The Good Place assisted living, but called it off so I could stay with Dorothy. Ken called me last night and we'll get together on Friday.

Yesterday, Friday, Ken came after me and we drove to Horizon, more of an assisted care center than a nursing home. It was very nice, but a very hot afternoon. We got there early so Ken could set up his amplifier system and a couple of microphones. There were close to 40 people in the large room to hear us. There were July 4 decorations, flags, etc. to celebrate the holiday. We did an hour-long program. I sang 3 or 4 songs with Ken, but he did most by himself. I did a go-go dance with one lady who danced all the time we were singing.

They all seemed to enjoy it, and Ken and I did, too. Afterward there were snacks, cheese crackers, some seven layer dip, etc., and Ken got a cold drink which we shared. When we got back to the house, Ken came in for a little while. He was very tired. I realized he works awfully hard, and I talked to him about it. He just has a lot to do. I was glad he seemed to relax for a few minutes before he went home. I left to go to Phil and Sherry's for supper and a few episodes of Benson.

Ken had brought some pictures of him, taken while he was in New Hampshire. He gave me one. It was one that had been printed on regular typing paper, but was a really good shot of him.

Today, Pauline Rice and I went to see Phil and Sherry, and I took the picture Ken had given me. Phil printed the picture on a sheet of photographic paper, and also put it on Facebook. I'll frame it in a day or so.

I talked briefly to Dorothy this morning. She said J.B. had been put in a room at the hospital today, and is doing better. I talked to my friend, Randall, two days ago. He's still not doing much better, still taking medicine, can't taste or smell anything. He had to get off the oxygen, as it was hurting his ability to breathe well and inflaming his sinuses. I'm very worried about him and miss our conversations on the phone.

I went this morning and picked up Manda to stay all night here. She is anxious to go to church with me tonight for a scholarship supper and fund raising, and also for Sunday's services tomorrow. We came back this morning by Joe's Diner for brunch and sat with Ginger and Claire Bertholf. Ginger is doing pretty well, walking some with a walker, and sometimes without. We saw several friends from First Baptist Church.

Yesterday, my friend Nicole came with her two little girls, and we went and had lunch with her husband, Matt, and his dad. I always enjoy the family; they are great friends.

I went to Manor Care twice last week, but it looks like I'll be going once a week now, as Betty is much better. My friend J.B. is better, still in the hospital, taking therapy, and day before yesterday, surprise! I got a long call from Randall. He is not much better—his sinus problems stay with him—but he was excited and happy. He had had a call from Joyce at Ginger Brown's, and she wanted Karen and Jeff's phone number. So, sounds like they may be wanted back to play there—so we exulted together and enjoyed the long talk we hadn't had in a long time. He just hasn't felt up to talking on the phone much. And also I got an e-mail from Alan Cook. He was a little down, hadn't had the greatest success with the neo-bladder he'd received. Hopefully it'll just take more time, but I can see how he could get discouraged. He is usually so upbeat. It's unusual for him to feel this way. I e-mailed him back, and told him I'd keep praying for better days ahead. He has to go back to the doctor soon.

I finally got Jann to cut my hair. It's a World War II look, long, shaped around my face, and not permed, but doing well. I'm rolling it twice a week again and pleased with it. I never had it long enough to fix like this before.

Phil and Sherry were here for supper last night, but he couldn't get the DVD to work so we could watch Benson. He called and they're supposed to bring me a new cable box, I don't know for sure when. It's a dark, extremely hot day.

Looks a little like rain. We really need it. The roses are not blooming at all, and the grass isn't growing. It's been 100° for more than two weeks.

I need to catch up on the last two weeks or so; a lot has happened and for some reason, I just couldn't write about it. First I got an e-mail from Alan—he isn't doing so well, and has had to go back into the hospital for more procedures. He is making little progress. And I've talked to Randall a couple of times. He still is having the same trouble with his sinus condition. We are planning to get together, some of us, at Ginger Brown's soon, although there hasn't been anything definite about Jeff and Karen playing there. We just want to get back together and visit.

I met Ken at Ridgmar Mall last Thursday, and we went out to a nursing home and heard Brian play. Ken had received a lot of electronics equipment, and had it all set up for Brian when he got there. Ken and I sat in the back and visited, while Brian did the program. They served punch and cake. I visited most of the residents while Ken and Brian packed up all the equipment and loaded it in Ken's car. Ken & I drove to the Cotton Patch restaurant in the Hulen area and had a shrimp supper and a nice long visit. We seem to be very compatible, agreeing with each other in almost everything. I am growing fonder of him every time we get together. He drove me back to the mall and had me sit in his cool car while he started mine and it was cooling off. It was very hot that day: about 105°. I drove on home, and knew I wouldn't hear from him for several days because he was having company until sometime this week. I did enjoy Brian's singing. He has a very nice voice.

Last Saturday, Sherry went to Tennessee with her mother and dad. She wanted to help her dad with the driving. Phil called me Saturday afternoon and told me he'd like to take me to eat supper. When he got here, he brought me an early birthday present from him and Thom: a new television! I was so thrilled! My old one was not an HDTV, and was not sufficient. He got it all connected, and we watched a movie. I called Thom and Debby and thanked them for it, and was very grateful to all of them. Phil took my picture standing next to the TV, and sent it to Sherry. She texted Phil every little while—they had stopped somewhere to spend the night. The trip to the Smoky Mountains is a long one.

I went last week and bought a new phone from T-Mobile. I'm still trying to learn to use it. I talked to my friend Dorothy Glover, and learned J.B. is back at HealthSouth and doing very well.

I walked out my back door yesterday and saw where some little varmints, probably an opossum or maybe a raccoon, has dug large holes in my yard and got under the fence, into my backyard, and under the utility building there. So I called animal control. They said if I would come and give them a $55 check as a deposit on a cage and catch the animal, the city will dispose of the animal I caught. I just put it out for the first time tonight.

I made an appointment with an eye doctor in the morning at 10:15. I thought this eye problem would go away, but it hasn't. I made one appointment, canceled it, but figured I'd better get it checked out since there hasn't been any change in it for several weeks.

The first night, my trap didn't catch anything; it may be that I didn't set it well, but on the second morning I got an opossum. People from animal control picked it up and left me another trap. I haven't caught any more, but today, Monday, there was a house cat in it. He was very happy to get out when I released him. He ate the bait: a can of tuna.

I called the doctor's office this morning and have an appointment for this bump on the left eyelid to be lanced and drained at 1 PM Tuesday. It's beginning to show more and grow a little.

I got the eyelid procedure done yesterday, Tuesday. Sherry went with me. It's a simple procedure, but I will have to keep up with the hot cloths on that eyelid for another week. I called Thom last night. We are looking forward to my visit to Virginia in November. Ken Elliott called me last night. He will come after he sees the dentist this morning. We'll do some rehearsals and go to Green Valley rehab later, and see if they'll let us perform for them. We planned to have lunch.

I'm getting e-mail messages from Adam in Albuquerque New Mexico. He's ready to take his written flight exam (nearly). I'm so proud of him, he seems to be doing well with his flying. He says he wants to take me with him to Oshkosh, Wisconsin in a couple of years for the huge fly in and air show.

I went to Manor Care. Saw J.B. Glover, Mary Jo Clardy, and Rose Jones, and then played millionaire with several residents and had a chance to talk to Gaye, the director. Betty is gone and will be replaced. Gaye said they'll hire someone in-house; they want me to keep coming, but can't buy me any gas, so I'm considering not going back, just visit occasionally, or maybe going once a week. I reminded her there are many nursing homes all around me, and I can volunteer at any of them. And also my car may play out; it's making strange noises and is an old car. I don't want to buy another one; I can't afford it and won't get this one repaired till I have to, so I don't know what I'll do.

Today, August 4, 2011 is my Daddy's 116th birthday. He was born in 1890 and died in 1949 at 61 years. My brother, Louie's birthday is August 5. Also I remember it's my cousin Annette's birthday, the fifth, as well.

I've had a busy week, and a good one. I hear from Ken frequently, and we have a few singing engagements. We're planning to get together soon for more rehearsing, singing together. Betty, the activity director of Manor Care has gone home; some of volunteering is at most a little shaky. I was there today, Thursday, and some of the residents there are upset that I'm leaving. But I promised to go back and visit them, and I will.

Our choir met today, the Sweet Spirit Singers. Nine of us were there, and we're planning to sing at Green Valley on the 18th of this month. Ken is planning to come and hear us. He and I are scheduled to sing there beginning next month. I've stopped going to Manor Care on a regular basis. Will go back to visit occasionally, as I'm attached to the residents and have promised to do so.

Yesterday, Thursday, we had 10 or 11 for Sweet Spirit Singers rehearsal. We go to Green Valley next Thursday, and Ken is coming to hear us. After rehearsal yesterday, he came here and we spent the afternoon. We're getting better, I think, and we're excited about learning more songs together. I had made some coconut pies, and we had iced tea.

I sat against a heating pad most of the afternoon to relieve my back. The arthritis pain has been so bad. But it's Friday. I go to Sherry and Phil's tonight for supper, and will watch a DVD of the old Dean Martin shows. I'm taking a coconut pie and a bowl of green beans with me, which I cooked today, and we'll eat them with whatever Sherry cooks.

I'm having a hard time trying to find time to write in this book. I'm feeling well enough; I'm staying pretty busy, but writing takes time and patience, and most of all, self-control. So I resolve to do it, and then somehow it doesn't happen. So here I am to catch up.

August 22, my birthday, and sharing with my old friend Robert Rice, now deceased. When we were kids, we used to always celebrate together. But the 23rd is Sherry's birthday. My daughter-in-law, Sherry is a very dear and beloved daughter to me, although she has a great mother. The two of us used to include Paulette; her birthday was August 18, and we went out to a restaurant every year. Robert and I used to contact each other by mail or telephone. He lived in California.

Thom and Debby always send us a check for lunch, and this year was no exception. Sherry drove us to Dallas, to the YO Steakhouse. We met Phil, and we had a great lunch. Phil and I had a buffalo filet mignon, my first, and Phil's too, though he and I have had ground meat of Buffalo.

After we ate, Phil went back to work and Sherry and I went to the shops on Harry Hines. I bought a beautiful three-piece pantsuit, bright purple, and a pair of earrings to match. Also got two other pairs of earrings. Sherry didn't get anything—she said it was all too flashy.

Later the next day, we had a supper. Jonathan, Jamie, and Emmie were there, and we had barbecue. It was good. When I got home, I washed and rolled my hair because I had plans today.

Ken and I went to Avalon and did a one-hour show. I was glad to see everyone there. I've known so many before, when Johnny was there and later, and most of them remembered me. After the show, Ken and I went to Ginger Brown's. He had a sweet roll, and I had coffee. We talked a long time, and he took me back to Avalon after my car. We've had many days without rain and there seems to be none in sight. Trees and grass are dying, and the heat is oppressive. Tomorrow is Thursday. We'll have Sweet Spirit Singers tomorrow, Friday, and Saturday. Ken and I will do two more shows.

Last Saturday, Karen, my neighbor across the street and I went to the Grapevine Opry. I haven't been there in so long. It was a great show, and the last half was a tribute to George Strait. Other singers sang his songs, and all of them were wonderful. The show was just a little long, so I may need the next two days to rest, but I loved the show and plan to go back. I'd love to have Ken go with me, and I know he'd love it—but don't know if he will or not. He hasn't.

We saw and talked to Jeff and Pam. I was so glad to see them, and they looked so good. They called me later and wished me a happy birthday. I got between 80 and 100 birthday wishes on my Facebook.

Our wedding anniversary has come and gone, mine and Sherman's—65 years! Sherman died 11 years ago. I'm now 82, August 22 of this year! Thankfully, I'm still living alone, doing most of the things I want to do, and still driving my car.

It's been an extremely dry summer. Water is becoming scarcer, and now the lakes are getting very low. The temperature is in the 80s, and that's a relief, but we're still praying for rain.

Phil and Sherry are leaving tomorrow for a vacation camping trip. They'll be going to Albuquerque, New Mexico to see Adam, and I'm not sure where from there. I'll be in touch with them.

Thom and Debby are taking a trip to England and Scotland, and should be home this next week. Ken and I are still singing — we will sing at Ashwood Nursing Center tomorrow and at Green Valley next Friday.

Thursday we'll sing at Manor Care and other places, not all determined yet. I'm enjoying singing with Ken, realizing a long-held dream and thankful for chance to do it now. Phil and Sherry will be home this weekend, and Thom and Debby are back. Thom called me yesterday while Pauline Rice and I were having lunch at Denny's. I've asked him to write a story for me to include here, about an experience he had in Ireland. He promised to do so.

Pauline Rice and I went to a couple of nursing homes to see if we could get dates for Ken and me to sing. We left material at the two places we visited. I called Ken last night to tell him about the visits, and he'd had a call yesterday— got three more engagements for us. We were elated and had one of our nice long phone conversations, and discussed some songs we want to learn. We're singing at Manor Care tomorrow and at Green Valley on Friday. Three dates in October are listed, and it looks good for us to be pretty busy.

We were happy to see Randall and Dee Burns last week. Randall is better but not well. He'll have the sinus surgery as soon as possible. I had a flu shot two days ago, but I didn't feel any ill effects until today. I'm feeling really bad, and I hope I'll be okay by tomorrow. I'm singing with Ken at Manor Care. It'll be the first time we've sung there since we found each other after 31 years, except that day when he came to entertain and I recognized him and we found our voices blended well. We seem to be very close now, Ken is not very verbal about our association (I am) but we agree on so many things, and we kid a lot and have a lot of fun with others. People take for granted that a couple singing together are a couple in other ways too. We aren't.

The show we did at Manor Care was a good one. The women enjoyed it a lot. They have no paid entertainment; these days so it thrills them to have someone visit. Ken and I are both comfortable performing. I guess he has been all the time, and of course it's second nature with me, but it helps a lot that we kid each other and have a good understanding—I think—of one another. But at Manor Care, the women asked us if we were married. We told them no, we had been married, but not to each other. They were disappointed and some of them cried, as they agreed with each other that we should be married. Ruby, an Alzheimer's patient, was crying as she begged me for a recording, and finally said, "My husband is a minister. All I have to do is go and call him, and he'll be here in a few minutes, and you can be married right here." I said, "Ruby, wait a few minutes about that phone call". Instead of leaving right away, we went to Rose's room and sang three songs for her. She was unable to get up in her wheelchair. Jackie Clark had come to hear us and was in Rose's room with her. Later, Rose's daughter Linda e-mailed me and expressed her gratitude for our coming in to Rose's room.

Singing with Ken

Chapter 6

"Do you mind if I come in here and see your legs?"

My good friends when moving to Sansom Park in 1947 were Ed and Irene May. Their son, Terry was 12 when my Tommy was born in January of 1948. The first time I met Irene, I went to visit her in the little concrete building they had built on a lot behind us. These were makeshift buildings which later would be built onto, and used as a garage. It was right after the war was over, and we did what we could to scrape by until the country could rebuild the economy. But it was okay—we were happy to have a country at peace, and be free to find jobs and rebuild our lives as well as our homes.

I was a little shocked when I knocked on the door and Irene asked me in. She was dressed in a pair of underwear, no bra, nor anything else. She seemed to be unaware of being undressed and later explained that Terry, 11 then, should know all about people, so she said she and Ed didn't always get dressed at home. This was a shock to me; I was completely taken aback. Our family was always as careful around each other, as anyone else. Irene and I became very good friends. She was so good to me, much older than I, and in a lot of ways looked after me, gave me things—I especially remember a beautiful blue stripe suit that I wore a lot. We were much the same size, although I was pregnant at the time.

We used to go places together. I knew her mother and dad, her brothers, Johnny and Howard, and their families. Irene's and mine were close until they moved away, not long after my Tommy was born.

Another shock I had was one day when Irene told me that some of our neighbors were going to a nudist colony on weekends. I'd heard of these places, but never associated them with anyone I knew. Wow! Talk about a babe in the woods! I was one! Irene told me that she and Ed were invited to visit the colony, and maybe join it. I gasped; I expected her to scoff at the idea, but she told me they were going to visit one weekend. Later I learned they did, but decided not to join it.

Irene was with me during my long stay at All Saints Hospital, the old one on 8th Avenue. There were some complications, and I was in labor 24 hours. But Tommy (later Thom, named after my daddy) was born on January 23, 1948. He was fine, 6 lbs. 8 oz., my sweet little firstborn. The Mays moved away to find work elsewhere. It was nearly like part of the family leaving. I saw them only a couple of times after that until Ed had retired and they moved back into her mother's house. Many years later, we were to be reunited with them, and when you read about Johnnie, my sweetheart, it's Irene's brother.

Irene was happy when Johnnie and I started going together. She said that Johnnie had been totally devastated when he lost his wife. They'd been together 62 years and his three children, Janet, Kathy and Jim Ed, told me they felt the same way. They are all very sweet to me. Johnnie was 84 and I was 72. We were a good match, but never considered getting married. Johnnie was the sweetest, most thoughtful man, and we were very much in love, but we realized that marriage is not always the answer. I could never consider marriage at my age, now 82.

Later, Ed and Terry died. Irene's parents had died, and Irene went into a nursing home: Fireside Lodge. She was there about 20 years, and passed away a couple of years before Johnny and Howard. She was 97.

I used to visit her at Fireside. Johnnie's wife, Esther had died two years before Sherman did. Johnny and I got reacquainted, and began going together after Sherman died in 2001. Johnnie was 84 and I was 72. Johnny was the sweetest, most thoughtful man, and we were very much in love with each other. Still, we never actually considered getting married. I'm so thankful we didn't. Sometimes marriage is just not the answer, and I feel that it could never be right for me again. As an 82-year-old woman, I'd never consider such a thing again. It's not too late for me to love, and I'm still certainly capable of loving, but I'm too old to have the responsibility of another person. I'm barely able to take care of myself. I was glad to have Irene back in my life for the time being, even with her in the nursing home.

In December 2009 Janet, Johnny's daughter, called and told me her aunt, my friend Irene, had gotten very sick and wasn't expected to live. She is 97 years old. Pauline Rice and I went to see her a couple of weeks ago and she was fine. She talked and laughed with us like she always had. Pauline was amazed that Irene looked so much like Johnny. The next day, on Sunday afternoon, I went to see her. The nurse told me she hadn't been expected to live through the night before, but I talked to her a little and told her I loved her. She had oxygen on her, and was breathing hard. She died at eight Monday morning.

A flood of old memories came back as I left her on Sunday. Sherman and I moved into our house on July 4, 1947. The first neighbor I met was Irene. She and her husband, and their son, Terry, lived in a large garage, and all through the years we were close. But she had been away and soon after they moved back, moved in with her mother. Terry was grown and divorced, a father now, and Ed became sick and died. Then later Terry, who took care of Irene, died of brain cancer. Irene broke a hip and went into Fireside Lodge where she lived about 20 years before she died last Monday morning. She had been lying in bed most of the time, for several years. Aside from a few incidents and a wild imagination, she had been quite well. I used to visit her often, but hadn't in quite a while. She never complained about it; just was always glad to see me. I'm going to miss her. We were best friends a long time.

I don't know if Johnnie and Howard know about her death. Janet said Irene's grandson was going to tell them, but Johnny can't hear at all, or at least he can't hear me. And I don't think he'll remember very long, but I think it will go hard for Howard. He's just lost both his sons, and his grandson is taking care of him. He hasn't been able to stand up since he broke his pelvis a few weeks ago, and he seems downcast now, maybe depressed. The funeral is Saturday morning at 11:30 at Greenwood. I doubt that Johnny will be able to go, but he may, and probably they'll take Howard.

Irene had made some provisions about what she would be wearing for burial. Her granddaughter had chosen a beautiful black dress and some shoes, and she was absolutely beautiful in the casket. Again, in the face, she looked so much like Johnny.

My Friend, Bill Gaby

Bill was about 21 when I first met him. He was a brother of my next-door neighbor, Earline. She, with my help, arranged a date with him and my friend, Nora Foster, to go to a church party where Nora was singing Silver Bells. They were married about a year later. Never had their own children, but helped raise nieces and nephews, and finally adopted two little girls who they raised to teenagers before Nora died with cancer. They were both adopted as newborns.

Bill and I have always been good friends. We've gone to shows, restaurants, etc., but never intimate with each other; much like a brother-sister relationship. Bill treated me well always, and our families were very close. After Nora died, Bill took good care of his teenage daughters. He'd always been a great father, and they couldn't have loved him more. They were all devoted to each other, but Bill's health began to deteriorate. He lost a lot of weight, but the diabetes took its toll on him. He worked as long as he could at a kiosk at a mall, selling Dippin' Dots, a special type of ice cream. His girls and their husbands helped him as he lost one leg and then the other, and finally died. The last few years, he had lived in an apartment, then an assisted living place, and finally, a nursing home.

Bill was a wonderful cook. He had no qualms about doing any kind of housework, taking care of sick folks, or caring for children. He used to leave work and drive across town to feed his mother-in-law her lunch at a nursing home every day at noon. Her family was all gone, and he took such loving care of her. She and her husband loved him dearly, and he was a great son to them. He was one of the best friends our family ever had. Sherman was as fond of him as I was. Nora died several years before Bill did. I'd known Nora since she was 12 years old. She had the most beautiful soprano voice, and we used to sing together at Broadview Baptist Church. Her mother played piano. Her father, Leon, was a drunk, lovable, but only when sober. I used to cut his hair. My kids all loved him.

On April 14, I had been to Phil and Sherry's, and when I got home, I had a call on my phone. I called back. I had no idea who it was, and it was Joyce Wells! I was so surprised! I'd wondered how they were for some time. It was 1983 when I met Bob Wells. I'll never forget it. He was a tall slim man in his early

60s, I suppose. When he drove up to my A&P School in Arlington, he drove a strange looking homemade truck. He and his wife Joyce had come from New York, had parked their trailer home, also homemade, at a trailer park close by, and planned to stay till Bob got his A&P license.

Bob was, I believe, the most interesting student I've ever had. He fascinated me, just talking about airplanes and his career with them. He had flown for the Rhinebeck Aerodrome in New York State, and knew more about all the older aircraft than anyone I've ever known. He knew so much about the antique planes; admittedly, he neither knew nor cared about jets.

He and Joyce, his wife, visited us, Sherman and me; we visited them in their trailer home. He got his license, and meantime he loved working in the shop. They were thinking about moving to Texas, which they ultimately did. Later, when Bob came back to visit, he had shaved off a long beard, and I nearly couldn't recognize him. He looked 20 years younger. A time or two, they parked in our yard so they could use our electricity. We always enjoyed them, and one night we, the four of us, went to Granbury where Bill and Paulette were playing at the Cuckoo's Nest.

They were avid square dancers. We ate at the Nutt House later, and then went to the Cuckoo's Nest. We all had a good time.

Later, after Sherman and I moved to Watauga, a couple of times they came and camped at Grapevine Lake where I went to see them. Bob was always full of stories, and I loved listening to him. They moved to Donna, Texas, where Bob worked on airplanes as a volunteer for the Civil Air Patrol. He loved dope and fabric work.

In 2003, he got sick, and was on full oxygen. Joyce told me he had died in August, 2006. She said she was moving, had sold the trailer they had bought (the homemade one had long since gone), and she's moving to Greenville, South Carolina, or a small town close to Greenville. She hates the ice and snow, but their kids live there. She promised to write me when she gets settled later.

One of my favorite memories of Bob is when he came to my school the first day. He rode his motorcycle and brought a propeller, holding it in front of him on the motorcycle, his beard nearly to his waist. What a picture! He was bringing the prop to me.

Joyce said she was cleaning out all the papers, etc., collected over the years, and she found the letter I'd sent him about his coming to school. She had meant to call and tell me of his death, but that cinched it, so she did and I'm so grateful.

Nine months after our divorce, Sherman and I decided to go back together. He had expressed the desire to try again to make our marriage work. After all, we were married from 1946 to 1990—44 years! They were good years, and would have continued if we had tried harder and hadn't let circumstances interfere. Our interests had been opposites, and neither of us was willing to comply with the other.

I was working for Dalfort at the time, and was still under contract with them after selling the school to them. They sent me to Tulsa, Oklahoma to talk to some people, and to visit a school or two there, and Sherman wanted to go with me. So I agreed, and we had an understanding that he would not be drinking. He declared that he would give up drinking entirely if I would go back with him.

Sherman and me

So we had a good chance to be together again and talk things over. I didn't readily agree, but I could see that he was not real well and needed me to look after him.

We visited the aviation schools there, in and near Tulsa. One of my good friends (a former student) and his wife lived there. He was a teacher in one of the schools, had been divorced, and had come to Tulsa after marrying again. We went to have supper with them, and I was so glad to see him, and was very impressed with his workplace. He was over the jet engine department, and showed us through the school, which had been a public school. It was so well equipped, and I've never seen so many turbine engines, all in various stages of assembly and disassembly. We flew home, and set the date in May, shortly after the Tulsa trip. We bought our new house on Lyndale Drive. Paulette was with us when we bought it, and she and Thom came out the next day and made several decisions about decorating. Paulette was an excellent decorator. I hate to think about what the place would have looked like without her decorating skills. She also helped select furniture and drapes, etc., and loved doing it. And then, it was time to plan the wedding. Meanwhile, Paulette was divorced, and Bill had married Becca. Paulette was dating Jeff Agnew and working downtown, and sharing custody of Matt.

We planned our wedding at home, very casual. Brother Wrinkle, our pastor at Azle Ave. Baptist was to officiate, and a few friends were invited. Paulette, Thom, and Phil sang "Today," and Jeannie sang a great song afterward, "Sweet Beulah Land." Paulette learned the song, and made it the title of her gospel album that we produced after her death.

We were happy in our new home, and for a while, everything was fine. One day soon after, Sherman tried to work a few days at Greenwood Cemetery, where he had done a lot of marble work. He lasted a couple of days, and had to give up. He just wasn't able.

Sherman and I went to a movie one afternoon. As we were driving home, I got a call on my cell phone, and it was Paulette. She was calm at first, but got emotional as she told me to call her as soon as I got home. I knew it was a bad message, and dreaded what she had to tell me. But I called her and she told me. It had just been determined that she had breast cancer. They had thought it was calcification, but the biopsy showed it was cancer. She was 37 years old. She began surgery and treatments immediately.

Paulette never stopped singing. Sometimes, while she took chemo treatments from a little container that hung at her waistband or belt, she sang on the Johnnie High Country Music Revue. She sang on the show regularly for several years, as a soloist or with others, and always in a back-up group, and was a favorite of many there. Many of her fans had her on their prayer lists at churches. For a while, she had radiation treatments as well, at the HEB hospital in Hurst. Part of the time, there were intensive treatments, there at Baylor in Dallas, and at Arlington Memorial Hospital in Arlington. She faced her illness, treatments, and what we hoped was recovery, with grace, thankfulness for her friends and family and others, and a love for everybody that was remarkable. But we, her close family, and Jeff's parents, as well as Jeff himself, knew her anxiety and angst, and concern for Matt. Paulette was a Christian; she knew the Lord, but was a young woman with a child, and wasn't ready to give up.

When a year and a half had passed, Paulette and Jeff got married. The wedding was in their house in Grapevine, where Jeff had taken her and was taking care of her. It was a small wedding with Sherman, me, and Jeff's parents attending. Matt was there, and Rusty Gribble played his guitar. It was a sweet but rather sad ceremony. We were glad to see Paulette happily married; she had loved Jeff for a long time. They lived together a year and a half before she died in 1993.

I looked at the roses out in front; the red ones were spectacular, and the yellow ones were nice, but not as large and don't last as long as the red ones. Also, the yellow ones have so many buds to get open that I couldn't cut them. But I cut all the red ones, about seven or so, and a couple of the yellow ones, and took them to Greenwood Cemetery. I cleaned out the vases on the two graves of Sherman and Paulette, and then I drove to Angelo's and had lunch—a chopped beef sandwich, a package of potato chips, and a glass of tea.

October, 2007

This particular time, a lot of my life was spent taking care of Margaret, and her family. I was having some medical problems of my own, and the hours I spent looking after others were rather trying; especially when I seemed to have the responsibility of JJ. I loved him, and wanted to help him, but I kept coming to a dead end.

On Monday morning, October 1, I got ready and went to North East Mall. I went to Office Depot and made some copies of my letterhead, and got some good quality copy paper for my printer. I went to Hancock's and looked around a while, didn't buy anything and came home.

I ate some spaghetti and had some shrimp, I cleaned up after JJ, washed the bed linens, etc. I went to Target for a prescription and came home. I sat down for a little while and dropped off to sleep. I woke up and looked up some recipes and I found a good one. It was a ginger cake, so I made it. It's very good. I had a piece of it when it was still hot.

I cooked some chicken breasts, potatoes, and Ritz crackers. I found some okra I'd frozen, and had supper. I cleaned up, went back to my chair to read the paper, and watched TV. Sherry came over. She was looking for a particular type can for a science experiment, but we didn't find any. She was homeschooling Kyle. She put the printer tape in my printer and it works fine now. I gave her some cake to take home. She tasted it and liked it, and I had another piece.

I went to bed, and just as I was dropping off, my phone rang. It was JJ, and he was very upset. He had worked from about 7 AM to 3 PM, and he and his friend were moving Jacky and Manda into the new apartment. Some guys—I'm not sure, but later a policeman said six, jumped on him. He said he was bloody all over, and he wanted me to come after him soon. He was at Lancaster and Beach, the worst part of Fort Worth. I told him I couldn't drive there at night; I still couldn't see too well, but especially in that area. I told him to call the police. I kept getting calls from him, and then a cop called and said they had had an ambulance take JJ to the Peter Smith Hospital. He had a cut lip, but there was a lot of blood.

I finally got to sleep; it was after midnight, and I was worn out. I got a call from JJ at 4 AM, wanting me to come and get him. He said he'd been waiting all night in a chair in the emergency room, and hadn't seen a doctor yet. I told him I couldn't come after him. He called again at six, but I still couldn't go. I finally relented around nine, and went after him. He had been released after putting something on the cut on his lip, and he was supposed to be waiting for me at the main entrance. He wasn't there. I waited a while, and then went in and looked around. He was nowhere to be found, so I just started on home.

My cell phone was ringing, and he was wondering where I was. I told him I was going home; I had brought him some food, but couldn't find him, and he'd have to catch a bus. I went home. I had lunch, and later in the afternoon, when JJ called me again, he'd come home and couldn't get in the apartment. It seems that Jacky and Manda had left about nine, and hadn't been back. JJ still had his bloody clothes on, and hadn't had anything to eat, so I went and picked him up.

He was supposed to go to work at 4 PM, but couldn't get in to get clothes, bathe, or shave or anything. I took him home with me, and I went to Walmart and got him a pair of black pants, a black shirt, a T-shirt and another pair of black shoes like the ones that I'd bought him before. By the time I got home, he'd decided he needed to call his boss again, so he called him and said he'd be late. They told them he needed to come tomorrow instead. He said the shoes I got him at first were too large. So he spent the night. After he went to bed early, I went to see Phil and Sherry and got my A&P info sheets done and copied, and I had supper with them. I came home about 9:30 PM. I went to bed and had a good, uninterrupted night.

While we were at the apartments waiting for Jacky and Manda, we saw Manda. She saw us and ran away. We never could get them to come to the door. We went to the apartment on Hudson Street to see if Jacky was there, but he wasn't, so I brought JJ home with me. The next morning I got up about six—I'd heard JJ up for a little while, but he's awfully quiet when he's here at night. He's in such a state, any time I don't agree with him or try advising him, he goes bananas. I have decided he is psychotic. He has a tantrum, and loudly. Just goes to pieces, and then I lose it. He ironed his pants and got ready, and I took him to the train. He wanted to leave the other clothes because it was raining. I said no, because I couldn't make another trip to bring them to him. He went all berserk again. I put his shirt and other pants in a plastic bag and made him take them. He was determined to not take them on the train, and he finally decided he could wear the shirt and T-shirt. He already had on the black pants, so that's what he did. He was going to try to get into the apartment first, then go see his probation officer, and go to work at four PM.

I haven't heard from him at all, and it's nearly 7:40 PM. I hope he is okay and working. It's not that I hate him being here; I want him to be independent, but I don't like him yelling at me, and I know my blood pressure goes up high. I am sorry for him. I love him, but I get extremely frustrated.

Armando Cortez was supposed to be here to study for his oral and practical exams. He was here right on time at 10 AM, but he had to be somewhere else for lunch so we just had time to talk a while. I was surprised—he nearly aced all three exams. I loaned him a book with oral questions and practical projects. It turns out, he's had a lot of experience and needs a good job. I called CJ Sury and left a message. After he left, I made a few phone calls and got some school info sheets and cards in the mail. I called Jimmy Nixon, and he said they were busy there at American Eurocopter, and Armando could probably get a job there if he'd bring a resume. So I called Armando and told him.

I made it clear to JJ again—I was to do no driving late at night to pick him up. He was upset, but I can't help it. I can only do so much. I pick him up at 6 AM— He can work till 11 or so, and spend the night in the locker room—wherever that is. He said he slept on a hard wooden bench until time to catch the train. We went by the doughnut shop where I got him some breakfast and half dozen doughnuts. We came on home. He went to sleep, and I woke him up at 1 PM so he could leave. He wanted to go by Jacky's and Manda's to pick up his clothes, but time was running out. After he brought his clothes out and put them in the car, I took him on to the hotel to work. I was exhausted, and we were snapping at each other again.

After dropping him at the hotel, I drove to Penny's to pick up my new glasses. I was a little disappointed at the way they looked, but took them anyway. From there, I went on to see Johnny a while before going to Ginger Brown's, and stayed just a few minutes and left. When I got to Ginger Brown's, the tables, many of them, were set up for two large parties, one of them for Carly, Karen's granddaughter. She is eight, so she had quite a party. We didn't know the other honoree or her party. But it was all fun, and we had a good time. Dan and Betty were there too. Laurine had called me and left a message on my home phone. She sounded upset, and I tried to call her back when I was visiting Johnnie. I left her a message. We all missed Randall. It seemed to me that he may have said he was going with Dee on a trip or something, but everyone asked me about him.

When I got home, I had another message from Laurine. She said to call her, no matter how late it was when I got home, so I called. She told me Nick, her brother was dead. He'd killed himself in the room he rented from a friend. He was an alcoholic and had become something of a hermit. The county would bury him; no one else had the money,

Of course.

But we would have a memorial later. She was still pretty upset. He'd lived with Laurine and CJ for three years, was converted and saved, but went back on the booze. We talked until 10:30 PM.

The next day, I got up early and went to the train to pick up JJ. I waited at the station until the train came, but JJ was not on it, so I left and came home. On the way, he called me and said he had missed the train, would be on the next one.

I went out again, and by the time I got to the station, the train had gone and he obviously wasn't on it. So I sat out there until about 7:30, and finally it came, and he was on it. I brought him home, and we had a distinct understanding; no more arguing and getting mad and yelling. We agreed, and the whole day was much more pleasant.

I left and went to Penny's. I figured I couldn't wear these awful glasses frames and would see about getting some more. But she finally got them adjusted, and they feel okay. Not pretty, but my sight is much better. I'll get some better-looking ones someday, when I find a good sale. I came back and had some brunch at Denny's. When I got back, JJ was getting ready to go to work, so I took him back to the TRE. I let him out and came on home. I rested a while and had a milkshake, then I went to the grocery store and got some stuff. I had called Jeanne yesterday and asked her to let me know if she saw my ad in the River Oaks News. She called me, and we talked for a long time; nearly an hour. I ate some Spam and beans for supper, and watched a great movie with Peter Falk (Monk).

Angelo's Barbecue is celebrating 50 years of being the number 1 barbecue place in Fort Worth. I can remember them from many years ago; it used to be a favorite of Sherman's and mine. Right next door to their parking lot is Teague Lumber Company. It used to be Castleberry Lumber Company, where we bought the building material for our first house in Sansom Park in 1947, after we had married in August, 1946. We had bought a lot, $10 down and $5 per month. So we borrowed $300 from the bank and had Mr. Good, his boss, sign the note so we could build a house: two rooms and a path out back. The lot was 75' x 180'. It was not finished when we moved into it.

I was just thinking about all this as I ate my lunch. Afterwards, I went on to Fireside Lodge. I went in, and recognized the lady standing there close by, and she seemed to know me. It was Dorothy Witcher and her girls, Janice and Carolyn, who had gone to school with my kids. We both went to room 38 where Irene was, and I introduced them. Dorothy went back to her room, room 28. Irene was having her lunch, and I sat in her wheelchair while we talked. She said she hadn't heard from Howard, and didn't know if he had moved into one of the apartments there. I laughed so hard when she told me the following story:

> An old man walks in the hall, and looks in at Irene. One day, as she was getting out from the covers, she uncovered her legs and he saw her. "Do you mind if I come in here and see your legs?" he asked. "I just love to look at legs" She said, "No, you can't look at mine! Get out of here."

When I left her, I went to room 28 to talk to Dorothy. We visited a while, and I left to go see Johnny at Manor Care.

I didn't stay long before I came on home. No Ginger Brown's tonight. I had called Randall earlier, to see how Dee was getting after her knee surgery. He said she was a little better. I told him I wasn't going to Ginger Brown's tonight, and he said he wasn't either. He's going to stay home with Dee. I cooked some chicken, baked potatoes, and green beans for supper, and went to pick up JJ. He was in a rotten mood, and I figured it was because he knew that tomorrow was his last day to stay here. But he thought his car would be ready before he got off today.

I came home feeling good, and now I would be free. As it's been, I can't go anywhere at night, can't have company, can't watch any TV in the evening, etc. I read the paper and took my bath. I washed and rolled my hair and got my bills all ready to mail. I dried my hair, fixed it and went out. I went to the post office for stamps, mailed my bills, and went to Big Lots. They had lots of new stuff in; I got about $25 of groceries. I did a small load of laundry. After I started supper, JJ called. His car wouldn't be ready until tomorrow, so I needed to come to the station after him. He was upset the rest of the evening.

Well, the weekend passed. I haven't written in here because...maybe I'm lazy, but I stay busy in the evening. Maybe I should start doing my writing in the mornings, when I usually have more time to myself and am not so tired. JJ hasn't got his car fixed yet, and is still here. I'm hoping it will be another two days at most. I haven't seen Johnny since Friday. He calls me every day.

I went to the Johnny High show Saturday night. I met Alan Cook at the Arlington Steakhouse. We had supper and went on to the show. Alan says he's fine, but he never complains about himself. He paid for my ticket, and I plan on paying for his next time. The show was okay, but not great. A lot of the regulars were not there.

Sunday services were good at church; I also went on Sunday night. But in the afternoon, after resting a little while, I went to the store and bought some groceries at Walmart. I got a large picnic ham. I cooked it some today, but it's very fat and I think I may cook it a little more tomorrow.

I got a call from Sherry last night, and she told me Matt is home from Chicago. He has come home to go to school, apparently. I'm so glad. He hasn't called me yet, but I'm sure he will. Tomorrow we have choir practice in the morning, and then I promised to take JJ's car flywheel to be resurfaced. So if I go see Johnny, it'll be late tomorrow.

When I went to the mailbox today, I heard someone say, "Pauline." It was Ken Bino; he came on out to see me. He told me he had met an old girlfriend and was thinking about going to North Carolina, where he's from. His folks live there, and he said this girl was interested in North Carolina, too, so he is thinking about going there—maybe for just a vacation, maybe to live, but his kids are all here. I'd like to see him happy—he seems lonely. But what a neat guy he is, I think. Thom called me today; he's making plans for my trip—only a month away! (Later, I found that Ken Bino really is a great guy!)

I took JJ to the train this morning, thinking this should be the last day I'd have to do this. I knew I needed to go as soon as possible to Calloway's, to see what was wrong with my car. I let him out, and went back home. I was tired and rested a while, tried and failed to take a nap. Just couldn't drop off. I got a call from Matt, and I was so glad to hear from him. We decided to go to lunch, so he said he'd call me back. He did in about half an hour, and I went after him at his dad's. He told me he was still tired from the trip home. He'd come on a Greyhound bus, a 22-hour trip from Chicago. We went to Applebee's and had lunch. I was a little shocked to see that Matt was hyperventilating, and having a real bad spell with it. Finally, he calmed down, but it happened again before long. He had lost his driver's license and was afraid he would have a lot of trouble getting it replaced. But I took him to see about it. He had no trouble at all; it only took about 5 minutes, and he was so glad. I took him by his house to take some medicine, but after we started back to my house, he was feeling bad and thought it best to go back home, so I went to take him back.

I came back by Calloway's to see about my car. They checked it out, and Gordon told me it needs a new tire. And after they checked, the timing system needed replacing. It cost me $168 altogether, and I'm so glad; it is so quiet now, and runs so smoothly. Sherry came after me and we went to the mall, but I remembered I had left the ham cooking in the crock pot. We went home, and I gave her some ham. She gave me a check from them to help me on expenses while JJ was there—$135. What a blessing they are to me!

I found out that Carl, the owner of Calloway's, is bad, in the hospital, but still alive. I'd heard that he died. I told Mark I really liked him and was so sorry he was so bad. Mark said he is the best man he ever worked for.

JJ got his car, so he called and said he wouldn't come back, so I could go to Ginger Brown's tonight. I got home late, and slept so well. He had said he'd sleep in his car, but I doubt it. He had gotten a haircut and some new T-shirts, and I didn't question it.

The next day I got up late for a change, and enjoyed being home doing a little work, then I went out. I had several errands to do. I got home around 3 PM, and very soon got a call from a detective from the Haltom City Police Department, detective Whitley. He informed me that JJ was dead. He was found hanged in a Haltom City motel. We promised to keep in touch; he gave me his cell number, and said he would talk to me anytime. I was so shocked, I called Sherry, and I called Jack Senior and he was shocked; he told me he had been working at a Whataburger for four months. Manda wanted to talk to me, but she was very short, just said, "What happened?" I said as little as possible to her. I made several calls and got several. Sherry came after me, and I went to their house and had supper. They brought me home, and my good friend

Randall called me later. Delores Rivers called about JJ. I talked to several people, and finally got to bed around 11 o'clock.

On Saturday, more calls. I finally talked to detective Whitley, and he told me JJ had committed suicide by hanging. I have had several theories, but they have so far become this. Phil got into the computer today and discovered JJ had been contacting all kinds of people, a lot of prostitutes, and it all explained what he was doing. He had obviously made a date with someone he'd met at the motel. The person, or persons, had taken his car and left him dead on the bed. I'm sure they detected that the car had been stolen, because he wouldn't have parted with it at all, so it could be there was no woman, but maybe a man who could have robbed him, but that's only my idea.

I talked to Laverne. She told me there were lots of young people these days using the hanging process to get a sexual high, and died doing it, but I doubt that in this case. Phil and Sherry came and took me to lunch at Cotton Patch. Then we went home and Sherry started doing extra cleaning, mostly in the front bathroom. JJ had broken the seat, so I made the bed after Phil turned the mattress over, and he did several things to the lights, etc. He left in my car for a while, and came back with two new tires. Bless their hearts; they are so good to me.

After about five, I went to Home Depot. I got a new commode seat and some Raid. We had found a swarm of ants at the window, and I'd used the last drop. Also, I got some cleaner for the refrigerator in the garage. Tonight I washed and rolled my hair. I have to admit I am so totally relieved and glad to be alone, to have my house back. I am here part of the time, and I love having the house to myself. Selfish? I guess, but it's going to help my blood pressure go down to normal.

I went to church on Sunday, and from there I came home, got an apple pie, and went to the Sullivans for lunch. We had a great pizza and desserts, and a good visit with everybody, and I went to see Johnny. When I came home I rested a while. If I sound like I'm indifferent to JJ's death, I'm not. He's on my mind continuously. I wake up at 2:30 to 4 AM. On Monday the alarm clock he used went off, and again today at 5 AM. I haven't figured out how to make it stay off. I don't know how to turn it on.

I made many calls on Monday to relatives and friends who know JJ, and they found out some facts, I guess. I talked to detective Whitley, and to the man who did medical exams. He works for the Tarrant County Medical Examiner. I got a call from a man from a funeral home, and learned this: Nobody knew about the car (??), but the man told me all the information on the car: the model, the Vin number, etc. JJ had all the papers in the glove compartment, and when I talked to his boss, he said he'd seen JJ counting his money, several twenty dollar bills, and he gave him some extra, so he had well over $100. As far as we know, no money was found on him. He had been dropped off by some motorists, and was very deeply distraught and distressed, the detective said. He bought and paid for one night, went to the bathroom, and there was a large mirror on the wall. He took it down and took it into the bedroom, broke it, and began to use the pieces to cut himself, his arms and I don't know where else. He must've sat on the bed and waited a while, decided it wasn't killing him fast enough, so he tried to hang himself with a telephone cord, and it broke. He then took a sheet and somehow fashioned a way to hang himself. I don't know if he got back to the bed or died in the bathroom—a lot of unanswered questions remain. I was out of patience with the detective of the Haltom City Police force, but may call him again for a couple of answers. I didn't believe a lot of the story I was told. Some of the details had to be imagined, and it was plain that it was just that somebody decided it happened this way.

The man from the funeral home called me and wanted me to bring slides for a slide presentation at the memorial next Thursday. I have all Margaret's pictures here, so I got a bunch of them together and took them to the funeral home.

I went to choir practice this morning, our Sweet Spirit Singers. It's so good to sing again, though my voice is bad. We sang "Everybody's Gonna Have Religion in Glory" and some more, and Rita and I went to Joe's and had lunch.

By the time I got back from the funeral home to take the pictures, I rested a while and then fixed a really good supper. I found this recipe in the paper and decided to make it. It's called cornbread and beef skillet pie. I had a piece of apple pie for dessert, and then I went to Bluebonnet Hills, to visitation for Mary Arrick, Dennis's mother. She had died a couple of days before.

Thursday, May 15, 2008

It was the day for JJ's Memorial service. I fixed myself a hamburger steak with gravy, and had a piece of the chocolate cake I had made the day before. I got ready to go, put all my other interests aside, and went to the funeral home. I got there just as Sherry did. Kim Ballog, my deacon, got there, and Manda and Tim, her brother was there. We went in, and I'll try to list them all: Jacky and Manda, Tim and his mother, Tim's wife and daughter, Boni Fraustro, James Klinkscales, Dan and Betty Shiro, Sherry, Linda, Cindy, three other people, and the pastor from a Methodist church.

The pastor of the Methodist church officiated, and we saw a good DVD they had put together of pictures from the family and the funeral home director. After it was all over, Jacky and Tim's family went to the grave site where they had buried JJ. It's a cemetery in Mansfield. Jacky thinks JJ was murdered, not suicidal, and so do I, but I can't pursue it. I'm too old, among other reasons.

I left there and went to see Johnny. We visited for a while, and I went on to Ginger Brown's. We were celebrating Sam Griggs' birthday. I got him a card and a T-shirt that read, "Texan by the grace of God." Everyone else gave him cards with money. All their folks—Karen's two sets of parents, her daughter and granddaughter, Randall and Dee, and I, were there. But Karen and Sam were late, and got there after 8 PM. Sam is Jeff and Karen's son. Their older son is Dustin.

But Jeff, Karen, Karen's dad and I all sang "On My Mother's Side," and it sounded good. I love the song, and love it when I get to sing with them. Karen's dad was using a walker instead of his wheelchair now, so he's a lot better.

The next morning I got up early, before six, made some biscuits, and had biscuits and butter for breakfast. I got myself together, and watched Steven Colbert on TV, and got a call from Matt. He asked me was it okay if he came to see me, and of course it was! I was excited to see him. I had taken some chicken out to thaw, and asked him if he'd rather have dumplings or pot pie. He said dumplings were his favorite, so I made a large batch of dumplings. They really are good; we enjoyed them for lunch, and I had more tonight. We went to the church to take books and some clothes for the garage sale tomorrow. The gym was full. We hung up the clothes, and then I needed to go to the grocery store. Matt drove me to Albertson's; I got a few things, and we came home.

He had another bowl of the dumplings. He loves them, and we just had the nicest time. Bill and Becca gave him their Acura to drive, and he was so happy about it. He worked yesterday, his first day here, and he was told he could be in line for a supervisory position. Also, he won some kind of award for being the best dressed at work. He dresses in Levi's and does look great. After he left, Sherry and Howard, my next-door neighbors, mowed the yard and edged. Our yards both look beautiful. I took them the rest of the cake. They were playing rock music on the Wii.

Chapter 7

"Look, it's a big world. Start your own school!"

My personal life was fine as I recall. I was working hard. It was easy enough to keep working for Steve. He was happy for me to do the instructing, and he even hired other girls to do the office work I had been doing for so long. I was still taking care of getting the work done, and he was still hiring a new girl every couple of weeks or so, but they didn't know how to do much, and sometimes didn't try.

He found and hired girls from a café nearby, from the lunch bar at Kmart, and even one from a Meacham Field competitor. Most of these girls only lasted a few days. One, a nice girl named Tina, became my good friend, and was there quite a while. Steve told many stories about these girls, including Tina and even me, to his wife. I knew this later. He even told Tina and me things about each other, totally false. He was obviously going through the men's menopause. We realized this as we talked to each other later and compared stories. Later, Tina went into real estate and, I understand, moved to Florida.

One of our students at Steve's, Bill Bedinger, a good friend of mine and a helicopter pilot, taught me how to teach the IA course. He had been instructing the course at Steve's after getting his own IA. I thoroughly enjoyed teaching this one- or two-week course for the mechanics who were qualified and had had their A&P's for three years.

We had other airmen from Carswell AFB come to school. One of these was Col. George Kentosh; he was here from Sheppard Air Force Base in Wichita Falls,

Texas. He and I became good friends, and used to go to lunch together. Later, Steve and I visited him in Wichita Falls to see about teaching classes there. We failed to make a deal (I don't think Steve really wanted to). George had an appliance store in town, and sold me, at cost, and delivered later, a beautiful radio and phonograph console. About a week later, Sherman and I had him spend the night with us when he delivered the console. When he started to leave the next morning, he gave me a bottle of nice perfume he had gotten at St. Thomas Island in Kwajalein.

George was a great guy, and I was very fond of him. I helped him get his IA three years later when my school was in Arlington. He was still single, having been divorced for several years. He was retired, living in Florida. We parted rather sadly, and I've never heard from him again.

And there was Tino—in his own words, a hot-blooded Latin. I wasn't teaching then, but Tino and I were friends. He made me laugh a lot because of the things he said. He was a lot of fun. He finished his A&P course in a short time; he was very intelligent and was temperamental. He had about finished, and was waiting for some results to come in. He was sitting in a chair in my office, and seemed to sink deeper and deeper into a depression, afraid he may have failed part of it. Then the mailman came. Tino asked me to open the letter and tell him the "bad news", which turned out to be very good. You could see him turn into an extremely excited state. He rushed over and gave me a quick kiss, in a completely different mood. He soon went home to Italy.

This entry is about my trip to Washington between June 8 and July 5, 2008. This last month has been a few of the most exciting weeks for me, thanks to my two sweet boys and their families. Here I go—trying to get my thoughts together about my world-shaking trip to Virginia.

Thom sent Sherry and me copies of my plane ride itinerary. You don't have a ticket; everything is done electronically now, and I'd be hopelessly lost without someone to look after me, but I started packing. My trip was to start on June 11, at 11 AM from DFW and on the 30th, at 8:30 PM—really it was 9:30 PM after the time change. I used my medium-size suitcase; Phil and Sherry had bought me a nice set of two some time ago, and they roll, so that makes it nice. I packed and filled the suitcase up and just quit, but I had enough. I left DFW on a Super 80 plane, and came back on a same type plane. The flight was perfect, and I landed at the Baltimore airport about 3:30 PM. Thom met me at the baggage station. We had a little to eat and drink. They don't feed us on the plane any more. I did get a small glass of orange juice, and I had put a small candy bar in my bag. That was my lunch, so I was hungry when we landed.

We drove home to Thom's house in Fairfax, Virginia. What a place that is! Huge! The first floor is kitchen, dining room, den, formal dining, living room, an alcove with another TV, recliners, patio (just built off the kitchen up high and back), and a great place for the nice grill. There is a large round table with dining chairs, a larger umbrella, and sitting room furniture with cushions. The cushions come off, and they have a large plastic trunk to store them in when not in use.

It rained all the time I was there, just a shower at night except one or two nights. It's a beautiful yard, and Thom works it every Sunday. Debby works in it, too, most of the time, but the yard is small. The upstairs has four bedrooms, three bathrooms, and another small alcove sitting room. The basement has a large bedroom which they had just furnished, and the large living room with two couches, chairs, TV and DVD player, and a wall full of shelves with books— many, many books.

The house is in a neighborhood of the same type houses. It shares a common wall with another house just like it, so I guess it's like a duplex, but the houses are bought and sold separately. They are well built, so you never know other people are living that close to you.

In most every area I saw, the houses are multiple, and there are many townhouses. But Fairfax is an old town, and part of it has a lot of older one-family houses.

The first week I was there, from Wednesday to Friday, the two cats, Ernie and Abby shared the house with me. They became fond of me, in spite of the fact that they are spoiled and expect to have full use of the house. I had to try to keep Abby off the table and cabinets, and she resented it, but just mainly gave me dirty looks. But then they would take turns getting on my lap, and forgiving me for interfering in their lives. Their litter box was in a downstairs bathroom. Thom had built them a cat ladder to get from downstairs to the first floor where their food was, near the kitchen. I think Ernie was the only one to use the ladder so far.

Ernie had been named Earnest because she was mistakenly thought to be a guy. But when they took her to be spayed or neutered, lo and behold, she was found to be a girl, so she was named Ernestine and still called Ernie. Then when they got Abby, the other cat, their granddaughter Maddy would call her Abby-ka-dabby, so she is Abby.

On Saturday, Lesley, Jordan, and Jacob came to and spent the night. I hadn't seen them for some time, and was so glad to see them. They left on Sunday afternoon, and I went with them to their home in Williamsburg. What a beautiful city! Small, but historical, and I loved every minute there. They showed me all over the area.

Their house is a two-story one. Ben had been working on it. He put down hardwood floors, and painted the wall around the fireplace and bookcases a nice red color. The house is small, but compact and very homey and comfortable. Lesley's office was downstairs. She had made it into a bedroom for me. I had the half-bath across the hall, and took my bath each morning in Jordan's bathroom upstairs. All three of their bedrooms and bathrooms were upstairs.

We went out a lot. Lesley, Jordan, and I went to the shops, small nice places, and ate lunch at a small place, but we spent most evenings cooking. We made rolls, pies (a couple), and always cinnamon rolls. They love them, and Jacob would always say they were awesome. I used to go out on a small patio at the back of their house against the dense wooded area. Ben had put some snake repellent out, and it smelled pretty strong. It didn't bother me; I figured anything was worth keeping snakes away.

There was the Presidents Park not far from there, where we went one day. It was extremely hot, but we really enjoyed seeing all 42 presidents' busts, and we made pictures of them with both my camera and Lesley's. This had to be the hottest day while I was there. We went home from there, to a Mexican restaurant and had some food like no Mexican food I had ever tried, but it was pretty good. I guess Tex-Mex here is just different from any other kind of Mexican food.

We left on Thursday. Ben, Lesley, Jordan, and Jacob drove me to the Cracker Barrel, where Thom met us and bought our supper, and he and I came on home to his house in Fairfax. The cats were glad to see me, and greeted me when we came home.

I was beginning to wonder how things were at home—not really homesick; I was having too good a time. Wendy had been at Thom and Debby's when I first got there, and had interviewed for a hospital job. It sounded like it went well, and she was hopeful. I was a little concerned—I didn't mention it to her of course—but she and Bryan had jobs at the Dallas Baylor Hospital, and the kiddos went to day school and kindergarten there. It was unlikely they would be situated the same way anywhere else. Also, they have a very nice home in Waxahachie. But she went home and will be called later about her interview. As a matter of fact, later, as things turned out, they both got very good jobs and had a situation as good as the one they had had before, and are now well situated in Winchester.

I had been back at Thom's a few days before Amy and Jeremy and their family came. They came on Thursday, stayed Thursday and Friday nights, and left on Saturday. Thom and Debby had fixed up the two rooms and bath downstairs, and it was so nice. I had a great time, as we all did. The kids are all so sweet, all six of them. During their visit I got better acquainted with them, and really enjoyed Amy. She's still the same sweet girl she's always been, both she and Lesley.

I was amazed at Thom and Debby's house. It was so large, comfortable, and private. You couldn't hear from one room to another, it was so well insulated.

I have not formally started my book. I have been home, but have about stopped keeping up my journal, so I plan to get a little more organized, maybe gradually. I have started working at Manor Care on Skyline drive. I volunteer two days a week, two hours each, on Tuesdays and Thursdays. So far, I'm enjoying it a lot. I go often to see Johnny anyway, and I just help the activities director and have fun doing it.

Our Sweet Spirit Singers are planning to go to Manor Care next Tuesday. We're going to sing at 11 AM. Johnny's hospice nurse said she's going to come and sit with Johnny while we sing.

There was a letter from the US government, saying JJ's stimulus check was coming, and sure enough, it came in a few days—for $433.00. I tried to find out how to get it cashed, so I could give the money to Jacky and Manda, but couldn't find out anything until I got to talk to Gaylen, my attorney. What a good friend he is! He said to get the check to Jacky, and he could deposit and cash it. So I took it to him. He was broke; hasn't been able to go to his job because he still has a drain. He showed me. As an aside, JJ was dead at this time: He had also got a letter, saying they were supposed to arrest him, because he was driving without a license. I was advised not to call and report that JJ was dead, because the police already knew it.

Phil and Sherry got back yesterday afternoon, after their bus trip to Tennessee. Sherry was worn out. Phil and I baked; we made two chocolate and one apple pie. He made the crusts, and I did the filling. Adam and Kyle had gone with them, and the Sullivans, Haskell and Sylvia, drove. They were on their way home.

Phil and I went to Braum's for a few things, and had a good time cooking together. Thom called me first thing this morning; he was having coffee on his front porch, and thought about me.

Later this morning I got two of the papers, The Senior Gazette, and sent one to Thom and one to Carolyn. I got the craziest card from Ray Simpson yesterday. He is always sending me something crazy! This was a picture of a roll of toilet paper made out of a grater, saying things could be worse than having another birthday!

My life has been so busy lately—but finally I'm feeling so good, and I'm thankful. I seem to be really straightened out as far as my health is concerned. This is just one of the many problems solved during this last 6 to 7 weeks.

I gave JJ a deadline. He has one month to stay here, find a job, and find another place to stay. The time was up on February 18, and he made it. So last Sunday, I took him to a friend's apartment. He had signed a lease for an apartment close by, and had to wait for some repairs to be made so he could move into it. He called me three days ago; he has a new cell phone now. He's obviously getting more money than expected on his job, and likes it and the people he works with. I'm proud of him and the way he's been pretty good here.

Phil and Sherry have found their house, a beautiful place near the TRE, and will sign the papers next Friday. I have seen it, and was really impressed. Some work is being done, though it should be ready in a few days.

Margaret is getting worse; she's getting hysterical when upset, but I'm trying to take care of her as much as possible. Johnny is much better, is going to church now, and we have Sundays together, plus other times when I get a chance to go see him. He loves to take me out to eat when possible, and is now walking pretty well without his walker. But I found I can load his good walker in my car, and so we started taking it when he goes anywhere with me. He went to Ginger Brown's with me last Thursday.

Jeff and Karen played at a place on Highway 377 last Tuesday night. It's only 3 miles from me, and I think they'll start playing regularly there. It's called Clear Creek, and is a Cajun place.

My good friend and attorney, Galen Groce, met me at Fireside Lodge and helped me get a power of attorney for Margaret. I just need to have it. I gave a copy of it to Fireside, so if (when) I buy something for Margaret, they'll pay me what I pay for it, as long as I have the receipt.

Galen has married again to an Italian lady who owns a restaurant on Magnolia Street downtown. He helped her get it going, and was her chief dishwasher for a while, to get started. She is a marvelous cook, and has a great, if small, restaurant.

I asked him about my house, and how I can be sure I can leave it to Thom and Phil. He's going to fix up a trust to ensure I can do that. He said he'd be fixing it up, so I told both boys. Thom said it was a great idea, and to make sure Galen doesn't forget it, so I'll call and remind him.

The Sweet Spirit Singers are meeting again on every Tuesday morning at 10:30. Jay Biles is directing, and we're enjoying it. I won't be going next Tuesday, because I'll have a refresher course to teach. I'll have two or three men here for eight hours. There are more, but that'll come later. I'm ready to teach them any time they can come. The deadline for renewals is March 31.

As I write this, I'm here alone. Kyle is gone for the weekend with the young people at church, and Phil and Sherry are out. Sherry will be spending the night with her mother, in Baylor All Saints Hospital. She has had more surgery on her hip. She had cancer and surgery before, but has been in an awful lot of pain, and finally they decided to operate again. They did hip replacement surgery and found cancer again, but think they got it all out this time. So hopefully she'll recover, but it'll take time. Haskell and the kids are taking turns staying with her.

Matt hasn't contacted me but once. He is in Chicago, and from what little I've heard, he wants to come home. He's been out of a job for a few weeks and probably needs money, but we don't know what to do until he calls.

Thom and Debby still haven't sold their house, so they are still living apart. They spend a lot of time in Washington on weekends.

Thom called me and we had a nice talk. I got a large set of pictures on MyFamily.com of Thom's family. I found out that Michael is home from the hospital, but has Crohn's disease. He will be treated for it, and will have to stay on a strict diet for the rest of his life. Hopefully, because of his young age, something can be done for him so he can get it under control. Michael is quite athletic, and loves to play football.

I have had quite a week. I made a double batch of candy, the dipped chocolates, and took several gifts of it to Ginger Brown's on Thursday. Also took Johnny some, as well as Joyce, Karen and Jeff, and Randall and Dee. I got a beautiful basket from Joyce, containing some great Christmas ornaments, a small tray with sugar and creamer, and pretty grape salt and pepper shakers. I love Joyce, and so does everybody else. She is a hostess at Ginger Brown's.

On Friday last week, I went to the mall and walked, and also bought some Christmas gifts while I was there. I saw my friends in the food court, and visited with them for a while. Then, when I was walking back to Dillard's where I was parked, I saw Bill Hartmann. We visited for just a few minutes; he was going to meet Becca somewhere there in the mall. I came on home and called Phil at work. Sherry was sick and was home; she had been to the doctor and had found out she had bronchitis and a sinus infection. I asked Phil about going to have supper at the Olive Garden where Matt works. He had a late appointment for a haircut, so I called Jonathan and Kyle, and they wanted to go with me. We met there, had to wait a while, but the food was good. Matt was so glad to see us, and I was happy to see him. He seems so cool, calm, and sociable with his customers. He'd lost a little weight, and looked taller. He looked great, and I was proud of him, but I always am. He plans to come to see us at Phil and Sherry's on Christmas Eve. He's moved out of his parents' house and now lives with a couple of his friends in a house not far from there.

On Saturday, I slept late. I got a call from Jay, Sandra Evans' husband, and he told me Sandra was coming to see me in a little while to bring me a gift. In a while, Nicole and Lily came. They brought me a gift: a nice set of kitchen towels. Later, Sandra came in and brought me a nice gift. I got a call from Alan, confirming our date tonight to go to the Johnny High show. When I was alone,

I bathed and redressed to go to the show. I was to meet Alan there at 7:15, but always went early to see everybody. I had a copy of the FBC Gazette, where I'd written the story about Phil and Paulette years ago. They had sung one night, and I'd written about it for the paper, and knew Johnny High would like it; he was so fond of Paulette.

I decided I couldn't very well comb my hair with the cast on my left arm, so went to the salon on 26th Street. They advertise taking walk-ins and would wash and set my hair for 15.99. So I went and had my hair fixed. I'd already washed it. Mary, the owner, a Mexican lady, fixed it. I was happy with it, and got home in time to get ready to drive to Arlington.

I got there early. I found out Johnny High was sick and had stayed home. I gave the paper to Wanda, his wife. I had seen Kevin Bailey on the way, so he read the article and took me to see Wanda. She promised to give the paper to Johnny, and said he'd be glad to get it. Later, I told Mike Stewart and Maurice Anderson the story. They'll see it, I'm sure, when Johnny comes back.

Pam, Jeff's wife, was there and I was so glad to see her. Her mom and sister were there, too. I introduced Alan to them. I saw Ashley, too, and she looked beautiful. She had helped Mike "the wild man;" they had planned the whole show, and it was pretty good. Alan and I left after the show. He went back to Dallas, and I came home. It was late, and I finally had to take a Xanax to get to sleep. I felt really bad all day today from lack of sleep, but felt better later in the morning. After church, I went to Walgreens and got a bottle of Tylenol, then went to Joe's to eat. At last I started to feel much better, but was weak from hurting so bad. I went home and rested, slept a little, and read the paper.

Then it was Christmas 2008! I didn't do much cooking; I spent Christmas Day at Janet's house because Johnny was there. He wasn't well; he spent the day mostly in bed. He ate a little, but was very tired. I went in to see him, and he wasn't asleep, so we exchanged gifts. I gave him a black sweater, and he gave me a beautiful silver necklace with tiny diamonds and a cross on a delicate silver chain. Kathy had picked it out for me, and I loved it. She put it on me.

Johnny is getting worse; his hearing is just about gone, and so is his memory. I said my goodbyes to everyone and left. I went to the Sullivans. Everyone was still there, and I stayed for some time. It's always fun to be there. Sylvia gave me a beautiful Thomas Kincaid calendar.

I spent Christmas Eve at Phil and Sherry's. We had turkey and all the stuff that goes with it. They are so generous with me, and so good to me.

Laverne called me and said she's having a big dinner on Saturday and wanted me to come. I had just received a package from Thom: a large cheesecake. They sent Phil and Sherry one, too; they'd taken theirs to the Sullivans. I told Laverne I'd bring mine to her dinner.

Laverne's dinner was attended by fewer than usual—Dan and Betty, Janice and me, Rhonda and Marvin, and Rhonda's daughter, Candy. Candy had married after becoming pregnant, and married a man with three children, so now there are four children. Quite a family; Candy is only about 19 or 20. She seems very happy, and the children seem well-behaved and sweet.

Kearney was there, of course, and we played music after a big dinner. It was Saturday night, and my hair hadn't been fixed for a week. I should've gone to the beauty shop, since my cast was still on my arm, but I stayed too long and had to try to fix it myself.

I got home, and after a lot of trying and failing to get my hair rolled, finally got it sort of rolled and went to bed. I was thankful I still had a permanent, so it didn't look too bad. I made it to church, and then went to see Johnny at Manor Care.

When I got there, he was really stressed and worried about me. He had called me, he said, and some man answered the phone and told him that I had cancer and was pretty sick. I don't know if he'd heard something from the bed next to him, some people were visiting his roommate who had cancer, or maybe he heard something on the TV, but he had already called both Janet and Kathy and told them about me. I assured them I was fine, but it took the rest of the afternoon to convince Johnny I was. His hearing is so bad, and he was totally convinced of hearing someone on my phone. I called my phone, gave the phone to him, and although I could hear my voice message, he never heard a word.

I came on home. Church service was called off for a few days, but we were to have a memorial service for Barry Webster (Elaine's son had died on Sunday) on Monday morning.

I went to the memorial service. It was a little long, and, I thought, a little cold. There was a lunch for the family afterward, but I came on home, did a little cleaning up, and took a nap. I needed sleep badly, and felt better afterward. I went to Phil and Sherry's for supper.

And now, it is the last day of December, 2008. I got ready to go to Manor Care for their New Year's party at 3 PM, but when I got ready to leave (about noon), I went to Phil and Sherry's. Phil was off, and I had wanted to wear the necklace Johnny had given me for Christmas. There had been a knot in the chain; a small one I couldn't get out, but I knew Phil could. He always managed to fix things for me the way Sherman used to do. When I got there, Phil was making bacon sandwiches. Sure enough, he got the knot out of the chain, and I went home and then to Manor Care. We had a nice party for everyone, and I was totally exhausted when I got home.

Another year has gone by. It seems we just see the years pass so quickly. I sold a set of A&P books this morning to a young man getting ready to go to Iraq for four months. He hopes to be ready to test when he comes back in April.

I talked to Carolyn this evening. We always have fun talking, but we are both very concerned about the war situation. Israel has sent ground troops to Gaza, and is still bombing. Just like the Bible predicts. It looks bad, and people are blaming Israel for taking up for themselves. But the Palestinians are still sending rockets into Israel. It is strange how people never see what's causing Israel to fight.

I was watching the History Channel recently, and saw a program about D-Day, the invasion of Normandy in1944. I remembered that I had been 14 at the time this happened. It was during World War II, and I was in McKinney, Texas, where my brother Robert and his wife Omia were. Robert was in the Army, and had fallen out of the tree at home and broke his back, and was sent to the G.I. hospital in McKinney. I was staying a couple weeks with them. I remember the newsboys shouting about D-Day. I asked Omia what it was all about, and she told me it was a huge concentrated effort to invade Normandy. 150,000 American GI troops led by General Dwight D. Eisenhower were on their way to Normandy, a crucial effort to winning the war. It was a sad but true story of heroism, and a great amount of death and injuries, with victorious results.

I was about to deliver my second baby. We were excited, Sherman and me. I'd had a hard time with my first baby, Tommy, and long hours of labor at the old All Saint's Hospital, but my doctor, Dr. T.L. Childs, had helped me get through a very difficult pregnancy. He thought I might have to have a Caesarean section, but I finally came through, and they got the baby awake with much difficulty. My labor with Phil was shorter, only about 12 hours. I had very little sedation, had less pain and problems, and he was lively and frisky from the moment of birth. We named him Philip Marion. He had dark red hair and large brown eyes: a beautiful little boy.

As Phil grew up, he loved to read, watch TV (after it became popular), and play quietly. He was sociable, but was fine when he was alone. He didn't talk early; he could, but he waited until he could use proper pronunciation. He learned to sing by the time he started talking, about two years old. He sang perfectly, the proper tunes and words to certain songs, and never would try the ones he didn't know. When he spoke, he used totally proper pronunciation.

He was a cute little boy, a couple of cowlicks in his red hair, a smile always, and a sweet nature. He loved to laugh, sing, and read. He had a vivid imagination, and could play and pretend for hours, and loved everybody. He was an independent, very stubborn child with his own convictions, and seldom could be swayed from his beliefs. As he grew up, he retained his qualities, a lot of them.

My two boys have been a joy to my life and Sherman's, and I depend on them more and more as I grow older. They truly are special, and I know that's not just because I'm their mother.

There are three years between Thom and Phil. Two years after Thom was born, I became pregnant again without realizing it. Sherman's parents were here for a couple weeks, and we enjoyed their visit, as we always did. Mama and Daddy were gone at the time, back to Oklahoma, getting a home place sold to make room for the large lake to be built later, and getting rid of the furniture, etc. that they didn't want to move. And then, they were to move in with us.

I woke up one morning. Sherman and I were sleeping on a quilt on the floor; there were only two rooms then. I was lying in a large pool of blood. I had no pain or even discomfort, but I realized what it probably meant. I hadn't had any indication that I was pregnant when I had missed a few days. I wasn't even sure about that, but this made me more certain.

My mother-in-law was also sure. She had had so much experience with pregnancies and childbearing. She took good care of me, and sat by my bed and spoiled me. When it was evident I wasn't going to be okay, Dr. Childs told me to come to the All Saints Hospital where he did the curette method procedure, and I was okay. He thought it was a tubal pregnancy, and he told me I should not have a pregnancy again for at least a year.

So after a year, I wanted to have another baby. Jacky, Margaret's baby was born: a little redhead. He was a year younger than my Tommy. Janice, Ruby's youngest, was also born that year, 1949. Then Phil, in April 1951. Mama suggested the name Phillip, and I chose the name Marion with it. His hair was deep red, his complexion rather fair, some freckles but not many on his face.

By the time I realized Paulette was on the way, two years later, Earl and Mable, Sherman's brother and his wife, were staying with us for a few days before finding a place to live. I became very ill. I had a bad perpetual cough, and was always nauseated. Again, Dr. Childs was taking care of me, assuring me I'd be okay. He was, nevertheless, concerned that I was having some complications.

Paulette was here, finally, a dear tiny little girl, blond, with beautiful features and growing up so fast I could hardly keep up with her. She loved her brothers, and tried to spend all her time with them.

Love A & P

We opened our school, Love A&P in Dallas, at Love Field, September 1, 1981, Morris Dixon and I. For a few days, there was only the two of us, giving us a chance to get organized, collect a little equipment, and get ready for the classes. Morris did a little teaching at first, as we began to get a few night students, but was working days for Southwest, a newly-organized airline there. I taught days and nights too, whenever we had students. We began to get more as time passed.

While I was still instructing at Steve's, a man I had known, one of my superiors from Braniff called. He asked me to send some good mechanics to Southwest, as he had been asked to fill positions for them. I had sent Morris and a couple of others, and they were now working for the company. So Morris was there days, and helped me at the school nights. He also took care of the bookkeeping and accounting. We worked well together, and made a good team.

For a year, everything went well. I had cooperation from the FAA and others, always enjoyed my students, and also made friends with people who worked nearby. I was visited by a man who was interested in the school and promised to help me obtain approval to administer exams if I would move the school to Fort Worth, or near the DFW airport. It sounded good; it would be closer to home, although I knew it would be quite a task to move at this time, and of course, a terrific expense. Also, I wasn't really excited about giving exams. But we continued to investigate the possibilities. There was also a consideration for those who worked as instructors for me.

I had hired Don Deyo, a man who had worked for Braniff Airlines, now defunct, for many years. Don was a good friend, a good man, as helpful as could be, and worked for me quite a while.

Gary Laney, one of the best men I've ever worked with, a great, experienced mechanic, had been at Aviall for some time. He was eager to learn everything he could about aviation, and taking every course available in aircraft maintenance. He was a faithful employee who would teach any hours I asked him, driving wherever he was needed. I was fond of Gary and his wife, Fay, and also one of their sons who was my student at one time. I used to warn Gary about his smoking. Most people smoked at that time, and Gary spent very little time without a cigarette. Don, too, smoked, but advised me, and did his part, to make the school a non-smoking place in the classrooms. It was allowed in the shop.

I knew that Gary sometimes smoked in the classrooms at night. Gary died of lung cancer after I'd sold the school to Dalfort in 1990. He was a great guy, just kept on smoking.

I hired Raymond Butler, an old friend of Steve's. He had retired, and visited Steve before my school was started. He was hoping to get a job as instructor in aviation. We talked, and I got his phone number just in case I needed him. He and I were good friends, and his wife was sweet to me, too. She used to make dresses for her daughter, who was in the Miss America pageants. She must have made other contestants' dresses, too. She was an outstanding seamstress.

Another good friend, Bill Jewell, did some instructing for me. Bill and his wife, who was in the insurance business, became friends of my family and Paulette. Bill got his A&P, and then later his IA, and then his DME for giving practical exams. Bill and Betty, his wife, went to the country music shows with Sherman and me. When Paulette and I went with A Johnnie High group to Branson Missouri, we found Bill and his wife, Betty, at a big department store. We went to one of the shows together. Bill passed away not too many years later.

Reuben, one of the greatest instructors, was a good man. He knew aviation well, an experienced man, and respected by students, in spite of his bad habit of cursing. It was offensive to the students, and many of them complained to me about it. At least twice I talked to him about his language, and also advised him against his smoking. He agreed with everything I said, and promised to clean up his language. He was such a good instructor. He told me, "Pauline, you won't believe this, but I'm a Christian man. I go to church regularly. My wife is always getting after me, the way I talk, and I promised her I'll quit the cursing, but it's just a habit I can't break!" I told him I would pray for him, and he said, "Please do. I know I need to quit." A little while later, he left to work at a rival school in Dallas. About two or three months later, he called me. Sadly, he said, "Pauline, I have to tell you something. You warned me about smoking. I should have listened to you. I'm dying with lung cancer. Nothing can be done. I've got about two months to live, and I just wanted you to know I'm sorry I didn't listen to you and others, but thank you for your warning me, and I enjoyed working for you." That was the last time I heard from him.

Another instructor, Howard Snowden, was a good instructor. I liked Howard, and I never heard anyone complain about him. He was a good employee, and taught regular classes in the certified course.

Also, Charlie Stephens, Steve's son, was a super instructor. He has always been a great friend to me and all my family. He's instructed for Steve, me, and Braniff Education Systems. Now he works for American Airlines.

One instructor, an older man who will remain nameless here, had worked for a rival's school and was a good instructor. He could turn the air blue with profanity (and I thought Reuben was bad). He turned traitor to me, and was part of a plan to make me look as bad as possible, ready to testify against me in a trial before we settled out of court. Later, at a veterans dance at Meacham Field, I saw him and his wife. I said, "Hello," and he said, "I'm surprised you'll speak to me." I replied, innocently as possible, "Why would I not speak to you?" He never answered, for obvious reasons.

So, after operating the A&P School for a year in Dallas at Love Field, I started to look for a place closer to Fort Worth. Raymond Butler, a part-time instructor now, found a place in Arlington, part of a well-known storage company. Available space included a large carpeted area, several offices, some classrooms, and even a nice kitchen area. There were several storage areas if we wanted them, but we didn't need them. Later, we got an area next door for part of the shop. It was a nice place, and I began the paperwork immediately to get an approved certified school. There were some people in the area who resented a woman having such a business as this. Morris had left it with me, and I started to think about what the "friend" had promised me if I'd move closer to where he worked. He'd approved the location, so I thought it was probably settled. But suddenly, this "friend's" attitude changed. I asked him about it, and he tried to cover his embarrassment, explaining to me that a man was more suited to be a practical designee than a woman, and that the powers that be wouldn't go for it. However, he said, name any man I would recommend for this rating, and he would be designated to be my DME. I realized then that my name was obviously a dirty word among the government, and I would never be allowed to have such a rating. I knew it wasn't my friend's fault.

The man I recommended was approved, and became the practical examiner for the school. Later, he proved to be less than the friend I thought he was, and was gone. The next man I recommended for this was a really super friend, honest as the day is long, and a good man for the job. He worked for me the rest of the time I had the school, and afterward when I sold it to Dalfort. Shortly after I left Dalfort, my good friend, Carl Maas, died at home alone.

We had the school going good now in Arlington. Paulette and Bill were both working for me. We got it FAA approved, and even NATTS approved. Also, we had some students' financial assistance available. There were still some who were envious. One man from Thailand approached me about going into business with me, having a flight school combined with my A&P and IA, making a fortune, and building a structure he had in mind. I was skeptical about it, and didn't agree to anything. But I let him talk.

This seemed to be his proposal. He, along with his wife and 2 or 3 other fellows, would buy into the place, buy aircraft for the flight school, and share in the whole thing. He brought plans for a new building they had designed, and started talking about what a good businessman he was. He and his wife, along with their little girl, about 2-3 years old, came out to inspect the office equipment. The baby ran around, trying out all the office machines, and they, I realized, were deciding where his wife would plan to run the whole show! Paulette whispered to me at one point what his wife had said to him and I decided on a plan.

They left. I was teaching a group of IA's at the time, and I assigned the students something to look up, while I began to compose a letter. I finished it and gave it to Paulette. "Type this, and send it special delivery," I instructed. I had completely declined to share the school we had built with anybody else. It was my school, and would stay altogether in my possession and under my supervision. Paulette happily took the letter. She was so glad to comply!

Of course, they were there bright and early the next morning. What in the world had happened? "Nothing has happened," I told him. "I have worked hard for this, and it's my school. I don't intend to share it with anyone." He began to tell me how lucrative it could be with the help of him and his friends. It all boiled down to this. His "friends" had no money, so he was going to pitch in $500 apiece, and he'd have $1,000 to put in for him and his wife. She would run the office, (now Paulette's office, with the new furniture I'd bought). I could teach, and he and his friends would take care of the flight school. There had obviously been no plans for Paulette or Bill, who were my rocks. I said no, thanks, I won't have such an arrangement. We're doing fine as it is. I said, "Look, it's a big world. Start your own school!" He said that was his next plan. He said they'd already bought a small aircraft, I think a 152 Cessna.

Later, I heard they did start a flight school with the one aircraft, but it had crashed when somebody put oil in the gas tank—or maybe gas in the oil tank. Anyway, as positive as he sounded when he told me how they were going to have the new school going, and taken into nations overseas, I guess it didn't pan out for them. Apparently, none of them had any maintenance experience. They were all pilots, and all from Thailand.

I have had others who wanted to get into the business with me, but I was not tempted. It was a little unusual for a woman to have such a school. I've had women students who were good mechanics and good students, but not many. The work is heavy and a little rough, but not as hard as automobile work, nor as dirty and greasy. Unfortunately, neither is the pay as high, unless it's for the airlines. I was, and am, proud to be a part of the industry, and I realize I couldn't have accomplished what I have done without the cooperation and friendship of the people involved.

Bill and Paulette returned from the East—New York, South Dakota, and Minnesota—where they were performing as a duo in such places as Holiday Inns, etc., to settle back in Fort Worth where they were raised. They wanted a baby, and to settle here while still staying active with their music. Paulette was anxious to work in the school, and very shortly, Bill was interested, too. They were invaluable to me and the school! Both knew computers, and began to use them for the A&P programs.

My ex-partner, Morris Dixon, came to the school and videotaped me instructing the IA course. It took a while to catch on; I usually sat with the students and taught. But eventually, it did catch on, and a lot of the students asked for it. I was grateful to Morris; I have always liked and appreciated him so much.

There was an auction place about two doors down from us. We purchased several Commodore computers, printers, etc. from the man who ran the place, and he was very helpful to us. He also sold us desks, chairs, and many other items we could use. The technology era was here, and thanks to several, mostly Bill and Paulette, we took full advantage of it.

Then it was about time for Matt to be born. I had gone to Fort Hood, Texas to teach an A&P course. I had been there several days, and was about ready to come home, when I got a call from the school. Paulette said she was about ready to go to the hospital and have her baby. I told her I would be there after the last class tonight, so I taught the class; I just needed to get on the road and get back to Grand Prairie where she was in the hospital. Just as I left, a storm began brewing. The sky was dark and ominous. I was a little frightened, and wondered if I should stop at a motel and spend the night. But I thought of her having a baby, and I couldn't do it. I kept thinking of her in the hospital, and I wasn't there. Once the rain was so strong the magnetic signs were washed right off the side of my car, but I kept driving. I turned off the highway toward Fort Worth, and drove into Grand Prairie without incident. I went into the waiting room where Thom, Phil, and Bill were waiting. They said she had been in delivery about 20 minutes, and Sherry was with her. I was a little relieved, because I didn't want to go in there with her. The baby was a little boy, and fine. Paulette was fine also, and so proud of her beautiful blond, blue-eyed son. His name was Matthew Konrad Hartmann. We went in to see him, he was so sweet.

He looked around, and Thom said "He looks like Paulette, thank God," and we laughed, all relieved Paulette was doing well, and so was her baby. He was a little jaundiced, but was fine except for that, and in a few days we could take him home. I went with Paulette to get him, and Paulette put him in the car seat in the back, and she put a pair of sunglasses on him. I expected him to object, but he readily accepted the sunglasses. His eyes were so blue, she was afraid of the sun's glare. From that time, she never took him out without the shades, and he always accepted them.

A short time, probably three weeks or so, after Steve and I started Stephens Aircraft School at Meacham Field, one of the men who had worked at American Flyers, where Steve had been working before starting the school, came in to enroll and start the course for A&P mechanic. His name was Gibson. I asked him his first name, and he told me he went by a nickname, "Hoot". American Fliers was an airline company that had started, and was based for a time, at Meacham Field in Fort Worth. Gibson was a mechanic for them for several years. Steve had worked at the same airline a while before. We began to get others from American Fliers as people learned about the school. He and I talked as I was enrolling him, and he told me about one of their airplanes crashing into a mountain in Ardmore, Oklahoma. There were several people killed; it was a terrible tragedy, and he had helped work at the wreckage with the ground crew, getting bodies out and getting pieces of the plane together. It really was a traumatic experience for him.

I felt that Steve knew about the plane crash, but he never said much about it. I began to realize the serious business I was getting into. And I could see that

Hoot was very sensitive about the people being hurt or killed in the crash. These things happen, and I gradually put it out of my mind as time passed. But I'll always remember Gibson, and how troubled he was over the accident, and I could always remember the anguished look on his face as he talked about it.

A few weeks ago, I met LaVerne and Janice, my two nieces, and we went to Ridgmar Mall, west of downtown. We went into Dillard's there, and were looking at shoes. As I was looking at some that were my favorites, the saleslady explained to me that the price would probably be marked down soon. She said she'd call me if that happened, and would save me the ones I wanted. I gave her my card, and she said, "Oh, you're an aircraft mechanic! Do you know anything about American Flyers?" I explained to her that my boss back then had worked for them. She explained to me that her stepmother was the supervisor over all the flight attendants, and had quite a lot of authority in the airline. She had arranged for the plane that had had the bad crash in Ardmore to make the stop there, and was to pick her up. Obviously, she had never boarded the plane. But then it crashed, and she somehow felt responsible for the disaster, and this feeling left her devastated for the rest of her life. Her name was Jan Fielder, and the stepdaughter I talked to is Gretchen.

Looking this incident up on the Internet, I found out that Reed Pigman, the owner of the airline itself, was pilot of the crashed plane. He was carrying 80 or more passengers, military personnel, and everyone on the plane was killed as it crashed into a mountain near Ardmore. Reed Pigman was a prominent aviation man in this area. But he had kept silent about a bad heart problem and his diabetes, or he'd have been grounded by doctors doing his medicals. So actually, the fault was his, not Jan Fielder's. It was an interesting story. American Flyers is still in business, but it is no longer an airline. They do have a flight school at Meacham, in Fort Worth. I have been instructed to call it by its real name now, Meacham Airport.

I did visit Gretchen again, and we have become friends. Also, the shoes did come down, and I bought them. But I've never heard from Hoot Gibson again after he got his license.

The following story was taken from an account I found on the Internet:

"80 plus military transients killed, flown by owner Reed Pigman, also killed.

Reed Pigman, owner of the airline, died at the controls of the crashed plane, of a heart attack, in the plane. He'd kept this, and the fact he had diabetes, from the medical staff, at his annual physical exams.

The plane was being flown under a Department of Defense Contract Charter, en route to Fort Ord, California, with a service stop, and crew change in Ardmore, Oklahoma.

Reed Pigman was an early aviation pioneer, was instrumental in developing the VOR Navigation System, currently used world wide today.

Many employees of the airline and its related aviation school had a very affectionate relationship with Pigman, who frequently piloted AFA's Lockheed Electras and on military charter flights nationwide".

Achilles Van Neerboom, a man from Belgium, presently working in Kinshasa, Africa, came to school at Steve's before I left to start Love Aviation with Morris Dixon. We called him Van, and he was a good student. He must have finished quickly, because I can't remember exactly when he was getting his A&P. He was a pilot in Africa, and he was here several times. He and I became good friends, and he came to my house to wash clothes and to eat with us, always at our invitation. During the time when he was here, he went with Sherman and me to a place or two to hear Paulette and Bill play.

He took us out one night to Cattlemen's, one of the finest places in Fort Worth. Someone else was with us, probably Thom and Jeanne, Thom's wife at that time. We had a good time. He rented an apartment on Highway 10, a nice place, and later he went back to Africa for a week or so. He brought back a lady he introduced as his wife, although I was very doubtful. We still had a lot of segregation here, and he noticed it, and thought it was bad. He had asked me what I thought about it before, and I didn't encourage him about bringing a black wife to his apartment at this time.

I explained to him that I would be OK with it, but I didn't think his landlady would just yet. Somehow, I think he was trying to prove something; I'm not sure what, but he acted a little defensive about her. We were fine at the school, and welcomed her. She never spoke English, and was definitely an African woman, with the big afro hairdo. He told us the people had lost both of their passports or visas, and they were trying to get them back. We, several of us, went out to eat lunch with them. They left soon, and went back to Africa.

Sometime later, I got a 13-page letter from him. I have wished so many times that I had saved the letter and could read it one more time. I thought I had saved it, but have never found it. I cried, and read it over so many times! But he was nervous and sick, he told me. He had been in the middle of the civil war there that had been going on so long. I guess I'll never know what has happened to him since. I don't know if he is still alive; I think he was about my age. I pass the place he lived in the apartment every time I go to Phil's house, and I always think of him.

And there was Woody Lesikar, a very young man, introduced to us by Brady York. Woody was an exceptional man who owned an airport and a flight school in Houston. He had inherited the business from his dad, and seemed to be an excellent businessman, especially for such a young man. We at Steve's school were all very impressed with him, and became good friends. He used to visit us often, and we'd go to lunch together. Brady York, who died several years ago, was very fond of Woody, and they kept in touch through the years.

Woody hired a new mechanic, a young man named Steven Hinson, and sent him to us to get his A&P. Woody used to send me a Christmas card every year, an airplane that would fold flat when put in an envelope. I'd save them, and still have seven of them from that many years, but when his daughters complained and wanted him to send another kind of Christmas card, he did it. I stopped saving the cards that were different.

Many years later, after I had moved to Watauga, I got a call from Woody. He had come to Alliance Airport for some refresher flight training, and was staying in a mobile home he had for sale. He asked me to come and have dinner with him, and directed me to where his mobile home was parked on the airport.

It was wonderful to see him again. He had a couple with him that was looking at his mobile home, to buy. We visited for a while, and had a glass of wine, and Woody took us all for a ride. After we came back and they left, we drove to Denton and had dinner. And, although we have talked a time or two, I think he's retired now, and may be married again. He was invited to my 80th birthday party, and sent me a check.

One day, after I'd moved the school to Arlington, an Egyptian, Shaban Morsey, came in to enroll for his A&P. He had been in the country for a short time, and was working as a waiter in an upscale restaurant in a hotel in downtown Fort Worth. He was a friendly, likable man, and I used to hear him reading his A&P books aloud, alone in a room. He said he learned better that way, and when he needed me to help, he'd let me know.

He brought me a gift–some really nice makeup, too expensive for me to buy for myself. He arranged and paid for a nice champagne brunch at the hotel where he worked one Sunday for Sherman and me, Paulette and Bill. We really enjoyed and appreciated it.

We became good friends quickly. Our family enjoyed him, and he came to see us often. He sometimes cooked for us, especially at Paulette's, and sometimes he fixed meals for Paulette and me at his apartment. After he got his A&P, he stayed, and shortly, he got his American citizenship.

Paulette went with him to receive his citizenship papers, and we were all proud of him. I don't know how many wives he had, or had had. He is Muslim, and I know the Saudis are allowed 4 wives, but most of the guys I talked to about it said they could only afford one. I do know he spoke of one, maybe more, and a son or two. Occasionally, he made the trip back to Egypt for a while, and came back here. He said he owned some property in Cairo. He was Egyptian. I guess that rule means one wife at a time.

Once, when he went back and returned, he started a pizza parlor in Arlington. He seemed to be experienced in many things, including cooking. But before that, I'd helped him get a job at Braniff, in sheet metal. He did well for a while, but quit because he wanted to go back to Egypt for a while and they wouldn't let him come back to the position there. He had worked for the Egyptian Air Force. He made us pizza several times, but would never charge us for them.

Later, when he came back from Egypt, he brought back a wife and a baby. They settled in San Antonio, and soon had another girl and a boy. Shaban became injured, and began drawing his Social Security for the disabled, and his wife supported the family. She drove a bus for a while, but must have found a much better job. The children are now either in or finished college, and doing fine. Shaban calls me about every 6 months or so.

About three months after Paulette's death, Shaban came to town. He called me, and wanted to go to her grave. So he came out, and we drove to Greenwood Cemetery and went to her grave. He knelt by her grave, cried, and began to talk to her. I had suspected he was in love with her, and he'd admitted as much. "She hears us talk to her," he said. "She knows when you come to see her. Do you believe that?" I hedged. No, I don't believe she's anywhere in the ground, I explained to him, I thought she was in Heaven, not hanging around a dreary cemetery. He disregarded my comments, and insisted, "She's here. She hears us and knows when you visit her." Shaban is not a Christian. I'd talked to him about becoming a Christian, but he only laughed at me, because I'm a Baptist, and he's Muslim.

Chapter 8

"Try again, Phil, we can't lose."

Shortly after we opened Love A&P School in Arlington, we began to prepare to make it a certified aviation school. I worked on the training material, according to the plans in FAA publication #145, and started to collect all the materials, parts, and tools to set up the programs. I received training aids from many friends and past students. Ben Seale, a friend and former student of Steve's, sent me from Louisiana a complete combustion heater system, never used. He flies helicopters, and doesn't trust the heater systems, so he took out this brand new one and sent it to me. Gerald Moffett, a good friend and parts man, helped me a lot, and had many things for me, which he helped me with. Lucky, a man who has been a longtime friend and has an airplane salvage yard, gave me a whole fuselage and other things.

I started building up a shop in a hangar next door to the one we were occupying for classes. Several people helped me, and some of the students really enjoyed helping to get the shop ready. We had special displays for all of the different projects, and were careful to get everything in the right place. I knew we would be carefully watched for any discrepancies. We got lots of cleaning supplies to clean the hangar, because the shop that had been moved out was an automotive garage. It was greasy, and needed a lot of heavy cleaning.

In 2012, January 23, I called Thom to wish him a happy birthday. He was in Cancun, and we reminisced about the trip we took to Cancun back in 1989. I had sold the school, and wanted to take my three kids to have a 3-day trip together. Thom was a bank president in River Oaks. He arranged for the trip, and came to my house to pick us up in a limousine and take us to the airport. We had a great time, and will always have good memories–also some mementos. I compensated the spouses, except Sherry, who wouldn't take anything; was happy for Phil to get to go. But I gave Jeanne a check, and bought a set of tires for Bill, for his van.

The rift between Sherman and me had grown wider, and he seemed to be unconcerned. Our marriage was over before long. And so were Thom's and Paulette's. Not because of our trip, but trouble had been brewing in each case; but not Phil and Sherry's. They have always had what seemed like an ideal marriage.

Lives change every few years, which is not to say marriages change that often. Ours, mine and Sherman's, picked up the pieces 9 months after our divorce, but things were never the same. I'll always have some regrets, and I know he did too.

Sometimes I feel a little lonely, living alone. I have many friends, but everyone is living their own life, completely separate from mine. And then, maybe an old friend calls, and I realize how much this means to me. I believe there is nothing so heartwarming as just talking to, or visiting with, an old friend. So many of my friends are from Broadview Baptist Church, and also from my school at Love Field or Arlington, and even from Stephens Aircraft at Meacham, and others from Azle Avenue Baptist, this community, and First Baptist Church in Watauga.

Sherman died in April, 2001. He'd had several bad spells, a bad heart, bad back, and prostate cancer. Each time I rushed him to the hospital, I was afraid it would be the last. He died at home. Hospice was taking care of him; I couldn't lift him at all by that time. And then he was gone. We'd been married 54 years. Sometimes, I wonder just what he would say now about those years! I know he was the real love of my life. But at times, months would go by, and I felt if he'd only hold me and express his love for me, I'd have never looked at anyone else. But those last years it never happened, and made me wonder if he still loved me at all. This, of course, didn't happen in the earlier years; we just seemed not to value each other the way we used to.

A few weeks after Sherman died, Johnnie called me and asked me if I'd go to lunch with him. I agreed. After being hopelessly lost for a couple of hours, he got here, and we went to a place on Airport Freeway: Harrigan's. We had a nice lunch. After that, we began to go to lunch nearly every day. We found a church nearby, and he always came after me on Sundays. We joined the First Baptist Church, Watauga, and loved it. After a couple of years, Johnnie was disabled. We were together as much as possible.

The Jet Engine

After months of preparation, collecting parts, training aids, and shop equipment, we were hosting the FAA Inspectors for our school certification. They came, three of them, to go through all of it. Each inspector would have an instructor to accompany him through the three phases: Airframe, Powerplant, and General. I can't remember which ones were there, except Mike, who was with me, and we were going through the Airframe section. He was a young man, still in college, I think, and it was his life's calling to give me a hard time. He knew very little about the whole thing, asked the same things over and over, and totally irrelevant.

The inspection took the whole day. They gave us a list of things to be explained or corrected, which meant another day of inspections. But we took care of it quickly, and before the day was half over, we had the last project to do: the jet engine run.

The jet engine, a great little APU, had been tested by us and run several times. It used kerosene for fuel, and someone had decided it needed a boost pump. I was given a new fuel line by my friend, Bill Jewell; it was small, not insulated well. I had turned on the engine once to run it, and fortunately, turned on the fuel before the ignition. The fuel line blew, and I was soaked with kerosene. It would have really been a tragedy if I had turned on the ignition first, which was the proper thing to do.

So with much hope and ceremony, we rolled the engine outside on the parking lot, and Phil B. went through the steps to start it. It belched, blew a huge cloud of black smoke into the air, and died. I said desperately, "But it did run a little." Ray shook his head and said, "No, it has to run 100%".

Phil, the instructor, was very frustrated. He turned everything off and began to roll the engine back in the shop. Bill, my son-in-law, came to me and said, "Pauline, why is he taking the engine back in the shop? Are we just giving up, just because it didn't start that one time?" I said, "I guess so." Frustrated, he said "We can't give up. We've worked too hard. And it's run before. Let's try again!" He turned to Phil, "We're not giving up! Try again, Phil, or we can get someone else to try!" Phil, resigned, said, "It's not going to start. We may as well give up!!"

But Bill wouldn't give up. He insisted. (Thanks, Bill! I love you for that!) And Phil asked me what to do. "Try again, Phil, we can't lose".

So, back to the yard. We waited, and Phil turned it on. It ran the 100% Ray had been adamant about. We rejoiced, applauded, and some of us hugged and knew this meant we got our certification! The next day, Ray brought the certificate and presented it to me.

Ray Moore presenting me with the FAA Certified School certificate

Love Aviation Training Center was a certified school, a dream come true! I remembered that the Lord had promised to go with me, to bless this school. And I remembered Morris, who had helped me from the start, and I wished he could have been there with me to accept the certificate presented from the FAA.

August 22, 1929

I am only vaguely aware of what the world was like in the year I was born. My dad, William Thomas Fagan, was known by everyone as Tom Fagan. He had been deserted by his first wife, Laura, when he and their four children became aware of her new lover, a man named Turner. Daddy told her to let him go, or go with him, but she couldn't take the kids with her. So she took the man. She left Ruby, aged 3, crying after her, Leona, 5, aware of the affair, and Lewie and Addie, the two oldest ones. Addie had had spinal meningitis and polio (I think it was called infantile paralysis) which left her crippled and slightly retarded, but completely disgusted with her mother. Leona was angry as she watched her mother leave, seemingly uncaring of her kids.

Daddy and Lewie went to find work. Some of Laura's folks kept the girls a few weeks, but found that Addie needed professional care, and advised Daddy to take Addie to what was known as a "state school" at Enid, Oklahoma.

It became very hard for Daddy to take care of them all, so he contacted the place in Enid, and they accepted Addie. Actually, the "state school" was not a school at all, but a mental institution. This was common in those days. This occurred in about 1925. So Daddy took Addie to Enid. It must have been a heartbreaking task for him, and it surely was for Addie. I'll write more about this later, when Addie's story continues.

Daddy and Lewie continued to look for steady work. Such jobs were hard to find in those days, and they eventually settled in Okmulgee. Daddy became a custodian in a school there, called the Lee School, and leased an apartment there for the family,

Mama married very young, as they did in those days. Her husband, Nick Shiro, was about 20-21 years older than she. He worked for the railroad. She had a son, born dead, and later, sons Richard, Louis, and Robert. Robert had a twin sister who only lived a few minutes. Her name was Rose. Then, soon after Robert was born, there was a railroad strike, and Nick was without a job. Richard, little more than a child, worked as a telegraph operator. Mama left Nick, and she and her three sons moved to Okmulgee, Oklahoma.

They lived in the same "rooming house" where Daddy lived.

Mama and Daddy married in 1926, and Margaret was born in July, 1927. Two years later, I came along. I was born at home in Okmulgee, August 22, 1929, the same year of the stock market crash, the birth of "Popeye, the Sailor Man", health insurance, penicillin, and the forerunner of American Airlines, "Texas Air Transport," operating from Meacham Field. They carried a load of 5,544 passengers. It was the year before women's cosmetics were no longer considered risqué. Vogue magazine: "Even the most conservative must now concede that a woman exquisitively made up yet may be a faithful wife and devoted mother!" Whew! That's a relief!! Saved by a year!!!

3 popular songs that year were: "Ain't Misbehavin'," "Honeysuckle Rose," and "Stardust," and the first musical comedy film was the "The Broadway Melody." A movie that got the first Academy Award in 1929 was "Wings," a saga of WWI shot in San Antonio, Texas, starring Janet Gaynor. My friend, a man I worked with at Dalfort and dated briefly, had that movie. We watched it at his house many years later, and I've seen it on TV.

TV was invented in 1929, but the screen was the size of a postage stamp. In June, 1929, Delta Air Service (later, Delta Air Lines) began passenger travel with 3-6 passenger Travel Aires between Jackson, Mississippi and Dallas, Texas via Shreveport and Monroe, Louisiana. These planes had been built to spray cotton crops.

I grew up knowing nothing at all about aviation; never imagining having a career in it after all those years. Nothing could have meant so much to me as being in aviation. I have enjoyed every bit of it, and have been anxious to learn all I could. I also enjoyed the other people involved. I still teach when I have a student, and I enjoy it and the IA renewals that I have been certified to teach since 1994.

I get the paper and read it right after breakfast. I was surprised to see the first person listed in the obituary column in 2011 was a cousin of Sherman's: Carol Jean Albertson , a 63-year-old woman born nearly a year before Thom. We had never spoken at all, as far as I knew. Her parents, Oliver and Jean Albertson, had finally given up trying to keep her at home. She had been in a mental hospital in Denton, Texas since she was a young teenager, probably 12 or 13 years old.

When Sherman and I were engaged back in 1945 and 1946, we had gone to a family reunion for the Albertson and Miller families in Paris, Texas, where I first met those families. Later, we went nearly every year until after we got settled in our home in Fort Worth, so we had seen Carol, as they also moved to Fort Worth. She was a beautiful little girl, very active, had a big smile on her face constantly. But it very early became evident that she was mentally inept, and would never be a normal child.

Later, a sister was born named Judy, a little blond girl, normal in every way. Oliver was the son of Olin, brother of my mother-in-law. There were 12 children in that family. Most of them would come to the reunions in Paris each year, so I had soon met them all, except one or two who lived in California.

I had known about Sherman's first marriage. He had told me a lot, but of course, not everything—I didn't care to know much. He convinced me that he didn't care for her, and had turned her down when she wanted to get back together with him. But I knew nothing about her background or her family. I used to resent the way Sherman's mother kept pictures of Viola on her walls, some in the box with all the other pictures, but some of her alone, and some with Sherman. But time went on—the pictures still on display.

Ironically, after both Mr. and Mrs. Ruffin died, many years later, we were given all her pictures of all the family. I finally took all those of Viola out, put them in a manila envelope, and put them on top of the refrigerator for Sherman to throw away.

We went to a Chinese restaurant that evening, just the two of us. The kids were all grown up by that time, and had gone somewhere else. I told Sherman what I had done, and asked him to please discard the pictures. I would if he wanted me to, but I'd rather he would. He immediately became very angry, and we had one of the worst arguments we'd ever had. I held my ground, and he held his. Upon returning home, he got the pictures, went and sat on the back porch, and, using his pocket knife, cut the pictures in strips, and threw them away. The loss of the pictures was a relief to me, but he stayed angry at me for a long time.

We really never had many discussions about Viola, only that he'd been faithful to her all the time he'd been in the Army and gone to France and Italy, and she'd been unfaithful to him. Many marriages were broken this way, during and after WWII. Some of the details of theirs were so bad I never thought we'd ever have to worry about Viola again.

And then, after starting my school in 1981, Sherman began to resent me. He told me "No, you're not starting a school!" I told him, "Watch me." He finally seemed to be resigned to the fact, but resented it the rest of the time we were together. But shortly after that, he became withdrawn and moody, and I asked him if he wanted to see Viola. He admitted that he did. So I told him to arrange to see her, but not expect me to be here waiting for him when he got back.

Paulette and Bill Hartmann had married and had been pursuing a music career as a duo in hotels. They were in St. Paul, Minnesota, performing at a hotel there, and I went and spent a week with them. When I flew back, Sherman met me at the airport, and as we walked to the car, he told me he had gone to see Viola's parents at Lake Texoma. He had had a great time, he said, and they wanted him to bring me to meet them. I said no, I cared nothing for these people, and certainly wouldn't visit them. He was mad, but so was I. I didn't worry about Sherman—he was beginning to be completely detached from me.

We didn't talk much, and didn't sleep together any more, and had quit having sex long before.

Our school, still in Dallas, was growing. Margaret, my sister, sometimes went to my house and cleaned it. On one evening, she had been there, and Sherman had talked to her. Although I don't know what all was said, she told me he'd said he was in love with Viola. So the next morning when I got up, he was in the kitchen, drinking coffee. I told him I was leaving him. He was mad about Margaret telling me what he'd told her, but admitted it was true.

I called Thom. He and Jeanne lived in River Oaks at the time, and he came after me. I got some clothes and makeup ready. Amy had spent the night. She was small, about 3 or 4, and she heard us and started to cry. Sherman held her and talked to her, and she was OK. Thom, Amy, and I left after I'd reached over the fence and petted our dog, Casey. I got in the car as Kermit was singing about rainbows. I spent the night at Thom and Jeanne's, and went to spend the next 3 weeks at Phil and Sherry's. They were going on vacation. I never heard from Sherman, and then 3 weeks later, Sherman sent me a long letter saying he loved me and wanted me to come back home.

As we went into the house, Sherman was being so sweet to me. He told me he had gone to see Viola, and she had said to him, "You and Pauline had 3 kids together, there must be something there." So he'd obviously told her he didn't care for me any longer. But she didn't want him either. Something in me died. My love for him had taken a mortal blow, and I'm afraid I never recovered. I never knew why he told me that.

Much later, when I left him and moved out of the house for good, where we'd lived for 52 years, it wasn't because of Viola, but because he had started drinking heavily. I could take that for a little while, but enough was enough.

Viola's maiden name was Upchurch. When I read Carol's obituary, her survivors included 2 uncles named Upchurch. I know there are other people by that name, but I knew Jean and Oliver had lived fairly close to the area where Viola had lived when she and Sherman met, so I was shocked! Now, Sherman had been gone since 2001, but I felt betrayed. Jean, my friend for so long, was kin to Viola, and nobody had told me.

I called Thom and talked to him about it. And then he and his wife, Debby, looked up the family history, and found Viola's obituary. She was buried there at Atoka, Oklahoma, and she had two brothers, so I figured she and Jean were sisters! Jean and Oliver, Sherman and I had been good friends and I couldn't understand why they had kept this a secret from me.

I got ready and went to Carol's funeral. Oliver had died in 2004 and this was 2011. Jean is a little older than I, and she was so upset and so tottery, my heart just went out to her when I saw her come in, leaning heavily on Judy. I went to her, and told her I was sorry, and I knew how it was to lose a daughter. It was a beautiful, simple service. There were some men there with the family, but somehow, it didn't matter any more. I'm guessing Jean may be Viola's cousin, or something more distant than I had thought. So now, it has become a mystery that may never be solved. I came home, and felt safe and comfortable.

I loved Sherman a long time, and still do, but it doesn't seem important to me any more whether or not he loved me. I know there were many times he did not. But I also am aware that love is bound to wane at times, and we can't have that same exciting feeling constantly, and sometimes it's hard to recapture. I always have to recall the good times we had. Sherman was a good provider and a good husband–a good man. He was respected, and resourceful. He could do most any kind of work: carpentry, electrical, plumbing, masonry, auto repairs, etc.

I looked up Viola's obituary to see her picture. She was a nice-looking old woman, born in 1925. I am rid of the resentment I've had for years. I'm alive now, and life is good, and the past is past.

I don't think these things will ever be a burden to me again. They belong to another time, and will remain just a memory. It's a strange thing, our love for someone when we're young, and the deep feelings we have are so strong, so life changing. We know they'll always be the major force in all the rest of our lives, and then as time goes on and changes take place, we find that our lives change in a lot of ways, as do others, and we become so different.

Chapter 9

"Are you MY Alan Cook?"

I'm going back today, to 1947. Sherman and I married in August, 1946, and had lived in apartments until we discovered Sansom Park Village, a place not yet incorporated as a city. It was mostly a hilly area, with no rules about buildings, seven or eight miles from town. It had just opened up for a residential area, after having been a pasture for a dairy for some time, and still had ample supplies of Johnson grass. We fought that Johnson grass all the time we lived there, but it was heaven to us. We loved the large lot, and we could only see four or five houses from our place. But very soon, others began to build, grocery stores and churches began to come in, and it wasn't long until there were no more vacant lots.

We knew our neighbors pretty well. These were people who had come out of World War II. Most of them that we knew were getting settled, starting their families, and having children, easily getting acquainted with each other, and many going to church. We were a quarter mile from the Jacksboro Highway, #199, which was one of the most, if not THE most notorious gang hideouts in or just out of town. Crime was rampant.

Police were paid off. It was easier, obviously, to pay them off than to face trials and pay fines. Gamblers and criminals were busy at their games, which were well-organized and fine-tuned. If they were caught cheating or breaking any of their rules, it was common for them to be found dead, sometimes in shallow graves, along the sandy beaches around Lake Worth, or maybe drowned or other fates befalling them. But still, it kept happening, and many were paid off.

We knew very little of this at the time it was going on. It was a totally different life if you didn't deal in these activities.

Our neighborhood was quiet, with many churchgoers, children in school, and adults working to take care of their families and building homes. We used to go to Oklahoma often to visit our relatives there. We'd stay weekends and come back home to find our house exactly as we'd left it. I can't remember ever locking the doors until sometime later, when Sherman's little garden plow disappeared. It didn't even have an engine, just a push plow for the garden he raised in the back yard. We also had some chickens in a large pen in the back. But the plow was the only thing we ever lost, even though we always left the house unlocked. But after that, we decided to start locking up before we left.

One day, Sherman went out and was looking at his garden. We didn't have a fence anywhere except around the chicken pen. Some of our neighbors also raised chickens, and they didn't have a fence either. An old hen had got out of a yard, and was enjoying her ample supper from our garden. She was happily going straight down the rows eating everything she saw, and Sherman idly picked up a clod of dirt (he thought) and tossed it at the hen. Suddenly, the hen dropped dead. Shocked, Sherman realized there must have been a rock inside the dirt. He picked up the now lifeless hen, and took her to the closest neighbor. He apologized to the lady, and she said it was OK; she would fix it for supper.

The next day, after the family's good meal of chicken that night, she was talking to a neighbor, and it was discovered that he had given the chicken to the wrong neighbor. So there had to be more apologies, but I doubt if Sherman ever lived that down.

When we first moved to Sansom Park, I didn't have children yet, so I did a little exploring on my own. I wasn't yet driving a car; I was waiting for Sherman to help me drive, and we only had one car. He needed it to drive to and from work. We had a bus, the Lake Worth bus, which I could ride to town and back. Later, Margaret's husband Jack drove that bus for some time. I rode to town one day, and when I got on, I sat by a lady who lived across the street from the church, Broadview. We got acquainted, and I saw out of the corner of my eye a little movement on her shoulder.

My attention was drawn to a tiny little varmint on her shoulder. It was a lizard, and he was alive! Now, I was used to seeing lizards in the country, but never riding on a woman's shoulder. I must have gasped as the thing raised his head up and looked me right in the eye! I couldn't talk for a minute, but the lady, Doris, smiled at me and said, "My Chameleon?" She reached up and petted him. I could see that he was being held by a chain around her neck. It was later explained to me that these chameleons somehow become whatever color their environment is; for instance, if you wear one with a green dress, they turn green, or if it's a red--------you understand. I never wanted one.

Doris and I became friends that day, but I never again saw a lizard like that around a woman's neck, and Doris and I didn't see each other much either after that. She went to another church.

Stephens Aircraft School was created in 1966 at Meacham Field, Fort Worth, Texas. Alton E. Stephens offered me a job as secretary, to help him get the school started. I was looking for a job at the time. I'd had some experience working at dry cleaners, mostly doing alterations, but also checking, cleaning and pressing. I hadn't stayed in one place very long at a time, and didn't particularly care for the work. I was glad for the chance Steve offered me, and felt that I could really get into it, although I realized that Dot, Steve's wife, was very much against my going to work for Steve. Also, I knew nothing about aircraft, and didn't realize where this job would lead me in a few years, or what the future held for me eventually.

Steve was good to me, and helped me learn all I could about the mechanics of aircraft. We enrolled students, and he had classes at night at first, but some fellows worked nights, and came and studied days. There wasn't a lot for me to do in the daytime, so I could talk to the ones that came days. Charlie, Steve's son, came sometimes, and he was helpful to us in a lot of ways. He was a fun person, and I enjoyed him. He was a year older than my Thom, and he soon learned to do a little instruction, and soon became one of the best.

I had never learned to type before, but I began to get much better as time went on. We had an old type machine that would make copies. It also got ink all over, but was the best we could do at that time. Charlie and Steve worked some for the man who owned the hangar, doing maintenance on aircraft in the shop, for the rental of our office and classroom. The owner had a flight school.

After a while, we moved to a large hangar on the airport. It had plenty of shop space, and a nice office with 2 restrooms. I enjoyed it, and although I was the custodian and did all the work keeping the place clean. I was learning a lot, and getting more acquainted with the world of aviation. And then Steve replaced me with Dot. I'd known she was still upset that I was working with Steve, but she had the twin girls, and they took up all her time. So I was totally surprised at this new development. She couldn't do the things I'd been doing, had never typed, and never tried, but she had brought a hot plate and groceries in, and was making their meals there. By this time, the girls were just beginning to walk.

Steve called me one evening, desperate. One of the twins, Jeanette, had climbed up on a piece of equipment in the shop, had fallen, and was in the emergency room at the hospital. She was badly injured, and had a concussion. They didn't know if she would make it. I was needed at the school, and went back immediately. I loved these girls. I had taken Dot to the hospital when they were born, and had been concerned about them being in the school, which was no place for small children.

I was replaced several times, but that was Dot's first and last time to try to work with Steve. Jeanette got well, but she was awfully sick for a long time. I was glad to be back, working at a job where I was beginning to learn a subject that was about to take over the rest of my life. Steve soon bought a lot, and hired a couple of contractors to build a nice, new building where we moved the school. This location lasted until he died, many years later. It wasn't on the airport proper, but across from the airport on 36th Street.

This was the location where I first began teaching in 1977. I continued teaching there until 1981 when Morris Dixon and I started Love Aviation Training Center.

May 21 is Debby's birthday. I was going to lunch with both my daughters-in-law in 2007, and had decided to make them both an apron. I went to Linens n Things to see if I could find two dish towels to make them out of, and maybe something to make pockets out of. But I could see that the dish towels were much too small, and it was a bad idea. So I decided to go to Hancock's—I figured they would have something I could use there. They weren't selling out as I'd thought, but as I was looking, I spied the perfect fabric for aprons. It was aprons, stamped with Elvis Presley all over. Beautiful, his head on the bib part, a large lifelike shot of him with his guitar on the front, and a great shot of him on the pocket. All ready to hem and put together!

I started early the next day, and was soon finished. I looked for some cards, and found some with some airplane shots on them. Then I wrote a poem for each.

For Debby:
It's your birthday today, and I know it,
And tho' I'm not much of a poet,
I love you like Elvis,
Loved music, I'll tell this,
But maybe this gift will help show it

For Sherry:
For Sherry, no special occasion,
But imagine my instant elation,
To find Elvis' face
In the big fabric place,
Where I gazed in complete adoration!

Later, I bought several yards of the apron material, and gave away as many as 8 or 9 aprons. I haven't found any more of the fabric, but I have looked many times. I obviously got all that Hancock's had. But I didn't write any more poetry with the other aprons I gave away!

After Mama died in 1987, I was telling Paulette about Addie, the sister I had and had never seen. She knew about Addie, vaguely, but became more interested, and we resolved to try to find her. I had gone to see her once when Sherman and the kids and I drove through Oklahoma, and decided to try to see Addie at the "state school" in Enid. The people in the front office there refused to let me see her, and were very obstinate about it, trying and succeeding to make me feel guilty because they didn't know Addie had any family alive. I asked if I could see her if I made previous arrangements, and they said they didn't know.

So I asked what I could send her, and they said I could send money. Afterward, I had sent her some clothes, and was told she didn't need anything like that, only money. I couldn't get any information from them, but the rest of the family suggested I not contact her again, since I got no cooperation from the people there. But Paulette, true to her nature, began to write letters and make phone calls.

On the last day of 1987, we got a call from a nursing home in Wilson, Oklahoma. They told us they had Addie there at the nursing home, she was a very sweet lady, loved everybody, and seemed to remember her family. They said she talked about Lewie and Leona, and that was all, except Daddy. We could see her any time we wanted to, and she'd be happy to see us.

I immediately called Lewie and Lennie; we all cried and made plans to go to Wilson the next day, the first of January, 1988. I asked what we could bring her, and was told she could wear jogging suits and loved dolls. They said she talked about Lewie and Leona. She had told the people there that her brother Lewie was a barber, and lived in Oklahoma City.

So we met the next morning: Bill, Paulette, Matt, Ruby, Lewie, Margaret, and me. When we got to Wilson, a short distance from Ardmore, Oklahoma, we had quite a crowd waiting for us. The Ardmore newspaper and TV station reporters and others took our pictures, and interviewed Lewie and me on TV It seemed that everybody knew Addie's story, and was glad to know she did have a family after all. Addie was overjoyed! She loved us all, but Lewie most of all. She asked about Daddy, and seemed to understand he was gone. He had died in 1949.

As time went on, we visited her quite often; we always took her dolls, jewelry, and clothes. Lennie went the next time, along with Leona, Carolyn, and Janice. We took her to the hospital once, and had a skin cancer removed from her face. She used to ask to come home with us, and Leona was tempted, but we talked her out of it; she wasn't able to care for Addie. The financial manager at the nursing home made arrangements for me to get Addie's checks, and I took care of her burial arrangements, as well as her needs there at the nursing home.

Addie became very ill at one point, and they took her to a hospital at Hearne, a few miles from Wilson. She had good care, and eventually was taken back to Wilson where she regained her health, for the most part. But in a short while, she died very peacefully as they were putting her back to bed for a nap. We took her to be buried close to Daddy, in the Moran Cemetery in Oklahoma.

Through the years, Steve began to do a lot of woman chasing. He talked about his escapades to me, but I wasn't interested, and told him so. I think a lot of it was his imagination, but some of it was true. I know he talked to Dot, and told her things not only about me, but others who worked there. There was no way I could tell Dot the tales were untrue, but I could sense that she was getting cooler to me as time went by.

After Morris and I started our A&P School, I began to get the paperwork ready for the Texas Education Agency and the FAA, who would need to check us out. After a few weeks, Steve sent his friend, a Middle Eastern man, to check us out. He was interested in the whole operation, and I showed him around and explained it to him. I'd known him before at Steve's, and knew Steve had sent him, hoping the TEA would shut us down

I'd done the work to get Steve's school approved, including getting the catalog ready and implementing the records and rules concerning the continued approval. He assured me he hadn't turned us in, but I knew he had. "It doesn't matter, Steve," I told him. "I've already started the process, and I'm getting my stuff ready." And, sure enough, I got word from the TEA that they were coming to visit me.

The man came right on time. He was very cooperative with me, and gave me plenty of time to get all my schedules, records, and lesson plans ready. Also, he said they'd give me a break, and only charged me $500.00 instead of the regular $1,000.00.

After that, I got us approved by the FAA, the VA, and approval of the county for some of the students' tuition. During this process, Steve came to see me, this time on good terms. He'd wrecked his airplane, flying at night with no airport lights, and had broken his neck, so I took him home after I closed the school for the day. He was wearing a brace to hold his head erect. Someone had brought him to see me, I forget who, and left.

Steve was still involved with the Basket Case. I later learned she was with him when he'd wrecked his plane; not in the plane with him, obviously. He'd called one of their sons to come and get him and take him to the hospital, and they'd put the brace on him, and also told him if he'd moved his head just right, he could have been paralyzed for life. He had just recently gotten his private pilot license, but had flown many years without it. But certainly, he would never fly again.

He and I talked that evening when I took him home. He had closed his school, and never got his DME back. He told me he was proud of me, and hoped there were no ill feelings between us. I replied that there were none, that I appreciated all he had taught me, and I was glad I had made him proud. I really meant it, and I do now, that whatever my accomplishments, they were not easy to come by, and I couldn't have done them at all without his help.

He told me he was sick, and would never be well again. He wasn't. He developed cancer, and lived a couple of months or so. After his death, Dot, his wife, and I had a good talk and made up, sort of, after all the lies he'd told about me to her. I guess we were never the same friends we'd been before, but we were friends the rest of her life. She died a few years later, of high blood pressure. She'd had a violent stroke, and couldn't talk for a long time. Ironically, they put her in Manor Care, in a room right next to the Basket Case. I don't know if she was aware of that or not, or if the Basket Case knew the difference.

Steve's school had been closed for some time and she had sold the building.

It was 1983 when I met Bob Wells. I'll never forget it. He was a tall, slim man in his early 60s, or maybe late 50s, when he drove up to our school in Arlington. He was riding a motorcycle and carrying a large propeller in front. His white beard was down to his waist. He was bringing the propeller for me to use for the school. He and his wife had come from New York, where he had been working and flying for the Rhinebeck Airdrome there. He had written me about going to school, and I had corresponded with him. He and his wife had driven (would you believe this?) a homemade trailer from New York. They had parked the truck and trailer at a trailer park in Arlington, and he was ready to start to school.

I believe Bob was one of the most interesting and colorful students I ever had. He had lots of experience working on old aircraft, all reciprocals. He neither knew nor cared about jets, but he knew more about old aircraft than anyone I've ever met. He was fascinating just to listen to. He loved the antique planes. While he was here, he, another student, and I went to an air show where we saw all kinds of the old aircraft, such as a Storch, a Jenny, and others. The student, Patrick, and I asked him about a lot of them, and he was delighted to tell us all about them.

Bob and Joyce, his wife, visited Sherman and me, and we visited them in their trailer home Bob had built. He got his license in due time. He loved working in my shop. He tore down and built up a reciprocating engine while he was in school. They were thinking about moving to Texas, which they ultimately did.

When they came back later, they were on their way to Donna, Texas, but stayed here a few days before moving on. I hardly knew Bob. He had shaved off the long beard, and looked 20 years younger. They parked their trailer on our place this time, and we really enjoyed their visit. While they were here, we took them to Granbury, where Paulette and Bill were performing as a duo at the Cuckoo's Nest there. It was a private club, but open to everybody when Paulette and Bill performed there. We ate at the Nutt House there, and they danced a lot. They were avid square dancers.

We heard from them occasionally. Bob was retired, but went to work there for the Civil Air Patrol, on the old aircraft. Bob got to do a lot of dope and fabric, a job he loved doing. A couple of times they went camping at Grapevine Lake. They'd call me, and I'd go visit them there. It was always fun to talk to Bob and to hear his great stories.

One day I got a message on my phone. It was Joyce Wells, and she told me Bob had died. I knew he had been using supplemental oxygen, even while he still worked. She told me she was moving, had sold the trailer they had bought (the homemade one was long gone), and she was moving to South Carolina—a small town close to Greenville. She hates the ice and snow, but their kids live there. She promised to write me when she gets settled there. She said she was cleaning out all the old papers, etc. collected over the years, and she found the letter I'd sent him about his coming to school. She had meant to call and tell me about his death, but that cinched it. So she did, and I'm so grateful.

Charlie Stephens and another instructor from Braniff Education Systems, Inc. started a small A&P school near Meacham Field after so many of us had left. I was looking for a job at that time, and eventually, they asked me to come to work for them, and try to recruit some students to get their A&P ratings. I did so, and in a few days, they were both contacted and hired elsewhere to do mechanic work. They left, and told me, "Pauline, it's all yours," so I found myself with a school. There was one student who came in about that time, and I enrolled him for classes. I worked with him, and helped him get his license. Then another man came in, a young likable man named Alan Cook. My good friend, Bill Taylor, had told him to come and see me about going to school. I knew Bill had been in Vietnam. That was during the crisis there, and Alan and Bill had been two of the last ones to get on the last plane leaving there when it was all over.

Alan was the only one left. He and I worked together, and he finished the course, and was successful. By this time, I had another 2 or 3 students there, and I got Alan to work for me and finish the students we had. By the time we got them finished, I was out of money, and had to tell him I couldn't pay him any more. Alan and I had become very close friends. He and Paulette went out together once, but it didn't work out well. I told him later that I thought he was too worldly for her, and she was just an innocent young girl. But he left, and I somehow felt that he'd probably gone back to Nebraska, where his mother and some of the rest of his family lived. Meantime, I closed the school down for lack of money to keep it going.

Very soon, I was back at Steve's, and teaching. I asked Alan later about what date was on his license, and he said it was about 1974. 17 years later, I was at the Baylor Hospital in downtown Dallas with Paulette, who was in her last stages with cancer. The cancer had spread, and was now in her spine. The stem cell treatments had done nothing for her, and she was now in the ICU. One night, I was in the family room eating supper, when a lady who was sitting by me began talking to a man sitting at a desk nearby. She told him she was a volunteer, to come only on Thursday nights. He answered that he, too, was a volunteer on Thursdays. I had seen him a time or two, and was curious because he looked so familiar to me, but I couldn't place him. The lady said, "Is it OK if I ask you questions if I am confused?" and he told her it was fine, anytime. "So what is your name?" she asked. And he said "Alan Cook." I did a double take. "Alan Cook!" I repeated, realizing who he was. "Are you MY Alan Cook?"

He laughed, and I knew that laugh so well. He said, "Well, I don't know. Tell me who you are," and I told him. It was his turn to be surprised. He got up and I got up, we met and hugged. We were so glad to be reunited. He came back often after that and sat with me a lot, and took me to eat frequently. He kept up with Paulette's progress, but she became worse. The time came that her lungs had holes in them and couldn't hold air. She was subsisting on the medicines they were giving her. The last time she could talk, they were taking her for a test. She was crying, and told me goodbye.

When they called me at home and asked me to have the family come in to see her, we all met there, and Alan was there, and held my hand. What a dear friend he is! I stood by her side, and her husband Jeff was on the other side as she breathed her last. Even as I write this, it seems to tear the heart right out of me. The date was December 20, 1993. She was 40 years old. And she was my sweet little baby girl. I believe she's singing with the angels tonight!

Alan has been one of my dearest and closest friends. We see each other, and keep in touch. He has had many physical problems but seems to be doing well at this time. He reminds me that he is MY Alan.

Chapter 10

"The Aurora Encounter"

A few months after Paulette was born, and I was about 24 years old, I began having some stomach problems. They were mild at first, and I didn't think too much about it, but the trouble seemed to worsen as time went on. I was working at church, Broadview Baptist, and doing everything I had been, and loving it, so I wasn't about to give any of it up. Eventually, when it would be especially bad, I'd go and see Dr. Childs, our family doctor. He was interested, and did all he could, but had no idea what was wrong. At first, he had me go to the hospital and have tests run which, at that time, was the barium enema, and then checking the upper part of the stomach by drinking the barium solution.

The tests didn't show up the problem. At one point, he said my intestines had slipped down, and I should try wearing a girdle to correct the problem. It didn't work. I tried a couple of medicines, which didn't help either. My nerves suffered, and there were other symptoms. Once, I went to see our pastor, Bro. S.R. Garrison. He reminded me that the Lord would take care of me. I told him I knew that, but I was worried about my kids, and I didn't want some strange woman taking care of them if I died, which seemed very possible at this point.

He reminded me that the Lord would take care of my kids the same as He would me. He really made me feel so much better that I began to be a little more optimistic. I made another visit to Dr. Childs, and we agreed something had to be done. He made the arrangements, and I was admitted to the hospital. He contacted a cancer specialist, a Dr. Gooch, to perform surgery. I was kept in the hospital 12 days while waiting for the surgery. They found the problem; it was a huge tumor in the colon, which had been completely stopping up my colon. No wonder I was having so much pain! But they needed the 12 days to build up my system in order to have the surgery. I had lost a lot of weight.

The morning I was having surgery, our pastor, Bro. Kelly Moseley, came to see me. He had been visiting me regularly, as some others had been. He started to read the 23rd Psalm, and I stopped him. I said, "Bro. Moseley, that scripture will make me cry. Please read another one." So he read John 14. The nurses came in, told me goodbye (they said later, they never expected to see me again), and ate my candy.

I had asked Dr. Childs to please be there for me when I was taken into surgery. "I know Dr. Gooch is doing the surgery, but you're my friend. I want you to be there for me." He promised he would. And sure enough, he was waiting, and when they were taking me into surgery, he was standing there in the door, waiting for me. He took my hand and held it to his bosom, and held it until I was asleep.

I woke up several hours later, and saw Sherman coming into the room. I could see his wide, happy smile. He assured me everything was fine. They had removed the tumor, cutting out 6 inches or so of colon, and I should be fine. I had asked the Lord to take care of me, whatever that meant, and I knew my life belonged to Him, whatever happened. After 3 days, I was feeling so well, and the kids, Thom, Phil, and Paulette, came to see me. They sang, "Meet Me at Midnight, Mary," and Dr. Childs came in. He assured us they had checked the tumor thoroughly, and there was no sign of cancer! I was elated, and never had any problems with the ailment again.

In 2009, it was getting close to my 80th birthday. I knew my sons and their wives were planning a party for me. Thom and Debby were here for a couple of days before, and were staying, for the most part, at Phil and Sherry's. They planned it at the church, and gave out lots of invitations, not only in the church, but had mailed several out to non-members of First Baptist, Watauga. Some were sent to people from Broadview and Azle Avenue. Thom had ordered a huge bouquet of large red roses. They decorated tables, and Sherry made some of the best punch I'd ever had. Phil had fixed up a montage of pictures of my whole life, starting with the house where I was born in Okmulgee, and so many others, along with people who had shared my life through the years. He also gathered many more pictures, and had put them up on what looked like a TV screen, which was scrolling constantly to show them one at a time.

The attendance was good. Many old friends were there, and the food the girls had fixed was great. Everyone loved the punch, and I loved it all, and enjoyed visiting with everybody. The gifts (we had asked for cards, and maybe some incidents written down) were piled on the table, and there were some nice things, as well as cards, gift cards, etc.

Unfortunately, I got some of the cards and gifts mixed up, but I enjoyed them all. The only written words I received were from my next door neighbor, Sherry. I've read it over many times, and it always brings a tear or two. It will be included here. After we got home, Thom and I went through it all. My niece had taken an old picture of Sherman and me when we first married. It was 1946, at Forest Park, and what was never noticed before were 2 ghostly-looking women, one looking over each of our shoulders. Laurine had had it enlarged and framed, not even noticing the extra people in it, but now it's quite a curiosity to anyone who sees it up on my mantle.

My good friends, Nicole and Matt Sherrick gave me a nice electric skillet and two screen skillet covers, and there were several other nice gifts. Much jewelry; most people know that I love jewelry, the costume kind! Thom and Phil took care of cleaning up after the party.

When Thom enlisted in the Army in 1967, he received a letter guaranteeing he would go to Transportation Officers Candidate School. He went to basic training in Louisiana, then as preparation for OCS he was assigned to Advanced Infantry Training at Fort McClellan, Alabama. Around the time he was to graduate, all of the non-combat OCS classes were temporarily shut down. Thom was told he could reapply, but since he had received advanced infantry training, he would be assigned to an infantry unit in Vietnam.

Fortunately, he was reassigned to Fort Bliss, Texas, went to Drill Sergeant School, and was assigned to a missile training unit as part of their training cadre. But in December, 1967 he received orders for a missile unit in Germany. Once in Germany, Thom auditioned as a music arranger for the 7th Army Soldiers Chorus and got the job. As a member of the chorus, he became friends with Dave McCubbin. Dave had recently gotten divorced and he was having a rough time with it. Thom suggested that he write to Paulette. The two became pen pals. A few months later when Dave left the Army, he sold his Volkswagen to Thom. Thom brought it home with him when he came back to the states in 1970 and drove it for several years after that.

Paulette and Dave became good friends, and later, while Thom was still in Germany, Dave came to visit us when we lived in Sansom Park. He became part of our family, although we didn't see him any more. And that was 40 years ago.

He still sounded the same. He had lived in Kansas City for years, and still does. He planned to come by to see me, and take me to supper in a few days. He said for me to choose the place. I called Matt to see if he would like to meet Dave. He'd never met him, and he was thrilled! We could sit in his area, where he worked at P F Chang's in Grapevine. Dave drove. He was familiar with the restaurant, he said. There was one close to where he lived in Kansas City.

He'd called me when he was on his way to my house. I was so glad to see him. He came in, and we talked a while before leaving for the restaurant. He had a GPS in his car, and drove Hwy. 121. We were seated in Matt's area. Before we were seated, he saw Matt and recognized him; he looked so much like Paulette! Matt was known there as Konrad (his middle name). There were too many Matts. I was so proud of him, and we had so much fun together. The food was outstanding, and finally, Dave and I left and got back here at 11 PM. Dave is a diabetic, and had to go to his motel and take some medicine. He took one of Paulette's tapes, and is going to make some CDs. I also gave him a Senior Gazette that had my story of Paulette and Phil singing Unforgettable. He said he'd call me and let me know he was OK when he went home, but promised he'd come to see me every year when there's a reunion of the 7th Army Chorus in Big Spring, Texas.

Plainview School

Our school, with grades 1-8, was a one-room facility. It had a platform, raised about 10 inches from the floor, to accommodate a teacher's desk and chair, and a couple of benches to serve as seats for classes in session. Otherwise, the room was wide open, because there was only one teacher for all 8 grades.

There were two outhouses for bathrooms, sometimes called privies, well away from the classroom; one for boys, one for girls. These were built over open pits. We were far out in the woods, and there was no sewage, and neither did we have sewage in the homes at that time.

Later, a place was partitioned off, just large enough for a small kitchen. Eventually, it was finished, and we began to have hot lunches served every day. Once that got started, there were no complaints from the students. I don't remember any of us taking a cold lunch to school again. At first, we were served bowls of navy beans with saltine crackers and a glass of evaporated milk, diluted half and half with water. We had some butter with the crackers.

We had one cook who prepared all of it, and she would sometimes make a sheet cake for our dessert. We loved it! I loved helping "Birdie", the cook. A few times, she was sick, and I was in charge. The food was so much better than what we had at home for lunches, and we were thankful. Birdie was good, and did all she could to make the meals more interesting.

I remember, before I started to school we visited there where Leona, Ruby, and Robert went. Their teacher was Buis Cooper, whose parents owned the hotel in Valliant. He was good to us, held Margaret and me on his lap, and talked to us. He also questioned us about Leona and Ruby, to tease them. But when I started to school later, he was not there. The school had burned, and had been rebuilt.

My teacher for the first grade was Miss Henry, a good friend to my family. I remember her being a sweet person, but when I started the second year, she was gone. It was decided that I should skip it, and go on with Margaret, who was in her third year. My teacher was Miss Denny. I didn't know where Miss Henry went, and she never contacted us after that, but I was happy with Miss Denny. I guess I just liked school and enjoyed learning. I'd learned to read, write, and do arithmetic before I started to school. Margaret helped me a lot.

We got new teachers regularly. After Miss Denny, there was Mrs. Slocum. She was a large lady, good to us, but not personally close as the others had been. She lasted one year. She had some big boys in class who sometimes got in trouble, but she handled the situation well. She used to threaten to "land on you!" and it got to become a joke with us because of her size. We were a little sad when we didn't see her the next year. The next teacher was Minnie Coffey. She used to board with Lennie and Lewie, and they lived close to us. So she, Margaret, and I were good friends.

A couple of times, Lennie and Lewie went away for a night, and she'd have Margaret and me to spend the night with her. We always enjoyed her, and then one day, Minnie got married! She married the mailman, Sam. He'd never learned to read or write, and she began to teach him at home. But somehow, he delivered the mail, and never let the handicap deter him. She was there, as a consequence, more than one year, and had a baby before long: a little boy.

Many years later, I visited her in a nursing home at Valliant. She was glad to see me, and we had a great visit. Her son was grown, had a family, and was living close by. I think Sam had died several years before that.

Last of all the teachers I knew at Plainview was Pauline Harris, a single lady not much older than a teenager, and a really special friend to me and Margaret. We were pals, visited and gossiped together. She must have taught about 3 years, and settled later, married, not far from where we lived when Margaret and I were in High School.

In those days, the local school building served as a community center. The war was going on part of the time, and Plainview (sometimes called Mudhole, because of the wet climate) is where we held war bond drives, dances, pie suppers, school programs, etc. It was also a place for church services on Sundays and revival services, and eventually, Vacation Bible School a time or two. Whoever the teacher was at the time never failed to ask Margaret and me to sing, dance, or whatever was needed for a performance at the school. Mama was always good at making the costumes needed, and we were never shy about performing.

During the war, when we had functions to sell war bonds and stamps, we usually had dances, because we could raise more money that way and draw a larger crowd. I loved to dance, and this was right up my alley.

When there were church services held in the school, we always went. Church buildings were few and far between, and it wasn't easy to have a preacher come out so far; there certainly was no money in it, but sometimes, a preacher would come anyway. We had some people in the neighborhood who couldn't quite decide if they wanted to preach or make moonshine whiskey, so they settled for both. While one brother was preaching the gospel, another one was selling bootleg whiskey close by. This whiskey was illegal until sometime after we left there in 1946, maybe the last state in the South to legalize alcohol.

My Dear Sherman,

So many years ago, in the 1940's, I grew up from the kid you used to know as Ruby's little sister, who whined about the sand being hot as we walked home barefoot from church, and you would pick me up and carry me, while Ruby, your date, complained that I just wanted you to carry me. It was true. I'd take off my shoes so I'd have an excuse. I loved you then, and my love never stopped. Oh, we, (I) grew up, and you and Ruby broke up. You went into an NYA camp, and a CCC camp, where young men worked on public projects, building roads, bridges, and parks.

Later, you went into the Army, you volunteered, got married, and served in the Cavalry, going on to France and Italy, and were in there over two years. At age 15, I saw you once, home on furlough. I knew you were married. You were so handsome and as we talked, I felt the same thrill I'd known before. Although I knew we couldn't be together, you were my ideal, and I knew I'd never be so attracted to another man. Meantime, life went on, and so did the war.

In September of 1945, we were having a party at our house. The war was finally over, at least for us, and some of the soldiers were returning home. I'd been dating once in a while with a few of the younger boys my age, and a couple of times with Taylor, who was home from the military service. I liked him, but wasn't too excited about him, and I knew he was fairly unconcerned about me.

Another man I'd carried a torch for, for some time, was Jerry. He was nearly 10 years older than I was, and so was Taylor.

But this was a festive night, and we were all excited about having peace in the world at last, after 5 long years of war. There was a knock on the door, and I went to see who it was. I must have stared at the sight of you standing there, handsome as ever, with your brown leather jacket on. My heart gave a leap, as I was held close for a moment in the arms of my idol. We were all glad to see you, and my family was especially happy to see you. You and I talked a long time; you told me you were in the process of getting a divorce from your wife, Viola. Details of your problems were not divulged until much later. It was enough for me to rejoice in the knowledge that you were home again. The Ruffin family home was a little over a mile from us.

So we began to see each other frequently. I was also dating others, as you rarely got out socializing with the rest of us. I went with Jerry some, and had also been seeing Don, a man from Ohio, who had been in the service with Robert Musset, and had come to visit Robert. We dated, Don and I, with Joyce and Leonard. Leonard was Robert's cousin.

My crushes were over when I fell for you all over again, but our relationship was not a regular thing with you. You would be at home for weeks, but I might see you only occasionally. You seemed to be crazy about me when we were together, but didn't seem to try to make time to be with me. You gave me a beautiful pen and pencil set for Christmas, and were thoughtful of me—sometimes.

Your birthday was March 14, and we were together more at that time. I made you a birthday cake, but my icing was a failure, so Mama made a new batch of white icing and saved the day! It was about that time that you told me you were falling in love with me. I was overjoyed! You told me your divorce would be final in the summer, I think it was July. So we settled on a date for the wedding in August of 1946.

I realize now, more than ever, I was awfully young, and certainly knew very little about life. I thought I was pretty wise, I'd grown up during a worldwide war, with its horrors, sacrifices, injuries and death. But really, I knew very little about the ravages of war. And much later, the realizations of all these things were revealed to me from the stories on TV, and some movies, meeting people who had first-hand experiences, and the 2 times I went to the holocaust museum in Washington, which was a real eye opener.

But Sherman, as young as I was, there's nothing I would change about you and me. I know you've been the real love of my life. Things change, and we change too, and I'll always wonder…what really caused us to grow away from each other? Maybe someday we'll have a good visit and discuss our life together. And maybe you'll tell me how you really felt about me. And you and me. I know you loved me from the start, and for many years. But for the last few years, from about the time you wanted Viola again, I felt the rift grow too wide between us, and I never felt you close to me again. I would never put the blame all on you; I know I didn't really try, either.

Last Wednesday, my friend, Nicole Sherrick came over, and we cut out a poncho for her to make for her mother-in-law for Christmas. The fabric was a beautiful black velvety material. I cut it out, and, because I'm ambidextrous, I used my left hand, not realizing my right hand wasn't working well. After getting it cut out, Nicole was going to sew it while I ate supper and rested a few minutes. When I went back in, I put the neck band on, and then realized I couldn't get my right hand to work right with the scissors or a seam ripper. It scared me, and I stopped and rested. I called Sherry, and she said I needed to call 911. I called Dr. Kallal, and he urged me to go to the emergency room. He said I could ride in a car if someone else would drive me there. Meantime, Sherry called Phil in Ohio, and he insisted I go to the hospital. So Nicole drove me to HEB, and Sherry met us there and stayed with me while a group of nurses started a whole battery of tests.

The hospital was being overrun with new patients that night, so they put me in an ER ward—many patients and one bathroom. The room I was in had a curtain between me and an old lady who moaned with every breath, and two women and one man in the room with them, and they were talking and laughing in normal voices. It was nearly midnight, and I never slept at all.

It was after 3 PM the next day when they moved me to a very nice room with my own bathroom. The nurses were a lady from India and others, all very nice and helpful, and I had a great bed. About 7 pm, Tim Ballog, "my" deacon, came to visit me. He'd spent the night before with his wife, Katy, whose blood pressure had spiked. He stayed a while—I always enjoy him so much—but he was worn out from having no sleep. I advised him to go home and rest, and he did so.

I had a good night's sleep, and had a visit from a therapist who took me for a walk in the hall. She said she was impressed that I didn't need her any more. But the only part of my body affected by the "stroke" was my right hand, mainly my thumb. It's still affected, but it's also affected by arthritis, so I don't know if I had a stroke or a TIA. That, the doctor explained to me, is the one that is not a stroke, but a lesser one that nearly was. I haven't had any more indications, and my blood pressure is fine.

I was waiting for the doctor, a Dr. Kane, to dismiss me so I could go to Irene's funeral. He was going to come early, then it was to be 12 noon, but it was 4 pm before he came. But before noon, a great friend came to see me. It was Jay Evans, my friend Sandra's husband. He'd come to see me after getting an e-mail from the church office. I was so happy to see him, and I asked him if he could bring me home after I saw the doctor. He assured me he could; he didn't have anything else he needed to do. Sandra was in South Carolina, visiting some of her folks. He talked to her on the phone, and let me talk to her too.

It turned into several hours, but Sherry got there in time to take me home. I am so grateful to Jay for staying with me and being so patient. He and Sandra are such sweet friends.

Sherry and I came back by Sandy's, a café on Rufe Snow, had a sandwich, and got here about the same time Phil, Jonathan, and Kyle got here with a load of furniture from Adam's apartment. Adam will be here a few days; he's got a trailer to live in. Jonathan is looking for an apartment, so he can probably use the furniture.

It was good to sleep in my own bed, but the doctor was afraid the Celebrex was what had caused the TIA (light stroke) and told me not to take it any more. But I took Tylenol and was OK. I got up and got ready to go to Irene's funeral. It was today, and I hadn't missed it after all.

I got ready to go to the funeral. I didn't realize it was so cold out; I wore a jacket, but it wasn't nearly warm enough. But I went on to the grave site after services in the chapel, and Jim Ed put his coat around me and walked to the car with me when it was over.

There were very few there for the service, partly because Irene was 97 years old and had been in the Fireside nursing home for more than 20 years, and at that age, had outlived a lot of friends. But Janet, Kathy, and Jim were there, one of Howard's grandsons (both of Howard's sons had died). Mark, Irene's grandson was there, and had made the arrangements. I was surprised—I knew she was a pretty woman, but she was beautiful in the casket. She had shown me the dress she had had for some time for this purpose. It was black and lovely, with a single strand of rose-colored beads. She wore bright red lipstick and dark eyebrow pencil, all of which she had designated. She looked remarkably like my Johnnie. Neither Johnnie nor Howard was able physically to come.

Janet handed me an envelope from Johnnie. He had sent me a check for $100.00 in the most beautiful card I've ever seen. I know the girls had picked out the card, but he always sent me such sweet ones. He is so dear to me. I hope he understands why I haven't been to see him; Janet said he does. I'll try to go and see him after going to the Sullivans' Christmas dinner.

On a Thursday night, after going to Manor Care and then to Avalon to see Johnnie, I went on to Ginger Brown's. I knew Jeff and Karen would be performing, and we were to have a birthday party for Jeff, who was now 44. Karen had made him a cake, and a lot of her relatives were there: her mother and step-dad, her dad and step-mother, her sister and her family, Dusty and Sam, Karen and Jeff's two sons, and Dusty's baby boy. Also, there were a couple of girls from Broadview: Donna Bolton, and Jeanette Wycoff, and her three girls, and many others. Randall came in late, and only stayed a few minutes. I was very tired. Before I'd left home, the tree trimmers had come, trimmed the tree in back, and even the one in front.

The yard man had come, mowed the yard, and trimmed the hedges. The yard looked great. My roses were blooming beautifully. My mind began to wander back to the time when Jeff was born, now 44 years ago. I had been at the hospital with LaVerne; this was her first child. I was working for Steve at the time, but I'd not started instructing yet. We were in a large hangar at Meacham Field, on the south side of the airport. There was a lot of aircraft work going on in the hangar. I did secretarial duties, janitorial duties, and also some shop work I could learn, and was a willing pupil.

Two men came in and enrolled for school. These classes were refresher courses for experienced mechanics to help them get their A&P (Airframe and Powerplant) license. It usually took 6-8 weeks to get through all the FAA exams, get results back from Oklahoma City, and take a practical exam. They were then issued their certificate.

These two men were Bob and Joe. Joe was a younger man, but they were good friends, and Bob seemed to look after Joe. Bob was an Air Force "lifer," and was soon getting out of the service. He was stationed in El Paso, Texas, and was a master sergeant. He had recently quit drinking, but his wife was still an alcoholic, and he said they were breaking up. We talked a lot, and the three of us became good friends. They told me they were not Christians, but both men discussed this with me, and asked me lots of questions. I was very happy to explain all I could at length: the plan of salvation and living the Christian life.

There was a distinct attraction between Bob and me. I was about 37, and Bob was 40. He was a tall, slim man, I guess not really handsome, but had a rather quiet, gentle manner, and seemed to be a very kind man. I'd never been unfaithful to Sherman, and certainly didn't intend to start now, but I was so happy to be with Bob. We never got any closer than a small hug or two, but he let me know he was falling for me, and I was feeling the same toward him. But my conscience was bothering me. I knew I'd not give in to this temptation. It was strong, but my family was too solid.

Paulette was about 13, and suspected something when Bob had Thanksgiving dinner with us. I assured her that everything was OK. Actually, Sherman was in Louisiana for a few months then, and didn't call me for some time. It was one of those dry times we went through, which happened throughout our married life. But I knew things would get better. I was determined to hold our marriage together, and he was, too, but had his moody spells, and this was a long one.

And then, my Lord spoke to me. He told me to decide. If I wanted to win Bob to Him, I had to give up any claim to him because Bob couldn't have me and Him too. I promised Him I'd take "hands off," figuratively speaking.

And then, one day I went after some supplies, and Bob went with me. We were talking, and he said he was ready to accept the Lord. We parked at a 5&10 cent store, and I explained that he just needed to pray and accept God's promise. I prayed; Bob said he just didn't want to right then. I think he couldn't because he needed to be alone, and not be with me. So I told him not to worry, to wait until he got into his motel room tonight, and he said he would. I went into the store where we were, and bought him a Bible. I wrote on the flyleaf to read this scripture: "He hath shown thee, oh man, what is good: and what does the Lord require of thee, but to do justice, to love mercy, and to walk humbly with thy God."

Bob announced to me the next day that he had prayed and had given his life to Him, and he knew now he was God's child. Soon after that, Bob was finished with his tests and had his certificate. The three of us went to lunch, and we said goodbye, as he put his arm lightly around me. We walked to the hangar door together. He'd already told me he wouldn't ever be back, and likely, I'd not hear from him again.

For several nights, I cried a little, but not from regret. I knew I'd chosen this because God had given me victory for Him. I knew I'd never have Bob anyway—and then Sherman came home, and everything was fine with us again.

A few years later, Joe came by to see us. He told me Bob had divorced his wife, married again. They had a new baby, and he was going to church regularly, working for an aircraft company. I called and talked to him for a few minutes.

Fifteen years later, Sherman and I flew to Fort Myers, Florida to visit Paulette and Bill, who were appearing at a club there. I'd made a dress for Paulette to wear on stage. We had a short, but great vacation. We saw the attractions there -- Thomas Edison's laboratories, Henry Ford's home, and many other sights. The last day we were there, we went to play miniature golf. It was the most beautiful golf course I have ever seen. It looked like something from a fairy story. Afterward, we flew home.

I stole some acorns from the banyan trees at the Edison plant in Florida. We had a large lot, and somehow I got the idea I could grow a tree, but probably not, because it grows out in all directions. But it didn't matter, because I put the seeds up at home, and they were lost forever. I could never find them.

We got home on Monday, and Wednesday Sherman began to mow the yard. At one point he came in, complaining of pains in his chest. I asked him if I should take him to the hospital, but he refused, and kept saying, "Just wait a while." Finally, I said, "What are we waiting for? You may be having a heart attack." He gave in, and let me drive him to a hospital. I drove as fast as possible to the hospital, and sure enough, it was a heart attack. They kept him for several days, and sent him home with a lot of directions for me to take care of him. Later, I felt that he blamed me for not calling an ambulance. He obviously didn't realize I wanted to, but he wouldn't let me.

After that, he started drinking again. It's a shame that a man with Sherman's abilities, intelligence, and talents would part with all that for a bottle of vodka. He seemed to give up after I started Love Aviation with Morris. I'm not innocent of some of his concerns, but I was true to him, working hard to have something and to take care of us.

I was concerned about him, and was also concerned about the school. And I guess I was also concerned about my own needs. We didn't love any more, and didn't share our lives as we once had. I had friends and a job to do. He was all alone; he had neighbors, but was alone for the most part. He took care of Matt a lot as time went on. He took him to school and looked after him while Paulette worked with me. Matt loved him dearly and we depended on him. Also as far as I know, he never did any drinking while he was caring for Matt.

But Paulette married Jeff, and she and Bill shared custody of him. Matt went to school in Grapevine, and was with Bill on weekends, After Sherman spent two weeks at the Schick Center, he never took another drink, but sat quietly and read books or watched TV. His back was hurting all the time; also he did have a lot of arthritis. Later, he just seemed to sit and brood. Paulette had died in 1993, and he never seemed to recover from her death. He lived until 2001.

On November 24, 2010, I went to Washington, DC. Thom had sent for me to come to Virginia to spend Thanksgiving with him and Debby. My good friend Randall Burns and his son-in-law took me to the airport to board the plane, American Airlines. I was a little apprehensive. I'd heard a lot of criticism about security and making passengers have pat downs and full body scans. They had arrested foreigners with bombs on another plane, but there was nothing unusual this time, just the metal detectors we always had to go through. Thom had made plans for a wheelchair for me all the way there and back home. I really appreciated it; I knew there would be a lot of walking to do at the airport.

My trip was good aboard the Super 80; I didn't even have a seatmate. I read and worked on a crossword puzzle. When I arrived, I was pushed into the baggage area. Thom came to meet me and tell me a reporter and photographer was waiting to interview me. They were from the local Fox TV station, interviewing people about their Thanksgiving travel. So they got a shot of me, still in the wheelchair. I got out and went to Thom. We kissed, the reporter introduced himself to me, and we talked briefly. What a thrill! This is such a popular station, and the interview went all over the place, and many friends saw it. Phil recorded it from Cincinnati and sent it to Facebook, where many people I knew saw it. They teased me about it, especially after I got home.

We got my luggage and went to Thom and Debby's house in Fairfax. Thom picked up some things to take with us. Then we went to Olive Garden, and I had some great soup and drink. We drove to Winchester, to the new house where they plan to retire in a year or so.

What a beautiful house! Right in the edge of the large grove of trees. Wonderful architecture! As we went in. we were able to see some of the Fox interview. It was a thrill to me, and I'm sure it was to Thom, too, although he was cooler about it.

We found out later that Wendy taped the program, and Phil told us the next day (Thanksgiving Day) that he'd put it on Facebook. Sherry was with him in Cinnncinati, but left a couple of days later.

On Thanksgiving Day, Lesley, Ben, Jordan, and Jacob came, and so did Wendy and Bryan. We drove downtown to eat Thanksgiving dinner where Thom had made reservations. We had a good dinner and walked through the downtown area of Winchester. Afterward, we went to Wendy and Bryan's house where Wendy played the TV program back to us. Later, we shopped at Best Buy, and Thom got me a charger for my cell phone—I'd forgotten to bring mine.

On Friday, we drove to Strasburg, VA and ate at a quaint café and hotel: Thom, Debby, Lesley, Ben, Jordan, Jacob and me. On Saturday, Debby, Jordan, Lesley and I all went to a gift shop and saw some great Christmas stuff. Lesley got me a scarf that I plan to use as a pattern to make more. Debby had cooked a hen, and when we got home from the shop, she used canned biscuits and made a large pot of dumplings. It was very good, and we had some left over. Sunday evening, Thom and I in his car, and Debby and the cats in hers, all went to the house in Fairfax. They were going to work on Monday, and I was to come home on Tuesday.

I spent Monday alone at the house in Fairfax. I had no yeast, so didn't make rolls this time. On Tuesday, I got up about 4:30 AM and got ready to leave about 6:45. Thom dropped me off at the airport and went on to work. It was a good flight again; rained a little, but the clouds cleared soon and the weather was beautiful.

Nicole came after me. Randall had told me he had to take Dee to the doctor, so I'd called Nicole. She's a super neighbor and good friend. We went by Cheddar's and ate lunch. I got home, got all my suitcases unpacked, washed about everything in them, sorted mail, and put stuff away.

I was surprised to see my e-mail. I had a lot of messages from friends who'd seen my TV interview. Phil could always be counted on for that sort of thing. He had spread the word on my Facebook, and his too, and I confess I'm not too proud to do a little bragging.

I don't usually spend much time watching TV, but on Saturday, for some reason I became glued to the set, watching The History Channel .They were telling the following stories, with pictures and some (much later) news headlines:

In 1897, before UFOs and space travel (that we know about), there was a strange airship flying around several states in the Southwest. It was reported by witnesses that the ship was cigar-shaped, could fly at very high speeds, and some fairly high altitudes. It crashed into a wooden water tower at Aurora, Texas, a small place about 20 or so miles from Fort Worth, in Wise County. Debris was scattered all over as the airship came apart, and it seemed to be all metal, some aluminum. It had one occupant: a pilot. He was small, decidedly "not of this world," goes the story. He was dying, and some of the people in this small community got a doctor to come out, who tried to save him. He failed, probably because he didn't quite know what to do to save him. So the alien died, and was buried the same day.

They buried him in the Aurora cemetery, and put a small, crude stone at his head. The people then proceeded to clean up the place, where metal was strewn all over. Most of the metal, it was claimed, was thrown down the well nearby, where the windmill was destroyed. Keep in mind, these are stories told by residents of the area, some claiming to be eyewitnesses. They were questioned later in 1948, when UFOs were being reported all over the United States. The details of the stories varied, and some claimed it was a hoax to draw attention to the small town, where there were very few people and not even a post office. And now, there is only the old cemetery, and a home-style restaurant called "Tater Junction."

The investigations went on for some time, but in the 60s, others started to try to find out more about it. Earlier, the metal was found to be primarily aluminum with a little iron. The iron proved to be 5%, which is way too much to be in any aluminum that flies. Another family moved onto the place with the well that supposedly held so much of the metal that had been thrown in it. I saw on TV the horrible way arthritis had caused his hands to be affected. They looked grotesque, and didn't look at all like arthritis. It was impossible— the well had been filled with concrete, and this obviously had been poured on top of all the metal. So certainly the water could never have been used, and wasn't even tried; it was learned later that it was a hoax.

Eventually, it was investigated further, and some went to court to try to exhume the alien's body. The court agreed, and when they went to do it, the stone was gone. The body seemed to have disappeared, and the metal was not to be found. They had found and tested a small piece or two of the metal, and that was all they found. The sheriff of Wise County, where Aurora is, decided to let the incident die and told them not to try to exhume the body. They've never found it. The cemetery shows no sign, and the headstone is gone. There is now only a marker, not a grave, with some of the history written on it.

My niece Alice's husband, Kearney and I went to the cemetery and looked around. It was donated to the city of Aurora just a short time before the airspace incident, and is still being used. It's a very nice, clean, and well-kept cemetery, and an interesting one—easy to walk in, with concrete between each row of graves. The town itself hasn't grown much, even in light of all this.

Now there are many expensive houses being built, but still no city growth yet. Who knows what's in the future?

There is a movie about this incident, not factual, and not popular, purely not just fiction, but bad fiction. I have it, and also have read 3 books written about it, still fiction. But who knows what happened or did not happen in 1897?

I've read a lot about UFOs; the Roswell, New Mexico incident as well as here close to us, in Watauga and Aurora. I have to tear myself away from the computer. The stories of these UFO landings and the Alien pilots (?) in them are pretty convincing to me. When these things took place, or if so, there was no way they could let the rest of the world know. The people who claimed to see them in the Roswell incident were warned, actually threatened, to say nothing to anybody about them and what they knew about it at the time. And this, by the US government who came out to the sites, although everything gradually leaked out. Now, a world of information can be found, but the eyewitnesses at the time have since died. There seems to be very little, if any proof of any of it.

Meanwhile, life goes on. I find myself getting a little lonely now, so many of my family are gone. Phil and Sherry are in Ohio. I try hard to face life alone without self-pity, but I miss talking to Ruby, Margaret, and others, and I think how life changes. I remember neighbors and friends who were always visiting, sharing time with each other, and kids playing with your kids, but it doesn't happen any more. We have neighbors, probably as lonely as we are, but staying home, or in most cases, working away from home, and so busy with their own lives, they have no time for us old retirees.

Sometimes, I wonder how lonely it must be to have no church affiliation. What do people do for spiritual help, found only in God's house, worshiping with His people? We have every means of communication available, but we live mostly to ourselves. Church members are not perfect people, but they are involved in the same circumstances to a great extent, and find much comfort in having prayer, worship and fellowship. I think of these things, and I can forget any frustration and aggravation of being alone.

I can always make a phone call to check on a sick person, or just talk to someone, be a volunteer in a nursing home, and these things are very rewarding. And although I fail to be faithful in my writing, I find a great satisfaction in putting my thoughts down on paper, and it saves me a lot of money. When I'm involved in writing, I have no time for shopping. Also, it's easier on my terribly arthritic left foot!

I went from Manor Care, to see Johnnie, and as always, he was glad to see me. I sat with him while he ate supper. He is beginning more and more to slip out of reality. Once, he said thoughtfully, "I haven't gone to see Mama in a long time; I really need to go and visit her." Later, he said, "I don't know what I'll do after I visit Mama." He made several similar remarks, and seemed genuinely concerned about his Mama, who had died a very long time ago. I hated to leave, but was a little relieved as I walked out to my car and went to Ginger Brown's.

It was a great night. Not long after I'd arrived and was drinking decaf coffee (they always made it fresh for me), Dee and Randall came. Shortly afterward, Jimmy and Patty Youree, and Donny and Judy Crites, followed by Richard and Chere Bradford, my good friends from church in Watauga. Donny and Judy paid for my supper, and he walked me to my car.

The next day, my niece Laurine, her daughter Janet, and I drove to Idabel, Oklahoma to see my brother, Robert and his wife, Omia. We went in Laurine's car, and she drove.

Since she doesn't believe in driving speeds below the speed limit, we made good time. It rained on us some of the way, but very little after we got there. We got a room at the Microtel in Idabel, and went on to Hill Nursing Home to see Robert and Omia. There was very little difference in their conditions since the last time we'd seen them. I was under the impression that Robert had dementia, but was hoping it wasn't Alzheimer's. That hadn't been diagnosed yet, but by the time I write this, I've had to concede that it obviously is. Omia is forgetful, and shows signs of some dementia, but she is 85 and he is 90, so that can be expected. We took Roy with us—it was his birthday—and ate supper at the fish place in Idabel. The next day, we drove to Valliant, and on to Moran cemetery, but we didn't stay long. It rained on us, so we came on back to Valliant, and ate lunch there.

I was tired when we got back home, but felt better after soaking in a tub of hot water at home. Sherry had come home from Cincinnati with Phil, and they went to her mothers' folks in Tennessee for the 4th of July. Sherry had called me on Thursday and told me the movie I had asked Phil to find for me about the Aurora incident had been ordered, and was at their house where I could pick it up. So I called Kyle at home. We watched the movie, "The Aurora Encounter," and I went from there to Avalon to see Johnnie.

The critics had said the movie, made in 1986, was fiction, bad at that, and cheaply made, which was evident. I am glad to have it, however. We enjoyed it, knowing there were no real incidents portrayed. I don't begrudge the

$22.03 it cost me. I appreciated their finding it for me, and they got it for $10.00 less than originally priced.

September 11, 2008

Today, 7 years ago, I was staying at Fairfield Inn on Loop 820, on the northeast side of Fort Worth, Texas, approximately 5 miles from my current home. It was a temporary arrangement for me. Sherman, my husband of 54+ years had died on the 25th day of April, and I lived alone in the house we'd bought in April of 1990. We had been separated for 9 months, from August, 1989 until May, 1990 when we were reconciled. Our neighbors' sewer had been obviously misrouted through the sewer system, and had flooded my own system, and had damaged my house so that I couldn't stay there for a while. I took a room at the Fairfield Inn for a couple of weeks.

It was about 8 AM when the TV had a news bulletin as I was going to bathe and get dressed. I was paying little attention to the program. I finished, and went downstairs to breakfast when I suddenly took notice of what was happening. The terrorists were bombing buildings—the pentagon in Washington, the twin towers, and others in New York City and Washington, DC. Reporters were giving accounts downstairs on TV, and lots of people were gathered around, many with their cell phones!

I had something for breakfast—probably a bowl of cereal—and started home to see how my house was coming along. Traffic was terrible. Everything seemed to be in an uproar. When I got home, my house was reeking with the smell of sewage. I opened doors and windows, made some calls, and stayed outside as much as possible. I didn't try to cook or do much else in the house.

I had the house professionally cleaned and new carpets installed. I had Gary, Sherman's good friend and his helper, also my student at the school, to install marble tiles in the front entry. Sherman had bought the tiles for the entry and the front porch when we first bought the house, but after he did the front porch, he became unable to do any more. But Gary did a beautiful job of the entry, and coordinated the pattern with the way Sherman had done the porch.

My friends, Gene and Vivian, put some linoleum in the front bathroom, and I had new carpet installed in the master bath and the rest of the house. I had the house repainted inside, all the same color as original. Thom and Paulette had chosen the wallpaper in the master bath and kitchen; it was a little unusual, but beautiful.

So today, these years after 9-11, many changes have taken place in my life. It's incredible! I live alone. I've been alone for these 7 years, and most of my family is gone. All of my brothers and sisters except Robert are dead, and he and his wife live in Idabel, Oklahoma. Their two sons live in Idabel, and their daughter, Betty, lives near Dequeen, Arkansas.

My daughter Paulette died in 1993. She was my constant companion, and it was so hard to give her up. She suffered with breast cancer that went into her spine, and had treatments for 3 years. A lot of that time, she was living what seemed to be a normal life. She had been married to Jeff Agnew for one and a half years. Matt was seven when she died. She is buried beside Sherman at Greenwood Cemetery.

Phil and Sherry live in Hurst, Texas with their two younger boys, Jonathan and Kyle. Their oldest boy, Adam, is working, living in Austin, Texas in an electronics place. He's been in the US Marine Corps. They are sweet and good boys, all of them, 5 years apart.

Our son, Thom, our eldest was born January 23, 1948. He is married to Debby Seibert, and they live in Fairfax, Virginia. He works for Greystone, a commercial mortgage company, and Debby works for BAE Systems in DC. He was married many years to Jeanne Butler, and has 2 girls: Lesley Cook and Amy Pent. Debby also has two girls: Wendy Johnson and Suzanne McHale.

My children are all great. Thom is 60, Phil is 57, and Paulette would be 55. She died at 40 years, one and a half after marrying Jeff Agnew. She and Bill Hartmann had been married about 17 years when they divorced in 1989. Thom and Jeanne divorced in 1992.

Sherman and I were divorced in September, 1989. He lived alone in our place in Sansom Park, and I moved to an apartment in Benbrook, close to Phil and Sherry and Paulette and Bill. When Paulette and Bill separated, she and Matt, her 3-year-old son, moved into my 2-bedroom apartment with me. Matt couldn't adjust—he missed his Daddy—and Paulette and Bill finally went back together. Meanwhile, Paulette and Bill both worked for me at Love Aviation Training Center.

Chapter 11

"No," I said. "We'll try one more thing."

In 1966, I needed a job. I had some experience in several dry cleaning establishments and had done some sewing at home, but I was looking for something other than work in a dry cleaners. I felt like I could do most anything I had an opportunity to learn, but I'd decided to decline the warehouse at Striplings Department Store where I'd been offered a job.

I really hadn't wanted to work away from home much. My three kids still needed me at home in the summer time, but when Steve (A.E. Stephens) called me, I was glad to hear what he had in mind. He was starting an A&P school, Airframe and Powerplant mechanics' refresher courses. I would be helping him get the school started: typing materials, setting up an office, and just generally helping to organize classes, etc. Steve was an experienced A&P mechanic, Authorized Inspector, and Designated Mechanics Examiner. He could actually issue the license when the students passed all their written and practical exams.

So we planned it, and he acquired a small office and larger classroom in a large hangar that belonged to a prominent flight school owner, Jack Robinson. Steve was working for Jack, and did mechanic work on the aircraft in exchange for the rental space. We shopped for office supplies, furniture, etc., and started night classes with about 16 or 17 students. I only worked in the daytime after helping the first few nights getting the students enrolled, but Steve taught at night.

After a few days and nights, we started getting students in the daytime classes. I started to study the materials, and since I was typing the lessons, began to learn more and more about aviation. Steve brought his son, Charlie into the school, part time. Charlie was an apt pupil, and did lots of work on aircraft. I always loved Charlie. He is one year older than my Thom. I've known him all his life, and we always joke and enjoy each other.

Steve was truly an aviation devotee. He'd been a mechanic for many years, and had worked for American Flyers, Braniff Airways, and Frontier Airlines, as well as several private schools and maintenance shops. I began to get very interested in aviation, myself, and it became my lifetime occupation.

I'd never flown until one day when one of Jack Robinson's pilots was going to fly to Dallas, and he asked me if I'd like to go with him. I hesitated, but Steve encouraged me to go ahead. So, excited as a kid, I agreed, and it was quite an experience! First, I called Mama, who was at home, and it scared her. She reminded me I had three little kids at home; I needed to remember that, as if I'd be leaving forever. I assured her that I'd be with a good, experienced pilot, and would be OK.

So we flew to Redbird Airport in Dallas, a small airport, and then on to Love Field. As we took off from Redbird, I realized my door was a little ajar. I alerted Jerry, the pilot, so he landed the Cherokee, closed the door, and we were off again. What a thrill it was. I'll always remember that first flight, although I've flown many times since then!

It wasn't long until we moved the school into a larger place. It was a larger hangar; there were several planes and some work was going on in there. The place belonged to a couple who'd been active on the airport for several years. I learned to do "dope and fabric" work, and I watched and learned how to do many more tasks. In the meantime, Steve's wife, Dot, who'd been my best friend since 1949, began to want to work with Steve, doing what she could in my place. For the first time, I was laid off, and she moved in. She had her 2-year-old twins with her, playing in the shop, and it proved to be a dangerous situation.

Through the years, Steve became more apt to chase women. I never knew what to believe about what he said, but I decided it didn't matter. I didn't care to hear about his conquests and told him so, but he seemed to need to tell me. I was not interested. I knew he talked to Dot and told her whatever he wanted to. I wanted her to know I was in no way involved in his escapades, but there was no way to diplomatically let her know, and she only grew cooler to me as time went on.

And then he settled, somewhat, on a woman who was not capable of working, but was involved with him. He bought her a car, took trips with her, and didn't try to hide the affair from anyone. We dubbed her "Basket Case." Dot knew about her, and it softened her attitude toward me. She caught them together several times, threatened them, and at one point, put all of Steve's clothes in suitcases and left them at the school. She finally relented and let him come back home.

She explained to me and others that he was the one who was working, and she needed him to take care of the family financially, so she just kept trying to get him to straighten up, which never happened. Then one evening, he went out to a small airport where he kept his plane. After all this time, he had got his private pilot license. He took his airplane up—the airport had no lights, and it had become dark—he crashed his airplane, and broke his neck.

Little by little, we learned that he'd called his son to take him to the hospital. They installed a brace on his head that reached down to his shoulders to keep his head erect; he wore it the rest of his life. We also learned that Basket Case was with him at the airport, but obviously not on the plane with him when it crashed. Before long, he contracted cancer, and was bedfast. I went to see him near the end, and we talked. He seemed a little apologetic, but I didn't hold a grudge. I was sorry he had hurt his family, and actually himself in the process.

He died soon after that. I took Dot to the hospital when it happened. I told her I'd missed her, and hoped she knew that I hadn't been involved with Steve. She said she knew, and there were no hard feelings between us. A little while later, Dot had a bad stroke. She was sent to Manor Care on Skyline Drive. Ironically, she was put in a room next to, of all people, Basket Case. Dot couldn't talk any more—she could laugh, but didn't seem to be mentally alert any more. She died a few years later. Steve had closed Stephens Aircraft School, and she sold the building after he died. He'd never regained his DME.

The first heart attack Sherman had was a few days after we had gone to see Paulette and Bill in Fort Myers, Florida. It was the first of several. At one point, he had surgery, replacing 2 valves that were stopped up. I was warned that his disposition could sometimes be affected, so I should be ready to accept changes in his personality.

I think Sherman had been depressed since he was 36 years old and never recovered, except for short periods, with long intervals between. Like some of the rest of the Ruffin family, he had a curt way to answer questions, and he didn't seem to realize that this could be hurtful at times.

Many times after that, he had to be rushed to the hospital to be cared for, and I never knew if he was going to make it or not. A few times, he was sent for some extra care to a part of the hospital called a skilled nursing center, and would stay 20 or 30 days. Then he'd recover and go back to work. He retired at 65 years.

Maybe retirement isn't exactly the right way to tell the story. He had been taking strong pain medicine to relieve pain from several crushed vertebrae, and had been adding alcohol to enhance their effects. Complicated with severe arthritis and emphysema, he was in a pretty bad physical condition. He had just bought a new truck after wrecking his several times when he came home and announced that he was now retired. I only later learned that he had been fired that day.

He had repressed his alcoholism all these years. It's a shame that a man with Sherman's abilities, intelligence, and talents will throw it all away for a bottle of vodka. He seemed to give up after I started Love Aviation with Morris. I am not wholly innocent of causing some of his concerns, but I was true to him, working hard to have something and to take care of both of us.

I was concerned about him, but I was also concerned about the school, and, I guess, about my own needs. We didn't love much any more, and didn't share our lives as we once had. I had friends and a job to do. He was home alone; had neighbors, but was all alone for the most part. I used to go to the places where Paulette and Bill were playing: clubs, restaurants, and such. Sometimes I went alone, sometimes I went with some other family member or friend. He stopped going with me because he realized the drinking was getting a little tough to handle. Still, he drank at home when I was gone.

One day in September, 1989, I came home from work and found Sherman in his recliner, drunk and angry. He had broken the stained glass lampshade that Thom had made for us, and the multi-colored shards were scattered throughout the living room. I began cleaning it up as Sherman complained about the neighbor having given us a dozen eggs, two of which were bad. The neighbor came over, and I explained to her that we appreciated the eggs. I also told her that I was leaving Sherman because of his drinking. I gathered up clothes and makeup, loaded my car, and left.

I rented an apartment in Benbrook and bought some appliances that I needed at the nearby Walmart. I had two bedrooms, and Paulette and Matt soon moved into the apartment with me. Paulette left Bill at that time, but they continued to perform together. Matt was very unhappy. At three years old, he missed his Daddy. They soon got back together.

After a while, I saw Galen, my lawyer. He was helping me with the sale of my school to Dalfort, and I instructed him to draw up divorce papers for me. I didn't want any property except my car, and I had paid for that. I used some of the proceeds from the sale to pay off Sherman's truck and to return the $10,000 he had loaned me from a stock liquidation. The rest went into investments and a vacation with my kids in Cancun. The divorce was final a few months later, and the school was moved to Dallas Love Field from Arlington. The buyers built a beautiful new school facility in the old Braniff building, and I was to be the director for three years.

During this time, Sherman and I were on cool, but friendly terms. He would come and watch Matt while Paulette and I would go out for the evening.

Dalfort sent me to Tulsa to check out some schools there, to see if they wanted to buy them. Sherman wanted to go with me on the trip, and promised there would be no drinking. He had begun to talk about us getting back together. I felt guilty, but mostly I worried about his physical condition and didn't want to be responsible for any more hurt. We flew to Tulsa together, and talked seriously about getting back together. We visited the schools together. Nothing came of the school visits, but Sherman and I were back together within a week of returning. We married again a few weeks later. We bought a new house in Watauga, and waited for it to be completed inside. Thom and Paulette were our decorators, selecting furnishings and other touches to make it special. Margaret hung the drapes and curtains.

Several weeks later, Sherman fell off the wagon. He seemed to want me to find that bottle in the paper bag in the pantry by the garbage can, as if his guilt needed external guidance. He had been acting strangely, and I should have suspected, but I guess I closed my eyes to it.

He told me, "I guess you want me to leave now."

"No," I said. "We'll try one more thing."

I took him to Charter rehab in Grapevine, but he was totally unimpressed with the facility. We went on to Schick Hospital in North Richland Hills where I issued the ultimatum. He would come out dry, or we were through.

After our nine-month separation, Sherman took care of Matt a lot. He'd take him to school and go back after him. Matt loved him dearly, and we depended on him. Also, there was no problem about the drinking, because I saw that he went to the center to help him quit drinking. And it did the job.

Paulette married Jeff, and she and Bill shared custody of Matt. Matt went to school in Grapevine close to their house. He was with Bill and his wife, Becca on weekends.

Sherman missed him, but watched TV a lot, read books, or just sat quietly. He was hurting all the time with arthritis and bad discs. Paulette died in 1993, and he never seemed to recover from losing her. He lived until 2001.

It's a beautiful fall day—about 65 degrees. Summer is about over, and it seems that it had hardly begun. I had my 83rd birthday August 22, less than 2 months ago. Nothing spectacular—I had wrangled a birthday lunch from Ken Elliott. We met at Ginger Brown's, and went to Applebee's across the highway. It was a very nice lunch, and a couple of girls sang Happy Birthday to me.

Another time, Ken and his drummer and I performed at Fireside Lodge. I had talked to the activities director, and she called Ken. He called me and asked if I wanted to sing with him. Of course I did. We may have talked twice since then, but I guess our getting together or even talking to each other is over. He didn't answer his phone when I called him, so I've quit calling him. It's hard to give up on a good friend, but sometimes necessary. As it turned out, we got back together later.

I've been taking a study course, Experiencing God by Henry Blackerby at Karen and Gary's, taught by Alice Bradshaw. My neighbor and good friend, Ken Bino has been going some. Ken is a good friend, and we have become close. He said he is through with Natalie, the girl who stole from me.

It occurs to me that for so many years, I've been looking after so many people, I've missed a lot of any life I might have had. I don't really feel that I've missed so much, and I wouldn't change anything, I guess, but sometimes people take advantage of you, and it can get worse and worse.

I loved Margaret. We grew up together, and being whole sisters, we had a lot in common. Margaret was smart, pretty, and helped me as we grew up, her being 2 years older. I depended on her. There was just a touch of something wrong. I didn't know, of course, how to analyze the actions she took or remarks she made, etc. But finally, in later years, I've thought about it and can see things clearer.

I could see, early on, that there seemed to be quite a difference in Mama's attitude toward us. She gave a distinct preference to Margaret. She was good to both of us, but I could tell she trusted me to be more independent. She expected me to understand why she preferred Margaret to me. In a way, I guess I did, but still, it was more of acceptance than understanding. I can see much clearer now, after so much time has passed, why she and Daddy were trying so hard, and trusting me to help.

Margaret was jealous of me all my life. I never knew why, except it was finally clear to me that she had a slight emotional disorder. She was much prettier, had a good personality, and in a lot of ways was very attractive. We sang, were talented, and loved music and social gatherings. But we rarely agreed on anything, and grew apart, and lived different lives altogether. We kept playing music and singing, but not together much. She never seemed to like my playing and singing, and I never heard any compliments from her. When Sherman and I were together, I could tell she was jealous, and I didn't know why.

Margaret worked all her life. A lot of the time, she sewed. She could tailor, and did beautiful handwork. But as time went on, we grew older and she lost the ability to do the delicate work she'd done so many years. She had always had the responsibility of taking care of her family, being the only one who worked to make a living. After her husband, Jack died, she had the responsibility of taking care of her son and her grandchildren.

She came by my school, the last one I had, at Meacham Field, and I could see something was badly wrong. It was the first indication I had that her old problem had become a mental problem. Maybe I'd been blind to that fact, but now I could see plainly. About this time, she had been seeing a doctor or two at John Peter Smith Hospital, and they had kept diagnosing her with dementia. Eventually, they decided it was Alzheimer's disease. But I could tell it was a misdiagnosis; she had no symptoms of Alzheimer's. For a time, I let her live with me, but it was a bad situation, and eventually she had to go back home. Finally, they located the problem. She had brain cancer. She'd had to have a breast removed, and the cancer reappeared in the brain. Later, they'd decided it wasn't cancer after all, but the effects of mini-strokes and other stresses that had caused damage.

We closed the school down, Boni and I, and by the time Margaret had come here, Sherman had died. I knew if he'd been here he'd never let me move her in. But it was a disaster; I just didn't know what else to do. I'd always had to care for her.

Margaret had a sorry life and died at 80 years. We took her to Moran Cemetery in Oklahoma for burial next to her husband, Jack, and close to Mama and Daddy.

I received some of the money that had been sent to Fireside Lodge. It was a nice sum. I gave some of it to Jacky and Manda, and the rest I spent for a double headstone for Margaret and Jack. I now had the responsibility for J. J., but I have had it all along. Ten months after Margaret died, J. J. was killed, as I've already written, and was buried in the county cemetery. I've never seen his grave. Jacky and Manda live alone in the downtown area.

Phil, Thom, Sherman, and me

The only times I ever heard Daddy use really bad language were when he was working with the mules or horses. His words would turn the air blue—he'd hold nothing back. I asked Mama about it when I was very young, and she explained to me that somehow, men thought they were the only words the mules or horses understood. So I guess it was understood that they were the only words they knew. I wasn't convinced, but I knew that was the only time I heard him say those things.

Actually, Daddy loved those animals, and was very affectionate with them at times. Much later, he sold the mules and got Beauty, a beautiful black horse, and another one or two. For the most part, though, he had given up on using a team of two, and did his plowing with "Ol' Beauty." Once, he bought a great little spotted pony. I loved Tony (as we named him) but we couldn't keep a horse just to ride, as I wanted him for.

I loved to ride. I rode Ol' Blue a time or two from the field after a day's work. The first time I rode Ol' Beauty, I went to the store in Rufe. I didn't know why some men laughed at me. When I got home, I found out why. I had put the work bridle on her, also called a "Blind" bridle. It had blinders to keep the mule focused only ahead. No wonder I had drawn attention and been laughed at! I was mortified when Daddy pointed it out to me.

The Wilsons were our good friends, Ocie, Roy, and their two sons, Juandell and Beverly. They lived a mile or so from us. They had traded for a fine horse called Prince, who was a very large tan and white horse; it was said that they gave 2 pounds of butter for him. I didn't know about that, but I loved Prince. I rode him and I felt like I was 50 feet high, he was so tall. But he was fun—a little frisky, but I'd been told to always be the "boss" with horses, and it works. I heard someone say that Prince had killed someone before. I didn't know if it was true or not, but I was happy to ride him. But they sold him before long.

I was never the "boss" with the mules. They were "boss." I'd be running a planter with Ol'Blue, laying seed where Daddy had plowed; he'd look over and see Daddy with Rhody, and regardless of my yelling at him, he'd go to the extreme right or left, to wherever Daddy and Rhody were. I was totally unaware of what to do, and Daddy would laugh and get Blue back in the row where he belonged.

I loved working with Daddy. I hated parts of working in the fields, but I enjoyed our talks, and Daddy was a lot of fun to work with when it was just us. I didn't like working in the field with Lewie; he was too bossy!

Robert was fun, and not very prone to do a lot of farm work. We'd mess around, stop and rest, find bugs, etc. I loved being with him. Sometimes I worked alone, hoeing a field, picking a little cotton; I never accomplished a lot, but did a lot of daydreaming and writing novels in my mind, sometimes creating lyrics to a song and immediately forgetting them.

I always loved to cook, especially pies, cakes, or cookies, but I could also cook other things. I wasn't too fond of housework, but I could wash, iron, and sew. I even worked in the garden some. Mama and I didn't work together much. I loved her, and she was a good mother, but she talked incessantly and wouldn't listen when I talked. I'm sorry now that I wasn't quiet and more interested in what she was saying. She was a wise woman, and I guess I didn't realize then just how wise she was. It wasn't that I never heard her, and it's amazing how much you hear and remember later. She used to remind me that she could talk with the other girls, but I was a little impatient with her.

I wish now I could ask her about so many things I'd like to know; some things about the family I wonder about. And I'd also like to know more about Daddy's family.

When Sherman and I moved out of our one-room apartment on East Belknap, we moved into a two-room apartment at 912 West First Street, right off Henderson Street. Henderson Street was a continuation of Jacksboro Highway, State Highway 199. Sherman's sister, Effie and her husband, Andy lived there at the time; it was a large home, converted to one- and two-room apartments, with one bathroom downstairs for all the tenants on that floor. There was a small laundromat right outside our back door.

The first time I went out back to the laundromat, someone told me about a sewing machine for sale next door. I really missed the Singer we had at home. I went next door to see about it. Sure enough, it was an old forerunner to Singer—a Wheeler-Wilson, and it was an oldie. But I got it for only $20.00. Someone there helped me get it home to our apartment. It was a treadle. We got it there, and I was excited! At last I could sew.

In those days, fabric was so cheap, I could make a dress for very little, and patterns were also cheap. A while later, we had an electric motor installed on it. That made it into a portable—easier to carry around, but not an improvement in the performance of the machine. Much later, we traded it in for a nice cabinet machine: a Singer that lasted until 1989. That's when Paulette and I decided to get a better set-up for our dry cleaning shop, and we used it to do some sewing. Paulette learned to use it and the serger that came with it. I gave up on that, and got a whole new set-up after her death in 1993.

While we lived in the apartment on First Street, we enjoyed being with Effie and Andy, who only lived there a short time. Andy lost his job, and they separated. Effie moved to California and married Harold Stevens. They lived in Oroville, California in a double-wide trailer, and raised two of Harold's grandchildren: Paul and Carrie. Andy died several years later in Fort Worth. I visited him in the funeral home, and was a little surprised to see how good he looked.

In 1980, Sherman and I visited Effie and Harold. I was disappointed with Harold. He was overbearing and a nag to the kids and Effie. I understand Effie became an alcoholic and died sometime after Harold. The granddaughter, Carrie, took care of Effie until she died. I loved Effie. She was a dear person, and we were great friends. She had wanted to come to Fort Worth, but Harold had convinced her that if they moved, or even if they came on a visit, he would automatically lose the pension he was drawing. She believed him. He was her 5th husband, but she had married one twice.

Effie was a beautiful girl—naturally blonde, blue eyes, and lovely features. She never had a child of her own, but helped with others, and always wanted her own. She was sweet-natured, and laughed a lot. No wonder I loved her and we got along great.

I learned that Paul, the sweet boy with whom I climbed a mountain nearby, got on the wrong track and the family quit hearing from him. I was so sorry; I remembered the fun we had climbing the mountain together. But right after that, I remembered Harold going into a tirade and browbeating him. I could hardly keep quiet. Paul took it, but I could see the resentment building in him.

In later years, Sherman and I visited Richard and JoAnne, but we didn't visit Effie and Harold. I hated to miss them, but had to admit I didn't really miss their tirades. We always enjoyed Richard, Sherman's brother, and his wife, JoAnne. They had great kids. Richard retired from the Army, and he and JoAnne remained in Moses Lake, Washington. Richard died a few years ago. Their son, Scott, was badly injured in a car accident on the night of his high school prom. He is paralyzed from his waist down, but makes his own living and a life for himself. He lives alone and is independent, but a heart goes out to him for what he has been through, and still goes through, all these years. JoAnne and I are good friends, although we don't talk often.

Sherman's brothers, James and Earl both moved home after Earl's wife, "Tommie" died from complications of a miscarriage. The rumor that it was a botched abortion are probably false. Their little 4-year-old girl, Earline, and 10-month-old Robert were raised after that by my mother-in-law, Agnes Ruffin. Earl married a young girl, Helen Harrell; they were married a short time, divorced, and he married another young girl, Mable. They stayed together until Earl's death in the '90s, and had two other children, Alvin and Mary. The oldest daughter, Earline, died with bone cancer several years before Earl's death. Mable and Earl raised a son of Earline's, Gene, who never knew Earline was his mother until her death. He had been raised to believe he was Earl and Mable's son. It was a tragic discovery for him. He was already grown, and had thought Earline and Joe's two girls were his nieces, but found they were actually his sisters. Earlene had had an illicit affair in California while Joe was deployed elsewhere in the Air Force. A great-looking blond girl, lonely and away from home, she immediately gave her son to her parents. He was not told the secret until her death.

When Earl and Mable moved to Fort Worth, they both worked. Mama kept Gene for a while after Mrs. Agnes Ruffin, my mother-in-law, died. Gene was a sweet, chubby, little redhead. Mama got really attached to him. She also kept a neighbor boy, and always was available to keep Jacky, Margaret's child. Earline died in a nursing home after suffering a long bout of bone cancer. Earl died much later of a heart attack, not long before Sherman's death.

James was married to Bessie Watson, and they had 2 kids: Minnie Bea and Troy, the same ages as Earl's two. After the war ended and James was discharged, he brought the two kids home. Bessie had left him. Mrs. Ruffin helped raise them for a while.

Sherman came home then, too, and all these families were living there for a while. I feel that I wouldn't have given Sherman a second thought if he'd had children. Who knows? But, as much as I loved kids, I was only a year older than the wives of James and Earl, and I knew I was too young to raise children.

Minnie Bea and Troy came home with us once and stayed a few weeks. Minnie Bea had grown to be a pretty young lady, and fell for a neighbor boy, Truett Campbell. Truett went into the Navy, and they were married. Soon, they divorced, and Minnie Bea went to live with her mother, Bessie. They both became alcoholics. James married Fredaline Whatley, and they had two sons, Gordon and Jimmy, and a daughter, Yveta. Troy became a preacher, and has been pastor of a church for many years. He also preaches funerals at a funeral home there in Valliant. His church is between Valliant and Idabel, close to Wheelock Academy, a school built for Indian children years ago.

James divorced Fredaline later and married Georgia. She had a little store where she sold handiwork, and had a room full of birds she bought and sold. I haven't seen her since James died with lung cancer. It's always a challenge for me to try to remember family history, so many things happen in a family over the years.

Two or three years ago, I got word that Earl's son, Robert, had died. He'd been living about 15 or 20 miles from me, and I hadn't seen him in several years. He "broke" horses, and taught people to ride and care for their horses. He had been married three times, always to someone named Linda. He was taken back to Oklahoma for burial. The funeral home owner had called me (we are good friends) and told me Robert's funeral expenses here were never paid, and his wife had never made any payments toward their taking care of his body. He was buried in the yard of their old home in the country.

In 1947, Sherman and I were already a little weary of one- or two-room apartments in a crowded building. It was just too many people, all sharing a bathroom, with mice, rats, roaches, and other undesirable creatures. We'd been living at 912 W. First Street for a few months when Margaret came to Fort Worth. She stayed with us for a few days, and looked for a job and a place to live. She and the guy she'd been dating in Oklahoma, Tom Barnett, had broken up, and there was some mystery that involved the two of them, Daddy, and Vernon.

I knew she was unhappy, because she'd been crazy about Tom. He'd gone to Colorado where his brother, Jerry eventually followed him. Margaret never heard from him until much later, but she started going to some dances. That worried Sherman and me. She eventually married a fellow she met there, Jack Nordin.

She and I started out walking one day, just to see Fort Worth and some of the places of interest. We walked and kept planning to catch a bus, but never did. We walked until evening, took some pictures, and went to 6 points in Riverside. We decided to go down Main Street, and kept going until we got to Diamond Hill. We turned right off Main Street onto 28th St. and to a little house where my friend, Nadine Steele lived with her new husband. They'd just built the house, a small 2- or 3-room building, cute and little. They planned to build on later.

We visited quite a while. Nadine had lived next to us in the apartment house on W. First St., where we'd become good friends. Nadine was older than I, maybe in her 50s.

She told me about a place in the west part of town. She said you could buy a good size lot for $10.00 down and $5.00 per month. She also told me the lots were large, there were many of them, and the place had been a pasture for Boswell Dairies. I was very interested, so she told me how to find out about it. We arrived home, tired from walking all day. The next day, I went downtown to see Sherman, who was working in the building then occupied by Monnig's Department Store. We both, Sherman and I, wanted to check out the lots Nadine had told us about. Sherman said he didn't have $10.00 to pay down on a lot, and also was afraid to try to take our old Plymouth that far. So, the answer to many of our problems, my brother, Richard loaned us his '33 Ford and the $10.00 we needed to pay down for the lot. A while later, he sold us the Ford for a small price. It was a very dependable car. We sold our Plymouth to Leon Foster, who drove it for a long time.

I'll always remember the first time we went out to see 5609 Buchanan Street in Sansom Park. We never even considered another place; we loved it from the start. There was some Johnson grass to deal with, and many wildflowers blooming. It looked like Heaven to us. The lot was 65 x 180 feet, large enough for a garden and some chickens!

We'd also seen on the way there a little 12 x 24 house, partly finished on the inside. We decided to ask about it, and quickly discarded the idea. We made the deal for the lot. It was one-third acre, and as we'd hoped, Nadine had been right about the payments. The total price was $539.00

Sherman talked to his boss, Mr. Good, and he agreed to sign the loan at First National Bank for $300. We went to Castleberry Lumber Company on White Settlement Road for enough lumber to start a two-room house. Sherman surprised me; he was so good at building, electrical, plumbing, and all the other skills it took to make the little house livable. We used kerosene to cook with, and by the time summer was over, we had butane gas. I went to a furniture place downtown and got just enough furniture to get by—a bed, a heater, and a five-piece unfinished dinette suite. Sherman built a little cabinet and other things we needed, including a privy (toilet) out back, which our next-door neighbors also used. Later, people began to move into the neighborhood, which merited a city hall in the next block. We also got a school two blocks down, where all three of our kids went to elementary school, part of the Castleberry School District. And shortly, we did gain a sewer system for the area.

There were only a few neighbors nearby, but we did have a couple next door who were friends. Meantime, at one of the clubs Margaret went to, she met Jack Nordin. He worked at Container Corporation in Fort Worth. Before long, they were married. We tried to talk her out of it, but she was determined. Jack was a lot older than Margaret, and antisocial, partly because of his eyes. They were crossed, and he was very self-conscious. Margaret continued to work, as she did all her life.

Margaret and Jack lived in an apartment in town. Jack soon quit his job, encouraged to do so by Margaret, to get a better one. But he couldn't find one, and resorted to bus and cab driving. Margaret arranged for his eyes to be operated on and straightened. The surgery was a success, but it didn't do much for his antisocial attitude. I had a feeling Margaret thought since Sherman could do well at a job, Jack could too. But it never happened. Before long, Jacky Junior, a little red-haired boy was born.

The year was 1949. My Tommy (Thom) was a year old (actually 23 months) when Daddy died. Janice, Ruby's youngest daughter, was born December 28, that same day. Jacky had been born in October.

Tommy, as we called him until his first year in school, was very fond of his Tom Daddy, and Daddy was so proud of him. I know Daddy was thrilled that we named Tommy after him. He'd take Tommy out in the yard, and if he got into the road (which was not widely traveled), Daddy would follow him with a stick in his hand. We all knew he'd never use the stick on Tommy, but felt like it would discourage him, but he always knew his Tom Daddy wouldn't use it.

The name Tom Daddy was carried down with the other two who knew him by that name, but never actually knew him, because Daddy was gone before the other two were born. I remember once Daddy told me, "Pauline, I know Tommy needs a spanking once in a while, but I wish you would wait till I'm gone—I won't live much longer, and I just can't stand to see you or Sherman spank him. It hurts me too bad." So we promised not to spank him while Daddy was still with us.

Daddy was digging post holes for Dale and Rose Jones next door when he had a bad stroke. He never walked again. Dale had crossties for his fence posts; they raised chickens and some other fowl, and he wanted a high fence to keep them in their yard.

Daddy became very ill and lived about 10 days after that. We sat up with him nights, because he was so ill. One night, it was my turn, and Charles Russell, pastor of Broadview Baptist Church, stayed up with me. We spent the whole night discussing my relationship with the Lord and my affiliation with the church back home, which was not Baptist. Since Charles Russell had a great influence on me, and I had been seeking for some right answers to the questions that plagued me a lot, I promised to read the Bible and find answers for myself. I began to read the Bible in earnest and to find some facts I had been looking for. Charles and Ora, his wife, were our good friends for many years, and still are. He retired several years ago, and they live in Mineral Wells, Texas. I'll always be grateful for his help, and their friendship.

Daddy died a few days later. His funeral was the first one Charles ever preached. He went with us to bury Daddy in Moran Cemetery in Oklahoma.

Chapter 12

"Get your own school."

The move from Love Field in Dallas to our new place in Arlington was quite an operation. Morris, my partner, had pulled out to concentrate on his career at Southwest Airlines and whatever his new life held for him. I missed him, but I realized he needed to go in a different direction. I asked him if he needed anything from the school, and he said no. He just wanted me to do well, and to make the business a great success.

I was amazed again at what a good man the Lord had provided for my business partner, and how he'd been exactly what I'd needed to get started. He and I talked recently about how risky it is to select a partner in business. He promised to come back the next week to make videos of my teaching the Inspection Authorization course. Over a few days, we completed the whole thing. We went through the entire IA course, with me explaining and showing materials. It was not an instant success, but as time went on, it gained more interest. I'll always been grateful to Morris for offering to do this, and for the popularity it eventually gained.

Paulette and Bill came back to Fort Worth the first day we were at Arlington, and we began to get the new place going. I could trust them to take care of so many things. Paulette had just found out she was pregnant; she was thrilled, and that was one reason they decided to come home from the east.

I had several employees, and the school was going great. We started working on getting the shop ready, and Bill took over a lot of the paperwork, all this for the certified school. I was teaching and doing other things, keeping the refresher courses going, and also helping to get things ready for certification. I bought equipment and parts, and worked closely with the FAA.

There were several men who wanted to buy, or buy into, the school. It was definitely not for sale either way. I turned down several offers, and I realized that some men thought I was doing a job that should be done by a man. I had the same response to each of them. I'd started the school, had put my heart into it, and did not feel that I needed to share it with anyone. "Get your own school," I'd tell them.

Celebrating the sale of Love Aviation to Dalfort

I know I was known as a stubborn woman, and that was OK. The more I had to fight to keep the school, the stronger I became. And it paid off, if not in money, certainly in pride and the satisfaction of accomplishing what the Lord had led me to do.

Paulette and Bill never gave up their musical career. They were a duo in Granbury and other places, although Paulette was the main one, the soloist. Bill was an ingenious musician, and sang some, too. They had left New York, Thousand Islands, South Dakota, and other places to come home, and they were so good to help me. My pride in the school included those who instructed: the office workers, the students, and others who were largely responsible for the success of the school.

Many of the students kept in touch with me long afterward. Some have visited me and called me. Paulette has been gone since 1993, and Bill is out of my life, but they are still a large part of my school memories and gratitude.

Nine months after our divorce was final, Sherman and I decided to go back together. He had expressed the desire to try again, to make our marriage work. After all, we were married from 1946 to 1990—44 years! They'd been good years, and would have continued if we'd tried harder and hadn't let circumstances interfere. Our interests had been opposites, and neither of us was ready to comply with the other.

I was working for Dalfort at the time, still under contract with them after selling them the school. They were sending me to Tulsa, Oklahoma to talk to some people, and to visit a school or two there. Sherman wanted to go with me, so I agreed, and we had an understanding that he would not be drinking. He declared that he would give up drinking entirely if I would go back with him.

So we had a good chance to be together again and talk things over. I didn't readily agree to go back with him, but I could see that he was not real well, and probably needed me to look after him. We visited two of the aviation schools in and near Tulsa. One of my good friends and a former student, Andy and his wife lived there. He was a teacher in one of the schools; he'd been divorced, and had come to Tulsa after marrying again. We went to have supper with them; I was so glad to see him, and was very impressed with his workplace. He was over the jet engine department, and showed us through the school. It was very well equipped; I've never seen so many jet engines, all in various stages of assembly and disassembly.

We flew home and set the date. In May, shortly after the Tulsa trip, we bought our new house on Lyndale Drive. Paulette was with us. She and Thom came out the day after we made the deal, and made several decisions about the decorating. They were both excellent at this; I hate to think what the place would have looked like without their decorating skills. Paulette went with us and helped select some furniture, drapes, etc., and loved doing it. And then it was time to plan the wedding. Meantime, Paulette was divorced, Bill had married Becca, and Paulette was dating Jeff Agnew and working in downtown Fort Worth. She and Bill shared custody of Matt.

When Paulette had the first surgery, they removed only one breast. She seemed to do well. I wondered a lot of times whether the cancer eventually became evident in the one remaining or, actually, if it really had become cancerous. It was some time later that the cancer doctor decided to remove the other breast; I don't know if the cancer reappeared, or they just thought it would later. But she had the other one removed, and also had reconstruction for both. She took it well. She seemed to be doing fine; she worked for me in the store, Paulette's Sassy Fashions, where I also taught some classes. I had signed a contract with Dalfort that I wouldn't start another school, but the contract was broken when they laid me off. Paulette was working for me, and she also worked in the office at Johnnie High's Country Music Revue, using her skills in computer work. At the same time, she and Sylvia White were singing at the funeral homes in and around Fort Worth. Their voices were a little alike; some people couldn't tell them apart.

Occasionally, a funeral would affect Paulette in a way that would make her sad, and swear she would quit, but she didn't. Once, there was an old woman about Mama's age, and it really upset Paulette. Also, if it was a young child, it would get to her.

She was having no symptoms of the cancer, except some back trouble. But after a whole year of freedom from pain, the cancer reappeared in her back. I was with her when they did a scan, and it showed up as a red angry-looking spot on her spine.

She took some shots of sharks' spinal fluid, which hadn't been approved by the FDA, but she was willing to try anything that might help. It didn't, obviously. She entered the hospital in October, 1993, for stem cell replacement. It was experimental, and made her extremely ill, but was a complete failure. She had chosen to go in October, because she hoped to be home with Matt for Christmas. But the day before Christmas Eve, we went to her funeral at Grapevine First Baptist Church, and burial at Greenwood Cemetery. Our little Paulette was dead at 40 years old.

It's nearly 8 PM, and I was watching an old movie on television. I prefer the old movies; I am not very interested in the regular TV shows. Thom and Debby came yesterday about 4:30 PM and stayed all night with me. Sherry and I fixed supper for them: Sherry, Kyle, Jonathan, and Jamie. Sherry cooked a ham and vegetables, and I made hot rolls and two coconut pies. Thom and Debby and I went to Joe's for breakfast before they left town the next morning,

We were going to watch the UFO movie last night, but my DVD wouldn't work, so Thom went out and bought me a new player. He also bought several movies, and we watched one last night. It was "An Affair to Remember," a great old movie. I don't think I'd ever seen it before.

Thom and Debby have made plans for me to visit them in Virginia for Thanksgiving—I'll be there 6 days. I have my ticket and schedule. I'll leave November 24 and come home on the 30th.

Matt was supposed to come and eat with us last night. He got busy and forgot, and was very upset when Jonathan called him. Then he talked to me, and I assured him that it was okay and not to worry. He was tired, and had a bad day. I'm worried about him.

The next morning, while I was busy getting myself together, my good friend, Nicole and her two little girls came. We had a nice visit. After they left, I finished my morning rituals and called Randall. I asked him for his opinion about an e-mail I got last night. Susan Hester, our pastor's wife, and another teacher where she worked, sent me a note asking me to come to their school for career day to do a presentation concerning my own career. I explained to Randall that I had dropped out of high school. I got my GED later, but I knew some of the students would ask me where I'd gone to college. Actually, I taught at Tarrant County Junior College for a couple of years part time, two nights a week.

Randall has done a little of everything in his working life, but his education was about the same as mine. So we discussed it at length, and I decided to call Susan and explain it to her. I went to Manor Care. It was about 4 PM when I left, so I went by to see Johnnie at Avalon. He was sitting up, but hurting, and wanting to go back to bed. He wouldn't eat, but they said he'd had a good lunch. After he went to sleep, I left, and went by Denny's for a little supper.

I came on home, sat down in my recliner, and turned on the TV. The phone rang. It was Sonya, my neighbor from across the street. She and the two kids came over for a little while. The weather is cooler tonight; supposed to be in the 40s. I called Susan—she was spending a late evening at school—and talked to her husband, our pastor. I told him my story, that I probably shouldn't do the presentation. He was surprised at my lack of education. We had a good conversation; he told me I surprised him every time we talked.

Pauline Rice called me today, and asked me if I could take her to her heart doctor next Tuesday. I assured her I could. I made a table runner for Sherry's table yesterday. She'd helped me pick out the fabric and the fringe. It turned out well. She sent a picture of it to Phil, and he sent it to me with one word: cute. So now, I'm getting ready to make myself a warm robe. I got the fabric yesterday. I need it to take with me when I go to Virginia for Thanksgiving.

Some good news: Sherry has a permanent job starting Monday at the same school where she had been working, and Phil had a long interview with a company in Houston that seems promising. It's much closer to home for him, so we're hoping it happens.

The next day, Johnnie was much better; I guess the pneumonia is about gone, but he's awfully helpless and contrary. Thom is supposed to be here on the 4th of next month. I guess he's passing through, haven't heard any more. Phil's Houston job didn't come through; they wouldn't pay his fare to go there for an interview. He suggested a video interview, but he hasn't heard anything about that for sure. But Sherry is about ready to sell their house and go to him in Ohio.

I got a call from Alan Cook. He's in the VA hospital in Dallas, waiting to see what they want to do next for him. His brother, Warren, also has bladder cancer, and has started taking chemo. Alan doesn't feel well, and for the first time I can remember, he didn't sound fine.

Ginger Brown's is tomorrow night, but due to the music licensing fee increases, she can't afford Jeff and Karen anymore. They'll still be playing at Tater Junction, as far as we know now. I'll miss going to hear them, but I doubt I'll drive to Aurora and Tater Junction on Saturday nights.

I got the news on Facebook that my brother, Robert, was in the hospital in Idabel with pneumonia. Sherry (my daughter-in-law) and I left the next day. We stopped in Valliant for me a cup of coffee and Sherry a soft drink. While we were there, a woman of 77 or so years of age came over and talked to us. She said she was from Powderly and was lonely, because her family had moved away. She was going to stay at a motel in Valliant next to the café for the next 5 years. I told her my Daddy had helped build the school at Powderly, and at the same time had cooked at our friend's restaurant. His specialty was making pancakes, and he used to make them at home after that.

We drove on to the Microtel Inn, and stayed in the same room Laurine, her daughter Jennifer and I had stayed in the last time we went to see Robert and Omia. We then went on to the nursing home, and saw Omia a while. I got a call from Thom while we were there in Robert's room. He told me he'd see me Thursday, and we would see him in Waxahachie for supper. I talked to Roy, and he said he'd meet us at Catfish King. We met him, had lunch, and then saw Robert in the hospital. As usual, we had a great supper at Catfish King, and Sherry and I went back to the motel.

We decided to go to Walmart to buy a pair of pillows. After sleeping on them last night, we were happy we got the pillows. We got up about 7 AM today, had a cupcake and coffee (me), and went back to see Omia a few minutes. We went on to the hospital, stopped at the gift shop, and saw some people I knew and some Robert knew or had known before. We got Robert a couple of books—he still could read—and we got him a bird vase with yellow roses, some candy, and gum. We saw Robert for a few minutes; he was hoping to go "home" in a little while (to the nursing home). We found out later that he did go back to the nursing home, so I know Omia was happy; she's been really worried about him. It rained all the way home.

I was sitting in my recliner, watching Mogambo, an old film starring Clark Gable, Ava Gardner, and Grace Kelly, plus a large part of Africa's population. It's been a busy afternoon. I talked to Randall; he and Dee were going to come and go to Joe's with me for lunch, but he was trying to make arrangements for Dee to have some surgery on Monday, and there were complications. Finally, he had her set up for a pre-op about noon, so our lunch was postponed for tomorrow. I ate some leftover pizza, and went to Joe Smith's funeral. He'd been at Manor Care a couple of weeks, and I could see that he was bad. He tried to talk to me, but couldn't, except to say "Hello, Pauline." Joe had been a deacon at Broadview years before they had moved to the church at Lake Worth, and his wife, Doris, had died a few months ago.

I was a little late getting the game started at Manor Care after doing some visiting first. We had several certificates made out for the veterans there. I passed them out, and expressed appreciation to the ones receiving them. Among them was my neighbor, Rose Jones, who had been in the Coast Guard many years ago.

We played a game, finished at 4 PM, and I went to see Johnnie at Avalon. I had supper with him, and didn't stay long afterward. I came on home, as it was getting dark. I was aware that time was going by fast, and I'm not making a lot of progress on my book. I've been getting ready to go to Virginia, but I'm lagging behind on that too. I'm to leave on Wednesday. Randall is taking me to the airport 2 hours early, as it's supposed to be the busiest day for air travel. They've started some extreme security checks for all passengers, so I'll have to deal with that. Also, Thom is arranging for me to have a wheelchair to get from one flight to another, so I won't have to walk so far and wait so long.

I went to see Johnnie before I left for my trip. He was very upset, thinking it was 3 in the morning and that I was running around with other men. It was 3 PM. I finally convinced him, but I doubt he'll ever quit thinking I'm going with somebody.

I went to the hospital Monday morning and sat with Randall and their daughter-in-law while Dee had her surgery. The surgery was successful, and Randall took her home in a couple of days.

Today, Wednesday, I took Pauline Rice with me, and we went to pay some bills, and ate at Joe's, then I took her home and went to see Johnnie. He was in bed, asleep, and I woke him up, kissing him on his head. He was so happy to see me, and I stayed a while with him, but had to leave, to buy some groceries. I had nothing to eat at home, so I came back by Walmart and bought $108.00 of groceries.

The last few days have been pretty eventful. I remembered, late, that I hadn't done anything toward getting my IA renewal authorization renewed. This is to be done each two years. I'd received the paperwork some time ago, but have needed a new ink cartridge for my printer, so I finally bought one. It's obviously wrong for my printer, so I enlisted some help from Kyle and Sherry. As it turned out, I finally got my stuff together and took it all to the office supply, and had it mailed to the man at the FAA who was over this part of the USA. He called me, and told me I was approved for another 2 years. I was elated, and now I'm planning to try and build up some classes next January, February, and March.

Last Friday, I was at Sherry's for our usual Friday night, watching several episodes of Soap. Jonathan and his girl, Jamie, came for supper, and told us they had become engaged. We were happy for them. Jamie has a little girl, 7, who is a sweet little girl, very hyper. She had some surgery when she was a baby, which caused her to be so hyper. They plan to be married July 3rd next year. This date is also the Sullivans' anniversary.

My friend, Alan Cook has had another series of treatments for his bladder cancer. He decided to have the regular Christmas party he always has, so he invited the usual friends, including me, Don and Janet Laughenhauser, the people who usually take me with them. They picked me up a few minutes after 5 PM, and we headed for Dallas. We were the first to get there, but soon after, the other usual ones came. Ron Knoll and Jan, Alan's two good friends, were there, and always were there to help Alan.

We visited, ate a lot, and sang Christmas songs. We left about 9 PM and got home about 10. I was happy to see Alan looking so well. He never complains, but when he talked to me, I realized he was just a little more discouraged than usual.

The next week I got some bad news. Bobby Moore, a great pastor from Broadview Baptist Church, for about 3 or 4 years, died suddenly with what was supposed to be a heart attack. His wife had had Alzheimer's disease for many years. He retired from his large church recently to take care of her. The Simpsons sent me a book he wrote about personal devotions some time ago. He was a great preacher, and a good man.

Some good news; Phil is home from Ohio, and now will be working in Dallas. He is so glad to be back with his family. It's good to have him home. And now, I am officially approved to keep teaching the IA renewals for two more years. These are 8-hour courses, taught every year to those who need them.

I went to the Sullivans for lunch today, and afterward I went to see Johnnie. This was the 3rd time I've had a very unsatisfactory visit with him. His mind is getting extremely bad. Today, he wanted to sell his wheel chair for $15.00. And he was trying constantly to get his shirt off. Finally, the nurses changed his shirt, and he wanted to go home.

Finally, frustrated, I came home. I got to thinking; I am at a complete loss about how to treat him. I've never been around an Alzheimer's patient before, and I'm handling it all wrong. I plan to go back, and change the way I treat him. I just need to let him talk, and give up trying to explain anything to him.

I made a big batch of dipped chocolates. I called Matt, and asked him if he wanted to come and help me. But I had to leave the message on his answering machine, so I was surprised when he rang my doorbell! I was so excited to see him. He was going to the cemetery. It was the 17th anniversary of Paulette's death, so he had to leave soon. He promised to come back soon and we'd have lunch at 3 PM, tomorrow.

Jeff called me. He always does, every year, at this time. He's so sweet to me. I've thought about Paulette a lot today, but it's been a long time since I visited the graves of her and Sherman. I'll go later.

I got an invitation to Bobby Moore's funeral tomorrow in the Broadway Baptist Church, Get Well, Mississippi. I appreciated it, but there is no way I can go, of course. Joyce Simpson said she and Ray would go very early because there would be an overflow crowd. He was an exceptional pastor, and was there in that church for many years. I talked to Ray tonight. He has a bad cold and can't go to Bobby's funeral, either.

Losing his mother (Paulette died when he was 7), Matt has had a hard time with it ever since it happened, 17 years ago. He is a waiter at an upscale restaurant in Grapevine. He told me yesterday that a family came in and ate, all wearing the same color, pink, which is the color associated with breast cancer. He asked them about it, and someone in the family had died of breast cancer. Matt went to his boss and asked what he could do for them, and his manager gave them their meals. Such a nice gesture of kindness!

Christmas is past, and it was so much fun. I've made a lot of candy, had lots of company, and heard from friends and relatives. Christmas day, I planned to go and see Johnnie first at Avalon, then go to the Sullivans for lunch, then to Johnnie's house, where all his kids were going in the evening. Johnnie wasn't able to go—I think Janet took him some of the brisket she had cooked for Christmas dinner. But plans were changed, as I'll explain later.

On Thursday, December 23, Richard and Chere Bradford came over. I was so glad to see them. I had mentioned to Richard that I needed new batteries in my smoke alarms; I could replace them, but didn't want to climb up on the ladder to install them. They visited with me, and we ate supper—they ordered pizza delivered. And we watched my movie: The Aurora Incident. Richard went to the store for me and got some things I needed. What good friends they are!

On Christmas morning, I got ready to carry out all my plans. My next door neighbor's sister, Cathy, from Missouri, came over and told me Sandy, the one who lived next door, had been taken to the Peter Smith Hospital. Her cancer, first detected in her lungs, and adrenal glands, had metastasized into her brain, and she'd had a bad stroke. So she was bad. Cathy stayed until nearly noon, so I decided not to go see Johnnie but to go on to the Sullivans for lunch. I got out into the street, and found my right rear tire was very flat. I drove back in, called

Phil, and he offered to come back for me, but I told him I'd call AAA. I did, and waited for some time, finally got very hungry and ate a piece of Phil's brisket he'd cooked for last night. Finally, AAA came, changed the tire, and the spare was the little "dough nut" tire. It had already been used, and was also flat. He aired it up, and said it was OK to drive. So I went on to the Sullivans, had lunch, and went on to see Johnnie. He was so mixed up, and still made very little sense, but I left early and came home because I was a little leery of the "spare tire".

On Monday, I went to the Discount Tire store, and bought two new tires, also got the old tire fixed, and now have it for a spare. The next day, Tuesday, I went to Manor Care. Betty is recuperating, and won't be back to work for a while. I delivered some mail, did some visiting, and Sheila, Anita, and I played Scrabble Slam. The weather was cold, and it rained all day—not hard, just damp, and drizzling. I found out one of the residents there had died on Christmas day. Such a nice, sweet man; his wife was with him nearly all the time. Before he got so bad with Parkinson's disease, he used to talk to me. One day, he said to me, "You are so nice. Every time I see you, I want to put my arms around you!"

"Well," I answered, "Go ahead. I'm right here." And he said, "No. You know how people talk. Someone is bound to say something about it!" I guess that was the last thing he ever said to me. He just smiled, part of the time. It's so easy to get close to the nursing home residents, and losing them is just part of life when you're used to going.

Time passes so fast, and I have become more careless about writing. Christmas 2010 is over. It was a good holiday period, and my life went on as usual—two times a week at Manor Care, but I did take off two weeks from Manor Care. Betty was off because of some surgery. She only comes in once in a while.

About the middle of January, I went to Avalon to see Johnnie. He was in the living room, and was violently ill. His son and daughter were called, and arranged to take him to the hospital. He was very ill, talked very little, and lasted about 4 days. As bad as he was, he never failed to hold my hand and say, "I love you." He had turned 94 the 19th of October, 2010. He was buried beside his wife of 64 years, Esther. But he was my sweetheart for over nine years.

It's been quite a few bad days for me. Johnnie and I had a great relationship for close to ten years, ever since 2001, after Sherman's death. So now I feel truly alone, but not to the point of being sorry for myself. I am so thankful that we had each other, and although he'd been disabled for nearly five years, we still loved each other, and were together as much as possible. I'm also thankful for our church friends, and the way Johnnie was loved by so many, and our experiences, spiritually, together with the Lord.

So now, I'll go on. Our lives do change, and we find ourselves in a completely different life situation every few years. I'll gradually quit going to Manor Care twice a week, and do more visiting closer to home. I am now working with a group of girls at church in an AWANA group.

I resigned my volunteer work at Manor Care. I hated to, but just need to drive less and I can find plenty of volunteer work closer to home. Now that Johnnie's gone, I don't need that long drive anymore. Anyway, when Betty came in last week, she was fired. I don't know who I'd be working with any more.

When I'm at home, I like to cook. I don't eat much, but the cooking helps me. I spend a lot of time making desserts and giving them away.

My friend, Pauline Rice has been in the hospital for over a week now. She had to have a double by-pass; her heart has bothered her for some time. She is a little better now, but she's had a rough time, not eating right or taking care of herself. I miss her. We are very close friends.

I'm busy with work at the church and visits to shut-ins, plus taking care of myself, which is not too hard if I'm feeling good. I'm doing OK now, I seem to have my arthritis under control and doing some walking—just have to rest frequently a few minutes at a time. I'm planning to go to Manor Care on Thursday afternoon. I had promised to come back, although not on a regular basis the way I had been.

I got a call from Randall this morning. He is still having trouble with his breathing. It's a sinus problem that won't heal. He's looking for another doctor, and another opinion about whether he should have surgery. I assured him I was praying for him and we both know that God has the answers, but sometimes it grows discouraging, waiting to know what else to do. Randall is a brave man, but is getting anxious about surgery.

I made chicken and dumplings, and will take some of them to Pauline Rice's and have lunch with her. She's home now, and doing better. We had lunch after the therapist had finished coaching her in her exercises; we heated up the dumplings, and had the cake I brought. When I left, I went by the pawn shop to see what kind of guitar I might find. I'd wanted to get one for a long time, to see if I could still play.

Sure enough, I found several, and, to my surprise, some of them seemed to be a good deal. I talked to a man named James, and he came down on the prices, so I plan on going back to tune and test one, and maybe get it.

I called and talked to Thom, and he advised me to do it, and later, when Phil came to my house to pick up some clothes they'd left behind last Sunday, he was happy about it too. I'm excited and will go soon, and see about it.

On Thursday, the day was full, and I was excited as I got ready to sing with the Sweet Spirit Singers, at Green Valley Nursing home and Rehab Center. We met at the church, and drove the short way to Green Valley, on Rufe Snow Drive. There were 8 of us, but two more came and met us there. My friend, Rachel was there, waiting for us, and many of the people sang with us, as they began to fill the dining room where we were.

We all sounded good, as the Lord blessed us and we sang some old familiar song we all knew and Carlene played the piano. Clair was there too, he had a doctor's appointment when we got through.

So when we finished, I took Doris home, went to the bank, at then ate at Joe's. After lunch, I went home, got the mail, and went to Manor Care. I did some visiting, but that was all. Nobody was up for a game in the dining room, but I saw Rose Jones come in and we visited the rest of the time I was there.

On Friday, I went back to the pawn shop on Rufe Snow; and looked again, at the guitars. I decided on one. It's a special one, brand new, with a connection for an amp, and also a connection for recording. I tuned it, and realized I could play it, after I got my hands toughened up. They gave me a good deal, a pick, and a tuner that connected to the guitar.

On Saturday, I went to spend the evening with Phil and Sherry, and Kyle. Jonathan and Jamie were there, and Matt and Leslie, his girlfriend. I took my new guitar, and they liked it, but nobody played it, we were too busy talking.

Monday morning, I got up, and became aware, vaguely, that something had happened. It had rained all night, and was still raining, with lightning and thunder. That was exciting, it had been so long we hadn't had rain, but when I turned on the TV, I was totally shocked! Osama Bin Laden was dead! The mortal enemy of the entire world had been shot in the head, by a Navy Seal! Bin Laden was responsible for so many deaths at the nine eleven bombing, and many more attacks on Americans and others during the presidency of Clinton, Bush and now, Obama. It was a day for rejoicing, and most of the free world would be doing just that.

Ironically, Adolph Hitler had died on May 2, 1945. Hitler's death was a suicide, but he knew he would die that day anyway, so he shot himself! His mistress, Eva Braun, had taken cyanide.

Reportedly, Bin Laden was buried at sea. They reported that it was customary to bury the dead within 24 hours in Pakistan, where he had been living within a short distance of the capitol, Istanbul. They said a positive ID was made, so there was no mistake about that. But there are doubters.

I called Pauline Rice as soon as I got home. While we were talking, my doorbell rang. I turned off the phone and the truck was driving away. There was a large box on my porch—it was from Thom and Debby, and was 2 dozen beautiful red roses, and a green vase to put them in. A great Mothers' Day gift! Later, I called Thom to thank him. They were having dinner with Debby's girls, and they all said for Thom to wish me a happy Mothers' Day for them. I have a great family! And it's a great Mothers' Day!

I knew I'd have to get up early on Saturday morning to meet Ken and Art at IHop at 7 AM; it's at least 15 miles away. I arrived just before 7, and both men met me in the parking lot. Ken had told Art that they were meeting an old friend; he didn't say if it was a man or a woman. Art was completely confused at first, then Ken told him who I was. He was glad to see me, and gave me a big hug. We went in. The place was nearly empty, but soon filled up. We had so much catching up to do, we stayed for over 4 hours. We took several pictures, and we realized it had been 31 years since they'd been to school at Steve's.

Ken asked me to sing with him often when he performs in the area close to me. I was glad to agree—I loved singing with him. He said he'd call me; he wants me to go hear a band somewhere that he was familiar with.

Phil and Sherry gave me a new camera for Mothers' Day. We spent that Sunday at the Sullivans. The pictures we took turned out good; I'd used my "phone camera." The ones I took at IHOP were great. I was so proud of them. Ken is such a handsome man—and so is Art. I took the pictures we'd taken to Manor Care the next week and showed them off. When I was there, I saw my friend, Dorothy Glover. She told me J.B., her husband, is in there. He has diabetes, and had lost some toes. He's had a rough time. He has always had the most marvelous voice.

Chapter 13

"Pauline, you'll be scared to death for a while."

When I started instructing a class of mechanics in January, 1977, I had a class of 7 or 8 students starting in General, the first part of the Airframe and Powerplant courses. We started in Weight and Balance, which I was more knowledgeable in, and since it was the first part of January, it was a new class. I'd asked Steve to please get started teaching. I had helped students before, in solving some problems here and there, but didn't feel like I could actually teach a class.

But Steve was talking to Brady York, a friend of ours who dealt with buying and selling aircraft, and Steve couldn't go in and start teaching. Feeling mildly uncomfortable, I went in and started. The men were so nice, and accepted my efforts with no criticism and good spirits. They helped me a great deal as I began to teach, knowing that this would be a permanent position for me. I knew that Steve would never do it as long as he knew I could handle it.

I remember Charlie Stephens, Steve's son, telling me, "Pauline, you'll be scared to death for a while. But it'll get better and better, and after 6 months to a year, you'll be perfectly at ease teaching. It'll come naturally to you; you just need to be patient." He was so right. I used to study the books every day and/or night, because I knew the students would know if I just acted like I knew all the material. I learned the subjects, and could even tell the students the page numbers, and even which paragraph in the textbook to find whatever they wanted. I tried never to teach just questions and answers as some schools. We had different aircraft parts in the shop, and students were also taught different projects in practical application.

I have taught students to weld, to do dope and fabric work, and several other works in the shop. Sometimes we had engines and airframes to work on. As soon as Steve saw that I was doing OK, he gave me a raise. I was paid the same as the other instructors there, all men, only they were part time. I was full time, because I was also doing the office duties that I did before, and sometimes I was doing overtime. Also, I went to Dallas to teach at Aviall, and to the Naval Air Station at Grand Prairie, and to Fort Hood, at Killeen, Texas. Another class or two was at Aerospatiale in Grand Prairie. Eventually, in 1977, I took the written exams myself, also the practical, and got my own A&P certificates.

I taught some night classes at Tarrant County Junior College for about 3 years, 3 nights a week. They were General courses: math, physics, weight and balance, etc. My friend, Jack Shafer, who had worked for Steve for many years, and now worked for the college, had recommended me to them. Later, we were to work together again at Braniff Education Systems in Dallas. I appreciated Jack; he was a good friend.

Meantime, I taught for Steve. We had a new building with 2 large classrooms, a shop, and a large office in the center. In 1981, Morris Dixon, a student from my first class, and I began to talk about setting up our own school. Many foreign students from the Middle East had been cheating on the tests. Steve, as well as the others at Meacham and other places, had lost their DMEs, so we had to send our students elsewhere to take their practicals. So attendance fell off drastically at Stephen's Aircraft School.

I've always been thankful to Steve for getting me started in the career that lasted all these years. It was a pleasure to work with students, helping them to get their A&P ratings, and helping so many get ahead in the field of aviation. Being a female in what has always been considered a man's world has had its drawbacks, as well as its advantages. Some people worked tirelessly to fight against my ownership and managing a school, which, rather than deter me, helped to spur me on. I fought that much harder to build my school, and ultimately, my reputation. There were no problems ever with students, who were mostly, but not all, men.

My problems were with other men who resented my place in "their world," and consequently, I won against the odds. I'm thankful for many who helped me along the way, and for many instructors and others who worked for me to build up the school. For Paulette and Bill, her husband, who worked for me several years, having left New York and other eastern states where they were a duo in several clubs and motels, bringing their music back to Texas and working days for the school. Matt, their son, was born here after they got back. I have taught classes with him on my lap, or on a pallet on the floor nearby where we could watch him. This was after I'd moved the school to Arlington. My partner, Morris left the school after one year. We worked well together, but he was a single man, and ready to go on to other things. I hated to lose him, but we parted friends, and there were no hard feelings.

All the time we had the school in Arlington, we were working on getting FAA certification, and it happened about 1984. This meant we could teach all the FAA subjects in a 1,900-hour course, and the students needed no prior practical work or other previous experience or education in the field. We still offered the refresher courses in A&P and Inspection Authorization. The latter was more complicated, and caused some trouble with the powers that be, but we won and came out victorious.

Meanwhile, my home life was falling apart, and although Sherman had resented the school from the start, he really hated it now and began to drink heavily. We were estranged, living in the same house and both of us unhappy—only I was excited about the school, and never prone to being unhappy. He was the opposite, and drank to avoid reality. Actually, Sherman had been unhappy for a long time, and (I finally realized) had been an alcoholic since his time in the Army. He did not drink because of the family, but started back when I started the school. We used to go to hear Paulette and Bill when they appeared in some of the motels and clubs in Fort Worth and Dallas.

They were a big hit in many places, such as the Pecan Plantation, the Cuckoo's Nest in Granbury, and a few other places on the west side of Ft. Worth. Of course, there was a lot of drinking in those places, and Sherman imbibed a little too much. He realized it, and stopped going to those places, but he didn't stop drinking.

For a 5-month period, after Steve sold his school to Braniff, I worked for Hartman's Real Estate in River Oaks. I did some rentals and rental inspections, management for rental places. I drove a little Volkswagen bug; it belonged to Mr. Hartman, had many leaks, and not much of a heater. As I recall, this was a very cold winter, but I didn't mind. Snow and ice are very rare in this climate. I enjoyed my work, learning about real estate, and making new friends. They even talked about helping me get a real estate license. But soon, I got a call from my friend, Jack Shafer. He wanted me to come and work with him at the school Steve had sold to Braniff.

Jack and I had worked hard to get that school certified by the FAA. But when Braniff moved the school to Dallas, they had no one to operate the office, do the records, etc., as I had done before. So I resigned the real estate management, and happily began the trip to Dallas and back home every day. I was put in an office, and not allowed to go to the school to get things I needed. The men in charge wouldn't allow me to see the students.

I managed to persuade my boss, Bill, that it was vital that I go and talk to the students and get the records I needed to report to the FAA and other government offices, so he agreed reluctantly and said, "OK, Pauline, I'm going to let you go this one time—and get back here just as fast as you can. I have work for you to do."

"Really?" I asked. "What work?" because I knew better than anyone else what there was to do. His answer was a vague, "I'll let you know. Just hurry back!" Meantime, the younger woman who worked with me was about 40 years old and pregnant. Her "work" amounted to reading the paper and sitting on the boss's lap. I went on to the school, enjoyed visiting with everybody, and took a lot of pictures. I got back late—no one ever knew the difference. They kept me about a year, and decided one of the two of us "girls" had to go. So it was me. I was sorry; they had paid me well, but I was confident I'd be OK.

That day in January, 1977 when I started teaching, I knew I'd never get out of the classroom after that. But I always enjoyed teaching, and had many good friends who came to get their ratings in aviation. Eventually, I started teaching the Inspection Authorization, which broadened my teaching skills. My good friend, Bill Bedinger helped me to do that, and was very helpful in lots of ways. He'd been teaching that course, but was glad for me to start, and was glad to give up the job to me. He lived in Weatherford, and flew helicopters for the Smelly Dairy.

Opening the new school the same time Braniff Airlines closed may not have been the best idea we could have, but Morris and I were both confident and excited. Counting every dollar carefully, we got enough large tables and folding chairs to furnish the classrooms. A friend gave us an old refrigerator for our break room where we kept cold drinks and some sandwich stuff. Water fountains and restrooms were in the hallway, right outside our door.

For a few days, very few people came in, which gave us a chance to scout around for supplies, books, and office material. Slowly but surely, people began to take interest. We had classes in the mornings and evenings, and sometimes in the afternoons, taking care of students whenever they could come.

I knew what was close; that we would have to be approved by the Texas Education Agency as Stephen's Aircraft School had. But I was not really worried, as I had handled the approval of that school, so I was ready to start making up the paperwork and catalogs for the A&P. So one day I realized that the man coming in was from the TEA. In a few days, we got our certificate of approval, and a little while later we got our certificate of approval for some financial assistance for students. By this time, we were teaching classes in both A&P and Inspection Authorization.

We advertised in some of the aircraft publications, some of them being sent overseas. So we got several foreigners, and I was working with the Immigration Service and some of the other organizers for financial help for the students.

After a year, Morris left. He was single, and wanted to do other things than teaching classes at night. We were getting ready to move the school to

Arlington, where Raymond Butler, one of our instructors, had found us a building on West Division Street that was large and had enough classroom space and shop area to accommodate our needs. It had been a church, and all the shop area had indoor-outdoor carpet on the floor. It even had a little break area, a cabinet, and a sink. Eventually, I rented the former auto garage next door, so we didn't have to be so careful about the floor.

We stayed until we had the place all fixed up, with the shops all arranged with the different subjects, and we got it ready for the first inspection for our certification. But meanwhile, Paulette had gone looking around for a better place, and she found one. So we moved again, to 111th Street. The City of Arlington gave us plenty of grief, and made us comply with many rules they put upon us and the people we rented from. We had to have quite a lot of new sheetrock, new glass for windows, and provide more parking spaces, etc. But finally, it was all done, and we had complied with all their rules. But we had the FAA Certification, and were ready to put everything into the school. We hired another couple of instructors and a girl to work in the office.

On this day in October, 2011 Kearney called me—we'd been talking about a pawn shop in Granbury, where he thought I could find a guitar I might want. The one I bought hadn't been what I needed; it was hard to play. My fingers were not able to press the strings, and I hadn't been able to play enough to get practice—I wanted to get one I could play easily, the way I could play Ken's Taylor. The Taylor guitars were expensive, so I knew I couldn't get one. But I'd asked Randall to look for one for me, and Kearney thought the pawn shop in Granbury was the place to look.

So we decided to go the next day in the afternoon. I was to meet Kearney in Granbury. He lives in Cleburne, and he offered to come after me, but I told him

I'd drive my car and meet him there. So I left right after I'd had lunch. I took him a sandwich and a few Fritos to eat, and went on to Granbury. It's about 30 or 35 miles from here and I didn't have the slightest idea where the pawn shop was. I drove into Granbury, and failing to find the pawn shop where he was, I went down a block off the square and parked in a church parking lot to try to reach him by phone.

As I drove in and parked, my car became extremely hot, with white steam billowing out of the hood. The temperature gauge was as hot as it would measure, so I turned everything off and called AAA. They informed me I'd have to have the car towed, and that was okay—I had the AAA insurance that paid for towing up to 100 miles. So I waited and meantime got in touch with Kearney, and he got to me before the tow truck. But the truck did come and took my car to the garage here close to home, where I always take it.

We left—Kearney and me in his truck—and drove to the pawn shop where I looked at the supply of guitars. I tried several, including a Baby Taylor, but finally, the lady who co-owns the place with her husband suggested one I might like. Sure enough, I was happy to get this one. It's a Kona; the people there are authorized dealers for that brand. It was easy to play, was used but not worn badly, and we made a deal for it. I also got a nice vinyl case for it, and Kearney drove me home.

So I got up next morning, and got ready to go to Sweet Spirit Singers' rehearsal. Mark from Calloway's called me. They had been closed when the tow truck brought my car in, so I explained to him what had happened. He promised they'd take care of it. I called Roland, and asked him to pick me up when he came after Rachel. He did so, and we went to the choir rehearsal at church. We had about 10 to 11 people there, including Zack, our worship leader and

Kevin, leader of the children's department, another preacher. Our pianists, Clair and Carlene, were not there, so Clara played. We were all surprised to hear Kevin; he sang a wonderful bass.

Roland drove me home, and almost immediately my doorbell rang. It was my former student, Jim Tubbs and his wife Sherry, to take me to lunch. Jim had gone to school at Steve's, and I was his instructor in 1981. I've seen him several times since then, and I appreciate so much those who keep in touch with me through the years. The three of us went to La Molcajetes, a good Mexican restaurant nearby, and had a great lunch. When we finished, they drove me by the garage and I got my car. The cooling fan had broken. No wonder it had gotten so hot. They put a whole new fan system in; it runs much better and quieter now.

The weather got worse. It kept getting colder as the day went on, and finally began to rain a little. I made a coconut cake this afternoon, three layers. Why did I do that? I don't know. I usually give most of the stuff I make away to neighbors. This is a really good cake, but a lot of my neighbors don't eat sweets.

I've tried to play my guitar a little every day to keep in practice. I cooked pork ribs and mashed potatoes, and made chocolate chip cookies. Phil and Sherry came to eat supper with me, and Phil and I picked 24 pictures I had on the computer to have reprinted—a free deal at Walgreens. Sherry did the dishes and read the paper; she is so patient with us. But we did watch one of the DVDs of the Dean Martin show before they went home.

I went to a party for Rose Jones; she is 90 and lives at Manor Care. It was quite a party; I'd taken several pictures, and so did Jerry Baker, Linda's husband. He also is a singer in nursing homes. He and I wanted to sing, but neither of us had a guitar, so we didn't. But he shot a lot of pictures, too, which he and Linda shared with me.

I also went back to Manor Care on Thursday. It's such a habit with me now, I just keep going back. I talked to Ken once this week. He's still waiting to see a cardiologist about his heart and a breathing problem. So we're done singing for a while, but I'm still practicing playing my guitar. I'm not successful playing the new one, but getting better on the old one that I got first. I'm working on getting my fingers calloused, so I can do better and play with less pain.

I finally got Jann to cut my hair last week. It's easier to fix, but not a lot shorter than it was; it looks okay. I prefer it long, but can't do much with it. I'm learning to wear it straighter like the style, but will never have enough hair to avoid rolling it.

The weather is finally getting cooler. Nice, still hot during the day, but when it's cooler and damper, my arthritis is worse. I'm getting ready for my trip to Virginia, and looking forward to it. I can't pack yet, since I'm wearing most of the clothes I'll pack to take with me.

Thom called me and told me the plans for Thanksgiving. He asked me if I would feel like making sweet rolls for Thanksgiving breakfast at Wendy's, and of course I will. Later, Thom, Debby, and I will go out for lunch.

My trip to Dulles airport in DC was a nonstop flight—very nice, uneventful until our arrival at Dulles. I thought Thom would be waiting at the gates where I went in, but he was not to be seen. After much frustration, I was taken by wheelchair to the station where I boarded the bus and rode to a part of the airport where, finally, Thom (who had gone to JFK airport) found me with my luggage waiting for him. Thank goodness for our cell phones. We drove to their home in Fairfax, collected Debby and the two cats, and drove on to Winchester. It was late, so we went to bed shortly. It was Tuesday.

We went out on Wednesday. Thom gave me spending money, and I did some shopping. While walking in Macy's, I met Michael, Suzanne son. He is in his first year of college and is doing really well. We recognized each other, but it had been a long time since we'd seen one another. Later, Debby and Thom came in, and we did some more running around. We went to the grocery store to buy some ingredients for the cinnamon rolls I was to make on Thursday morning for Bryan's family, who would be there for breakfast.

Thom woke me up at 6 AM on Thursday morning, Thanksgiving, and we made the sweet rolls. We made 25 large rolls for 12 of us. Since there were three kids, there were plenty to go around. Bryan's parents, two brothers, and their wives were there, plus Wendy and their two. They all went back to spend the rest of the day with Bryan and Wendy, and Thom, Debby and I drove to the place a couple of hours away and had Thanksgiving dinner at an old colonial place, very picturesque. They had been there before and love the place. I enjoyed it too.

My visit with them was a little short. Lesley called and wanted me to come on Saturday instead of Sunday, so Thom and Debby took me to the Cracker Barrel between Winchester and Williamsburg on Saturday. We all had lunch together before separating. Going to Lesley and Ben's is always fun too. We had from Saturday until the next Sunday, when I left from Richmond to go to DFW and home. My neighbor, Karen, was meeting me at the airport; she left our Sunday School Christmas party to come after me.

All during my visit in Virginia, the weather was beautiful. The sun was shining and it was warm with very little wind, and all this time the weather in Fort Worth had been cold and raining. I realized it was still raining as I waited in the baggage area for Karen. I was very hungry. I hadn't eaten in several hours, and hoped Karen would be hungry, too, so we could stop somewhere on the way home and get a bite to eat.

She drove right up to the door of the baggage area and came in after me. She was driving her new car, a Honda van; she'd had it only a few weeks. "At last," I thought. "Not long now, and I'll be home!" We got closer to home on the airport freeway, nearly even with the HEB hospital, and it was impossible to tell exactly what happened. A wheel appeared out of nowhere, we swerved a little, and it seemed that we were hit by another car. We made one complete spin, and hit a concrete wall head-on. The airbags deployed, the seatbelts tightened around us, and we both thought it was curtains for us. Not only did the airbags expand, but they also exploded, and it looked like there was fire all around us. I was vaguely aware that my right knee was pressed tightly against the dashboard, but obviously I quickly forgot about it.

We never did learn what happened to the other car, or even if there was another car. We were both terribly bruised and frightened, and sore all over. The police came, and called an ambulance which came and took us both to the hospital. Karen went with me, but said she wasn't hurt badly enough to be seen by a doctor. I could hardly move on my own, and was in a lot of pain. They did an X-ray on me, and decided if there were no bones broken I was OK. So Karen's daughter, Diane, took us home and saw that we were doing all right, before she left us alone.

It took us some time to recover. Karen had some good insurance which took good care of getting her car fixed, taking it in more than a couple of times to make sure everything was working all right. Her insurance also paid for my medicine and trips to the doctor, etc. But especially at my age, it takes some time to get back to normal, and it took me a while. They prescribed hydrocodone for me, and I took as little as possible because I am aware of how this can become habit forming.

Yesterday, I received 2 more Dean Martin DVD's, so Sherry, Phil and I went to eat at the Cotton Patch and then watched one of them. I'm feeling better, for the most part, and leaving off the hydrocodone. My appetite hasn't returned, but I guess I eat enough.

I got a call from a cousin, Adrina. She, her brother-in-law, John and sister, Melba are coming to see me this afternoon. I'm glad; I haven't seen them in several years. Their mother, Lucille died while she was at Manor Care some time ago. Their dad, Buck Burt and their sister, Barbara each committed suicide at different times. Their grandmother, Lelia Knoblock, who was married to my mother's brother, Leslie Knoblock, was either killed or committed suicide; the suicide theory was accepted, although there was some doubt about it. She was shot, and found in a shed near the house. Her daughter, Lucille was 17, and the boys, Leslie Jr. and Jim were younger.

Few people understood Uncle Leslie. He was a very serious, withdrawn person, not very sociable or outgoing like Mama's other brother, Uncle Jim.

The girls, Melba and Adrina, asked me a lot of questions about the family. I could tell them very little, because I was so small at the time, and completely out of character, Mama never told what she knew or suspected about the situation. We all went to a late lunch at Spring Creek Barbecue, and they had to leave shortly afterward. But we had a great visit; the girls mean a lot to me.

The weather has been cold, and I finally bought myself an electric blanket a few days ago. The sun is out today; it's cold, but beautiful. It's supposed to get up to 54 degrees this afternoon. I called my friend, Alan Cook this morning. He is better, but now has permanently lost some of his hearing in one ear, and has to wear a hearing aid. He's interested in meeting me at the Johnnie High show, as we've done many times before. I found out the shows have continued each Saturday after Johnnie High's death. I want to go, but don't care to go alone. Later, I have friends to go with, but I'll look forward to meeting Alan there.

My good friend, J.B. Glover died last Sunday night. I went to the visitation for him at Mt. Olivet. I saw John Dobbs, and Cecil and Beth Baker, but there weren't many there that I knew. It's been a while since we all went to church together at Azle Avenue. I saw J. B. often when he had his foot surgery and was at Manor Care. He was a great friend, he and Dorothy, and he was a great singer in churches in the Fort Worth area.

I did some inquiring, and found out the Johnnie High show was set for every Saturday night. Gary Johnson, a good friend from church, and Karen's boyfriend went with me. I made reservations for us, and I was excited. Johnnie High had died 2 years ago, and I hadn't been there since his death. Paulette was a regular singer there for many years, and was a favorite of many of the people there. I paid for our tickets to the show, and Gary bought our supper at Babe's, next door.

I saw so many of my old friends at the show, also many of the performers who were still there, and we really had a great time. The show was very good. Bill Brooks was the emcee. Michael Hicks was normally emcee, but he was gone somewhere. I saw Mike Stewart and Patsy Andrews and others, and got to talk and visit with several. So it was a great night, and I got home around 10 PM.

After church on Sunday, I went to the Sullivans. We had a Mexican lunch, and it was all great. I came home about 4 PM and found a message on my computer that Waylon Perry had died on Saturday night. Waylon was my cousin, the son of my dad's sister, Aunt Lizzie. There were several kids in Aunt Lizzie's family— Floyd, Harmon, Frankie, Omia (married to my brother Robert, but they were not kin, she was kin on Daddy's side), then Faye, Waylon, Robert, and Ruby. Ruby, Robert's twin sister, died when she was 12, from something like strep throat.

Waylon and Bobby had been living at Broken Bow together. Bobbie wasn't real bright, and the two lived together, never married, worked very little, and were drunks. There were 12-13 dogs in and out of their house, and it was terrible. I'd seen it once in many years. But once, long ago, Waylon, Faye and I went to school together for a time and had fun together. I worried when I got the message about Waylon's death, because I knew there was nobody in the family that could pay for a funeral. But I called Roy, my nephew who takes care of Robert and Omia, his parents. I found out that several years ago Robert had arranged for some of the money sent to Waylon and Bobby from welfare was sent to a funeral home in Broken Bow for both Waylon and Bobby.

What a relief! I always appreciated Robert and the way he was so thoughtful, but it really made me proud of him. And now his memory is so bad, he probably doesn't even realize Waylon is gone. Robert is now 91.

It was January 23, 2012. I called Thom to wish him happy birthday. After a few glitches with the connection, he answered—he was in the shower in Cancun! So he called me back a little later, and told me about their trip there, and said they'd be going back home in a day or two. We reminisced about the trip we took to Cancun in 1989. I took the three, Thom, Phil, and Paulette for a three-day trip to Cancun. Thom was a bank president in River Oaks, and arranged for the trip.

Phil and Thom in Cancun

Thom came to get us all in a limousine to go to the airport! We had a great time, and will always have good memories. We also took several good pictures, and got some mementos. I compensated the spouses, except Sherry wouldn't take anything; she was so glad for Phil to get the trip. But I gave Jeanne a check, and Bill a set of tires for his van. Later, Sherry reminded me that I had given her something.

The rift between Sherman and me had grown wider, and he seemed to be unconcerned. Our marriage was over before long, and so were Thom's and Paulette's. Lives change every few years, which is not to say all marriages change that often. And ours, Sherman's and mine, picked up the pieces nine months later, but things were never the same. I'll always have some regrets, and I know he did, too.

Sometimes when I feel a little lonely living alone—I have many friends, but everyone is living his or her own life, completely separate from me—maybe an old friend calls, and I realize this means so much to me. I believe there is nothing so heartwarming as just talking to or visiting with an old friend. So many of my friends are from Broadview Baptist Church, and also from my school at Love Field or Arlington, and even from Stephens Aircraft School at Meacham; others from here in the community and First Baptist Church, Watauga.

My friend, Irene was in the Fireside Lodge in River Oaks for many years. I've visited her, at times fairly regularly. One of these times, her brother, Johnny came in to see her. I hadn't seen him in a long time, but had read about his wife, Esther dying a couple of years before. It was good to see him again, and after a while, he and I left together to get to our cars.

I saw him a few times after that, and we talked on the phone, mostly about Irene and her family. Her husband, Ed and her son, Terry had both died, and she only had some grandchildren who looked after her besides Johnny and the other brother, Howard. Howard's wife had also died after years of being completely disabled in a bad car accident. She hated being in a nursing home, so Howard took her home and cared for her the rest of her life. She was completely helpless, but lived about 14 more years.

We agreed to have Johnnie's son, Jim Ed to help us take Irene to see Terry's grave. She had been to the funeral, but had to stay in the car because she had broken her hip and couldn't walk to the grave site. She told me she couldn't cry; as bad as she hurt, the tears just wouldn't come. So we met at Fireside; Jim got her in the pickup he was driving, and Johnnie and me in his car. We went to the Greenwood Cemetery and visited the graves for Ed and Terry. Irene was in her wheelchair, and did cry quite a bit as she saw the graves for the first time close up.

After we got her back to her room where they brought her lunch, Johnnie took Jim and me to a cafeteria for lunch.

Not long after that, Sherman died in April, 2001. He'd had several bad spells, and each time I rushed him to the hospital. I was afraid each would be the last. He died at home; hospice was taking care of him. I couldn't lift him at all, but was doing what I could. And then he was gone. We'd been married 54 and a half years. Sometimes, I wonder what he'd say about those years. I know he was the real love of my life. But at times, months would go by, and if he'd only held me and expressed his love for me, I'd never have doubted his love for me.

But it seldom or never happened, and he made me wonder if he still loved me at all. This was not the way it used to be, or at least not often, but the two of us just didn't seem to value each other any more.

A few weeks after Sherman died, Johnnie called me and asked me if I'd go to lunch with him, and I agreed. After being hopelessly lost for a couple of hours, he got here. We went to a place on the Airport Freeway, Harrigan's, and had a nice lunch. After that, we began going to lunch every day. Johnnie was the sweetest, most thoughtful man, and we went everywhere together—to church, shopping, visiting, and to Waxahachie to see Thom and Debby. We eventually discussed marriage, but never really considered getting married. And at our ages, we both had some medical problems. At those times, we stuck together. We both had families who helped us when we needed them, and, as time went on, Johnnie was disabled, and after a brave fight, had to spend the rest of his years in a nursing home. He only lived about 4 more years. We were going together 5 years before that, but he finally grew tired and old, and had lost a lot of his memory. I still miss him; we loved each other.

In 2004, Phil lost his job here and went to work for the Hermann Hospital system in Houston. Sherry went with him. They sold their house here, and they rented an apartment there. In a short time Sherry had some tests, and was told she had thyroid cancer. She had surgery, chemo and other treatments and suffered a lot. They came home after a year and a half; Sherry had some problems, but the cancer was a misdiagnosis.

When they came back from Houston, they stayed with me for a while, while they looked for another home. Phil had a new job with Greyhound. Sherry was busy for a few days searching the Internet for a new car. They got a house a few miles from me in Hurst. But it was a while before they found the one they wanted. The house they bought was a beauty, large enough and brand new. I was glad to have them here. They helped me, and we all helped Margaret and the rest of her family the way they always needed someone to look after them.

And at this time JJ was also staying here; he had been in jail for the last six months after stabbing a neighbor and being placed on parole. He slept on my couch, because there was no room for another bed. Adam was working in Austin.

During this time, I was having a lot of trouble with stomach pains. I'd had my gallbladder removed at the HEB hospital. I went first to North Hills hospital. They did a scan, and showed me a large gallstone inside my gallbladder and then, for some reason, sent me back home with no mention of surgery. I continued to have trouble; I could eat but very little.

Once, I started to a funeral for my friend, Peggy. She had asked me to help her plan the service, which I did. Peggy had cancer, and had known for a long time that she wouldn't live very long, and she had planned to play some of Paulette's gospel tape. When I was on the way, I had to stop and get gas. I got too sick to go, so I came on home and called Johnny. He went in my place, and he didn't even know the lady. He was so good to me -- no wonder I loved him so.

I went to HEB hospital then, and they removed the gallbladder. I was relieved, but soon after that I began having more trouble with my stomach. In a few years, I was hurting bad. As I started to the TRE to pick JJ up from the train, Phil had me come to their house first. He arranged for him and Sherry to pick up JJ, and then they drove me to the HEB hospital where two doctors questioned me. They said the trouble seemed to be my gallbladder, and I assured them I'd had it taken out there several years ago; they just couldn't believe me.

Finally one of them came up to my room and began to question me again.

"Are you sure you had the gallbladder taken out?" he asked.
"I'm not sure," I answered. "I was asleep at the time. But they told me they did."
"And where was it done?"
"Here."
"Who did the procedure?"
"I forgot."
"When was it done?"
"I don't know," I said. "About five years ago."

Resigned, he got up and said, "I'll see if I can find a record of it." So obviously he did, and came back and announced to me that I did have it removed here four and a half years ago, and it was a doctor in the same group as the two who were looking after me.

They prepared me for surgery, and it was performed in a few minutes. Two large gallstones were in my bile duct. They brought me in from surgery, lying on my tummy. They later showed me the gallstones. They were very large. I haven't had any more trouble since then with my stomach.

Wednesday, April 25, 2007: Sherman, it's been six years since you went away. I'll always miss you. I wish we had both tried a little harder to make things work. But I guess we just let things go, and quit trying several years ago.

In the middle of the storms last night, they sent Margaret to North Pointe in an ambulance. So I'll go and see her in the afternoon. The storms seemed to be over, and it's a beautiful day.

I took the flowers and went to see Margaret. I took a gown and robe for her; I figured I'd go tomorrow and get her stuff at Fireside. After I left her, I went to Johnny's for a while. Margaret looked good. She was sitting on a pillow and seemed to feel good, but already a little homesick. I went on to Johnny's and we had lunch at Moe's. Then we went to Fireside and got most of her clothes and stuff. I got her chair—the black one I'd got to accommodate company—and she kept telling me to get her blue one. I finally realized she meant her wheelchair; actually a Geri chair, sort of a reclining wheelchair that hospice furnished her. I had to load everything by myself. Johnny wanted to help me, but I knew he couldn't; he's just not strong enough. After I took him home, I was so exhausted; I went on home and decided to go early in the morning to take the stuff to Margaret.

The next morning I got up early, got her stuff together, and went on to the nursing home. She wasn't very happy this morning. I realized that hospice had really spoiled her, and she was missing it, but she said she was going to make friends. She liked the lady who was her roommate. She was still wanting her chair, so I asked a girl. She said hospice furnished the chair, but the nurse said she thought they had one there she could use.

I was still there when the chaplain, James, came and visited her. He said he lived close by, and would see her once or twice a week. He said hospice had called there, but they had such a long waiting list, he couldn't understand how I got her in there. I said I just used my charms, but we knew it was Providence—

an answer to prayer. I filled out some paperwork in the office and took a lot of it home to fill out later.

We're expecting Carolyn and Dale to come to town over the weekend. I got a package in the mail. It was memoirs Carolyn had sent me, written by Carolyn's aunt Bertie Mae. There were 23 pages, typewritten, all about the Jacobs family. It was interesting, and I read it through at once. I am planning to write a book about our family, and Carolyn and I will share some information as I get started.

The next morning I went to North Pointe. Margaret was okay and sitting up in her old chair. I took her out to the living room, so she could watch TV and all the birds in their cages in the living room. I took the papers to be filled out, and waited for Rosalind to help me with them. The girls, Tracy, Sherry, and Rosalind, were all really sweet to me, and so were the aides and nurses. I was impressed because the place was clean and very large, with no unpleasant odors.

I got up this Sunday morning, May 6, got ready for church, and watched for Johnny. He came right on time. I went outside to help him into the house. Jim had brought him, because he was unable to drive by this time. I was talking and didn't notice, but all of a sudden, Jim was out of the car, and saw that Johnny was not walking right. He admitted he was weak, a little dizzy, so Jim and I convinced him he needed to go on back home, and not try to go to church today. He hates to miss church, but finally agreed to go on home. I told him I'd be there as soon as church was over.

I got my stuff, and went on to Sunday school. I was teaching today (the first Sunday of every month), and our lesson was from Philippians. It's a great book, and we were teaching this quarter without books: purely from the Bible. It was a challenge, but a good one, making us study more, but I need more commentaries. I asked the class to help me discuss the lesson, which they did. It was a good time.

Our senior choir, Sweet Spirit Singers, were to sing in the service this morning. I'd had to be home last practice day, Tuesday, and forgot we were going to sing and wear our red and black vests—red out—but Mildred, who had made the vests, had one in her car. She got it and I wore it. I still had mine and Johnnie's in a dresser drawer at home.

After Sunday school, we went into the auditorium and sang in the choir—our chairs were in front of the regular choir. We sang, "I'm Gonna Wear a Crown and Walk Around," and some older songs. It was really great. So were the rest of the services, including the sermon.

It was a great service, and after the invitation, all of our seniors went back to the choir & sang, "Freely, Freely," completing the services.

I went straight to Johnny's. He was ready to go out and eat. Jim was gone and Johnny said he was feeling okay. We went to Moe's and had lunch. After we ate, we went to Fireside Lodge and visited with Irene a while. She was lying down, and had a really bad cough! I gave her a few mints and one cough drop I had in my purse. They helped a little.

When we left there, we went to Johnny's house to visit a while. We'll go see Howard next week sometime. When I left Johnny's, I went on to North Pointe to see Margaret. She was in bed, covered with the Hello Kitty blanket I'd made her (she loves it), and the kitty pillow was under her legs.

I went to her old room and got her Bible, phone book, and gold lap robe. Marjorie's husband was there. He got the clock and a lamp, and went with me to take the stuff to Margaret's room. He told me Marjorie had had a stroke, and that she'd been in Manor Care on Glenview Drive for a couple of weeks before they brought her to North Pointe. Margaret said she hollered all the time.

The girl who brought Margaret's supper said there were only two there to feed the patients on that hall. I told her I would feed Margaret so she could do the others. I fed her. She ate everything, still complaining, but admitted it wasn't too bad. I think she's getting a little more used to the place.

I came on home, fixed my supper, read the paper, and watched a great aviation movie about early aircraft and aviators like the Frenchman Bleriot. It made me think of my late friend Bob Wells, who died last August.

Tuesday, January 23, 1977

Today my oldest son, Thom is 59 years old. Quite a lot of memories! I've given birth to three babies, and lost one before I even knew I was pregnant, but it's so special each and every time. I was only 18 when Thom was born. He was named before he got here. I wanted to name him after Sherman too, but Sherman wouldn't hear of it. He said I could name him Homer, Sherman's other name, but not Sherman. So he was Thomas Homer, after my dad and his own. We called him Tommy, but the first day of school, his teacher Mrs. Carroll, sent me a note saying he wanted to be called Thom, so we did. Thom was a beautiful, healthy baby, with large brown eyes and white hair, which turned dark brown later on. He was Mama and Daddy's pride and joy, as well as our own.

When we brought him home three days later, the weather was bad. A five-inch snow was on the ground. We had a 1936 Plymouth with one window out, so the baby in a basket, and I on a gurney, rode home in an ambulance. Incidentally, they had a pink one and a blue one, but only the pink one was available for us that day. I doubt that the color of the ambulance has ever intimidated Thom. Our little house was only partly finished and was cold, so for a few days we were staying in an apartment house on Elm Street where Mama and Daddy had rented a place. But soon the weather turned nice, and we were happy to get home.

In April 2009, I went to Baylor Hospital in Grapevine and had a mammogram. I have a small lump in my left breast, the same breast that Dr. Mary Brian did the lumpectomy on about eight years before. It's very small, and today, Monday, I had a biopsy. It was a bit painful, but a little complicated. They put clips in my breast to mark where the tissue was removed, and the mammogram didn't show where it was, so I had to have a second one. It was successful, but I was curious about clips, and I asked Dr. Gregory what they meant by these clips. He had been watching World War II movies and heard the motto, "loose lips sink ships" which, misunderstanding what I said, he said, "They sink ships."

A little surprised, I said "And you put those in me?"

He kept apologizing, but later we couldn't stop laughing. After I went home, Carolyn called to see how I was. We laughed so hard; I guess it was easier to laugh than to cry.

The next day, Tuesday I was on my way to Manor Care, and Dr. Matt Gregory called to tell me the results of the biopsy. It was definitely cancer, not the worst kind, but not the best either. He broke the news as gently as he could. I didn't cry. I wanted to, but made myself control my emotions as well as I could, and told him "Well, you made a place for yourself in my book; I wrote the episode about the loose lips." We laughed, and he told me to please call them any time I have comments for him and the two nurses who work with him, and to be sure to ask any questions I had, and let them know how I got along. I went on to Manor Care. I told Betty, Gaye, and Jann I was fine. Somehow, I knew I'd be okay, whatever happened.

My dear friend, Sandra Evans took me to see Dr. Mary Brian. I was set up for surgery at HEB on April 14 at 11:15 AM.

I called Dr. Kallal, my family physician, to get some Xanax to help me sleep. I never cried, neither was I upset, just couldn't sleep well, so I guess I was a little nervous. The doctor told me to come in at 7 AM the next day. He was very upset about me. He's always been so careful about me, especially since my daughter died with breast cancer.

I had called him when I first found the lump, and he wanted me to see Dr. Brian as soon as possible, but now he seemed to regret not being the first doctor I had seen. Later he filled out the papers to admit me to the hospital.

Thom's company sent him to Dallas on the 13th and 14th. He meant to spend the night at home here, or I'd come to Dallas to be with him, but he came to my house on the 13th and took me to the hospital on the 14th. We met Phil and Sherry there. The company postponed his meeting in Dallas so he could stay at the hospital with me.

People, some from the church, began to gather. I counted about 16 who were in the waiting room for my surgery. Janet brought Johnnie in his wheelchair. She brought him to me, and he was so sweet and so glad to see me. My surgery was over, and I began to wake up. I was not in pain, and never had pain medicine after waking up.

Late the next day, the 15th, Thom brought me home. I was okay. I took some Tylenol as usual, and we kept the tube and bulb drained as needed. Thom is so good to me and took care of me so well. The next morning, Sandra came over and had coffee and snacks with us. Thom is going to write a story for the Senior Gazette and send it to her, about my being in Alexandria, Virginia, and going to the mall there. The taxi never came for me, and a strange lady gave me a ride home. It was a funny story, and funnier when Thom told it. Actually, I had had a taxi take me to the mall, and asked the driver to pick me up at the same entrance at a particular time, which he promised to do. So I stood at the entrance and kept waiting. No taxi. I had one or two of the clerks call the taxi company. Still no taxi. Several people saw me when they came in, and again when they left, and finally this nice lady I'd seen before asked me if I'd get in her car and show her where Thom's house was. I had no idea, but together, the two of us found the place. Thom and Debby couldn't believe it! Thom said he could have stood there all night and nobody would have offered him a ride.

Later, a sweet lady from the church, Judy Stillwell, came by Chick-fil-A, and brought us all sandwiches and cookies and little bowls of fruit. It was great; we had a nice visit. Thom had to leave for the airport for home at 4 PM. But he'll be back next week; his postponed meeting will be held in Dallas.

I'm doing okay—have had many calls and e-mails and phone calls. The most important call was from Dr. Brian, telling me all my tests were negative—I needed no chemo or radiation, but no more cancer! I made many calls, e-mails, and messages telling the good news to everyone, including the girls and Dr. Gregory at Baylor Breast Cancer Center. God is good.

When Thom first came before my surgery, we met Matt at the Olive Garden where he worked. I told Matt about the situation and he cried. He looked so good and was doing fine, but I was upset to see Matt upset. I told him jokes and tried to cheer him up.

Today, I let him know I was fine. He just wanted to tell me he loved me and didn't mean to be so busy, but was working on a new album he was doing. I assured him I understood, and was happy about his music going well, and always knew he loved me.

Kathy called me from Johnny's today, and Kathy took her phone and let me talk to Johnnie on the speakerphone. He could hear me well for a change. They fixed his room up and made it more home-like.

Randall called me and told me he took Dee to the Waffle House, but she didn't eat much. It made me hungry, and I decided to make pecan pancakes for my supper which was really good. I've got too much appetite!

Several days have passed. I'm about well, but still in some pain from the drainage. Last Thursday when I went to see Dr. Brian, she said I was still having too much drainage. Janet took me there, and when we left there we went to eat at IHOP. Then we went to visit Johnnie at Avalon. He was so glad to see me. He had been calling me two or three times a day, but he could hear me very little.

Dr. Brian told me I could drive now, but not to go far, just in my own community. I went to Ginger Brown's Thursday night. Roxie came after me and brought me home. We were a little later arriving than usual, and Randall called me while we were on our way. He said my fans all wanted to know when I'd be there! It was a good night. Joyce gave me a nice gift. It was Jeff's birthday, and we had a party for him.

I saw the paper yesterday, Saturday. There was to be a static air show at Meacham. It was a war bird display. Nearly all were WW2 planes, but some modern ones, and some helicopters. I called Jim and Donna and asked if they wanted to go. They did, and took me. After we had seen the show, about two hours or so, Wow! We walked all that time. We went to the Colonial Restaurant and ate, had a great lunch. I was awfully tired when I got home, but rested a while and went to the store.

I went to church this morning—enjoyed all the attention—and after eating lunch at home, I went to see Johnnie. We had a good visit and saw Howard and his friends, Sam and Gina, and later Janet and Jack and Randy came in. Randy brought his recordings and played them for us. He had sent Randall a couple, and Randall was impressed. They were pretty good.

Jim came by to see his dad, too. One of the ladies there who was about as deaf as Johnny began to show me how to direct music. She was very intellectual and knew what she was doing. She said she was going to test me when I came back to see if I remembered what she told me. We had a nice visit, but I had to leave and get home. I need to rest a lot these days, till I get over the effects of the surgery.

I am only vaguely aware of what the world was like in the year I was born. It was August 22, 1929. My dad, William Thomas Fagan, known by everyone as Tom Fagan, had been deserted by his first wife, Laura, when their four children and he became aware of her new lover, a man named Turner. Daddy had told her to let him go, or to go with him, but she couldn't take the kids with her. So she took the man, and left Ruby, aged three and crying after her, and Leona who was aware of the affair, Lewie about 10, and Addie, the oldest, 12.

Addie had had spinal meningitis and polio; I think it was called infantile paralysis back then. These two ailments had left her crippled and slightly retarded, but thoroughly disgusted with her mother. Leona, 5, also knew the circumstances and was very angry with Laura. She saw Laura and her lover leave, seemingly uncaring of her kids.

Daddy and Lewie went to find work—some of Laura's folks kept the girls a few weeks, but found that Addie needed some professional care, and advised Daddy to take her to what was known then as a "state school" in Enid,

Oklahoma. It became very hard for Daddy to take care of them all, so he contacted the place in Enid, and they accepted Addie. Actually, the state school was not a school at all, but a mental institution, which must've been common in those days. This occurred in about 1923-1924. It must've been a very heartbreaking task for him, because it was for Addie.

Daddy and Lewie continued to look for steady work, but such jobs were scarce in those days, and they eventually settled in Okmulgee, Oklahoma. Daddy became a custodian of the Lee School in Okmulgee. He leased an apartment for the family in a rooming house.

My mother, Margaret Mae Knoblock, was married to Nicholas Shiro and lived in Fort Worth, later moving to Texarkana. Mama married very young, about 14 years old, which happened a lot in those days. Nick was many years older than Mama. They had one son, born dead, then Richard, Louis, and Robert Shiro. Robert had a twin sister, Rose Pearl, who died soon after birth. Mr. Shiro worked for the railroad; a good job in those days, but there was a bad strike about 1923, and the railroad did not recover for many years. In the meantime, Richard found work as a telegraph operator in Okmulgee, Oklahoma. Mama and her other two sons joined Richard, and they lived in the same apartment house where Daddy and his family lived. Mama had left Nick because he never got his job back, so Richard was the breadwinner for her family until Mama and Daddy married in 1926.

Mama and Daddy married in 1926, and Margaret Lucille was born in 1927. Two years later, I came along; I was born at home in Okmulgee August 22, 1929. Other world-shaking events took place the same year: the stock market crash (which was known as the Great Depression), the birth of Popeye the Sailor Man, health insurance, penicillin, and American Airlines (first named Texas Air

Transport), operating from Meacham Field in Fort Worth. They carried a load of 5,446 passengers. The first musical comedy on was "Broadway Melody." The movie that got the first Academy Award in 1929 was "Wings," a saga of World War I aviation, shot in San Antonio, Texas, starring Janet Gaynor. My friend, a man I worked with at Dalfort and dated briefly, had that movie. We watched it at his house about 1990. I've seen it on TV since then. It was a silent movie.

In 1933, Daddy and Lewie came down from Okmulgee to the Southeast corner of Oklahoma to look for a place. Daddy had quit his job at the school because his employers had told him who to vote for, and Daddy wouldn't be told—he valued his freedom, and I'm like him. I like to think I'm independent, not necessarily stubborn, but maybe. Voting to me is a sacred freedom, and I don't think we should be told how to believe, even by the people we happen to work for.

Daddy and Lewie came to McCurtain County, Oklahoma, and found Rufe. This place is in the country, about 10 or 12 miles from Highway 70. It is, and was then, a truly deep wood. Oklahoma only became a state in 1907; it was settled rather sparsely since the land run a few years later. Many Choctaw Indians had settled later, after the trail of tears. But many whites had come to the state, and this territory was full of gunslingers and bootleggers. Prohibition was there much longer than in the rest of the states. Therefore, many distilleries were run and operating. This whiskey, illegal but rampant, was sold, and caused gunfights and crime.

They purchased an 80-acre farm in the community about 7 miles from Valliant, a fairly good piece of farmland. No house was on the property. Daddy paid the owner, Tom Davis; I'm unaware of the price of the place, but he traded his car off, an old Ford, for a team of mules.

Margaret, Leona, Ruby, and me

Meanwhile, Mama took Margaret, me, Leona, Ruby, and Robert to Texarkana, to Mama's brother Leslie's house, to stay until Daddy got a large tent. He set it up on our new place, so we could live in it while our house was being built. Mama's brother in New York City, Uncle Jim, who had, among many other talents and professions, a great knowledge and skill in architecture, drew up the plans for our large, two-story house.

Daddy, with some help from Lewie and others, built the house. It was, by necessity, built of rough lumber, never painted, nor did it have electricity in those days and of course, no water piped into the house, no sewage system, and no gas. There was a path out back, leading to an outdoor toilet, a well was dug for water, and wood was the fuel we used.

But despite all this, it was a comfortable house, and the way people lived in those days. This was about 1933 to 1934. About 1/2 mile away, our neighbors, the Rices lived in a rental house. Will Rice, his wife Laura, their children, William, Jesse, Robert, Buster, and Richard were our close friends. The Rices asked us to move in with them while we waited for the house to be built. We did, and stayed for a while, probably a few weeks, and then moved into our new place. Years later, they lost their house, and we had them move in with us while other arrangements were made. Later, their little girl Helen was born.

So Robert and Buster became our good friends, Margaret and me. Robert was four years older than I, and Buster about a year younger. Robert and I had the same birthday, August 22. Many years later, Robert remembered that I had given him a men's tie for his birthday. No ties were worn out there in the country, but it started the trend with Robert and me, and every year we gave each other some little birthday gift.

Chapter 14

"I think I just had a snake bite me."

I was about eight years old, and we were living in our farm in Oklahoma. Our house was isolated from others by a little over a quarter mile. Margaret and I were playing, creating our own games. It was about 1937, most of the world was dealing with war and the different aspects of saving certain things needed for building up war materials. The USA entered World War II in 1941.

We were playing that we had a restaurant, I suppose, and found that we could make colored water from certain substances. This colored water was put in fancy jars or bottles that we found stowed in the fruit house where Mama's canned foods were stored. I remember going out to the fruit house and reaching into a shelf to get a jar when I felt a sting on my middle finger, right hand.

Mama, spending most of her life in town and never being around snake territory, had warned us that if you got bitten by a poison snake you would die. No such problem if the snake was harmless, such as a garden or green snake, and even blue racers or black snakes. They were all harmless. Also king snakes, because they kill the poison ones. Chicken snakes are not poison. They swallow whole their prey, such as baby chicks or eggs. The poison snakes we had in Oklahoma were copperheads, rattlers, and cottonmouths. Any of these three were killers, Mama said, and she really believed that.

Anyway, I drew my hand back quickly, and there was that copperhead, lying stretched out on that shelf. I could imagine him leering at me, as if to say, "Good enough, Smarty. You practically put your hand in my mouth."

I wasn't scared—then. I went casually in the house and told my sister-in-law Lennie and Margaret, "I think I just had a snake bite me." Lennie got excited.

"What kind of snake was it?"

"I don't know," I said.

"What color?" she asked.

"A lot of colors, I think."

So she ran out to the fruit house and found the snake, which was now on his way to safety out of the little log fruit house. She grabbed a hoe and held him down, not daring to raise it and strike him because he would get away while she was about to hit him, so she held him down.

Mama had me put my hand in a bucket with about two inches of kerosene in it. She went to tell Daddy, who was plowing in a field nearby. Daddy left the plow and came home quickly. He went to the fruit house where Lennie was holding the snake. Failing to find anything to kill the snake with, he took out his pocketknife and cut off the head. He then cut off about 4-6 inches of the snake, split it, and slapped a piece around my finger. It hurt like heck!

As the snake died, the part around my finger drew the poison out of me. I'd been complaining, but now it wasn't hurting any more, and Daddy said it had done all it would do. They gave me some pure alum on a knife (we didn't have capsules).

They put a snakebite tourniquet on my arm that Uncle Jim had sent us from New York, and as one last precaution, Mama got peach leaves, cooked and thickened them, and made a bandage for my hand. Daddy said, "Now you'll probably get sick, but you won't die."

"But our school picnic is tomorrow!" I wailed.

Daddy said, "Well, I don't think you'll feel like going on a picnic, but you'll be okay."

I went to bed, and the next day I was fine. I had a fat hand and a good story to tell the other kids, but I was okay and enjoyed the picnic. By the next day my hand had gone back to the normal size. When Daddy related my story to the doctor later, he was commended. The doctor said he did all the right things, and it was good that he didn't cut crosses in my arm the way a lot of people did those days. This used to be done to bleed the poison out.

My hand carries no scar from the copperhead, only a memory, reminding me to look carefully into a dark shelf that may shelter a critter waiting to get revenge for the death of an ancestor long gone.

Life goes on. In 1931 Thomas Edison, the "Wizard of Menlo Park" died. My Uncle Jim had worked for him, and had a couple of inventions to his credit. Years later I was to hear much more about both Edison and Uncle Jim. Sherman and I got to visit Edison's park and laboratories in Fort Myers, Florida. Also in 1931, the Light Crust Doughboys, a group of country music artists, were on the radio, and also worked at Burrus Mills in Fort Worth, Texas, a great, well-known group for many years. And the new comic strip called Dick Tracy made its debut.

In 1932 The Great Depression was in full force. I didn't realize that until later, but times were hard for most everybody. Ours was the way of life for most Americans. Even wealthy people lost their savings and became poverty-stricken. But we knew little about bread lines, starvation, etc. We raised our crops. Our gardens and orchards gave us food. We also raised corn, beans, peas, potatoes, and we always had a cow or two and a couple of hogs. But everybody worked, and though our family was fairly small, as several lived elsewhere, someone seemed to always be visiting us or just staying with us for a few weeks or so.

As I grew older, I used to read everything I could. I learned to read at an early age. I was reading the Bible at five years old, and started to school shortly after age 5. I went to the first grade, and the teacher promoted me to third from there. She said I should be in the same grade as Margaret. So I was ahead one year throughout my student years, and started the ninth year at 12 years old.

But although Margaret and I were close—after all, we were the only two from both Mama and Daddy—we drifted apart as we grew up, and had totally different interests, although in the first new student years, we were pals. We used to sing together. We learned to sing harmonies, and the rest of our lives, we were thrilled to sing and to learn the different harmonies all by ourselves, and later, even to read music a little. Then we learned to play guitar, mandolin, and ukulele. Some of the first songs we learned to sing were, "If I Could Hear My Mother Pray Again" and "Beautiful Isle of Somewhere," and there were others. As we grew a little older, we used to sing some of the fast gospel quartet songs. This love of music was with us all our lives. We were always into the country music, from the first songs of Jimmie Rodgers to the years when a new type of rock music took over. My brother, Louis used to see that we had every country song recording that became popular. We had a large record player called a Gramophone, or, as we called it, a Phoneagraph, which had to be wound up about every record or 2 played on it. Really a great invention, spring wound, never needing a battery or electricity.

Eventually, we learned the songs, and learned to play them on the guitar and mandolin. So the Phoneagraph was not played as much as it had been, although we still needed it in order to learn the songs. Louis continued to send us records as long as we were still at home. In his later years, Louis and Murrell had many problems, and finally got a divorce after the kids were all gone from home. Louis stayed in his room all the time, playing records and re-recording the songs on cassette tapes. He seemed to be obsessed with this hobby, and seldom came out into the rest of the house. I believe that over the past years Murrell had been unfaithful to him, and they had finally been driven apart.

It was April, 2006. Phil and Sherry were moving into their new house. Sherry did a lot of cleaning in my house, washing and getting their stuff ready to go. I did my wash, too, mostly after they left. I called Jacky and told him I'd pick him up around 10 AM tomorrow to go see Margaret. He doesn't want to go see JJ, so I guess we won't. JJ was still in jail after having stabbed a neighbor, and I was having a hard time with that, but I know I can't do anything about it. Jacky is still mad at JJ. I talked to Jacky, and he said JJ had been indicted, and may get up to eight years in prison. But I don't know, and I doubt he will spend that much time in jail.

Next morning, I got ready to go get Jacky and take him to see Margaret. While I was still in the bathroom, I got a call from Thom; he was going to Dallas, and asked me if I wanted to meet him at Dunston's. I did, but it would have to be about 1 PM, because I would have to take Jacky home.

So I headed for Jacky, and we went to the nursing home. I don't know why Jacky won't go see JJ. JJ thinks he probably has spent his money (JJ's) and doesn't want him to know.

Margaret was up, but still had a gown on, and while we were there, the lady from hospice came to bathe her. Her glasses are lost now, as well as the skirt to her best 2-piece outfit. And of course, her two lap robes haven't been found. I reported it again to the girl at the desk.

We left pretty quickly. It's hard to talk to her. She can't hear, and now she can't read the notes we write, except she wore Jacky's glasses some and read some notes I wrote her. So I dropped Jacky off at home and headed for Dallas. I had asked Johnny if he wanted to go with me, but he didn't. He wouldn't go unless Thom specifically invited him. He thinks he's intruding.

I still got to Dallas early, so I went to the shopping strip on Harry Hines. I went to a store and found a lot of ladies' clothes. I got Margaret and me a couple of outfits for summer and went on to Dunston's and met Thom. We had a great lunch. He wanted to go to Sam Moon's, and so we went. He wanted to look for something for Debby (her birthday is in May), so we drove down Harry Hines. The traffic was terrible. We didn't buy anything, and he took me back to my car; it was awfully hot.

I drove home and was so tired, because of the heat, I guess. I watched TV a little, lay down, and took quite a nap. Then it was time to fixed supper, so I cleaned up the kitchen and fixed some meat and vegetables for my supper.

Sherry next door came over and brought me a dinner, including two small pieces of pie, chocolate and lemon, chicken enchiladas, and green beans. So tomorrow, lunch is taken care of. She and I talked a while, and I showed her the picture I had got, an e-mail of my new great-grandson Lee, Amy's last one.

I had a strange dream in the night. I dreamed I had to go somewhere for a night meeting and I had to have an escort. For some reason, it couldn't be Johnny, and I couldn't go alone. So the folks around me insisted on some guy I didn't know going with me. I refused, saying I wouldn't be unfaithful to Johnny. I woke feeling really uneasy.

I called Johnny, and he suggested he come here. I said, "Great!" We had a good visit and went to lunch at Joe's. He left about 2 PM and I got the mail. There were three letters from JJ. He had sent two of them to Margaret and one for me. He seems to be much more used to the jail, and a lot more adjusted to the situation. I left, went by to see him, and planned to go take his letters to Margaret. But I had to wait for them a while, and it was late when I left, so I went to the dollar store and got Margaret a pair of glasses and a pair of shoes. I came on home, rested a while, and found stuff for two lap robes. This time I put her name in big letters in each of the four corners of each one. I'll take them to her tomorrow.

JJ goes to court on Monday. His lawyer thinks he can get off with probation. JJ is still pretty mad at his dad, and he says Jacky doesn't really want to work. I talked to him about what hate does to you, and he needs to trust in the Lord, although I understand why he is so against his dad. I love Jacky, but he doesn't work. But we had prayer, JJ and I, and I left. He wants me to come and see him Sunday.

They're predicting rain, and it looks like it, but hasn't started here yet. It has been a great day, in the 80s. It seems to be turning cooler now. I walked out to see the clouds, and saw my neighbor Ken Bino putting fertilizer in his yard. We talked a few minutes, and he said he could spare some of his fertilizer for my yard. I watched for him a while, but it got dark. I gave up, shampooed my hair, and rolled it before going to bed.

It came quite a storm after midnight—a lot of leaves and twigs were down, and my trash can was missing. The trash had been picked up and the recycle bin was still there, just no garbage can.

I was about ready to go to the gym, but it was still raining, so I just used my exerciser. I did 40 pulls on it without stopping, and decided that was enough. I called Johnny and asked him about my bringing stuff for lunch to his house. Anyway, I had to go see Margaret and take her the stuff I got for her yesterday. Johnny wasn't home, so I went on and called him on the way. He said he'd go with me, so I took the chili, chips, and cheese that Phil had recommended, and all the stuff for Margaret's. I had made her two lap robes, got her some new glasses, shoes, the two capri outfits, and the two letters I had that JJ had sent.

Johnny and I went to the Fireside Lodge. We visited Irene a while and I went to find Margaret. She was in the beauty shop, and the lady was just finishing her hairdo. It looked really nice, like Margaret always wanted it. I took her to eat her lunch, read her letters to her (she heard very little of it), and I went to get Johnny and left.

We had lunch at his house and watched a little TV. He was going to meet me at Ginger Brown's, so I went on home. Barbara had said she and maybe Jim might go with me to Ginger Brown's, but she said not tonight. They were still talking about storms tonight, so Johnny and I decided not to go after all. After I had supper, I sat around a while reading, watching TV (bad). Kearney called and talked a while but the evening was long.

I haven't been to the gym all week. I need to start back, but the rain, welcome as it is, and as happy as I am to see my yard looking better, makes my arthritis so bad. I went to the store and to the mall, didn't do much, just walked and got a few things.

I went to Wild Bill's and had a great lunch. It was the first time I've been there. They were fairly new, and I promised myself I'd take Johnny there sometime. We had nearly stopped having lunch together except on Sundays, or whenever I went and got him, but he always insists on paying. He just isn't always up to driving out here, and I understand that. I just have depended on him for so long, I miss him when he's there and I'm here alone.

I get letters from JJ. I guess I'm all he has, and he depends on me a lot. He wants me to come and see him on Sunday, and Manda wants me to come after her to see him. I told her I would, on Saturday. And then I talked to Jacky, and he wants to go with us if he gets better; he has a tummy ache today.

I picked up some things from the store for the lunch on Sunday; got the stuff for my special dip and chicken for chicken pot pie. I called Manda and told her we would visit JJ on Sunday evening. I was going to need to go then anyway, and she said it was okay. Manda is usually very agreeable with me.

I was in the kitchen at the table when I heard the garage door open, and I knew it was Johnny. It was Sunday morning, and nearly time for church. I kept waiting for Johnny to come in through the garage, and when he didn't come in, I looked at his car out in front, and could see was still sitting there. I was alarmed, and went out to see what was happening. He had one of his weak spells (he gets upset when you say dizzy, but I always thought they were the same). Anyhow, I helped him in the house and got him a cup of coffee.

He sat in the recliner for a while, and I had him come in the kitchen so I could take his blood pressure. It was 100/53. I told him I'd take him to the emergency room but he said no, wait a while, so I took it again in about 15 minutes. This time it was 96/50. Again I suggested the ER, but he said no. Finally, he decided to take a couple of nitro tablets 5 minutes apart. He got pretty weak; I called HEB, and they said we could come on in if we needed to. So finally, he decided I could drive him in his car.

I called Barbara to see if they wanted the pot pie and some dip, and she came over to get it, along with some chips. I started to help Johnny out to the car; he nearly didn't make it. I was really struggling to get him into the car, and it appeared that he wasn't going to make it. I called out once, but nobody heard me, so as he leaned his head against the car, I dialed 911. He managed, with my help, to get into the back seat and sit there to wait for an ambulance. They came quickly. Barbara came over and went on to the hospital to meet us. I rode in the ambulance with Johnny. The attendants decided to take him to North Hills Hospital; it was closer, and they said since his blood pressure and heartbeat were so low, they wanted to get him there as soon as possible. So Barbara met us at North Hills Hospital, and I spent my time with Johnny and sitting with Barbara.

They took blood etc., and didn't find anything abnormal, so we brought him home about 3 PM. He was feeling a lot better. I gave him lunch; I didn't want him to try to drive, so I called Sherry next door and she drove behind us. We took Johnny to Braum's on River Oaks Blvd. There was a reason. Johnny didn't want his kids to know what happened, because he was afraid they'd decide to have his driver's license taken away. We made it okay, and he drove his car on home.

On Monday, April 24th I got up early, didn't accomplish much, but went to the gym—my arms were too sore to do the lifting exercise. I had really held Johnny when we went to the car on Sunday. I was so afraid he was going to fall, and didn't realize how heavy he was, and I guess I was so scared; I didn't feel the soreness until later.

Thom called; he'll be after me on Tuesday afternoon. We're going to Oklahoma to see Robert and Omia in Idabel. I took the food I had saved for Johnny to him. I visited with him a while, but he didn't want to go to see Margaret and Irene, so I went alone. I visited with both of them for a little while and came on home. I called Robert about 8 PM, and he said he's coming to Arlington to have some treatments or surgery for his prostate problem. I assured him he is welcome to come here and stay with me, and he said he probably would. He will hear from the doctor's office soon to let him know the schedule, etc.

On Wednesday, I got up and started getting ready for our trip. Thom didn't get here until about two, so I had plenty of time. We went first to downtown Dallas to the Plaza of the Americas. What a sight! Thom's old job was right across the street; he had some girl meet us outside and bring Debby's dark glasses. She had left them in Thom's office. We went to a fine jewelry store to pick up some of Debby's jewelry they had repaired. We looked around some—there is an ice skating rink in the middle, and many shops and fast food places all around.

After that, we drove home to Thom's house in Waxahachie. Right after we got there, Debby came home. Thom fixed us chicken sandwiches for supper. I got up about seven. Thom had knocked on my door, and Debby had already left. We got ready and left fairly early, and ate breakfast at a Mexican restaurant Thom likes. It was a good breakfast. We'd had a large cup of coffee at Thom's. He brought me a cup before I got up, and we had more with breakfast. We had a good trip. Thom drove his Toyota Camry. He's a good driver, and we stopped when we needed to. We got to Idabel in time to have hamburgers at Braum's in Idabel.

I was shocked to see Omia. She could hardly walk at all. She just crept very slowly, and she and Robert both talked at the same time. Neither can hear well, and they get aggravated at each other. They were glad to see us. Cindy, their granddaughter, had discovered the Schiro family (Robert said Mama had decided it should be Shiro) had moved from Albania to Sicily, and later came to the USA. Some of the apparently wealthy Schiros had started a very large and ritzy hotel, the Monteleone. This hotel is still a great, wealthy place in New Orleans. We saw some pictures, letters, etc. concerning this.

We rented a room at the Microtel, Thom and I, in the afternoon. I took a bath and we rested and watched a crazy movie, "The Jerk" with Bernadette Peters and Steve Martin. Then we went and got supper for us, Robert, and Omia at Kentucky Fried Chicken. We saw Mark, and later on, Roy came in for a few minutes before they both had to go to work.

When we left, instead of going to the motel, Thom headed downtown. He wanted to take me to the Choctaw casino to gamble. I thought he was kidding at first, but he wasn't. When we started, Thom had $20 to gamble. I had two dollars I dared spend. I lost it all of course, but when we left, Thom had $21. This was my first and last gambling experience.

Back at the motel, I was bushed. I promptly went to sleep, and Thom watched a few minutes of TV. When we got up, we got our things together, went back to Braum's and had breakfast. Then we visited Robert and Omia a while but left early, so we could go and visit the Moran Cemetery. There are always a lot of new graves of people I know, and some I don't. Our families' graves, Mama's and Daddy's and Jack's, were all okay, but we had to dig out a lot of leaves on Addie's. I could see that getting a flat stone for hers was foolish; nobody keeps this cemetery up, and headstones get lost too easily.

We came back through Valliant, didn't take the bypass around Hugo, but drove through it. We went through Powderly before we found a place to eat lunch. We found a nice restaurant, and were surprised at how nice it was. The decor was all New Orleans and stuff. The food was good, too. We had pork chops, beans, fried squash, and then large slices of strawberry cake. While we were on our way, Thom got a call from a man who's interested in hiring him at a great salary, so we reached Fort Worth on a high note.

Matt came on Friday at 11:30; he had a date for 2:30 p.m. We decided to go see the Civil War museum on Highway 820. It had been open a few months, and I had wanted to go, but Johnny wasn't too interested in history, so we hadn't gone. But Matt was glad to go with me, and it was pretty interesting. We saw a lot of stuff, but not much documentation. I made several suggestions about where we could go eat, but Matt didn't seem to be hungry, so he left without eating anything.

On Saturday, I went after Manda about 1:30 PM. She had obviously just got up and failed to comb or brush her hair. I neglected to tell her she needed some ID in order to talk to JJ, and I had thought Jacky would have told her. He had told me he was taking her to get her Social Security card, but he hadn't, so only I could talk to him. I think JJ is ready to pick up his life, but now he's worried about ever getting a good job, since he has a record now as an adult. We talked the whole 10 minutes allowed, and he asked me to pray, which I did. He also asked me if I could put $15 in his account. I would have, but I needed to go to the jail downtown to do it, and I was not feeling like going downtown. I was getting ready for more physical tests, so I would tell his dad today that he needed to do it.

We went on to Fireside Lodge and visited Margaret. On our way, we went to Braum's. Manda hadn't eaten all day, so I got her a meal and both of us a milkshake. I told her to tell her dad to take JJ some money.

I have seen Robert and Omia several times since then. Their son, Roy managed to get them in the same nursing home in Idabel. They share the same room, and they seem as happy as possible. I feel the food leaves a lot to be desired. Robert now has Alzheimer's. Omia has some dementia, but doesn't seem to be nearly as bad as Robert. He's forgotten he was a great cartoonist, and doesn't know what to do when I put a pencil in his hand, hoping he would draw something. He always knows me, but doesn't recognize whoever is with me, and when I leave he cries, which makes me cry too.

On Tuesday, May 2, I got a call from LaVerne, asking about Jeff and Karen. She thought he was off work on Monday and Tuesday. I said I didn't think so, normally, but I'd be glad to call and see. I was a little surprised—he answered the cell phone, the one I called. He said he thought they could come for lunch. He asked who all would be here, and I told him Dale and Carolyn, Laverne, Janice, and Johnny. I called Laverne, and she was excited. It was only a short time till Jeff and Karen got here. Karen helped me fix the sandwiches. She's so good at cooking and preparing food, and she made some super-good salad dressing with honey and mustard.

The rest got here shortly. We visited, ate, and Jeff got his guitar and banjo, and we sang and sang. They did several songs that they knew I liked, and I sang along on some of them. I am such a ham. They all left fairly early, and I got busy cleaning up the kitchen. We had used throwaway glasses (which I wash anyway) and plastic plates which I don't. It's funny; there are still always a lot of dishes to wash.

I went next door to sit with Ashley while her family was gone to a banquet with Jonathan, part of his graduation activities. I hardly saw her; she was working in the yard until 8 PM, and then bathed, ate, and went to bed. I sat in the den where Goliath, a blind and arthritic Chihuahua dog, very old, was stumbling around; a pitiful sight. Sherry walked me home, and we talked a few minutes. They're great neighbors and friends.

During the night there was a terrific storm in the Sansom Park area, Meacham Airport and Keller. I talked to Johnnie, and he didn't have electricity; a tree had fallen on the wires and knocked out the power. Mabel Troup called me, and then I called Rose Jones. A tree had fallen on her house, and our old shop on Jacksboro Highway had had the roof torn off. The building was nearly demolished or looked like it on TV. There was nothing in our edition of the paper about the storms.

I decided to go to the cafeteria for supper. I went to Luby's on 820. Just as I got to my table, I heard someone call my name. It was Tommy Drain and his wife Billy. I hadn't seen them for ages, so I got to sit with them and visit. Billie is in the late stages of Alzheimer's. I'd known them a long time and was very glad to see them. It's sad to see Billie so bad, although she's been this way for a long time. Their daughter, Barbara lives with them, and helps take care of her mother.

On Thursday, I got a call from Johnny, and he said the people were coming to repair the damage done by the storm to the electric wires, and maybe to the roof. I got a little uneasy about him, and I said to him, "Johnny, please don't go outside when they're there. They won't need your help, and it would be too easy for you to fall." Johnny was recuperating from surgery; he had had an aneurysm in his aorta, and was just recovering. Of course he assured me he'd be okay. Later I talked to him again for just a few minutes, and then after a while, I got a call from Kathy. "Pauline, I don't want to scare you, but I'm at the hospital with Dad. Somehow, he was outside, and got too close to the truck out there, and his foot got run over. He thinks he has a broken toe."

I had to stay close to home, because I was getting ready for a colonoscopy in the morning, but later the news was worse. Johnny had obviously fallen when the truck ran over his foot. His ankle and hip were also fractured, they told him, as well as the big toe and three ribs. He was in a lot of pain; she said they were taking a lot of x-rays.

I took the stuff I had to take for the tests, and it was awful, for most of the night. Finally, about 2 AM, I was ready to draw a tub of hot water, and afterward I crawled into bed and slept. I rested pretty well, but I was aware of the constant storming outside my window. I got up about 6:30 and got ready to go. I took my high blood pressure medicine and waited for Thom. I was worried because of the storm. When he got here, he told me he had seen some bad wrecks and traffic tie-ups. We got there right about on time. The place is new, and the girls were all nice and took good care of me.

I was out completely for the procedure, and when I woke up, I was told I was okay. Even the Barrett's didn't show up. He had removed one polyp from my colon. Thom took me to eat at Applebee's; we couldn't get breakfast, so I had a grilled cheese sandwich and coffee, and he brought me home. I waited a short time after he left, got in an unmade bed, and slept a long time. Whatever they gave me to sleep must've worked. When I woke up, I felt so good I didn't hurt all day long.

Johnny seemed to be a little better. They did surgery on his hip—only a one-inch incision, they said—and he'd had some company from the church. Randall called me this evening and said he'd be glad to take me to the hospital to see Johnny tomorrow morning. I may agree to that. Sweet of him, he is a good friend.

I felt fine next morning. I had somewhat of a shock when I read on page four of the Star-Telegram that the medicine I took for the cleaning up my colon had been causing patients to have kidney failure: 23 of them, in fact. But I got myself together and felt fine, so I went to see Johnny. He was in ICU, so I couldn't see him until 11 AM.

It was 10 when I got to the hospital, and very quiet, being Saturday, so I went to the cafeteria, had a cup of coffee and a pecan muffin. It tasted good, but I started feeling ill. I figured I'd be okay soon, and went on up to the waiting room. Jim was there, so we sat and talked until Janet came in. We went to Johnny's room; he was so glad to see me. It was the first time I've been there, because I'd been getting ready for my tests when the accident happened. They were keeping him pretty sedated, but he talked to us, sometimes a little confused.

I got very sick and had a terrible chill. I couldn't keep from shaking, so the nurses took me to the emergency room. We filled out a lot of paperwork, and they put me in a room in the emergency area, where I finally quit shaking. Janet and Jack came to see me before they left for home. I had an IV in my arm. It was right inside my elbow, so I couldn't bend my arm. I had to keep it down by my side to keep it from that eternal beeping. Finally, they said they wanted to admit me, so they put me in a room up on the fourth floor. I was the only patient in the room, and they took good care of me. I was on clear liquids and getting pretty hungry. They checked my blood about every four hours, and started at 4 am.

Wednesday, March, 2007. I am at home alone—Phil and Sherry moved into their new house on Riversprings in Hurst. What a great place—a small lot, as all of them are, but very roomy inside, and I like the room arrangements. They are all moved in now, and just busy getting settled. All three girls and their husbands, plus Justin, Jonathan, and Kyle moved everything, and the girls worked at getting it all straightened out.

I made a chocolate cake for them, and had made a large batch of rolls the day before. Sherry had made Sloppy Joes for everybody. I know they were all worn out at the end of the day. Sherry and Phil came back here and got a lot of stuff from my garage, and they straightened my house so well I was surprised. I met Thom and Debby at Mimi's in the Hulen area for supper. I was really surprised when I came home and Sherry had cleaned up so well.

I had nearly forgotten how it is to be by myself. It's hard to cook for one person, and I'm having to learn again how to plan meals. Johnny couldn't go to church with me yesterday. He's still not feeling real well, has a sore hip from the surgery. But I went after him after church, and we went to Furr's to eat, and then went on to Fireside Lodge.

Margaret is getting worse; she seems to be swelling pretty bad in her stomach area. I had found a lot of her pictures, and some of her papers, in my front closet. She didn't seem to remember exactly what they are, but I'll take him back to show her again in a day or so.

I've done a little planning about redoing my house. I decided to put the original drapes back in my living room, then plan to get a new bedspread outfit for my bedroom. I went to Linens 'n Things, and found exactly what I wanted for the bedroom. It's red and gold. The set included the comforter, bed skirt, two sheet sets, two shams, two odd pillows and the drapery set. I got it all set up the next day, and the bedroom looks great.

Johnny called me this morning early and told me that Howard fell and broke his hip. He is to have surgery tomorrow. He is 92 and nearly blind with macular degeneration.

I really am enjoying my house, and having things returned to normal, so to speak. I went to choir practice. Jaye was there today, but the pianist was still sick and Claire had gone for blood tests, so Beth played, and we sang the old songs from our regular books. We had a good time, and after it was over, I was invited to go home with Ginger, along with Jaye. We waited at her house for her son and his wife. They live in Denver, and were in Austin, Texas for a Film Festival, which included a book Ginger's son had written and illustrated. We saw the book, written for kids and it was all great. It was all about country singers, Jimmy Rogers to the present, funny and entertaining. When they came, we finally went on to the restaurant Jaye recommended, called the Wooden Nickel, a really good place to eat.

The next morning about 10 AM, I called Matt, and we decided to go to Grapevine Mills Mall just to goof off. I picked Matt up at 11:30. Since Matt hadn't eaten anything, we went to the Traildust Steakhouse, only it wasn't Traildust anymore, it was "Love and War in Texas." What a name! But it was great food—Matt had a good steak, and I had a salad and a small bowl of soup.

We went out into the mall and walked all the way around. We stopped a few places and looked, but never bought anything. But we enjoyed it, just being together and talking. He drove my car home, and is going to see about going with me to the Johnny High show on Saturday night. Tomorrow he's meeting Jeff and Pam for supper.

I came on home, and when I got here, Sherry (next door) and Zack and Ashley were working in my yard, and Donna was working in hers across the street. I had a call from Johnny and some mail, but went out and swept the front porch and part of the driveway. I couldn't do much, but at least I was able to help a little. Then I came in and got a large jar of cranberry juice with black cherry, and I took glasses out and poured for everybody, called Donna over, and she brought cake for everybody.

Afterwards I called Johnny back and talked to him. He hadn't heard from Howard today. I felt a little guilty about not seeing him since Sunday, but I'll go see him tomorrow.

I checked, and decided I can't hang those drapes in the living room by myself. Matt said he'd help me, so we'll see, but I've got to get a curtain rod that will work. This is one of the times I really miss Margaret. She's always done this for me.

I have improved a lot and went to choir rehearsal yesterday. We all went to Manor Care & sang old songs. Later I went to Ginger Brown's and had some lunch and visited Johnny.   He is satisfied there at Avalon, doesn't seem to remember Manor Care much at all. I left and went back to Manor Care from 2 PM to 4 PM, and we played a game. I had to learn the rules all over again. I left at four, because my student René was supposed to come to class tonight.

On the way home, I got a call from the student who was supposed to start last week and never made it. René called me; he had to make a visit to another Bell worker and will start back next Monday. I was so tired, I went to bed early.

I talked to Dan; he'd heard that Charles Russell had been sick, so I called Charles and talked to him. He said he was okay, and asked me to come to their house the next day. Ora's sister and her daughter were coming, Mary Jo and her daughter Paula. They lived near Hulen Mall. I went to Mineral Wells today and took two leftover pies, coconut and chocolate. It was a lot of fun, and I always love to visit Charles and Ora. I found out the sister who had a baby the night Paulette was born was Nell, not Mary Jo, as I'd thought.

I was very tired when I got home. The trip to Mineral Wells is about 50-55 miles. I had appointments with Dr. Mary Brian and Dr. Krekow. Dr. Krekow is an oncologist, a young, pretty lady, very sweet, and talked to me and listened to me for quite a while. She prescribed some pills I'm to take for five years: first month didn't cost me anything. I'll take them, and she gave me a second prescription of free ones after the first month was up. I got downstairs just in time for my appointment with Dr. Brian; she had a full house. I read all the magazines I could get interested in before I was called in. She said I was doing okay, but she did a sonogram and then drained a lot of fluid outside of my left breast or where the left breast had been. It's been hurting and swollen for a week or more, and I hadn't been sleeping well because it was hurting so. I left her office about five, and went home in time to go to Ginger Brown's. I stayed until 9 PM, felt bad, but hoped to feel better after a good night's sleep.

It's been a really rough winter. We had a snowstorm in January like we've never seen here in Texas. It destroyed live oak trees all over the place. I was told by Donny Crites, a deacon at church, that it was because most other trees had already shed their leaves, but the live oaks still had theirs. The snow stuck and weighed them down so the branch is heavier. My large live oak in the front lost two large branches, and another one is bent way over and needs to be cut. Fortunately, our power lines are underground, so we didn't lose power like a lot of others did.

All winter has been cold and wet. The advocates of so-called climate change etc. had been silent all winter. Those who were saying we were all responsible for global warming have been shown by the Master who's in control, and that the climate is out of our control. But they made lots of money by advocating this.

I've been pretty active most of these cold days. I'm still going to Manor Care and to see Johnny at Avalon. He is in a bad way—still knows me and his family, but losing a lot. His brother, Howard, also at Avalon, is failing too, and stays in bed a lot, as does Johnny. I have a lot of fun with the computer. I'm on Facebook, and have many friends on there—I think about 104. Several of the Broadview kids were at my birthday party in August. Phil put about 85 pictures on my Facebook that were taken that day.

My health is pretty good now. The arthritis is always with me, but a little better since I got over dropping the Celebrex. I still take a lot of Extra Strength Tylenol.

I've been waiting since Christmas to see Thom. Every time he's planned to come and meet me for supper, his flight has been canceled because of bad weather. He's supposed to be here Monday evening, and I hope he does, but they're predicting bad weather then, so we'll see.

Sherry and the boys, Jonathan, Kyle and I went to PF Chang's recently and saw Matt. He looks so good, and he has a new cell phone. He's called me once since then. He's still writing music.

My friend, Nicole Sherrick had her little baby girl last week. I haven't seen her yet. Her name is Larissa Joy. Nicole put her picture on Facebook.

When I got up this morning and turned on the TV, there had been a terrible earthquake in Chile, and afterward they were warning about a tsunami. This was the Atlantic Ocean, and the earthquake measured 8.8. It's now 8:45 PM and the news reports 200+ dead.

Chapter 15

"Mother, please don't cry when I'm home."

In 1990, Dalfort had operated Love Aviation Training for a year. They had bought my school, and therefore broke the contract, which included the agreement that I would work for them three years, and wouldn't operate a school for myself for three years after selling the school.

There were other aspects of the contract we had signed, but, along with my good friend and CPA, Mike, I was satisfied to take the money. It wasn't all that was due me, but fairly close, and figured the agreement was null and void. I was happy to leave, avoiding the drive to and from Dallas every day, and dealing with some people like Hugh Krull, the VP over me.

Immediately, I heard from Thom. The cleaners pickup station he had bought for Jeanne after their separation was for sale, and he thought maybe I'd like to buy it. He had borrowed some money from me, and would pay it back by helping me pay for the cleaners. Paulette and I decided it was a good idea. It was near Skyline Drive on the Jacksboro Highway, and we'd keep the business there, and so we made the deal.

We operated the cleaners. I had worked at dry cleaners before and done alterations plus a little of everything, so we did okay. We bought a new sewing machine with a serger and all the fancy stitching. Paulette had a ball learning how to embroider, etc. We decided to include a ladies clothing section.

We bought a van, and began going to Dallas where we bought ladies' clothes, costume jewelry, even got some hats and wigs to sell. The name was already Ruffin's Classic Cleaners, and we added Paulette's Sassy Fashions. We started to outgrow our space, and moved down the Jacksboro Highway to a log cabin shopping strip. I taught some A&P classes, along with our cleaners. Paulette did some work at Johnny High's office in Grapevine. She sang at the Johnny High show every Saturday night, and also sang regularly for funerals at Greenwood, Mt. Olivet, and occasionally at Biggers.

We went to the wholesale places in Dallas to buy merchandise to sell. We did pretty well, but it became hard to sell and make enough profit. We were inclined to sell at very low prices, so we made very little money; we sewed and did alterations, and made dresses, etc. and sold them. Maybe we spread ourselves too thin.

Paulette knew her cancer, although seemingly in remission, could come back any time, and she went to her doctor and the cancer center regularly. For a time, she wore a pain contraption that was electronic, and it eased some of the pain in her back. But she kept up her good spirits, and loved the clothing business. She was beautiful, and many of the wholesalers loved for her to wear their clothes. They always had something new that had come in, and they wanted her to try on different outfits, so we would get her a lot of the new things. She always had new outfits to wear when she sang on the show, and sometimes we bought three of the same things for her, Patsy, and Christy, the three who sang together a lot on the show.

We lost money, but I didn't worry about it. I was happy that Paulette was happy, and I figured it was worth whatever it cost to see her happy. We sold things to Kitty Wells, Sammy Smith, and other, sometimes famous people.

Cindy went with us to Dallas, and many times she went with Paulette while I stayed at the store. Cindy worked for me through the years, and was one of Paulette's best friends. She had worked for me at the school long before we had the shop.

We finally moved to a place on Davis Boulevard, close to where we both lived. We had the store for a few months; Paulette died in December, 1993. I went from Baylor Hospital in Dallas to the store the afternoon she died, and closed the store forever. I didn't want it without Paulette. Anyway, I'd spent so much time at the hospital with her, we had just about stopped buying merchandise, and the store was nearly empty. The economy was getting a little bad, and ready-to-wear was getting to be mainly jeans and tops for women. And now, after 19 years, it's still the same.

Paulette Joyce Ruffin, 8-18-53 to 12-21-93

Our daughter, Paulette was a tiny baby at birth, she weighed 6 pounds and 6 ounces, but, as most babies do, she lost a little weight in a few days. I took her home in about two days—the time had been shortened since my two boys were born. I had a very hard pregnancy. I'd had prenatal care, and Dr. Childs was a good doctor, and very careful with me. He had seen me through three pregnancies now, and since one had ended in a miscarriage, we took every precaution to get the baby here and well.

I remember having a terrible cough which persisted. I was nauseated much of the time and couldn't eat very well. Finally, I began to have pains that seemed to be early labor, and had to stay in bed a lot. Sherman's brother, Earl and his wife, Mabel came and stayed quite a while with us, and I suffered some nervousness. I loved them, but my nerves were bad.

Paulette was born in the same old All Saints Hospital that Thom and Phil were born in. I had a very long and difficult labor. Dr. Childs gave me strict orders to never have any more babies; he said otherwise I probably wouldn't live to raise what I had. I was taken to a ward where there were three other women, new mothers. The one closest to me was a sister to Ora Russell, our pastor's wife. I was excited, and I must have kept her awake all night, talking to her from about 10:30 PM until morning.

Sherman was ecstatic. He'd always wanted a little girl, and although he loved our little boys, five and two, he doted on our baby girl. Mama was with us then—it was 1953, and Daddy had died in 1949, so she was there with us, and was so helpful, and loved the family.

So Paulette grew; she was very talkative and walked and talked early. I was always surprised. She seemed to grow up overnight. I used to sew for her. A dress could be made from such a small piece of fabric, and she loved what I made her. The boys were sweet to her, and she used to stay right with them and try to do everything they did.

All three of them love to sing. I sang with them, and we sang all parts. We formed a quartet very early. Thom started piano lessons, and later played guitar as well. Phil started playing trombone in school. Paulette learned piano and clarinet, and she also played guitar. But we all sang.

Growing up when I did in the 1930s and 1940s, we learned how to live, to treat others, and how to raise a family. Women were supposed to be a little subservient to her husband, since he was the breadwinner, and to obey, as written in the marriage vows. They were never to make judgments contrary to what the husband had decreed.

Women were barely beginning about that time, late 1940s, to defy husbands at great risks, and sometimes to work in public, often hiring babysitters to look after the children. This became a necessary thing, since many men had left their families to be in the military. Some had to leave their families for good, were killed or crippled, and couldn't work any longer.

For whatever reason, women began to take over some jobs; they sometimes learned to like working, earning money, and being a necessary part of the workforce. This was resented by some, because it changed for so many families. I was instructed by Sherman that I was not to work at a job; I was to be a homemaker and take care of the family. It was okay. I wasn't going to work at a job anyway, and was glad to have a husband who loved to work.

So for several years, that was the way we lived. By the time I was 23, all three of my children were born, and I was still a young woman. I was beginning to be a little curious, and wondered how it would be to make money on my own and have a little to spend occasionally.

So six years later, Paulette was in the first grade at school, happily enrolled in Ms. Carroll's room at Sansom Park Elementary, the same teacher Thom and Phil had in the first grade. Ms. Carroll was a priceless first grade teacher; we loved her dearly all through the years.

I took some clothes to the cleaners, owned and operated by a man I knew well, James Clardy. He put me to work on the spot. I was very excited, because it was part time. I would work only when the kids were in school. James taught me a lot about the whole operation. He had the whole plant: cleaned, pressed, did alterations, etc. I was experienced in all types of sewing, and learned the other stuff easily. I worked for James for several months doing whatever was needed, and eventually was laid off because he had hired another girl in my place.

I worked at a few other cleaners—the work was okay, but very little money and no future. I liked some of it and hated some, such as alterations, but I looked for more opportunities.

I was faithful going to church with my family. I did several things there, always taught in Sunday school, training union, etc. My family was great friends with the AE Stephens family (one or more of them were charter members of the church), and this led to my working for Steve many years later, helping him start Stephen's Aircraft School at Meacham Field in 1966. All this working I was doing was fine with Sherman. He never seemed to get upset about it until I started getting my own school together.

I had always taken a lot of pride in the beautiful work Sherman did for so many years, and still do. It was hard, heavy, and grueling work. But he loved it, and would take me to see jobs he was so proud of. We would rejoice in the great craftsmanship he mastered and worked so hard at. He worked for several different companies, as it was hourly employment and not always easy to find.

But he wasn't proud of mine. After I started my school, he stayed miffed with me a lot, and actually criticized what I did, to other people. I heard him tell one man that I only "read to students." It hurt my feelings, but was just one of the battles I had to fight. Eventually, he was a little proud of me, when we went back together after our divorce. I made more money than he had realized.

Sherman was a few days from death, and had quit eating or drinking, and had very little to say. I was sitting with him and talking a little, and he said to me, "I'm surprised that you've stayed with me, and are taking such good care of me." I was a little taken aback, and I said, "I'm taking care of you because I love you. And I believe you'd do the same thing for me." He nodded and agreed with me, and I knew he meant it; He'd always been very good to take care of sick people. I remembered when he was so good to me when I was 8 years old. He stayed in the room with me, and I thought he was the greatest man alive. And again, after we were engaged, I had the measles and he took care of me.

It was the latter part of the year Sherman and I married, in 1946. Sherman was just out of the Army, and we had come to Fort Worth. We had been at my brother, Louis's house. He lived close to town and was a truck driver. He and his wife, Murrell had welcomed us into their home, and we stayed there for two weeks. We were anxious to find an apartment, and for Sherman to find a job. He'd been a mechanic in the Army, on motorcycles and other vehicles. He was an excellent auto mechanic, but starting in a mechanic's job seemed to be hopeless. Finally, the Texas employment office sent him to the Stripling's department store in town to see Charlie Hartley, who was setting marble on a stairway near the front entrance. He needed a helper.

Sherman knew nothing about marble, although when he was in the service he had the opportunity to see a lot of beautiful marble, in St. Peters Cathedral and other historical structures in Italy, and some other places. He had admitted at that time that he knew nothing about marble, but now he longed to see some of the same sights again.

Immediately, he became very interested in the work being performed, and in Charlie himself. They became fast friends, and their friendship lasted for many years. I met Charlie and his wife, and we, too, became good friends. Sherman and Charlie were employed by the Good Marble and Tile Company in Fort Worth. Charlie was pleased at Sherman's abilities to work well, and to learn the trade very quickly, and eventually, Sherman applied for training under the G.I. Bill. We got a much-needed check every month from the government to subsidize the pay from the company.

After a couple of years, Sherman got his own journeyman card, and became a member of the union. Plus, he got more pay from the company, so the checks from the G.I. Bill were stopped, but we were doing okay now. We were always grateful to Charlie for helping to make it possible.

Charlie and his wife lived on the east side of town. They had a daughter we met, and her husband, and they had a couple of boys, small at that time.

Sherman worked out of town a good part of the time. I was used to it, we were just grateful for him to have a job, and when he was out of town his expenses were paid. I have been to visit him, sometimes taking the kids with me. We've gone to see him in Pueblo Colorado, in Denver, where Sherman's uncle was a barber, and I went with him to Paris, Texas for a couple of weeks.

After Daddy died, Mama lived with us for quite a while. She wanted to live alone, but she tried that; we helped her get a place, a small apartment, but it didn't work out, and she was back in our house in a few days.

There was a small house about three doors from, us, nothing fancy, but two large rooms and bath, which seemed to meet her needs perfectly, and she wanted it. So Sherman and I made a deal for it, got it in our name, and paid the down payment of $250. She paid the rest of it at thirty dollars a month out of her small pension from Daddy's death.

We helped her, bought her some groceries and medicines, etc. She loved the place, and fixed it up so it was comfortable and clean. It was near us, so she could walk to our house any time. Margaret came to see her lot, and still depended on Mama for whatever help she needed, as she had always done.

Mama had had some radium treatments when she went through menopause, and I guess that's what made her bones brittle. She fell and broke bones several times. Once, after breaking her leg, she was in Manor Care nursing home near our house, getting the care and rehabilitation she needed.

We had some company. It had been years since we had seen Charlie and his wife, but this was Charlie's daughter, and her husband and 2 boys. Sherman was always a good man and has always been ready to help anyone who needed it; to a fault, really. We didn't know these people well, and what Sherman did was inexcusable. He told them they would be welcome to move into Mama's house while she was in the nursing home. I was astounded, and very angry. I told him he should have talked to me first, but I didn't know about this until they had already accepted the offer.

When Mama was ready to come home, she was also very upset. We both were angry at Sherman for making the decision he did, with no word from me or Mama. Mama stayed with us for a few days, and they left. They left the house in a mess, stole some things from her, and I don't remember any words of thanks being said. I made Sherman promise he'd never do anything like that again.

A few years later we began to get letters from a prisoner in Huntsville. This prisoner was one of the sons of Charlie's daughter and son-in-law. We got several letters, and Sherman answered one or two. I don't remember for sure, but I think Mama warned me we shouldn't give him a reason to think we would cultivate this friendship. For our own sake and that of our family's, we stopped that and never heard from him. I understood that he was in prison for life, and probably thought Sherman could help him get out.

After Sherman and I remarried, I sent him to the Schick center to be dried out; he had fallen off the wagon. It was successful, but he met a man there called Don; he decided Don needed help when he was through there with his two weeks. He was to go back later for two weekends. Don, his new friend who was an epileptic, couldn't pay for a trip back, so Sherman gave him (I still can't believe this) his credit card so he could pay his bus fare. But on the way here, he lost all his luggage and his ticket he'd bought with our credit card. Sherman bailed him out again, and told him he could stay here for three or four days.

At the same time, Paulette was having a biopsy to determine if she had cancer or calcification in her breasts. Sherman and I were at the hospital, and left Don here alone. Her news was bad. I was so shocked when I saw her, not knowing at the time that she had cancer, but she was as white as a sheet. I nearly fainted, and they made me sit down and gave me oxygen. I was sent the next day for a stress test, but everything seemed to be OK.

Meantime, we got back home, and the house was extremely cold. It was winter, and the house was fairly new, but when I tried to turn up the heat, the front part of the control was missing. We looked all over for it, and asked Don if he knew where it was, but he swore that he hadn't touched it. Finally, I called the company that had installed it, and they said it could be replaced for $250. I asked what else they could do, and they said they'd sell us another one for

$150. I ordered that one; we had to have heat, so they came in and installed it: an efficient one, just less sophisticated.

Don left the next day, insisting he knew nothing about the control, but the one we'd had installed worked fine, and gradually, you just forget these things.

A few years later, after Sherman's death, I decided to move furniture in the guest bedroom. I moved the nightstand, and lo and behold, there was the control plate that was lost for so long. Someone, I guess it was Phil, happened to be here, and reinstalled it for me. It's worked beautifully ever since. I decided that Don had probably had one of his seizures, and, trying to adjust the heat, had dislodged the control plate. If he was truly having a seizure at the time, he probably never realized what happened.

After a family moved out of the house next door, on Lyndale Drive, another family moved into the house. They were a couple with three children, and have proved to be wonderful friends all through the years. We've never had better friends. Sherry and her husband, Howard, and the three children have always helped care for our yard, never charging for it. They are just great neighbors in every way. Sherry and I have been close neighbors, and I am enclosing here a note she sent to Phil when I had my 80th birthday party. All the way through my writing, I am referring to her as "Sherry next door" because I have so many Sherrys in my life.

> I have been racking my brain trying to think of a good story about Pauline!!
> As her neighbor, our relationship is based on many 1 minute interludes.

Anyone that knows Pauline, knows that she is full of one liners!! For example;
"To make a long story even longer..."
"I have a great memory, it's just short!"
and so on.
She has so many more, and while I don't remember them, (because I too have a great, short memory) I do remember the times we stand out on the sidewalk and talking and laughing.
Pauline loves to laugh and enjoy life! That makes her not only a great neighbor, but also a great friend.

Pauline is also passionate about life. The Yellow rose bush in the front yard reminds her of her daughter Paulette, who died early in life. She was by her husband, Sherman's side till he died. She loves family deeply. I remember when her sister Margaret moved in. It was a tough time, but Pauline helped Margaret till it almost ruined Pauline's health. She also took in a nephew, when he needed a chance. She would drive him to the train station each morning, then pick him up in the evening. She spends each Thursday helping out at Manor Care. She regularly visits Johnny, and that keeps him going, whether he knows it or not. She is a saint!

Pauline loves music. Those close to her know that she goes to Ginger Brown's each Thursday night. How long did she go to Johnny High? I know she was there a lot, especially when Paulette was a regular. She sings in the church choir and even has directed it. She encouraged all my kids as they learned to play one instrument or another.

When I was talking to her about her big party, she and I talked and laughed about what would happen when she made it 80 more years. I told her that I'm sure it would be a great party, but that I didn't plan on hanging around long enough to celebrate it! However, if anyone could make it to be 160, I think it would be Pauline!!
"Gray hair is a crown of splendor, it is attained by a righteous life." Proverbs 16:31

What a joy it is to be able to honor Pauline today, on her 80th Birthday!!

Happy Birthday, Pauline
We love you, Sherry and Howard

It was 1966, the year Thom graduated from high school. We had looked into his going to Houston Baptist College, but decided it would cost more than we could afford. We didn't try to get a loan at the time, and he decided to go to the Texas Wesleyan, here in Fort Worth. After a few weeks, he informed me one day that he was unhappy with that decision, and he wanted to drop out and go into the Army. The Vietnam War was going on.

It was a blow to me. I guess I felt like any parent, thinking about the oldest child leaving home and going goodness knows where. But he was determined about it, and had obviously been thinking about it for a while.

I started to cry, and he said "Mother, please don't cry when I'm home. I can stand anything but that. You can cry when I'm not here, but I'm asking you not to cry again when I'm here with you." So I dried my tears and promised.

He enlisted and went for his examination, etc. He passed his physical, and asked for a job in aircraft maintenance, but they put him in the infantry. We took him to the bus station in Dallas, and I'll never forget watching him go in alone, the wind blowing his hair. Such a handsome boy, in his jeans and blue shirt. I didn't fight back the tears that now flooded my cheeks. I had kept my promise not to cry until then.

The Sunday before he was to leave on Monday evening, several friends were gathered at the house, and, as usual, we had been singing and recording some cassette tapes. After the rest had gone home and Paulette had already gone to bed, we decided we wanted to record a hymn we had learned; or rather the three of them would. Paulette gladly got up, and dressed (she was a ham like me). She took the microphone and said, "And now, the Shake-it-up Trio proudly presents, 'Jesus Is the Sweetest Name I Know.'" It was the first time we had heard the term, all her idea.

Thom was sent to a base in Louisiana where most of the boys went for basic training, those that joined the Army. He never knew where he would go next, but he went from the base in Louisiana to one in Alabama. He spent some time in El Paso, Texas. He was a squad leader part of the time, and because he was neither a drinker nor a smoker, had to look after other recruits, cleaning up after them and getting all the cigarette butts left on the ground at the camp.

He was finally sent to Heidelberg, Germany, where his job was arranger and composer for the Seventh Army Chorus. He came home on leave, and married Jeanne Butler, and the two of them went back to Germany for the rest of his time in the Army. The following letter was one I received.

November 16, 1968

Heidelberg

Dear Mother,

Tonight Jeanne and I had guests for dinner, and afterwards, we went to see "The Greatest Story Ever Told". To say that I enjoyed it would not be enough. I have to write you tonight and tell you how much I love you and how much your life means to me.

Mother, if one were to compile all of the things that Jesus said in the movie, and if he were to combine all of His teachings to fit just one person, that person would be you.

I am sure that Jesus has also said something like this, "I am very proud of her. She is one of my best children".

All my love,
Thom

Thom and Jeanne were glad to come home, but they had enjoyed Germany immensely, saw wonderful sights, and wanted to go back as tourists later. Thom worked at The Bedroom Shop for a while, and they settled in Arlington. Later, he began a career in commercial and mortgage banking. Their first child was born soon after they moved to Arlington, Lesley, a beautiful little girl, and about 17 months later, another little girl, Amy was born.

During this time, Phil and Sherry were married and had a family. They became the parents of 3 boys, 5 years apart: Adam, Jonathan, and Kyle. They were all 4 exceptional parents, and Sherman and I were proud grandparents. He had had to have some surgery, because of a ruptured ear drum that affected his hearing some. Phil never went into the military service. He was into electronics and sound systems, and Sherry was a schoolteacher.

Paulette has always been completely engrossed in music. She took some voice lessons, and was always active in singing and performing. In the first few years of her marriage to Bill Hartmann, they were into songwriting, as well as performing. I was into some writing also, and have a few songs to my credit, mostly just the lyrics to the tunes composed by Bill, who is still heavily into writing music. They, too, became parents of a son, Matthew Konrad, who was only 7 when his mother died in 1993. He inherited the talent for music from both his Mom and Dad, now has his own band, and writes a lot of the songs they perform.

My Daddy, Tom Fagan, was only 61 years old when he died, December 28, 1949. He'd had a series of strokes; he had suffered from high blood pressure for several years, he and Uncle Clem, his brother. They had tried different methods and medicines. Daddy had weakened his coffee with water, until he was only drinking hot water. He was eating no greasy foods or any salt. He wasn't doing much work; he still helped Sherman around the house, but was afraid to exert himself much.

He loved talking with the neighbors. He used to go with me to shop, or just walk with me and Tommy, the baby. He walked to the store often and liked to stay busy. He walked in the neighborhood and even downtown with me, and would carry Tommy when I know he didn't feel like it. He just loved doing it, and so did Tommy. He seemed to be exhausted a lot of the time, but he denied being tired. He never failed to go to church on Sunday; he loved our pastor Charles Russell, and Buel Russell, Charles brother, who was our music director for a while. He had been baptized in a Baptist church. Daddy and Mama had lived with us a little over a year when he died. Mama was 57.

A few years later, Uncle Monroe, Daddy's brother, shot himself at the home of him and Aunt Nellie. Uncle Monroe had undergone surgery for hemorrhoids, and had suffered from some treatments afterward, and swore that if he had to take any more of the treatments, he'd kill himself first.

He told us this when we had gone to visit him and Aunt Nellie in Alvarado, where they lived in a very small house on the road off I-35 going into the town. He'd been working at an old cemetery close by. There had been no perpetual care for the cemetery until he had taken it over several years before, and he kept it beautifully.

Uncle Monroe and Aunt Nellie never had children; Aunt Nellie had been pregnant and lost five babies. They always loved children.

I was awakened by a phone call a couple of days after we visited them, and was told that he'd shot himself with a shotgun, to the head, and we knew the reason. So we dressed quickly and rushed to Alvarado. He had put the gun on the ground, leaned over it (he was a tall man), put his toe over the trigger, and blew his head off. The roof had to be cleaned off where the gun had blown off his head. What a gruesome picture! And I remembered the way he looked at me as he said, "I'll never go through that again," and I knew he meant it.

Uncle Clem used to have high blood pressure. He'd go to the doctor, get a prescription, come home, and throw the prescription away. He would do the exercises, certain that such exercise as standing on his head would run his blood pressure down. It didn't seem to help, but he did the same thing the next time. He and Daddy tried the garlic that was thought to help, but didn't really seem to do any good.

High blood pressure is something that seems to run in our family. I am taking medicine for it, and have been for years, and several of my brothers and sisters have had it. But it seems easier to control now than it used to be.

All of my family was faithful members of Broadview Baptist Church until about 1981, when Sherman decided he wanted to get back with Viola. I left Broadview and went to Azle Avenue Baptist. Our separation lasted three weeks. I went back home, but I stayed at Azle Avenue Church. Sherman also started to Azle Avenue, and so did Mama. Paulette stayed at Broadview. Thom was in the Army, and Phil was going to Sagamore Hill Baptist, where he met Sherry.

We were happy at Azle Avenue, even though it was totally different from Broadview. There seemed to be no young people, and very few children. I was disappointed and surprised that the choir was full of older folks. After the death of the pastor, I was asked to teach his class of adults, which I did as long as I was there.

Broadview was full of children and young people. I was used to working with all ages; I loved it and the youth choir I had started several years before. We had good pastors, wonderful music and music directors, and many musical programs. We went to youth camps, concerts, and county-wide programs. We had concerts at our church, and we visited and were visited by different choirs. These are what I missed at Azle Avenue. But there are different programs going on now, at First Baptist, Watauga. I'm older now, and not physically able to work with young people any more.

My first few years at First Baptist, I taught Sunday school in an adult class. Now, for the first time, I'm only a member of an adult class. None of my family goes to the same church. Phil, Sherry and Kyle live close by, but Kyle is a singer, and we don't have a youth choir, so they go to First Presbyterian, downtown so he can sing in their youth choir.

Matt and his girl Leslie aren't in church, as far as I know. Matt is a Christian. We've talked about it many times.

It was so many years ago that I felt being led to start a youth choir at Broadview. My kids had always sung in school and church, and Phil also played the trombone in the band at school. We had many young people interested. We met one Saturday, just to get started. There were about 20 there and Thom played the piano. It was a good start; we learned a lot, and sang at our church many times, as well as some other churches. Our kids were all good singers, and glad to perform and have the good fellowship we enjoyed with each other. A lot of us are still in touch with each other on Facebook and by telephone.

Brother Kelly Moseley was our pastor at that time. He was so helpful to me and our youth choir, and did everything he could to help us. When we got our church directory finished, we saw a picture of our youth choir, and he had dedicated the directory to us, as stated on the very first page. Bro. Moseley later went into work as a missionary in South Carolina, where he stayed for some time. His wife had died while they were at Broadview. He later married a friend of hers, and she died the same way: had a heart attack. He married a third time, but he passed away in 2011. He and the third wife had visited us several times. He had pastored more than 50 years.

Broadview Baptist Church kids in 1992

While Love Aviation was in Arlington, we had some rather large classes, and a lot of my students were interested in finding new jobs in the industry. I did everything I could to locate places that were hiring, different companies, and we frequently got calls about sending prospective employees to fill these available positions.

Occasionally I would have students, either in school for their A&P or IA, who would invite that class to the shops where their work was performed. The trips for the students were successful as well as educational, and fun for the students. We were in close proximity to Bell Helicopter, and went once to see several projects in session, of people doing fiberglass structures. I had done fabric work before, but this was completely different and interesting. I had not seen the way fiberglass was used, and I think this was soon after the work had started on helicopters. Later, we went to Aérospatiale, which is now called American Eurocopter, where we saw all types of work performed on helicopters, including periodic inspections, engine build-up, rotor, and rotor systems, etc. We also visited the engine shop, Turbomeca, where all types of engines were being repaired and rebuilt. I have had several friends who worked there some for years, and I have also sent men to Bell Helicopter.

I have also taught several classes at Bell Helicopter and American Eurocopter, and some of those men, ex-students, always remembered me.

When my school was in Arlington, I was contacted about going to Egypt. I was told I was recommended to teach a certified A&P course, or part of it, at an airport in the desert. I was instructed to buy books and materials, and be ready to stay for a 6- to 8-month period. My students would be Egyptians interested in taking a 1900 hour course. This course was sponsored by American Eurocopter. I was recommended by a friend who obviously knew very little about the project, but I got ready, obtained my passport, and then the deal fell through. The friend who recommended me went to Egypt himself. He asked me to send books to him, which I did, a little relieved that I hadn't gone, since nobody seemed to know much about it. I didn't know much about it myself, or what was expected of the teacher.

A couple of months later, I acquired a class of 15 or so for the short-term course of A&P. They were Egyptians, and I never knew what happened in Egypt as far as the classes, but the ones I had for the course there at the school were sponsored by American Eurocopter. My friend came home way too soon, and I never found out what happened.

When I was teaching college students at TCJC part time, I had students from Carswell Air Force Base, they had some T-38s there. I don't know if they were based there or just there for some maintenance and repair. T-38s were flown by the group known as Thunderbirds, a wonderful group of pilots who were specially trained to fly these beautiful airplanes in precision flight. I had watched them several times, performing in air shows in and around Fort Worth.

The T-38s are small aircraft, very streamlined, with air inlets on either side. A student of mine, a small man, was just the proper size to climb in the inlets when there were repairs to make in that area. As small as he was, he was the only man who could fit into the inlet and do the repairs, but someone had to stand outside with a fan blowing air into the inlets with him so he could get his breath as he worked.

He arranged for our class at TCJC to take a field trip, so we went one night—I taught night classes. We had a great tour, and learned of both the airbase and the plant where work on the airplanes was performed. We saw where Danny worked on the T-38s, and we also got to go up into the B-52s.

The B-52s are so large on the outside, it's hard to realize that it's small on the inside. You go up the ladder to inside the cockpit, where everything is close together and seems very small, but most of the airplane is the huge bomb bay. The B-52s replaced the old B-36s, which were very efficient in their time, with both reciprocating and jet engines. This part of the tour was very impressive.

We also saw a lot of structures in the sheet metal shop, controls for the large aircraft, and much machinery for cutting, shaping, and forming the metal. My students and I were amazed and surprised to see it all close up. Such tours make us proud of our country's great strides in aviation.

It was Tuesday, August 21, 2007. My sister Margaret was very bad, had been getting worse for some time, and her body was beginning to shut down. She had stopped talking several days ago, and the people at North Pointe Nursing Center seemed to be taking excellent care of her. Plus, the hospice people, nurses, and counselors were looking after her as they do, in such a caring and loving manner. I was going as often as I could, but appreciated the care she was getting. On this day, the day before my 78th birthday, I woke up very early, which I do frequently. I got up and had a bowl of cereal, waiting to maybe hear a word about Margaret.

I didn't get a call, so I went on and got ready for our choir rehearsal at 10 AM. I'd been up a long time, and got hungry, so after I'd been to North Pointe to see about Margaret, I stopped at the donut shop and got 2 sausage rolls. We'd had a good rehearsal, although there were not many there. Afterwards, I went to see Johnnie. He was in bed, but was dressed and ready to get up. I noticed he was awfully weak, but still very careless about walking without his walker. He's very unsteady. We visited quite a while, and he gave me a check for my birthday. I asked him if he'd mind if I used the $100 he gave me on my new roof, and of course, he said no, whatever I needed to use it for.

Chapter 16

"Remember the monster on the taxiway that was so huge?"

It was probably late 1980.

Dave was a young man, about 45 or so, Latin looking, handsome, friendly and kind. He was married; I don't remember his wife, I may not have ever met her, but I liked Dave a lot. He was so patient with me, and so helpful to teach me several activities in the shop.

I was teaching at Steve's. Dave had had his A&P for a long time, and was also a pilot. He was employed by American Airlines Training Center, and taught flying in the pilot center. Dave and I talked a lot, and he told me he and his wife had two boys; one was completely disabled, physically and mentally, and had to have constant care. Any time I didn't have students to teach, I would go into the shop and work with Dave.

We tore down and built up small engines, and did other things in the shop that proved very helpful in my explanations to the students. Dave made arrangements for one of my night classes to go to the American Airlines Training Center for a tour of the facilities. It was a great tour, and he showed us many things used to train pilots.

He gave us a ride in one of the units called a Link Trainer. Half or more of my students there were or had been taking flight training, and we were all thrilled to get into the trainer that looked exactly like the inside of a 727. The students took turns acting as pilots, and the rest of us sat in as passengers. The airplane took some unexpected turns, and once we were alerted to a huge monster lying dead and bloody all over on the taxiway. It was startling to the pilot, as he had to deal with going around the monster. With all the alerts and bells ringing and sirens screaming, he brought the airplane safely to a stop, and I guess we all breathed a sigh of relief because it seemed like the real thing.

After the flight, we walked around in a large area with many maps, sectionals, all types of training aids, etc. Finally Dave told us, "Remember the monster on the taxiway that was so huge? I'll show you how it looks normally." Before being magnified during our flight, the monster turned out to be an ordinary housefly, magnified hundreds of times larger. It was hard to believe it didn't look so scary. This was just about the beginning of electronics becoming the norm in our lives.

Dave left after a while; he moved his family to Ohio. I was sorry to see him go—we never heard from him again. I'll always remember you, Dave, and appreciate you so much. You would've made a wonderful instructor in a mechanics school. We all need people like you. Of all the work you did for Steve, you never charged him at all, which helped to show what a really good man you are.

Lou was an Italian man, a good friend of mine. He taught classes at Tarrant County Junior College before I did. Among other things, he always did a lot of dope and fabric work, which I did too, on a much smaller scale. Dope and fabric was used on many airplanes, especially small, reciprocating ones, and some faster ones, like some spray planes, a lot of trainers, and older aircraft. It was truly an art to know how to shrink the fabric and apply it over wood or metal surfaces, to test the strength, etc. It is very important, as everything else is, to follow guidelines in everything about it, using the books and materials for the particular plane bring worked on.

The stitching is an art, too, as most of it is hand sewing, tying knots, stitches spaced just right, and applying a special tape to cover up the seams. At one time, Lou was working in a hangar on Meacham Field. He had flight controls for a large biplane to re-cover, and it was a big job. He had started on the controls, but still had much to do. He came to Steve's, and asked me if I would come help him. Steve said he could do without me for a few days, and to go ahead.

It was winter and very cold. The hangar Lou was working in was cold. Cold air was coming in large cracks in the building, and there was no stove because the dope doesn't like heaters, and some dope is very flammable. Lou said it was safe to work with the dope, with as much air as we had blowing in. Normally, when applying dope on fabric, there needs to be plenty of ventilation. I dressed as warmly as I could, but as I worked, the dope started to take a toll on me. I developed a terrible headache, which stayed with me for several days afterward. The job took us nearly a week. But I really, except for the cold, enjoyed getting those controls finished and ready to install on the airplane. I don't remember what the plane was, but it was a biplane that flew at higher speeds, so the stitches were about 1/2 inch apart (not about; the stitch spacing was very critical). I just can't remember for sure, but they were very close together.

It took several days, and it finally began to warm up a little by the time we finished. Lou paid me well, and I was glad to have the experience. Lou went to Hicks Field, an airport on the north part of Fort Worth. He had a flight school and a maintenance shop there, the last I heard from him.

Sherman and I visited him and his wife one day. I found out later that his wife had died, when I saw him once at a cafeteria near here. He may still be there at Hicks Field, but I have been out of touch with him since then. However, I have since heard that he is still operating his business at Hicks Field in Fort Worth.

I remembered a book that I'd read a long time ago, and I found it in my bookcase. It is a first edition of The Brutus Incident, given to me by a former student at Stephens Aircraft School. The student, George, and his wife were co-writers of this book, and he gave me a copy after the book was published. While he was still in school there, he was rebuilding an airplane, a stagger-wing bi-plane, a beautiful, bright red Beechcraft. He took many snapshots of the work being performed, and several flights, and showed them to me regularly.

After he'd finished getting his A&P, he started an airline company there at Meacham Field, with flights from here to Houston and back. Like many other airlines before, he soon closed the business down, and also like many others, had run out of money to continue. Some of the larger ones who had started there had succeeded, and moved on to larger facilities: for example, American Airlines, American Flyers, Central Airlines, and others. It takes a lot of money to operate an airline company. I think George had been an airline pilot before. I never saw him after that, and don't know how the book did.

Several years ago, Leona and her husband, Baustin, moved to Van Buren, Arkansas. Their daughter, Carolyn lived there with her family. Carolyn and her husband, Dale operated a service station and grocery store. Their daughter, Julia, had married Pepper, a boy from that area. Baustin, who had worked in construction for the oil companies, was about ready to retire, and they knew the best place for them was near their family. They had bought a nice, small house close to Carolyn and Dale. Ruby, Vernon, Sherman, and I decided to go and visit them. There were just the four of us. So we left here, and Sherman drove. The highway was good, it was an easy drive, and Sherman was both a good driver and a good navigator. We stopped and visited some friends who lived off Highway I-35, and got to Okmulgee early in the afternoon the next day, after spending the night in a motel in Marietta, Oklahoma.

My Daddy used to work at what was then Lee School, downtown. The name has been changed to something else, but Ruby remembered quite a bit about the school, our living there, and I think she had gone to another school.

She remembered the house on Madison Street where I was born. Downtown was Creek Council House, a very small establishment, a little like a museum with lots of interesting items in it. The Creek Indians were prevalent in Okmulgee, and I'm sure they have quite a history as one of the Five Civilized Tribes. I bought a beautiful bracelet and necklace, made by an Indian a little while before that. Later, I bought a matching pair of earrings in another town in Texas.

But the main attraction for us was the house on Madison where we used to live. I was born in that house. It had been very small, and had been enlarged since. The people were gracious, and invited us in, showing us the house and how it had been built onto. They also invited us to come back any time we wanted to, and said we'd always be welcome. They said there were more plans for adding to the house.

We did visit a few years later, and the house was still in good condition, or seemed so. But now, we continued into Arkansas, and to Van Buren to see Leona and her family. We went several times to visit them, and always enjoyed it. Julia's family grew, and eventually, Baustin and Leona both died. I continue talking to Carolyn, and keeping in touch with them.

I was sitting at my desk in our new office at Love Field. Morris Dixon and I had just opened Love Aviation Training Center at Love Field in Dallas, and I was waiting for a customer to come in and enroll. I can't remember having any misgivings or doubts about what we were doing. Ever since I knew this was the right thing to do, I was ready to start teaching. A man came in. I spoke to him, and he told me he was anxious to start A&P School. I asked him his name and where he was from. He told me his name was Joe Green, and he was from Okmulgee, Oklahoma. I held my breath when he said his home was on Madison Street.

"Madison Street!" I cried, "I was born on Madison Street!" It was an incredible moment!

He told me there were only three houses on Madison Street. But his house was painted green, so it had to be a different one from ours. This had to be one of the most incredible things that has ever happened to me. We marveled together how Okmulgee was such a small town, and we were both from the same street. I told him later that his coming in when he did must have been a good omen, because others began to come in then.

The first time we drove to Memphis, Tennessee, we visited our good friends from Broadview Baptist Church: the Bobby Moores, Ray and Joyce Simpson and their family, and the Stanfills. We had a great time; we'd just acquired a new little blue Volkswagen which Thom loved to drive. While we were at Jackson to visit the Simpsons, Ray made arrangements for Thom to go and play miniature golf with some of the young people from their church; Ray was their youth director. He knew a boy just slightly older than Thom, whose name was Ricky White. Ricky didn't get out much. Ray thought he needed more contact with his age group, and figured he and Thom would be good friends. They did hit it off, and we all liked Ricky. He lived in Brownsville with his dad, a buyer for a men's store, and his invalid mother. He was an only child, and seemed very lonely.

On our way home, we stopped at Bobby and Joyce's in Memphis. Joyce had fixed a good lunch for us, and we were to leave right after lunch. As we were about to sit down, someone looked out the window, and coming down the street was Ricky, carrying a small suitcase. He wanted to know if we'd take him home with us to Fort Worth. He'd come back later, he explained, and if we didn't want him to come with us, we could say so, and he'd go back home on the bus the way he came. We told him, of course, he was welcome to come home with us; we'd be glad to have him.

We were happy to have Ricky; by this time we nearly accepted him as part of the family. When he met Thom's friends at church and other neighbors, he made a good impression with them all. He loved our Broadview Church, teenagers and all. In a couple of weeks, he knew he needed to go home. He was never any trouble to us, and we weren't in a hurry to have him go, but he did need to go. He arranged to go to Dallas with Sherman; he could be dropped off at the bus station. Sherman came to me and said, "Honey, go talk to Ricky. He's crying because he hates to leave." So I went in the bedroom where Ricky was packing. He was truly crying; the tears were flowing down his cheeks, and he apologized for them. I held him and did a little crying myself as I told him he nearly belonged to us, we loved him, and wanted him to come back any time he could.

He came back several times. Meantime, he was going to college while Thom was in the Army, so they didn't see each other much those two years. But Ricky was happy to be invited to be Thom's best man when he and Jeanne got married. Thom and Jeanne left for Germany right after the wedding. I am enclosing a letter from Ricky to me just before he was to come, in time for the wedding rehearsal;

Dear Mrs. Ruffin,
That time is drawing near when you will gain a daughter. I am really looking forward to the big day. It's getting more exciting every time I hear someone talk about their first airplane trip.

We certainly did appreciate the invitation. I only wish I knew of something special that I could bring them that they could use. If you think of anything, just let me know.

I have been thinking, if the time my plane arrived in Dallas interferes with the rehearsal, just let me know. (I am at home now). That way, I can be sort of prepared when I get off the plane and can't find you. If my memory holds clear, the plane (American Airlines) is due around 9:23. I am really looking forward to seeing everyone again.

It will be the first time I have been there since Bill and Sharon married. Those Stephen's boys are really taking all the available girls. Maybe Paulette won't be married or engaged by the time I get there. If she is, how old are the Stephens twins?(Ha) Phil still dating my other girl friend? Tell him he had better be prepared for some real competition when I get there!!

We started In-Service Training yesterday. It has been hot as blue blazes, and the school is not air conditioned. I'm not used to this kind of weather. The teachers here have been real nice to this scared-stiff "freshman" teacher. I feel now that I may make it.

Mama and Daddy are doing pretty good. Mama's feet have really been swollen. Both her big toes are infected. (This is due mainly, to the diabetes) My High Blood Pressure is back to normal.

My new upstairs is real nice. You wouldn't believe it!! Daddy has really worked hard on it. I am surely enjoying it!!

Well, have to close now and get to sleep. See you in a couple of weeks. Tell all Hello for me. See you then.

Love to All,

Ricky

While Ricky was at college, Thom and I drove through Brownsville, Tennessee once, and stopped to see his parents. His mother was a very nice lady, and had us go upstairs and see the beautiful apartment Ricky's dad had fixed up for him. It looked wonderful, with everything a young man would need in his home. We only stayed a few minutes, and really enjoyed meeting his mother. She was in her wheelchair, and couldn't even go upstairs.

So Ricky came, and was here soon after the wedding rehearsal started. Soon after, he had to go home. He had really matured during his time at school and at college. It's very rare to see a young man so thoughtful, and we will always remember him as being part of our family. A few weeks after this letter, I received a very sad call. I don't know who it was who called me, but I'll never forget what was said: "Mrs. Ruffin, I have sad news. I know Ricky was always so fond of all of you. There is a railroad track right close to the house, and there are no warnings for motorists driving across the tracks. There's a lot of growth around the intersection, so Ricky probably never realized what happened when the train hit him. I hate to tell you this, but Ricky is dead."

Our Rick-----gone! And I had the task of calling Thom and telling him. It's a sad story, and I wish it could have ended differently, but one of these old days, Ricky, I'll be so happy to see you, and meanwhile, say hello to Paulette.

April 2005-2006

A little before this time, Margaret's health began to deteriorate. She had some of the same problems health-wise that Mama had suffered with the last years of her life. She had inherited the stomach problems, the diabetes, and something else that was peculiar to her. I don't know of anyone who had this particular ailment. She either never dropped off to sleep at night or awoke soon after, and went into the bathroom, and read the paper aloud, or talked in a low, guttural voice which made my flesh crawl. I didn't understand a word she said, and I doubt if she ever knew herself. I've never heard anything like it. It was an inhuman sound, and she denied doing it. I've gone to the bathroom and insisted she go to bed, but she resented it and complained loudly. Later, I've put my head under the covers and tried to ignore it. I hated to have her spend nights here, but she was living with me at the time.

She had called me one day, and said she couldn't live with her family anymore. I went and got her, along with furniture Paulette and I had bought, and now it had to be fumigated (it was full of roaches). She sold it soon. She paid me for a lot of living expenses and tried to help me with the work, but some things like her night sessions were getting harder to take. I always loved her; she was my sister after all, but she was not like she used to be. I was more worried than anything else, but I didn't know what to do.

Several times, we brought Manda here to spend a night and she slept with Margaret.

These sessions never failed to happen. Manda, sleeping in the same room, never seemed to know, but she did complain that Margaret kept her awake nearly all night, talking. I have never figured out what she was trying to say; there was no sense whatever in the way she carried on and the horrible, inhuman sounds she made. It was more of a growling sound; no definite words nor normal inflections.

I have never talked about this to anyone that I remember; it was a rather touchy subject. Since the '70s when there was so much ado about witches, evil spirits, demons, and such things, and I didn't want people thinking these things about her, or even me. Soon after that, I arranged for her to go back home with Jacky and his kids. This was not the first time I wondered about her mind and some of her actions. It was a long time later that the doctor at Peter Smith Hospital diagnosed her with brain cancer. And some time after that, they rescinded that diagnosis and decided it was a bad case of arthritis that affected her brain. She had had breast cancer, and I'm inclined to think the cancer went to her brain, but maybe her brain was bad anyhow, after the trouble she'd always been through. And, at the rate she was deteriorating, I was afraid it would affect my own mind.

Mama had died in 1987, but her mind was good until a couple of weeks before she died. She had been in ill health, but as far as I know, her brain was fine. She was a very capable, intelligent woman, and Margaret could have been the same way, but I don't know what happened.

Our little girl, Paulette, grew up so fast. I know the boys did, too, but Paulette surprised all of us. She walked early, and soon began talking non-stop. She loved clothes, and was thrilled to get a new dress, and I did a lot of sewing. But very soon she was sewing for herself, and she'd help me pick out a pattern; it always turned out to be the most difficult one available. So I had to learn a lot, along with her. We cooked and did many things together all her life. Her main talent was singing, and she was never without a song. She sang with the boys, with me, or just by herself, and would learn a song after hearing it only a few times.

She was a popular girl, partly because of her singing, and she had a great personality. She was a stylish dresser, and knew a lot about make-up and hair, which she started dying very early. Dissatisfied with her own hair color, she liked to dye it blond, and as she got older, she wore falls and hair pieces. But when she had cancer treatments, she hated wigs and all hair pieces. Once or twice at the Johnnie High Show, she wore a hat, no wig, but she was still beautiful, and there was a picture of her in the Memorabilia Room, of her, with her hat on.

During her senior year in school, she took some voice lessons from a professor at TCU. Her voice was giving her a little trouble, and she seemed to have a small node in her throat, which made her a little hoarse, and is normally attributed to sinus trouble. But the lessons helped take care of it, she learned well, and her voice was clear again. Right after she and Bill married, they started appearing as a duo in many clubs, motels, etc. One of the first places they played was at the Sands in Texarkana. Sherman and I went to hear them.

The Sands was about as close to a "honky-tonk" as they ever went. But we enjoyed it, Sherman and I, but some bad stuff went on after we left. I'd made myself a new dress, a plain black one of my own design. We met one of the students from Steve's, Ronnie, and his wife, Linda. Sherman didn't dance, but I danced once with Ronnie. They were booked at a place in Everman, a few miles from here, and did well. Paulette learned to project herself more into the performances and Thom advised her to smile more. She took his advice, and was a big hit. They were there for several weeks, and we, her family, got to hear them often. They also played for some time at Bryan, Texas, near College Station. I visited them, and Paulette and I would shop. Once, I went with Bill Gaby and his girls. We went to see ET, and also heard them play.

They played another night or two in Texarkana, and started getting more and more places booked. They became fairly popular, and made a few tapes to sell. They got several pieces of sound equipment, and as time went on, they went to New York, South Dakota, Niagara Falls, and other places. I visited them in Iowa, New York, and Minnesota.

They were ready to start their family. They came home to Fort Worth, and started working at Love Aviation in Arlington. Then they played here, close to home. They played at Granbury every Saturday night. At this time, they lived in Benbrook, not far from Phil and Sherry.

In July, 1946, after living in apartments for several months, Sherman and I moved into our very own home at 5609 Buchanan in Sansom Park, in the northwest part of Fort Worth. Sherman had started our house with only two rooms, a kitchen, a kerosene cook stove, small dinette, and enough cabinet space to get by and do the cooking, etc.

The couple who lived next door, with four rooms (not nearly finished) was Edgar Foster and his wife, Gertrude, a very unique woman who was very much in love with her somewhat younger husband. He had left his previous wife, along with four or five children, and married or not, I never knew for sure, now lived with Gertrude. He worked afternoons at the bomber plant, later becoming Convair, and then General Dynamics. Sometimes he just didn't go to work, which was an aggravation to his wife, Gertrude. She was much more ambitious than he, and believed in working hard all the time.

She was strange. One day my neighbor, Irene and I came from her house to the back of mine, and Gertrude was out there, viciously beating a little cat to death with a big stick. She said she couldn't make it go away. We were appalled, and came in the house quickly to get away from the gory scene.

We were all friends—I used to cook a lot in the afternoons, baking bread and desserts, and Edgar used to come over and watch, and we would talk while she was working.

Edgar was the son of Leon Foster, but Pauline was not his mother. Pauline also had another son from her first marriage. Pauline and Leon were parents of Nora, a girl of 12 when we first met them, and Nora was a good friend of mine who had a marvelous voice and was a sweet girl. Pauline was a special friend of mine, and it turned out that she had been married to the son of our first landlady, Mrs. Crocker. We had rented the first apartment from her, the one on Belknap Street. Pauline had been the "sunshine girl", singing on the radio many years ago, and a popular program in this area on KRLD. Another puzzle was put together later.

When our family had moved from Okmulgee to Rufe, we needed a truck to haul our furniture to our new place. I have no idea how it happened, but there was a man living at Rufe at the time who had his own truck, and Daddy hired him to use it to go and get our stuff and move it. The man's name was Ves Fuller. We knew him and his family for long afterward. Edgar had been married to a girl from Ves Fuller's family before Gertrude. Later on, he left Gertrude and went back to the Fuller lady and his kids that he had left. I never knew her, but always marveled at the coincidence. I saw Edgar once after that, when Leon died. He'd become a motorcycle rider by then, and had long, snow white hair, and a long white beard to match.

After Leon's death, Pauline went into a nursing home and spent her last years. Bill took good care of her. Nora had died much earlier with cancer. I've written before about Bill, Nora's husband and my good friend. He finished raising the two girls they had adopted, and was a great daddy to them. Bill lost his health after he lost a lot of weight because of diabetes. He had to have his legs both amputated. We were still good friends. I took Johnnie to visit him occasionally, and he always wanted to fix a lunch or supper for us. But I know Johnnie was a wee bit jealous of Bill, so I didn't go often, and sometimes felt bad about neglecting Bill all this time.

Soon after Gertrude and Edgar broke up and moved away, we had new neighbors. This was a couple, Earline and Elton Summers, who each had a daughter from a previous marriage. Elton was a war veteran, and had been in the Bataan Death March. His daughter was a little redhead, about 6 years old at the time, and Patsy was the daughter of Earline. She was a sweet little 12-year-old, in my Sunday school class. These people all became our friends, and Elton went to work as Sherman's helper for a time. Earline and I became close, and she started going to church with me.

We were getting ready for a Christmas party, and one day Earline said to me, "My brother is a young man, 21 years old, and is coming to see me, and I want him to go to the Christmas party. He needs a date. Do you know someone he could ask?" And, of course, I did. Nora was very close to his age, and I suggested they go together. Nora had gained a considerable amount of weight and I told Earline about it. She said, "That won't matter. Bill's a little overweight, too." So we fixed them up, and Nora, a good-looking, grownup girl by now, sang "Winter Wonderland" beautifully. They went out afterward, and Bill confided in me later that he'd got a ticket for "weaving". But he said he didn't mind.

About a year later, they were married. I was maid of honor. I made Nora's dress and my own, and helped Bill to attend to some details. The day of the wedding, I tried to talk him out of it. I was really worried, as I thought about how Leon was a drunk and sometimes abused his family, etc. But Bill was determined; he loved Nora, he said, and was sure they would be happy.

Bill and Nora were some of the best friends we ever had. Nora and her mother had encouraged me to go to church at Broadview, along with Gladys Campbell, who lived behind me on Biway and Landino. Bill also became a member. The Fosters, Gabys, and Ruffins spent holidays together, and sometimes went to hear Paulette and Bill perform. If one of us was in the hospital, we were all there.

In the early 40s, the Wilson family lived down on Little River, about 4 miles from us. Their house was a few feet from the water and isolated. A small place, but there were only four of them. Roy Wilson was an accomplished artist. He painted beautifully—mostly western art: cowboys, horses, and Indians. He didn't do much else that I'm aware of, since I was very young at the time. A nice guy, not a lot of ambition. He had a guitar, but as far as I know, never played it. He left it at our house, and we loved it. Margaret and I played our own and his guitars, also Mama's mandolin and a ukulele.

Frequently, our two families spent time together. Our house was open to whoever wanted to come, and was a second home to the Wilsons, as well as others, kin or friends. Mama worked hard and tirelessly to cook for everybody, but when the Wilsons were there, Ocie, Roy's wife, was always helping Mama cook good meals, or whatever needed to be done. She always stayed busy, and was willing to help Daddy, too, with whatever he needed help with. The boys, Juandell and Beverly, were like family, and we liked to play together. When we visited them, Ocie and Mama would be cooking lunch for us all, and the four of us kids used to get into a leaky old boat, and go rowing down the river. Neither Margaret nor I knew how to swim, and Beverly was too small, and hadn't learned how to swim yet. Juandell was the only one who could have swum if the boat sank. It was old and leaky, and we'd bail the water out with an old coffee can as we rowed down the river.

Later, Margaret learned to swim, but I never did. When the Wilsons moved up closer to us, to a house about a mile from us, I used to go and visit Ocie. We made goat chili, which was very good. I enjoyed helping her cook, and our families stayed close.

Once I went to a church that was about 3-4 miles from me (we used to go when we could). I never hesitated to walk long distances alone; there didn't seem to be anything to be afraid of, but Ocie asked Juandell to look after me, since he was going too, and he agreed, so we walked together part of the way. A man we knew, driving a truck, stopped and picked up several of us who were walking, and took us the rest of the way. After the church services were over, there was no truck waiting to bring us home, so we all started walking home. There must have been 8 or 10 of us, and, as kids did frequently those days, everyone stopped at a bridge not far from the Wilsons' to talk and goof off. I kept going toward home. Juandell asked me if I'd be OK by myself, and I assured him I'd be fine, and not to worry about me. Meanwhile, it was very dark.

So I walked on, past the Wilsons' house, and as I passed by a grove of trees in the darkness, I heard a low voice saying something to me from the dense growth. I could hear what he said, but I was grown and married before I knew what it meant. What I did realize was that it was Hubert, the only boy I knew who couldn't be trusted, and that he was standing not far from me with his horse, and his intentions were actually scary to me because I knew what he had in mind.

I told him I wasn't interested in him, and he should leave me alone. He didn't, but insisted I needed him. I turned around and started running back toward the Wilson home, hoping to get a head start before he could mount his horse. I ran (I'd never run so fast as I did then), and just about the time I got near the Wilson house, his horse, running the way he always ran his horse, passed me. He knew better than to linger, because he was afraid of Ocie. I stopped, went in, and told her what had happened. Ocie was indignant. We went out directly to find him, but we never did. The next day, she went out again, and followed his and his horse's tracks. She saw where he had gone into a culvert, probably to avoid her finding him.

Afterward, he rode his horse by our place at that fast pace, and Daddy went out and read him the riot act, and told him if he EVER rode his horse on our place again like that, he (Daddy) would shoot him. Daddy was mad at him anyway because of how he'd talked to me that night, and his voice was shaking. Hubert decidedly calmed down after that, and he began to act much better.

So we all grew up. Ocie and Roy later divorced, and she and the two boys moved to Ogden, Utah. Beverly, his wife, son, and Ocie all came to see us at Sansom Park once. Mama was with us, and we enjoyed their visit. Roy had painted and given us a great western painting that was in my home for many years. I always treasured it, but when I left home, I never saw it again. It was a snow scene with a couple of deer he painted many years ago. In January, 2009, Beverly called me to tell me Juandell had died from the COPD he had told me about a few months ago.

Chapter 17

"Would you like for me to come back later?"

It's been a busy week; everyone has finished their IA renewals, except Chris Beams will have another half day on Monday. Today I went to the funeral of a great guy—Dr. Hospers. He and his wife owned the museum at Meacham Airport since 1995, starting with the B-17, a beautiful airplane used in World War II so many years ago. He built the museum with more World War II aircraft, and many items collected over the years.

Dr. Col. Bill Hospers and his wife, Chuckie had been married many years. He had named the B-17 Chuckie after her. This was done to woo her into the field of aviation, which he loved, and it obviously did the job. She involved herself in all he did, and she took care of him when he became dependent on the wheelchair.

He was my student part time when I had my school in Arlington. He was a dear man, had a great sense of humor, and I'll always remember an incident at Love Aviation when he was going to school. He always asked for a snack, so we went into the kitchen, and found something to eat. He was an osteopath, and I asked him about a stitch in my side. He said, "I'll take care of it. Lie down on the floor on your stomach", so I did, and he began to feel my spine. "That's it!" I said as he touched the spot that hurt so bad. He put his knee on my back, and I yelled. It felt like he'd put all his weight on my back. Bill Hartman walked in. Bill's dry humor took over as he said coldly, "Would you like for me to come back later?"

The stitch was gone, and we all had a good laugh. The Hospers used to go to hear Paulette and Bill wherever they were performing, and he used to have Paulette sing at some of the osteopathic meetings. Later, he got injured and became wheelchair-bound. But he remained active in his museum and the activities he still sponsored. They had a big dance every year in the hangar, with dinner and a World War II theme. All of the aviation community will miss him greatly

In 1948, right after Thom was born, Irene, my good friend and neighbor, used to visit me. She would bring her niece, Janet, and Janet's brother, a little boy nearly one year older than Thom (Tommy then). This little boy, Johnnie and Ester's little boy named Jim Ed, was a favorite of Irene's; she was so fond of children. She had lost her little girl in a tragic accident at 14 months, and it was years before she even partially recovered from that. She was the driver of the car, and much later had to have some psychiatric help. Johnnie and Ester also had two girls, Janet and Kathy.

So, many years later, after Ester died and Johnnie and I were going together, his family and I grew close. The girls and I are still good friends. They all went to school at Castleberry, where mine went. Jim Ed, the boy, went into the military service, and I believe was into law enforcement as an MP. He married, had two sons, and divorced. He was visiting a girlfriend recently, and had a massive heart attack.

His sister, Janet called me last night, and told me about the services planned. He will be buried in the military cemetery between here and Dallas on Friday afternoon. I was a little startled when I saw his picture in the obituary this morning.

I knew Jim was a handsome man, but this picture of him is outstanding. He is truly one of the best-looking men I've ever seen. He was 65 years old.

My son, Thom came to see me last Monday evening. We went to have dinner at Olive Garden, one of his favorite places to eat. Then he took me shopping at the mall, something he always does when he comes. He bought me some costume jewelry and a couple of great tops. But he had to leave right afterward. He had a room at a hotel on the airport, and had to leave early the next morning. I am writing this on Wednesday, 12-12-12.

There is some more GOOD news from yesterday. Phil, who has been out of work for some time, had a good interview yesterday, and I am praying, as I know others are, that he'll get this job. The next day, he got confirmation. He goes to work January 2.

There have been so many dear people in my life, I can't write my story without listing some who have meant so much over the years. I used to tell the young people at Broadview that each one of them meant something special to me. I feel the same way about others, especially former students, some who have remained friends over the years since. I still get Christmas cards, some calls, and some have come back for an advanced course. I teach the IA Renewal course, and some students come back year after year for this. The same is true with former church members, pastors, musicians, etc., and some young people who were once "my young people" in Sunday school, and in training union, GAs, and youth choir.

Some are gone. Several have died. I was only 18 when I first went to Broadview Baptist, and for years, the youngest adult to work with so many young people. But there are also those from Azle Avenue, and even some from First Baptist, Watauga. But I was puzzled about Azle Avenue; there were so few young people. I'm no longer physically able to work with these groups, and I have only taught older adults since Broadview days. Now I really enjoy being a pupil in the older adult classes. It's good to know that some of these people I've known so long still remember me and stay in touch via Facebook.

I'm still in touch with many who were students and want to stay in touch. I live fairly close to Meacham Airport, and go back there sometimes to eat at the café and see people I've known, and who still remember me. I guess every industry has a certain feeling of camaraderie for the people who have been involved in the work, and aviation is a special "club"; a small world. I am thankful to be in this group.

It was about 10:00 AM, when the big jet I was on landed at JFK airport in New York City. What a thrill for me! I guess everybody dreams of seeing this huge city, with so many large buildings that look like they are close together enough to touch. The airport is, or seems to be, right in the heart of the city, and the plane was seemingly barely missing the buildings as it wended through and finally touched down on the tarmac, totally clear of the structures all around us.

I had taken a few days off from work at Steve's at Meacham Field. We had always been in touch with Uncle Jim's family who lived in Queens, New York. Uncle Jim had died a while before, and their daughter, Annette still lived in the house where they had lived for many years. Aunt Annabelle was still alive; a strange woman. She mostly kept to herself. Annette lived with her, but each one lived her own life, together, but apart in so many ways.

Annette had lived for several years in another house with 2 or 3 other women who were doctors. I knew very little about her life. I just knew Annette was a good cousin, very sociable, but I think few people knew her very well. She had been a director of nurses for a long time. She confided to me once that she had gone with some nurses to San Francisco. There was a convention connected to her work, and she had met a man there who won her heart, and she said was the love of her life. They had parted, and she never heard from him again, but she was very sad any time she heard the song, "I Left My Heart in San Francisco".

She was in her 50s at that time, never married, and obviously had little or no romance in her life, aside from the man in San Francisco. I had heard someone say she might be a lesbian, but it wasn't proven, and no one knew. And I didn't hear this until long after my trip there. I didn't have long to wait—she found me shortly, and had planned quite a weekend for us. She drove us to their house in Queens, and I did a double-take when I saw the house. It was designed exactly like the plans he had sent Daddy to build our house in Oklahoma.

Our house wasn't as fine as this one. Daddy had, of necessity, used rough lumber, and lapped the boards so the wind couldn't get through. Our fireplace was made of clay, and looked exactly like concrete, but proved to be extremely durable.

This one was 2 stories, had a bungalow roof, and very close to others like it. Queens was a whole village. The house was nice inside, but not spectacular; I guess I was expecting a little finer, but Uncle Jim had told Mama they had taken carpets, drapes, and other nice things out of their house and sent them to us, and that they didn't keep a lot of things for themselves.

On the way to their house from the airport, the scenery was magnificent! We crossed the Brooklyn Bridge, and we saw Shea Stadium and many other landmarks. I know that Annette was amused at me because I was so excited about everything. She took the two of us to eat lunch, and this was also quite a treat. We went to a fairly small place, and the first thing she ordered was a "split" bottle of wine. We didn't order food for a long time. I realized that meals in New York are at least a 2-3 hour affair, and always includes drinks.

I am not a drinker, but I tried to imbibe a little because Annette was so used to it. We went out for all the meals we ate. I don't remember any meal we ate at the house at all. We went out again on Saturday; Annette took me out driving, and we were intending to go to Long Island where she had purchased a place. She had made plans at one time to live there, but later sold it and bought a house in South Carolina where she lived the rest of her life. It was an interesting drive; we saw a lot of the ocean, and took some pictures.

On the way, we saw Jones Beach, and Annette showed me a large estate: a grand house and grounds called The Westchester Place. We had a tour of the house and grounds, and she told me all about the history of the place. It had been used during World War II for taking care of children. The people there arranged to care for German and Jewish children who were in danger in Germany, and who had parents in danger during the Nazi Regime. I never saw so many fireplaces; there was one in nearly every room. It gave me a feeling of gratitude for the people who had been so charitable. There were many others who wouldn't take these children, and it was thought that many people had been afraid for Americans losing their jobs, eventually, to these kids after they grew up.

On Saturday night, we went to a lady's apartment for a party. She had just moved in, and was celebrating with some friends. It was nice; the ladies were all amused at my accent, as I was with theirs. Of course, I couldn't mention that; I was in their territory. The hostess gave me a little cup and saucer set, and I have it still.

Early on Sunday morning, Paulette and Bill drove from upstate where they were booked at the Americana Hotel in Albany. The four of us, Paulette, Bill, Annette and I left soon and drove all over the city, including Brooklyn and

Harlem, and saw the sights. It seemed strange; there was very little, if any traffic in the city until around 2 pm. On Sunday, I was told, everybody slept until after noon because they'd been up all night.

So it was easy to get around. There was a strike around Harlem, and lots of trash in the streets, but a fascinating trip, just the same. We took lots of pictures. We went downtown, saw the Twin Towers, the Stock Exchange building, and the Statue of Liberty. We rode a few minutes on the Staten Island Ferry!

Later, we took Annette back home, said goodbye to Aunt Annabelle, and headed upstate to Niagara Falls. What a trip that was! We went by the Americana, where they were performing nightly; it's a beautiful place. But we left in a short time, and went on to Niagara Falls. We really enjoyed that. Paulette and Bill had been there, and had played for a time close to there. One side is Canada, and the other is USA. The USA side is cluttered with gum wrappers, cigarette butts, and candy wrappers, etc., but throwing trash on the Canadian side is strictly forbidden, and it stays very clean.

We took pictures, watched tourists, and finally started back to the city to take me to Annette's. Paulette and Bill went back to the Americana Hotel; I spent the last night with Annette, and got ready to go home the next day. I flew home from LaGuardia Airport; it was quite different from Kennedy. LaGuardia is right on the edge of the ocean, so the plane takes off right over the water.

Like all the other times I'd been off work for a few days, there was a new girl sitting at my desk. I'd been replaced. So I went home and waited a few days for Steve to realize he needed me back and give me a call. And, as usual, it only took a day or so.

While I was a young teenager, maybe about 13 or so, my Uncle Clem, Daddy's brother, his wife, Aunt Ophelia, and their two boys, a little older than Margaret and me, moved close to us. We were so glad. We hadn't had relatives live close, and these were some of our favorites. These two boys, Jewell, and the younger one, Marvin, were great friends. Marvin was a good-looking boy, full of mischief, and easy to laugh and make others laugh. Jewell was a very tall, rather droll boy, hard-working, and also fun-loving.

We all four had a good time getting together, playing dominoes, cards, etc. We always had to watch Marvin; one of his favorite things was to cheat at these games. We teased him, but couldn't get mad at him; he just laughed at us, and behaved—for a little while. Margaret and I had always wanted someone to run around with, and we couldn't have had anyone any more fun to be with. We went to parties together, and we loved to just get together at our home or theirs.

Years passed, and we all grew up. I married Sherman, and Margaret came to Fort Worth. We lost touch with the boys for months at a time. Uncle Clem and Aunt Ophelia had two older girls: Pearl and Hazel. Pearl had been married, and had a little girl, Alice Fay, a beautiful girl who stayed part of the time with Aunt Ophelia, her grandmother. Pearl was quite a wild woman; she drank a lot and ran around. She was a pretty woman, but not very close to her family because they didn't like her lifestyle. Hazel told me many years later that she had told Pearl she didn't want her to come and visit her (Hazel). Also, Hazel was the one to take care of Aunt Ophelia and Uncle Clem when they needed her, and Pearl wasn't good to them. Hazel was a great daughter, married to Winston Jones. They had 2 children, a boy and a girl. Winston died while he and Hazel lived in Dallas, and after that, Hazel moved to a place in Cleburne. She and I were good friends for a short time, but she died shortly afterward.

Pearl also died, and a few years later, her daughter, Alice Fay died of cancer. Marvin married a girl from Valliant, but couldn't stop drinking. He and Dorothy, his wife, had several children and divorced. He married another woman, and stopped drinking for a while. But his wife left him, he started drinking again, and died of acute alcoholism, and was found dead a few days later. I went to his funeral at Moran, and the stench was so bad we had to stand quite a ways off from the open grave.

Jewell, who had married Rowena very early and had two children, lived in Quitman, Texas. They stayed together, both great people. Jewell worked in the oil fields, and always did well. They were in close contact with Hazel, and with his parents, Uncle Clem and Aunt Ophelia, all their lives. I have been in contact with them for years, and the two of them came to Margaret's and Ruby's funerals here.

Jewell and I talked on the phone frequently. He died a few months ago, and I miss him badly. Here are some things he told me about the Fagan family. My grandmother on the Fagan side was Laura Perry, and she married Bradford Chapel Fagan. Her mother, my great grandmother, was an orphan, a full blooded Choctaw Indian. Her husband, my great-grandfather, Robert Fagan, was one-half Cherokee Indian and one-half Irish. Interesting. I'd thought we were more Cherokee. Phil figured it out, and said I was 3/16 Indian, which means my kids are 3/32, and their children are 3/64. Also, Uncle Tobe, who was Daddy's first cousin, had a father named John Perry, who had been murdered. Uncle Tobe was married to my Aunt Lizzie, his first cousin.

Uncle Clem and Aunt Ophelia had another son. He was the oldest, and was in the US Army for a long time during WWII. He was an escapee, and instead of being captured by the Japanese, lived with others who had escaped in the jungles, living the life of an animal at times. But eventually, when the war was over, got to come back home. I met him then, for the first time I could remember. He was probably about 26 by that time, and, like a lot of others who'd been through so much of war and its horrors, was a little testy and a fall-down alcoholic. But basically a sweet guy, and I was very fond of him. His name was T.C.

T.C. came to Fort Worth after a short time. There was no work there in Oklahoma, and we were glad to have him. He got a job very soon, and rented a room in a house downtown. He had quit drinking, or I thought so, and he came to see us often; we'd pick him up, and several times, take him to a drive-in movie.

I went after him one day, and he wasn't there. I made some calls, and found out that he had gone to Alvarado to see Uncle Monroe and Aunt Nellie. He stayed there a few days, went on, settled in Snyder, Texas, where he married a girl named Margaret. They eventually had a son. When the baby was a couple of months old, T.C. had gone out with some guys, and they were drinking, and had a bad car crash. As he was dying, T.C. asked someone to send for his mother. She was with him as he begged her to pray for his salvation.

I went to the funeral, taking Phil, who was 10 months old, and Lewie, Uncle Monroe, and Aunt Nellie. It was a very sad funeral, knowing the circumstances. I had talked to T.C. many times about being a Christian, but now it seemed like he never had called on the Lord. But who knows? I could only hope he had. How sad, when it seems that such a life has been wasted. I saw his son later, and was amazed at this handsome boy who was the image of his dad!

When I was 7 or 8 years old, the Rices, our friends for so long, had lost their place and moved. One place where they lived for a while was a quarter mile from us. The house was up on a hill from the road, across from our mailbox. At this time, they had a big, mean-looking brown dog, a barker, although they swore, as most dog owners do, that Ol' Jack wouldn't bite, he just liked to bark.

I've always been scared of dogs, as long as I can remember. I like the sweet, gentle ones, but when they act like they're hungry to sink those ugly teeth into somebody's soft flesh, I don't like them. The advice I always got was (1) don't look them right in the face; that tempts them to bite, (2) look them in the eye and stare them down, (3) don't ever hit them; that makes them fight, (4) hit them with a big stick, (5) pat them, only on the head, (6) don't put a hand on them; they'll bite for sure.

When I was little, my main goal was to (1) avoid ever getting around a dog you don't know, and (2) if you do encounter a mean dog, get away as fast as possible. So as I got through the fence and started up toward the house, I saw the Rice boys and their dad, Will, out on the front porch. Ol' Jack saw me and started running toward me, barking and coming at me as fast as he could run. Did I mention that Ol' Jack was big enough to eat a small person for lunch every day?

I stopped, turned around, and started running as fast as I could, back the way I'd come. The dog was running, too, after me. All at once, I heard a shot.

It was extremely loud, and must have been a shotgun at the sound of it. I stopped, turned back around, and looked. Ol' Jack lay dead, killed instantly. As I started back toward the house, I heard the other guys giving Jesse, the one who shot the dog, the dickens, and saying it was my fault for running, and he shouldn't have shot the dog. Jesse was still holding the gun in his hand. I was aware that they were mad at me; they insisted the dog wouldn't have bit me unless he realized I was running.

I had no sympathy for the dog, nor any gratitude for all the advice I got then or afterward. I am still scared of mean dogs, or dogs that look like they're mean, to this day, although I probably wouldn't run today. We have had some dogs, but never would have tolerated a mean one.

A few years ago, I was at the Rufe Reunion, at the Baptist church there, and I saw Jesse Rice. I asked someone there if it was Jesse, and they told me it was him and his wife, also an old acquaintance of mine. But I hadn't seen them in so long, I wasn't sure. So I went to them, and we got reacquainted. We talked about old times. I told Jesse he had always, since the dog incident, been my hero for all these years. I told him I had hated that his family had got mad at him about killing the dog, and he told me his family had stayed mad at him. He assured me that he would do the same thing again under similar circumstances, and not to feel bad about it. I told him I appreciated it, and he'd always be my hero.

Sunday, July 13, 2007

One year ago today, we had a small celebration at North Pointe Nursing Home for Margaret's birthday. She was 80 years old. James Clinkscales, a Hospice Chaplain, brought Jacky and Manda, and I went to the train station after JJ. When I left the nursing home to pick him up, Jacky and Manda left suddenly. I knew it was because they didn't want to see JJ Margaret was getting worse at that time, and was staying in bed. She only had a little time left, a little over a month.

In August, around the 20th, Margaret was just lying in bed at North Pointe. She didn't watch TV, or even talk any more. I went about every day to see her, and I knew that the nurses there at North Pointe, and also the hospice people, were taking good care of her. I was trying to let all the relatives know how she was doing, and she was having some visitors. I was also getting ready for Mike Stewart and his crew to redo my roof, which had been damaged in a hailstorm. The people at North Pointe were kind to me, and this night they gave me my supper. One of the hospice nurses who was there for another patient promised to look after Margaret, and she said I needed to come on home and get some rest, and she'd keep an eye out and let me know if Margaret needed me. But we noticed that Margaret would have a tremor at times, and the lady told me her body was shutting down because she was about to die. This was the 21st.

I went home and rested. The hospice nurse, a man, called me at 6 AM the next morning, the 22nd, my 78th birthday. I'll always feel that Margaret planned it that way, because she had been reminding me that it was my birthday coming up. I got up, got ready fast, and pulled into the North Pointe parking lot at 6:20 AM. Margaret was lying very still, breathing lightly, seemingly not conscious. I put my head down by her ear, and talked quietly to her. She took her last breath at 6:30. Trinidad, the lady in the room next to her, asked me to pull back the curtain between them so she could see Margaret one more time. What a sweet lady! I had talked to her many times. She loved Margaret, and I'm sure Margaret loved her. But she said she didn't know Margaret was so bad. Her family, she said, was moving her to another place, and she was apprehensive about it.

Margaret's chaplin from hospice, James Clinkscales was there, and after the Biggers had picked Margaret up, he and I walked out to the parking lot together. He had been faithful to visit her often, and she was very fond of him. And so was I. As soon as I got home, I remembered it was my birthday, and Lesley, Ben, and some others were meeting me for a birthday lunch. I was a little late, but Sherry came after me, and we had a great lunch. Thom and Debby gave me a couple of checks, enough to cover our trip to Oklahoma where Biggers would take Margaret for burial beside her husband, Jack and our parents, also our sister Addie.

We had visitation for Margaret on Thursday evening, and on Friday we went to Valliant to the Moran Cemetery. Phil drove. Sherry and I went to the store

Friday evening and bought some things for JJ, who went with us. Manda and Jacky went to the visitation, but didn't go to the funeral.

We went down I-35, and as we went through Paris, it began to rain—hard. The wind was blowing awfully hard. We met others at the café in Valliant: Jewell and Rowena, and their daughter, Lita, Carolyn and Dale, and others. We all ate lunch there, and drove out to the cemetery, about 7 miles. There had been a tabernacle built, and it was a welcome sight, since it was raining. It was also pretty cold, and we were wearing summer clothes. Sherman's nephew, Troy Ruffin, a preacher who had been a pastor of a church in Millerton, was there to preach the service. Just as we started, and one of Paulette's tapes started, the rain stopped. The wind stopped blowing so hard. Troy had put his own coat around me. The rain and wind stayed still for the rest of the time.

We all stayed at the Microtel at Idabel, which was where we usually stay when we go to Idabel. So there were breakfast items and coffee, orange juice, etc. there when we got up in the morning. These breakfast items seemed a little scarce by the time we all got up, but then we remembered: JJ had already been there.

We went to see Robert and Omia there in Hill Nursing Home before we left. They are both bedfast for the most part. They can get up once in a while, but both need help for most everything. Robert has forgotten he was a great cartoonist, and doesn't know what to do with a pencil.

Eight months after Margaret died, JJ was killed. Strange things happen. But Jacky and Manda had already turned against me for helping JJ, and they didn't speak to me again until we had the memorial service for him. But anyway, Margaret's birthday this day brought it all back to me. While I was in the bathroom, the phone rang. It was Joyce Simpson, calling me from Mississippi to tell me their oldest son, Michael had died early today. Trisha, Mike's wife had called them and told them Mike had died in her arms. I got ready—it was Sunday, and I went on to church. Nita taught our class. The lesson was from Revelation, and the title was number 666. She did a good job, she always does, and we discussed it, which is our usual practice. The church service was good. I came home, ate lunch, and went to Manor Care to have my T.B. injection inspected. It was OK. I went to Braum's, and got Johnnie and me a banana split.

I called Bill and Sharon Stephens later, and told them about Mike Simpson. I next called Charlie; he was at work, but I talked to his wife, Debby. When Ray and Joyce were at Broadview, Mike was a small boy, about 10 by the time they left and moved to Clarksdale, Mississippi. He was young when he died, in his 30s.

On Saturday, Alan and I talked on the phone, and made arrangements to go out to eat and then go to the Johnnie High Show. So we met at Friday's on Highway 157 and I-30, and had supper. Then we drove on to the theatre, and the show was good. He and I always enjoy seeing each other, being together for a little while. I'm concerned about him because of his illness, but he laughs at me and acts like he's perfectly OK.

I got home about 10 PM, but had a hard time getting to sleep. Alan had told me he had tried putting a bar of soap in his bed (it's believed that this will keep away leg cramps), so I tried that, and will see. Actually, I became a believer, and keep the soap there. Alan and I have seen each other fairly regularly ever since we found each other. He'd been to my school and gotten his A&P in 1974. It was 1993 when Paulette died, a few weeks after he and I met again. But we have been out to shows, the Johnnie High Revue, and have spent some holidays together.

Alan has had many physical problems, but he makes light of them, and always says he feels fine. He is faithful to go to church, and sings in the choir. He started having parties, and always invites me, and now it is an annual event at his house in Dallas to have Super Bowl and Christmas parties. My neighbors, Don and Jan always come after me for these parties. I enjoy them, the other guests, and Alan so much. I have about quit driving so far, unless I know for sure the route and can get where I'm going without any trouble. I used to go anywhere I wanted, but it gets different after so many years, and they get the highways all messed up with construction.

After I got up, had breakfast, and read part of the paper, I got ready to go to North Pointe with the Sweet Spirit Singers. Rita rode with me, and there were 17 of us to sing. We left our purses in the trunk of my car. Mine had my keys and my cell phone inside, and I was unaware of this until later. We went in, and the large dining room started to fill up. We sang several songs and met many of the residents there. When we started to go home, I realized we'd put our purses in the locked trunk, and my keys were in it, so I couldn't drive the car without my keys.

I borrowed a phone and called Sherry, my daughter-in-law. She said she'd go to my house and get some more keys and bring them to us. Meantime, we waited out on the patio. A man came out of the place in a wheelchair, and we got acquainted. His last name was Everett. As we talked, he said his wife was there, too, and her name is Karen Anna (Carter). I was surprised. Her sister Rose, her brother Jim, and their dad (called Dad), all constituted a wonderful quartet known as The Chuck Wagon Gang many years ago. I used to love their music, and was really thrilled when Rose came to church at Broadview Baptist Church and I got to sing with her. What a strong, great soprano she sang! Her husband, R.T. Carnes used to work on some buildings where Sherman was setting marble in downtown Fort Worth.

We went inside and met the man's wife, Anna. She was a sweet lady, and we visited for a few minutes. A very special time for me. Anna had Alzheimer's disease but I'd heard her sing with us, and noticed what a great voice she had. I went back outside just as Sherry got there with my car keys.

I went to Manor Care to do my volunteer work and to see Johnnie. I had a good friend there named Irene. She, Johnnie, and another friend, Pauline Wasser were to play a game, but it turned out to just be a talking session with the 4 of us. I enjoyed it, as did the others. I am so thankful I've been allowed to do this volunteer work. I've really felt that this is where I truly belong. When I got home, I had a message from Thom that he was sending a check for Sherry and me to have a birthday lunch.

When Sherman and I moved into our house in Sansom Park, it was 1947. We had bought the lot, a good size, 65 by 180 feet. There was no sewer system there yet, and we would need very soon to build a septic tank system. But meanwhile, Sherman was building the house and getting the whole place livable, and that required a privy out in the back. So he got one up as soon as he could. The couple next door was happy to have it handy to them; I don't know how they got certain things done before that. I've mentioned before that Edgar, husband of Gertrude, was not extremely anxious to work around the house, so he had neglected to build one.

Mama was living with us at that time. We were waiting for Tommy to be born soon, so she was with us. One day she went to the toilet out back, and was working hard to get the door open, when she finally realized someone was inside pulling on the door as she was outside trying to get in. It was Edgar who was inside, and she realized it and came in, terribly embarrassed. It obviously didn't worry Edgar as much; he still didn't build one of their own. But a few days later, I went out there, opened the door, and there was a long, dark-colored snake lying along the seat. It scared me; I didn't want to share space with the snake. I don't know what kind of snake it was; it was too intimidating to hang around and try to figure out his pedigree, so I'm afraid it was a while before I dared go out there again.

Very soon after that, we got the septic system in, and Sherman built an addition to the house. I went to River Oaks and talked to a tile setter who worked some with Sherman, Howard Williams. I visited them a while, and asked Howard about setting some tile in the bathroom Sherman had just built. He showed me some samples, and we chose some that were an oatmeal color, mixed with a pretty blue. He agreed to install it for us, and we arranged the date. It turned out very nice, and was so much better than the privy! And soon, they put in a whole sewage system. Later, we had more rooms built, and installed a half bath in our new bedroom.

As our children grew up, we enjoyed them so much. I was so young, I felt like I grew up with them. We had a lot in common, especially the music; we loved to sing together, and they were interested in playing musical instruments. I started Thom with a piano when he was 6, and I bought the piano. Later, he started playing guitar, and did well, although he was more into piano. Especially, as a teenager, the girls loved that, and their school, Castleberry was very much into music and voice. The high school, with a great director musician, Charles Duke, performed popular musicals such as Oklahoma, Fiddler on the Roof, Mame, and Flower Drum Song. They were all outstanding. Many of the students who played the various roles in these musicals went on to do this professionally, and became famous.

Thom has never been without a piano. He loves to play. He tells about when we used to have company, and his parents would persuade him to play for the company. I reminded him of the times he couldn't go by a piano without performing for us. He never needed persuasion.

We figured the others, Phil and Paulette would learn piano, too, but they were not interested in piano. Phil learned the trombone, but Paulette was more interested in voice. She sang beautifully, alone or with others. But she liked piano, and learned, and had some lessons. She also learned guitar, but didn't play it much. She loved piano lessons later.

Paulette was very good at acting, and was in several of the musicals, as were the other two. Phil played trombone in the band, and also sang with the choir. Paulette and Thom were in choir and sextets. Mr. Duke was fond of them, and called them "his" kids. Much later, Paulette was singing at several funeral homes. Mr. Duke, by then retired, worked at Greenwood, played piano, and Paulette sang there.

I never did as well as the kids, but always loved to sing whenever I had a chance. Usually I sang harmony with someone; not professionally, of course, just for fun. I sang with LaVerne's son and his wife, Jeff and Karen, at Ginger Brown's. I loved singing with Ken Elliott, but we don't sing together any more. In fact, he just told me a few days ago that he's not going to sing any more. But since then, he has changed his mind again, and we are back to singing together.

There was a man here for a while who used to come with Karen's family from Montana. He was a singer, too, very good; I liked him a lot. One night we sang, first with Jeff and Karen, and then he and I sang together. The song was

Edelweiss, and we did well, I think, having never sung together before. As we finished, we added a tag line. I'd never heard the line, but watched him closely, as we sang, "I will love you forever." Every time I hear that song, or just think of it, I think of singing it with this young man, Edward Eyestone. Eventually, he went back to Montana. There's no live music at Ginger Brown's any longer, but Jeff and Karen still perform elsewhere.

Cindy Wilson Arrick was one of Paulette's very best friends. She worked for me for several years, along with Paulette and Bill. She was married to Dennis, our good friend who also helped us on some projects at the school. She could do lots of things, including secretarial work, and I have even observed her giving students a quiz from their material. Cindy and Dennis both became like family over the years.

Nearly 19 years after Paulette's death, Cindy wrote to the Star-Telegram in answer to their quest for letters from friends about heroes who had had breast cancer. Following is the letter Cindy wrote. They shortened it some for publication, but this is the entire letter she wrote. She sent one for me, and one extra one for Matt. I had planned to write a letter about Paulette and her dealing with this, but didn't get around to it. I am so thankful Cindy did, and for the copies she sent.

My Hero, Paulette Ruffin Agnew

Here's my hero, Paulette Ruffin Agnew. At the time of her death, she was 40. She would be 59 today (8-18-92) and resided in Grapevine. I hope my words will do justice to my best friend's lasting legacy & memory. I knew, from the start, she would become a once in a lifetime friend, a true kindred spirit.

We did everything together, much like Lucy & Ethel, always getting ourselves into predicaments. Paulette was such a beautiful person, both inside and out, with such a magnetic personality that people were naturally drawn to her. She was so talented in so many ways, one being her amazing voice. Many will remember her from the Johnny High Country Music Revue,

At the age of 36, she received the devastating news that she had breast cancer. Immediately, she began a voracious quest to find out all she could about the dreaded disease. She took on a can-do attitude with such strength, courage and grace. Sometimes, I just didn't know how she did it—from radiation to chemo to the latest techniques, ending with a stem cell transplant. Early on, she decided she would look good and have a positive attitude. She didn't lose her sense of humor, either. She embraced her baldness, making a game of it, so it wouldn't scare her young son. He thought his mother was the coolest Space Alien ever.

One day, when she was driving, some guy (another driver) was making goo-goo eyes at her. When nothing would deter him, she slipped off her wig, stuck out her tongue and proceeded on. Needless to say, he probably thought twice about doing that again.

Paulette had a year of remission before her cancer returned and was told she would need a stem cell transplant. While she was waiting to go to the hospital, she would go sing at the Johnnie High show just long enough to do a song or two, and go home because she wasn't able to stay through the whole show. Though she was as weak as a kitten, and at great risk to her, she went on stage, and performed magnificently, thanking the audience for their love, support and prayers. Paulette finished recording the gospel tape she made, with Bill Hartmann, before entering the hospital on Monday. She wanted to impart her undying faith–spreading her ministry. She was always talking to everyone about preventive exams, living each day, and making it count, and loving family and friends.

Even in her darkest hour when she was put on a ventilator, she wasn't thinking of herself, but of her young son. Matt. She just wanted to hold him, reassure him, and tell him how much she loved him, most of all. So, the day she died, she left so many of us without that special light in our lives. As I get older, and have health problems of my own, I try to remember how she attacked her disease with such grace, beauty, strength, courage and inspiration. And I hope I can do the same.

Paulette comes to mind so often; I am so eternally grateful for having her in my life—my best friend, sister of heart, my forever HERO.

Even after all these years, I've shed many tears, reading this letter Cindy wrote. Thank you, Cindy, for always being there for her. We all love you and Dennis.

Today is the 22nd. Nineteen years ago, we were making final arrangements. It's still difficult to face the Christmas holidays without her, but we remember that we are celebrating the greatest gift of all, the birth of our Savior Jesus.

Chapter 18

"Your family is just complete when you have a little girl."

Today, it is Christmas day: Tuesday, December 25, 2012, and I am at home alone. I usually go to the Sullivan's and celebrate with Phil and Sherry, and all her folks. They are so good to me, and we are all family. I made a couple of coconut pies, and a great amount of chocolate candy, but I just didn't feel like going. Phil said they'd come back by here when they leave there. There's nothing I can tell is really wrong, just a little something. I just sit around, watch a little TV, and read the paper. And remember Christmases gone by.

I remember Christmas many years ago, when we were trying to decorate a little tree Daddy had brought home for us. We didn't have a thing to decorate with. We looked for anything we could find but there was just nothing. Finally, we gave up and went to bed. When we woke up, we had a happy surprise! It was Christmas morning, and we discovered my brother Louis and his wife, Murrell had come from Fort Worth while we were asleep. They brought presents and a box full of tree decorations! For Margaret and me, they brought warm hoods. Mine was wine colored, decorated around the face with white fake fur. Margaret's was blue, with white around the face area. Our climate was extremely cold, and these were perfect to wear to walk the ¾ mile to school every morning. And the tree was beautiful with the decorations. I think Lewis and Murrell were ecstatic to see us so happy! They also brought some food, candy, and other things.

We usually had Uncle Leslie and either Lucille or the boys, Leslie Jr. and/or Jim at our house for Christmas. They brought Christmas candy and other foods they knew we wouldn't have otherwise. We were so happy to have company at Christmas time. One special time, Mama had a great surprise for us; after we got home from school, she told us to go look in a big box in the living room. It was a package from Uncle Jim, and we hurried to see what it was. There were two wonderful dolls, large, with sleeping eyes: a little kid's dream! One had on pink, and one had blue. So of course, the one in pink was mine. I can't remember if Margaret was as fond of hers as I was mine, but I loved that doll for many years. I think those were the only really nice dolls we ever had.

When we had come from Okmulgee, we had a small doll apiece, but one day we played like one died, so we buried it. I think it was Margaret's, and it was her suggestion that we give it a proper funeral. But when we decided to bring it back to life, I guess it had been resurrected. We never found it, although we dug up a good part of the yard looking for it.

So went our Christmases. But we were happy anyway, and these things didn't deter our (or my) belief in Santa Claus for a long time. I didn't know for sure what Margaret believed; we didn't discuss these things with each other. Most other holidays came and went without much celebration. I guess that was partly because we were farmers, and hardly noticed a difference in the days. I can remember the old almanac Daddy went by to plant different crops. They usually grew fine, unless the climate was bad, not enough rain, or sometimes too much rain.

It has been hard for kids since then to realize what life was like in those days. And it's been hard to remember, for a lot of us, because we never have had to live that way since. But it was just that way in those times. We never felt like we were underprivileged; it was just the way we lived then, and as time went on, it was just so different. Life changes so much, and even now when we go back to that country, nothing is the same as it was then. We all live better in most every way.

This evening, Phil and Sherry came by, as they had promised to do. They brought me food, enough for two or more meals. Also, a present from Sherry's mother, Sylvia, a nice, warm, tan cardigan. I've had it on ever since. Sherry called me later, and reminded me to protect the outdoor faucets, which I did. It's been snowing all afternoon, and will probably snow more tonight and rain some more. And it is very cold, in the low 20's. I've put my electric blanket on my bed.

Several years ago, Thom and I decided it was somewhere around 1977, my cousin Annette Knoblock came to Fort Worth to visit. Annette is the daughter of my Uncle Jim, Mama's brother. They lived in New York City. We had been in touch with the family all through the years until Uncle Jim died, around 1965. After that, since Aunt Annabelle never did any correspondence, we would have lost touch except for Annette. And that was mostly between Thom and Jeanne and Annette. They had visited her in New York, and they were good friends. I'd never met her until then; my trip to New York was long after that. Annette was a spinster who lived with Aunt Annabelle until she died after Annette's trip to Texas. She stayed several days with Thom and Jeanne. But she and I made a trip once, to visit a place in Texas not too far from us where Grandma Knoblock had lived for a time with her three children: Uncle Jim, Uncle Leslie, and Mama. This was exciting to both of us. I'd never been to Chico where Mama's cousins lived, but had heard of the Nobles who lived there. I drove my car; I think it was a Chevrolet, our first one with an automatic shift. We did fine; I found my way easily enough. Annette couldn't believe her eyes, there was such a small amount of traffic on such wide highways. I'm sure that changed rapidly.

The first small town we went through with the traffic circle most all small towns have, we stopped, mainly out of curiosity. They had a large US Flag in front of the courthouse. It had been blown down about halfway. A man we later referred to as a handsome grey-eyed man, came up and talked to us. He said he was there to get the flag back upright. He also gave us some highway information. A while later, we came to Decatur, the seat of Wise County. About all we knew about Decatur was that a cousin, Ray Nobles, had been a sheriff of Wise County. We stopped, but decided to keep going and stop back by on our way back.

So we went on to Chico, another very small town with a town square and not much else. There was a residential section, but no courthouse, nor any place where we could check for records. No place to find out anything. We just gave the town a pretty good once-over and went back to Decatur. We had found out that there was an attorney in Decatur named William Nobles, and decided he must be kin to us. There was very little going on in Decatur. I've decided it must have been a weekday, otherwise the courthouse wouldn't have been open, and so many records available to us.

So we looked up William Nobles. He was a nice-looking, prosperous-seeming man, not very excited to see two strange women who were claiming to be kinfolks. I think if there was any excitement among the three of us, it would have been Annette. But William Nobles gave us some information. Some of the family, maybe his mother, was still alive and lived in Decatur. Annette and I left, and drove home. It was a good trip, and we really enjoyed each other. We gave the information we had to Mama, who began to make plans to visit this aunt of hers that William had told us about. Mama remembered her.

Annette and I visited some, but she spent most of her time here with Thom and Jeanne. We used to kid each other about the handsome, grey-eyed man. Mama shortly made a trip to Decatur to visit the aunt. She stayed a few days with her, and had a funny story to tell us when she got back. Mama was widowed at this time, and was in her late 50's, but the aunt she visited was much older. They walked around town, and one day they went to the courthouse. I don't know what all they did, but when they were going out, there was a long flight of steps to walk down, and the aunt stopped; her underwear or slip, I'm not sure which, had fallen down around her ankles. The stairway was the one going into the street, out of the building. Mama said it was quite a sight, and she helped her pull the garment back up. I think it was funnier to Mama than embarrassing to her.

I was a little surprised about that; Mama was always easily embarrassed, normally, but she laughed heartily about the way they must have looked to passers-by.

Annette had bought the place on Long Island, and was going to build herself a house on it. But she decided against it, and decided to buy and build in North Carolina. She designed it herself, and did a nice job of it. It was built by true Southern plans, with a great room in the center and the rest of the rooms surrounding it. She left the old place when Aunt Annabelle died, and Uncle Jim had gone long before that. She loved her new home, and decided to become a "southern lady" with a New York accent!

Not too long afterward, Annette died, leaving her home in North Carolina and possessions to Thom and Jeanne. Thom called me to meet him there. I did, and we stayed for a while, while Thom took care of some of her business. We enjoyed a few days there in the place she had designed. Thom had met some of her neighbors and close friends, which she had never had in Queens. Her house was very nice, but also very homey and plain; not quite what one would expect of Uncle Jim's daughter. But a little sad, considering that she was so alone. While we were there, Thom and I were invited to a small party of some kind. One of these neighbors was a woman who turned out to be kin to Sherman's family in some way. I don't remember exactly who or how she was related, but time passed quickly, and we went home.

It's funny, the things we remember, and sometimes the ones we don't. But I remember a little café there close to Annette's house where we ate a few times. What I remember vividly is the saltine crackers they served. They were homemade and delicious. I have no idea what was served with the crackers, but I'd love to have another serving of the crackers. Or maybe the recipe.

When Sherman and I got remarried in 1990 and moved into our new house in Watauga, we were asked to choose two trees to be planted in our front yard. Actually, there shouldn't have been but one tree in front and one in back. Our lot is too small for too many trees, as the roots grow out about as far as the limbs do. We had two trees in front: a live oak and a Bradford pear. In back, we chose a little apricot tree. In a short time, we had a bad storm blow in, and although there was very little damage, it twisted our little apricot tree down at the ground. It lay down flat, so there was no hope for it.

We went to a large store with a good selection of trees, and were told that apricot trees were very delicate and couldn't withstand bad weather very well, so we looked at others. We found among the oak trees a pretty little chinquapin oak. I questioned the sales person, because I didn't realize they were a type of oak. I was assured they were, and they were very hardy, though slow-growing trees. So we bought it, and put it in the place where the apricot had been. Although the tree is as bare as can be now, in the middle of winter, it has truly been a great little healthy, non-bearing tree. It is still growing and doing fine.

I remember, in the area close to our house in Oklahoma, we had a beautiful chinquapin tree between our house and the mailbox. It was umbrella-shaped, and bore many acorns which were edible. Lots of times, we'd go to the tree and gather a handful of acorns and eat them. We obviously overlooked small worms, discovered years later. I never had seen them, but was hesitant to eat any more because of what the others saw. As far as I know, nobody else ate any more.

But we were glad to know we could buy one. The trees are hardy, non-bearing, and therefore less messy, making a great shade tree in back. We had the Bradford tree in front cut down and destroyed, because it was crowding the live oak, which has made a great shade tree. We've had to have it cut back a lot, it has grown so fast.

While we were living in Sansom Park, Sherman got an acorn and planted it, kept it watered, and measured it every day. It grew ½ inch a day. It was in a large bucket when we moved it here, and now it's much taller than the house, and shades it well from the back, along with the chinquapin. A writer for our local paper says the chinquapin oaks are lovely and less common than other oaks.

When we moved here to Watauga, one of the most beautiful trees that were plentiful here was the sweetgum, also prevalent all over Fort Worth, and the kind we were familiar with in Oklahoma. They had beautiful shape, and when they bloomed in the fall, the colors were bright, various, and truly spectacular.

But somehow, they seemed to all be replaced with the live oaks. These trees shed leaves at different times than the rest, and stay green and plentiful during the others' shedding. But then, earlier than they shed leaves, they furnish bushels and bushels of acorns to be swept up. But they are nice shade trees.

Thanks to my son, Thom, I now have a better record of my mother's life, than ever before.

Going back—way back to the 1890's, Louis and Elizabeth Knoblock lived in or near Newton, Kansas, at the corner of Main Street and West 5th Street. Louis was a blacksmith by trade, and he also made wagons. In the financial panic of the early 1890's, Louis lost his business and their house. The family went to Texas to find work. He eventually left his wife and kids, James, Leslie, and Margaret (my mother, a baby) in Texas, and took a train to Colorado to find work.

Louis went to work in a blacksmith shop in Ouray, Colorado, rooming in his boss's house. After a few days, he got sick and soon died of pneumonia. Meanwhile, his family had gone to Wise County to live with Uncle Josh Nobles, and waited to hear from Louis. They never heard from him, and finally assumed that he had deserted them. Years later, they learned about Louis' death, and were able to obtain his trunk that had been in the attic of his former boss's house for many years.

Elizabeth, my mother's mother, married a farmer from Mineral Wells, Texas named Matt Reeves. There is no official record of the marriage. Reeves put the young kids to work in the cotton fields. Uncle Jim was the first to leave. He went to Dallas, where he got a job washing dishes at the Adolphus Hotel. He impressed the folks at the Adolphus, and got promoted to assistant chef. One day, he read a magazine, and saw an article saying that Edison's laboratory was looking for young boys to train as draftsmen. He took a freight train to West Orange, NJ and got signed up to go to work at Edison's. He worked there several years, and rose to the level of chief engineer.

There is a letter from Edison's private secretary to Henry Ford's secretary, advising that Uncle Jim would be in Detroit in a few days, and would Mr. Ford arrange for him to take a tour of the car factory? In the letter, he states that Uncle Jim is his chief engineer.

Rutgers University is compiling and indexing all of the Edison papers. They give Uncle Jim credit for designing the laboratory complex at Edison's. They have the drawings of the plant online now. While Uncle Jim was at Edison's in 1917, he and Aunt Annabelle were living in a boarding house across the street from the laboratory when Annette was born.

Meanwhile, Elizabeth, Leslie, and Margaret, my mother, who had been living in a small house in Grand Prairie, moved to Fort Worth, Texas. My mother, Margaret married Nick Shiro, and they started their family. Nick worked in a bakery for a time, later going into railroad work, a lucrative occupation until a railroad strike that never got settled. After my mother leaving him, he worked the rest of his working life as a shoe repairman in Fort Worth.

Before in this book, I told about Sherman and me going to Florida to visit Paulette and Bill, who were performing at a club in Fort Myers. This was in 1982. Soon after we got home, Sherman had his first heart attack. But while we were there, it was great to visit the Edison summer laboratories and the

Henry Ford place. The two places are very close together, and each one so very interesting.

The following was written and experienced by my son, Thom, who is our oldest son, born in January, 1948. He became interested in genealogy at a very early age. That interest was carried on until, after many years and his many travels to different places, lots of reading, etc., he decided to help me, for which I am very grateful.

I was in love with genealogy from a very early age. When I was 18, I went to work part time at the downtown Fort Worth Public Library. I had been curious about where my family came from, particularly the Ruffins, probably because I bore that name. I knew my Ruffin grandparents and their names. I asked my dad where they came from, and he explained that my grandfather, Johnny, or John Willis Ruffin had been born in Arkansas County, Arkansas, and his father's name was James Ruffin.

My grandmother, Agnes, had also been born in Arkansas County. Her parents were Frank and Katie Albertson. They had 12 children when Mother and Daddy married.

That was about all I knew about the Albertson family at that point. I was still curious about the Albertsons and the Ruffins. One day, after I'd finished my duties at the library, I went up to the genealogy department to browse. I saw folks doing research on the microfiche machines, so I looked around to see what records we had. I pulled up the census for Arkansas County 1890, and lo and behold, there were my grandparents AND my great-grandparents! It was emotional for me. I got a large lump in my throat, forming a mental image of these two families living there on those farms.

A question that entered my mind almost immediately was, I knew that Agnes and Johnny had married in Oklahoma, where they lived the remainder of their lives---was it just a coincidence that their families had both been right there in the little community of Point DeLuce, Arkansas, and then fast forward, they got together years later in McCurtain County, Oklahoma? Was it just a coincidence that both families migrated together to the same place?

Actually, Thom, I think I can answer that question for you. My mother-in-law used to talk to me, obviously more than anyone talked to you. When the families migrated from Arkansas, they were very good friends. They made the trip to Oklahoma and scattered out later. Oklahoma was an Indian territory, not a state until 1907. There were, however, many Indians living peacefully there. I don't know why many of the Ruffins and Albertsons moved away, but Johnny and Agnes got married at a very early age, had their family, took root, and lived there the rest of their lives. I hope this helps answer your question.

Also, there were some marriages in those days that, in spite of the hardships, or maybe because of them sometimes, marriages broke up. Agnes, my mother-in-law, told me her parents had divorced and never made up. I can't remember that there were any details; it had happened many years ago.

I couldn't understand why everyone seemed to be leaving Arkansas and moving to Oklahoma. My Dad tried to answer the question, but I don't think he really knew. He told me my grandfather had only gone back to Arkansas for a visit one time in his life. He took a train trip in the early '50s. I don't recall the reason. It may have been a death in the family, but his parents had been dead years before. Dad told me that I should get in touch with my great-aunt Jimmy or one of her 2 daughters. I thought, "Jimmy—what kind of name is that for a girl?" He had no idea how to contact these ladies.

I temporarily gave up, but my interest never went away—it even got stronger over the years. In about 1976, a postcard came to Mother and Dad's house, advising that someone had written a family history book about the Ruffins, and that the book would be on sale at the annual Labor Day Ruffin Reunion, in Point DeLuce, Arkansas. We made plans to go, and took Mother and Dad with us. I was very excited to meet my long-lost Ruffin relatives, and to buy a copy of the book. At the same time, I was a little nervous about suddenly being face to face with all these folks who probably knew each other; but I knew no one. None of my Ruffin aunts, uncles, or cousins would be there—just the Arkansas Ruffins.

The drive to eastern Arkansas was interesting. The terrain was flat and green, mostly farmland. Arkansas County is both blessed and cursed by being situated at the confluence of the American and Mississippi rivers. I used the term "cursed" because, prior to all the modern-day levies, dams, canals, and bridges, the country had been swampy, and serious floods were commonplace. Nowadays, it consists of beautiful, productive farmland, with great irrigation systems that use shallow wells or surface water from the nearby rivers and canals. But at the time the Ruffins and Albertsons left this part of Arkansas, it was not a good place to live.

When we arrived at Camp Doughboy where the Ruffin Reunion was held, folks couldn't have been friendlier. I believe our family won the prize for having traveled the longest distance to get there. Everyone wanted to greet us and visit with us. I couldn't wait to talk to old timers who knew my grandfather, and great-aunts and uncles, and ask them why my branch of the family had left this beautiful place and moved to Oklahoma. Most of the responses I got were the same, "We always wondered that, too."

It was a great experience for me, too. I got to be great friends with some of them, and keep in touch to this day. Many have died since then. They all seemed to be good, down-to-earth people, and I'm glad to be part of their family. And I did get answers to some of my questions. It turns out that my great-grandfather, James had lost a lung to tuberculosis when he was very young, so he had only one good lung. Once, there was a large prairie fire that was moving toward his house and barn. The weather was cold, and he stayed up all night, plowing with a team of horses, trying to keep the fire away from his house. He got sick and died a short time later from pneumonia. He was only 37 years old.

My great-grandmother, Irena soon married a second time to a man named McGahhey. I don't know this for a fact, but I get the feeling he was a ne'er-do-well. No one seems to know much, or at least say much about him. This generation complicates my Ruffin family tree. Here is why:

Irena was James' second wife. He had a family by his first wife then divorced. Then he married Irena. After he died, Irena remarried McGahhey. And after that, Irena moved to Oklahoma, about 1905. I knew one of these great uncles, Uncle Homer. He changed his name to Donnie Mac. I'm not sure why he changed it, but family stories indicate that he had gotten into a lot of trouble earlier in his life. When I knew him, he was a barber, and lived in Denver, Colorado. He had a wooden leg, having lost his leg earlier in life. There is a family photo from about 1907 where it is apparent that his leg was not normal looking. It was later amputated, and he was fitted with a wooden leg. It never seemed to bother him. He played games with my siblings and me, sticking a pencil just under his pant leg, so that it looked like he was pushing it all the way through his pant leg. But he was really just sticking it through the vent in his prosthesis.

Uncle Homer had lots of good stories. I think some of them were true, and some were either embellished or outright lies, but they were all entertaining to those of us who were 10 or 11 years old.

Thom continues to write, and tells the story of his dad's full name:

My dad was named after this uncle. The name given to him at birth was Sherman Ruffin, after Uncle Sherman. Later, when he was about 5 years old, his parents had gone somewhere without him, and he decided he was going to add the name Homer. He had another great uncle named Homer, and he decided his name should be Homer Sherman Ruffin. His parents approved, and the name became legal. The family still called him Sherman, and so did the rest of us. But when others worked with him, and when he went into the Army, he was always called Homer.

When I was in high school, college, and did some construction work with Dad, I was known as "Little Homer," which I didn't care for. Not that I was ashamed of my dad, but I was 1-3 inches taller than he, and proud of every inch! I didn't want to be called "Little Homer".

I guess nobody's ever been prouder of any accomplishment than Morris Dixon and I of our Love A&P School. We saw men daily come in to enroll and get started, from here in the US and even overseas. We had sent advertising to several papers, and it brought them in. I would have never thought of selling the school to anybody, but business became hard as time went on. Morris had left after a year, and I was doing OK, but not great, and people grew interested. They began to talk about it, and finally, I decided to look into the possibility. When I started talking to Ray Williams, I really did get interested.

But when Ray became interested, he brought along another vice president of Dalfort, Hugh. I understood much later that Hugh had been a salesman for a Jell-O company, and something else that I've forgotten. At this time, though, he was a junior VP over some part of the flight academy of which Ray was the VP. I had known Ray for many years, and he was a great man. He'd worked for Dalfort since the long-ago Braniff days, and was tops. I trusted him completely, but hadn't quite put much faith in Hugh.

As the time grew shorter, and we were about to complete our deal, Hugh asked me and Paulette, my secretary, to come and see the new furniture "we" had, which was in his office. So we went, thinking he was probably telling the truth, and he showed us the new desk and chair, and some more stuff. I was happy with it, until he introduced us to his secretary, a very modern-day girl with an attitude that seemed to warn us of trouble to come.

Can you believe that, of all the names I can remember with no trouble at all, I've forgotten her name? I've wracked my brain, and the only thing I can come up with is Janice. Janice is a pretty name, I'm sorry if I'm wrong, but, for the time being, I'm going to use it. We went ahead with the plans, and we soon realized that the furniture had been bought for Hugh, or at least, that was where it went. He was so proud of it, he showed it to everybody. I had my old desk, and the wonderful chair Morris had given me our first Christmas. I was happy with them, but after that I knew I couldn't trust Hugh.

I wasn't there very long until I found out just what had happened. When they had started talking about buying the school, I believe Ray was maybe trying to get Hugh away from the flight training area. Hugh was upset because he was making less money as assistant VP than the other VPs were making, and he wanted to make more than I'd be making there. So they raised his salary so that he was making $10,000 a year more than I.

This made him happy to order me around. Meanwhile, he knew little or nothing about teaching mechanics.

He soon ordered me to stop teaching my refresher courses, and then he said no more Inspection Authorization courses. I hated to give these courses up, and feel they are absolutely necessary in a school such as this, but he had the upper hand. He informed me I was not to be in classrooms, but needed to sit in my office and write memos. Sometimes I feel like I should have gone and talked to the President, Mr. Kiropolsky, a Russian gentleman. I feel sure he would have helped me, had he been given a chance.

And Janice? She proved to be just what we thought. She flirted, especially with Hugh, and got her way in everything. She didn't bathe often (UGH!) and smelled it. And I'm afraid she had people talking all over the place. They hired other people, girls usually, and they were all fine, but normally didn't like Janice. Paulette and Bill had separated, and Paulette got a job downtown with some of the Leonard's people whose parents had opened the Leonard's Department Store downtown. This time, she and Bill got a divorce, and before long he was married to Becca, a lady who had been their neighbor in Benbrook.

Before much longer, Paulette was going with Jeff Agnew. But when the company she worked for discovered Paulette might have breast cancer, and decided to fire her, she thought it might be because she had a good health policy. So she stayed at home, and wouldn't answer the telephone, afraid that it would give them a chance to do so. Her insurance stayed in effect while she was going through the awful chemo and radiation, and then, as a last resort, she agreed to have a stem cell replacement. So things went for 2 months, dreadful to have to tolerate, but I stayed with her when I could. By that time we had the store going, but there wasn't much business, and my heart stayed at the Baylor Hospital in Dallas or the hospital in Arlington, where she spent some weeks.

But I came home from Dalfort, which is what they re-named the school. I was empty handed. No pictures, no 9-cylinder radial, not even the chair Morris had given me. What a rip-off! But I got a good check in the mail, which was a little healing. But now, I was going to the hospital either daily or nightly, and someone else was helping with the store.

But the store was finished, too. The day Paulette died, Sherman and I came home by the store and closed it down forever. I feel seriously that ladies fashions have gone, and am not "in" any longer. I have never been impressed with the things that have come out since then. It's only pants and tops, sweaters and jeans. And you never see boutiques, different styles, and pretty things any more.

I sometimes wonder about the school. I know it was closed down after I left, but I haven't seen many, if any of the students. I did contact Gary, a student who finished, and was also Sherman's helper, to put down the marble Sherman had saved for the entrance here in the front of the house. He matched it to the porch Sherman had put marble on. It is a beauty, just the way Sherman would have done it!

I did hear a while later that Hugh had been terminated at Dalfort. He had somewhat of an objection to the action, whereupon he had to be bodily removed from the building. I was mildly curious as to what caused the action, but never heard any more. I did have a couple or more check with me. They had obviously dropped out of school before it was over, and the school was now closed. Also, a few of the students from Texas Aero Tech came by to check with me. I had to turn them all down. I have, however, had several students come in for the Inspection Authorization, which I can still teach, and every year I have students for the IA one-day renewal course. I still love teaching. And I still have a student occasionally for the A&P, and am anxious to teach, but not really able to publicize my courses.

When Phil and Paulette were in high school, they were both energetic and loved to work with kids. They started to go to the Edna Gladney Home on 8th Avenue, where there were many kids who loved for the older ones to come and spend time with them. There were many unwed mothers or single mothers who needed help with their little ones, and this was a great place for them. Obviously, they could take them home if things got better, and sometimes a child just might need a firm hand they could get there. Many unwed mothers had their babies there. And some left them there.

Phil and Paulette had their favorites. Occasionally they would, with the approval of Sherman and me, and the child's nurse at Lena Pope, bring one home for a weekend. This was something we had to be careful of. It depended somewhat on a child's personality. For example, Phil's little buddy, Governor, a cute boy, and seemingly sweet, suddenly went bananas when we started to take him back to the home on Sunday. He kicked, screamed, and went under the table, and wouldn't come out; he wanted to stay. They all did, but rarely did they go to these lengths. They all called Sherman and me Daddy and Mother. And all begged us to adopt them.

Paulette brought a little girl home with her for Christmas one year. Her name was Judy. We bought her several things for Christmas, and somehow, she thought we were going to adopt her. We tried, but she was not adoptable. Her mother took her home later. But Governor was the 17th child in a family, and their father was in prison for rape. I noticed that Paulette seemed to get close to the preemies a lot. She had such a heart for little ones, and so did Phil. Paulette used to beg me to have a sister for her, but I explained to her that it wasn't possible, and she finally understood, but still wanted a sister. As she grew through her teen years, she had many girl friends that were very close to her.

As she battled the cancer that invaded her, her main goal was always to be able to spend more time with Matt. She used to spend as much time with him as she possibly could, talking with him and visiting with him. When it was late, she could take off her wig and explain her situation to him. He seemed to understand at the time, and I'm sure he did afterward when it was all over, but not at first. Right after she died, he started to remember about the times he wanted to see her, and she was so bad, she preferred not to have him see how bad she was. This had to be explained to him much later, after he grew older and was able to express the questions he'd carried with him for so long. He and I had some long-overdue discussions as he reached his 20s. He is a great young man, now engaged to be married to a sweet, smart young woman, and I'm sure that Paulette looks on him from where she is, and is very rightfully proud of her son, as the rest of us are.

It used to be, it seems to me, that everybody came from a large family. Since I am the youngest one of 9, it's all I know. And I'm very proud of the fact. Maybe we had a special love for each other; I know we were always taught that we shouldn't ever consider that we had a different parent than some of the others. Of course, Margaret and I were from the same parents, but everyone got along, were taught the same values, and I can't ever remember any squabbles, just a lot of teasing, a little practical joking and kidding around. And of course, they teased us two some, since we were the smallest. But we learned to do the same, so they taught us.

Lewie was the "big" brother, at home. We loved him, but he was so much older, sometimes he got a little bossy, and referred to us as "these kids," which made us a little defiant. But as we grew older, he showed us kindness and consideration, which endeared him to us. And when I was married, and he came to Fort Worth and stayed with us a while until he got them a house and himself a job on the railroad, we began to talk more, and got as close as a brother and sister normally are. I learned, after all those years, that Lewie really respected me, and was a joy to have around.

Lewie's wife, Lennie never cared much for me. It was OK—the feeling was somewhat mutual. I thought maybe her attitude toward me would change as time went on, but it never seemed to. I really never minded. I was a little shocked when Mama and I visited them one day, and there she lay in the bed with their 3-day-old baby boy. We hadn't heard a thing about it. His name is Glenn, and he was a beautiful baby, and is still a good-looking man who looks a lot like Lewie. They already had Evelyn and Ronnie, the older boy. Ronnie died a couple of years ago.

Ruby's youngest daughter was born either the day Glenn was, or a day later. I know it was the last couple of days of December 1949, the day before Daddy died.

Lewie and Lennie started going to a Baptist church close to their house, a mission from a large church in Azle. Lewie and I went to Alvarado to visit Uncle Monroe and Aunt Nellie several times. These were good experiences for both of us, and we enjoyed them so much. We had some good heart-to-heart talks, and discussed such things as our relationship with the Lord, the church, and also to our relatives and to each other. When we were notified of Uncle Monroe's death, we went to help Aunt Nellie, to help with arrangements. We were saddened by the fact that Uncle Clem couldn't cry. He turned pale, and I was worried about him, but he said he hadn't been able to cry in a long time. I know that happens to a lot of people. But later, when one of his children died, he could. His whole family is dead now, since Jewel, the last one, died last year.

Aunt Nellie died a short time later. It was hard for her after Uncle Monroe's passing. They had no children, and she had no family. But she had been pregnant, and lost 5 babies.

Several times, Lewie and I drove to Oklahoma, and once to Bonham, where some of Lewie's mother's people lived. He'd tell me all about them, the ones he remembered. Once, we went to the cemetery where some of his relatives were buried, and we looked up their graves. And then we visited a couple of relatives, where I met them and learned more. Those times were so good, and I was so thankful for him.

Lewie was a good man. He was good to his family, wasn't a drinker, and didn't smoke. He had one bad habit that he never considered bad, and that was chewing tobacco. He'd smoked a little, but gave that up. He tried drinking a little beer, but decided that wasn't a good idea, so he gave that up. But he kept up the chewing tobacco. He was a hard worker; he worked for the railroad until he retired. Lennie, his wife, worked a lot of years, too, but finally died with cancer. I think we were better friends by that time. She was taken to Oklahoma to be buried at Rufe after a burial service here. Lennie had always been known as a beautiful woman, and she was truly beautiful.

Evelyn, their daughter, is the mother of 6 children. She was married to a man who was a great husband and father. Evelyn is a tiny little thing, a very sweet lady, and has a great family. She has had a hard time with her health, and so has her husband Bob, who now suffers with Parkinson's. Lewie was staying at their house after he collapsed at our old homecoming in Rufe. I was not privy to all the information, but have learned since that he had cirrhosis, I guess, because of all the chewing tobacco he'd swallowed. They said his liver was as hard as a rock. I went to see him at Evelyn's, knowing he didn't have long. We talked; he had about stopped eating, and had come there to die. He told me he was dying, we both cried, and I said for the first time I can remember, "I love you, Lewie," and he said he loved me too. He lasted another day or two.

I'll always remember that when Sherman and I were separated, I went to church with Lewie and Lennie. I enjoyed it, and later, after Lennie died, we went back together. I went to Azle Avenue, where we were members, and there was Lewie. He had come to Sunday school in the men's class! From that time on, he was a regular in our church! What a joy! And when he died, our pastor, Bro. Wrinkle went to Rufe with us for his burial in the Rufe Cemetery beside Lennie. As we started to leave, Sherman and I went back to see Bro. Wrinkle a minute, and Paulette, who'd rode up there with him, was wearing his hat. It was one of those colorful hats with a narrow brim, and she looked so cute. We laughed at her; it looked so funny.

It wasn't long after that that Bro. Wrinkle, a fairly heavy man, had to have surgery on one knee. He'd need to have surgery on the other knee soon. The doctor warned him that the work done would last 10 years if he lost weight, but if he gained any more, it would only last 5 years. Actually, he died shortly after that.

Lucille, Uncle Leslie's daughter, was 17 when her mother presumably committed suicide by shooting herself in the temple. Lucille found her there, bleeding from a small wound, and already dead. It made a lifetime impression on the young girl, who had been coached for a year by her mother to cook, wash, iron, clean, and do all types of household duties by her mother. She obviously had a definite plan in mind. This plan was slowly divulged to Lucille

431

as she dealt with the fact that her mother was gone forever, and all the work her mother did was given over to Lucille.

One of the first rules laid down by Uncle Leslie was that Lucille was to keep house and take care of the rest of the family as Aunt Lelia had done, including taking care of the two boys, Leslie Jr. and Jim. She was to forget about going to school any more, as her duties at home were too great. I understand that Jim had been spoiled, and was used to being looked after, and nothing was to change that. I do remember that the boys took advantage of Lucille, and were not always kind to her, and the same went for Uncle Leslie, who had expected the same from Aunt Lelia. She had told Lucille she had a hard time getting enough money from Uncle Leslie to run the household. Lucille always mourned her mother's death, and was known to be in a state of depression all her life.

Depression was not known to be an ailment in those days. I know Sherman was depressed so much of his life, and it wasn't recognized until very late. I can remember Lucille's depression all those years. She had so many children, and was a good mother, but some of her children didn't understand her. Some left home early, and we're not even aware of where they are.

When Sherman and I were dating, he would be at our house, and Lucille had one child at that time. She stayed with us for some time, and Melba, her oldest child, was 5 years old. She was a sweet little blond girl, and loved to kid with us. Lucille was pregnant with her second daughter, Barbara, at the time. I guess she went with her husband, Buck, after our house burned down, and they moved to Fort Worth, where they lived the rest of the years, and Lucille had more children. After Sherman and I moved here, Melba grew up, and married. Melba had one child, a little boy named Johnny. Johnny got into trouble at a young age, and has been gone from home for many years.

Melba became pregnant again, and a little boy was born. She named him Ricky; Ricky was a beautiful little boy, but was ill. Melba was having a hard time financially, and the couple was separated at that time, so Melba moved in with Lucille and started to go to nursing school. She took her baby, Ricky to the hospital, and had them check him out, because she knew he wasn't well. After some time, a lot of tests, and at her insistence, they discovered he was very ill, with holes in his heart. He underwent 2 very long surgeries.

He failed to live through more than a few days after the second one. During some of this time, my mother went to visit them at Lucille's and called me at home. She asked me if I'd be willing to have him stay with us for a couple of weeks or so. Lucille's small kids had measles, and they knew Ricky couldn't overcome this, and Mama assured her she could trust me to take care of the baby. Of course it was OK with me, we all loved babies, and would be glad to have this baby there for a while.

This was in 1961-1962; I'm not sure of the date. I just remember he was a precious little boy with blue eyes, and was a good baby, hardly ever cried, but was probably too sick. He died shortly afterward, and was buried at Rose Hill Cemetery in July, 1962. He couldn't overcome the 2nd surgery. Melba reminded me that I had stayed at Harris Hospital all day with them when he was having the operation. She also reminded me that my pastor at the time came with me, and we spent 5 ½ hours there. I took a mental inventory of our pastors—we had many—and have decided it had to have been Bobby Moore. That made me grateful for him. I can't think of any other pastor who would have done that for me, but there are probably more. I thought at first it was Harold Stanfill, but realized I was wrong when Thom reminded me he was at

Broadview the year he (Thom) graduated, and received a red vest from Harold. That was in 1966, a few years later.

Ricky lived to be 18 months, but spent most of that time in the Harris Hospital downtown. As I write this in 2013, I feel that, had this happened in the last few years, he could have been saved, but we don't know these things. There have been many strides made in the medical field for such things as heart trouble. Melba continued with her training, received her RN, and has retired after working all these years.

Sometimes, when your children begin to think of having a family and a life all their own, it's hard to realize that this new family will also include adults that will become not only part of your children, but the families of each one also. So suddenly, your family has taken on more adults, and eventually more children, and you are sharing life with many more people than you had planned on. Some of these added adults have been raised much differently, and have other values than what you have instilled in your own children. Such differences don't have to change everything; however, we all have to be ready for changes, and accept them as different from what we may have expected. And today, with the divorces, re-marriages, and single living, as this new age is going through, we undergo more changes than ever.

Thom and Jeanne divorced a short time after Sherman and I. Thom worked in Kansas a while, and Jeanne had a dry cleaners pick-up station. Thom had gotten her started with Ruffin's Classic Cleaners on Jacksboro Highway, but she gave that up soon. I bought it from her after Dalfort bought my school. Paulette had been laid off, and we got the cleaners, where we also sold ladies' clothes. Paulette and Bill had divorced, and Dalfort kept him on until they closed the school. We moved the cleaners and ladies shop to Davis Blvd., and I closed it the day Paulette died.

We always were friends with the in-laws; of course, closer to some than others. Phil's mother-in-law, father-in-law, and all the Sullivan family have always been very close friends. Sherry has 2 brothers and 2 sisters, all married with children, and we are all close. And now, with Sherman gone these 12 years, I have been accepted as one of their family. And I love them all.

We used to visit with the Hartmanns, and Sherman was free to deer hunt on their place. But Mrs. Hartmann died with breast cancer, which was a big blow to Paulette. She grieved for her mother-in-law for some time, and felt once that she had had a visit from her. And then, Paulette and Jeff fell for each other, and a little later, it was determined that Paulette had breast cancer herself. Jeff took great care of her, and they married one and a half years before she died. She was no less fond of Jeff's mother than she was Bill's mother.

Jeff's parents, Neil and MM (Margaret May) lived in Memphis, Tennessee. Jeff had a brother younger than himself who lived in Virginia, named Joel. He was married and they had one daughter. Shortly after the little girl was born, they divorced, and he married again.

Sherman and I were great friends with Neil and MM. They used to come often, and the four of us loved to go shopping together. Paulette and I had the store going, and they enjoyed shopping with us. It wasn't long until Sherman wasn't able to go with us, so he quit (he never enjoyed shopping anyway). But Neil was a woman's dream to go shopping with. After we lost Paulette and MM, he and I used to go to outlet malls together.

He never failed to want to look at merchandise. He and MM loved to go to Mikasa, and anywhere they sold fancy cut glass. They must have had loads of that sort of thing at their house. But he was also interested in ladies' clothes, and always helped MM and me to select the right things to wear. As time went on, in 1993 Paulette died, and 2 years later, MM died. She had a brain hemorrhage and died suddenly. And then Sherman died in 2001. Neil and I used to communicate by mail, and I worried about him. He fell once, at home, and messed up his face pretty badly. But he was all alone there in Memphis, and finally decided to sell out and move to this area, close to Jeff. His other son, Joel, still lived in Virginia, not very far from Thom and Thom's new wife by now, Debby.

I was surprised, a few months after MM died, to get a large box from Neil. It was several beautiful suits of MM's. Neil had packed them carefully, with tissue paper between them. They were packed so carefully that they didn't even need pressing. He knew MM and I wore the same size (nearly), and that I could wear them. They were nice outfits: suits, blouses, etc. I was thrilled, and wore many of them. Some I gave to Sherry; some I tried on for Neil when he came, because he wanted to see me in them.

Once when we were shopping, he told me firmly that I should never wear pastels; I should always wear dark or bright colors because of my olive complexion. I agreed with him, and still remember that whenever I look at clothes.

I took Neil to get some hearing aids while he was here once. He and I went to the Grapevine Opry once to see the show and hear Jeff, who is a great steel guitar player.

When Neil came back in his new Cadillac (he always drove a new Cadillac), he and I went to get his hearing aid adjusted and to look for him a place to live. We looked at a new apartment or two, and he seemed anxious to get my opinion. But I was going with Johnnie Hooper, and I couldn't keep it a secret because I knew Neil was thinking about our being together a lot.

So I told him about Johnnie and me. I explained that we were not even considering getting married, but we loved each other, and I couldn't break up with Johnnie. So he took it OK, although I could tell he was disappointed. We stopped and ate lunch, and after that we talked on the phone. He found a very nice apartment in Grapevine, a two-bedroom place that he kept immaculately. He was also a good cook, and several times invited me over for lunch. So we remained friends. He met a woman there in the complex, and they became good friends,

Once the two of them came here. Johnnie was here, and we all four went to the mall; I don't remember buying anything, but we had a nice visit. I could tell the lady Neil was with acted very possessive over him. And I could tell Johnnie didn't like it when Neil came and sat on the hassock by my chair to talk, and sure enough, Johnnie expressed his feelings about it when they had gone.

Neil became very ill. He had surgery, and was in the hospital several days. I went to see him, and stayed all day one day. He wasn't able to talk much, and when I bent over near him, he managed to kiss me on the mouth. I went to see him another day and he didn't seem any better. They moved him to another Baylor hospital, where he died a few days later. I went to see him at the funeral home. Jeff was there, and he let me go in to see him in the casket. I told him goodbye, and kissed him on the forehead. "I love him, Jeff," I told his son. "I know you do," he said. I truly missed him, and I still do. He was a true friend, and so was MM.

I've heard many people make this remark: "Your family is just complete when you have a little girl!" I know there are many families where there are only boys, and they seemed to be fine and well-adjusted. And I know our family, when we only had our two boys, was certainly happy and complete. But I also know we were so much more so when Paulette, our happy little girl came along, and we realized what she meant to us. I've mentioned her so many times here, but I'm going to tell her story here, since it needs to be told, and she will never be here to tell you herself.

Paulette was a tiny little girl; when born, she weighed 6 lbs., 6 oz., and as most babies do, she lost a little weight in a few days. When I held her on the way home, she was so tiny; she would roll up in a ball. Or maybe I was used to holding Phil, who was 2, and a husky little boy. The boys were proud of her, and so was I, of course, but Sherman was ecstatic.

He'd wanted a girl every time, and was now carried away. Paulette was a blond now, with large brown eyes and a beautiful face. She stayed small, but was a good baby, and adored by Phil. He would stand at her bassinet and gaze into her face, and if she cried or whimpered, he would shake the bassinet gently to help her go back to sleep.

Thom was growing up. He was 5 when Paulette was born, and most of the time was fairly indifferent to her, but at times, he would show her affection. I began to notice what a change there was between boys and girls. She walked early, as did Thom, but was more delicate in her movements. She talked early, and constantly. Phil didn't choose to talk until he could pronounce his words perfectly, and then he could sing all the words of a song the way he wanted. He got mad at himself when he fell while walking at 10+ months, and wouldn't walk again until he was 1 year old. Paulette, like the boys, was a breast baby, but when I had a bad case of flu, was given a bottle. She didn't accept it easily, but finally became OK with it, and she'd run around with the bottle hanging by the nipple in her mouth. She was very active.

When she was six, she started to Sansom Park Elementary School with Phil. She was happy, and made friends there that she cherished the rest of her life. She was a good student; she worked hard, and was interested in music as well as other studies. She loved to help me cook, sew, and anything else we did around home. She used to help Sherman, whatever he did. If he was working on the house, which he did often, she was right with him. I've cautioned her about going up on the roof with him, but she always stayed with him. I had started getting Thom into music when he was 6, and wanted to do the same with Phil and Paulette, as they were all showing a talent for it. I had bought an old player piano, we'd had it tuned and overhauled, and it was a good piano.

Phil wasn't interested, and dropped it quickly. Paulette had a lingering interest, and was later very interested. But she was more interested in voice, which became her lifetime career. She was interested in many things. She took some modeling lessons once, which helped her in such things as walking, and built up her self-confidence (as if she needed that). She learned to be a good cook, a seamstress, a decorator, and other things. She learned to crochet, to knit, embroider, and any other handwork. When she was about 14, she used to be a singing waitress at an ice cream place, where she sang with Bill Hartmann, the man she later married. He played the piano.

Phil wasn't interested in piano, but loved the trombone. After high school, he went to Tarrant County Junior College. He took music, voice, and also different types of musical instruments, and excelled in them. He sang beautifully, and we, the family sang together, but he didn't take it up as a career the way Paulette did. Phil and Sherry were married in Sagamore Hill Baptist Church, where Phil was doing the lights and sound at the time. He wrote a beautiful song that he sang during the wedding. He forgot one verse at the time, but nobody else knew the song, so we never knew the difference.

Paulette sang at school functions and other places, and she was in plays that Castleberry High School was famous for. Charles Duke, the choir director, was fond of my 3. Phil was in a cappella choir and band. He played trombone. Paulette tried playing an instrument, but gave it up, except for the piano. She also played guitar. She sang in the choir and double sextets, as did Thom. Thom also played piano for some of the programs. They all sang, and we were a quartet when I sang, otherwise they were a great trio. Thom and Paulette always played at our church, Broadview. Thom started playing guitar, and Paulette could play too, but they majored in piano. For a while, when she had some trouble with her voice, Paulette went to a voice professor at TCU who gave her some lessons, and the trouble was quickly overcome. She was quite popular even while she was still in school, for her marvelous voice.

She and Bill married in the chapel at TCU; Bill was going to classes there. After an unhappy romance, Paulette and Bill renewed their love for each other, and their mutual love of music. I remembered, as we gathered for the wedding to take place, the other time I had been in this chapel. It was August, 1953; I was having labor pains as my niece, Bobby and I had just come from Dr. Child's office. He suggested I go on home until the pains worsened. So we had come by this chapel, where Sherman and his helper were working on a stairway. It was a little hard for me to walk up and down a stairway with the pains I was having, and I just got home and had to come back to the hospital. Sherman was gone to another job by that time, but there was really no hurry. The pains would stop frequently, and eventually start again. Finally, after 23 hours, Paulette was here and everything was OK. But my labor was long and difficult.

After they married, and had lived a few months in an apartment and for a short time at our house, they made a decision. They would invest in some sound and music equipment, and do some traveling. They practiced at home, and got a few gigs around For Worth, and somehow acquired an agent who booked them some. They then got another agent who wanted to book them in and around New York. They played at Texarkana, mentioned elsewhere in this book, and played at Everman, at a large club for a while.

I have listed places they played when they traveled. I'm sure these are not all, but some I remember. I visited them at several of these places;

Des Moines, Iowa
Amarillo, Texas
Grand Prairie, Texas
Dallas, Texas
Black Hills, South Dakota
Colorado
Minneapolis-St. Paul, Minn.
Granbury, Texas
Bryan and College Station, Texas
Niagara Falls, New York
Buffalo, New York
Everman, Texas
Albany, New York

They moved back to Fort Worth in 1982. They wanted to start a family and buy a home, and Paulette wanted to work with me in my school, Love Aviation.

They got here about the same day I opened the school in Arlington. I had told Paulette I wasn't making enough money to pay her, but she was anxious to help me do better, and she and Bill were very instrumental in doing so. I was very thankful when they both went to work for me, and we really did get it going quickly. I paid them regularly, including their insurance.

Paulette soon became pregnant. They got places to play every weekend, and we got our Certified School Certificate, and started using computers in our programs. The years passed, and their little son, Matthew grew fast, and was, like his parents, involved in music. He was born April 30, 1986, and like his mother, was Sherman's pride and joy.

Paulette started singing every Saturday night at Johnnie High's Country Music Revue, and became a favorite. She and Bill divorced after a while, and shortly thereafter, she was found to have breast cancer. Meanwhile, she and I ran our Dry Cleaners Pick-up and Ladies' store. She sang at Bigger's, Greenwood, and Mount Olivet funeral homes for funerals. She, and sometimes Sylvia White, sang in the Grapevine Opry, where Jeff, Paulette's new beau, played steel guitar.

As her cancer progressed in spite of all the treatments, prayers, and good wishes of so many, Jeff took good care of her, as did Sherman and I. Bill married Becca, and they shared custody of Matt. Paulette sent him to school in Grapevine. Matt is now a young man, a waiter in an upscale restaurant in Grapevine, and has a group with whom he makes CDs and writes most of the music. He is a very sweet boy, a lot like both parents.

When Bill and Paulette first married and lived in the back room of our house in Sansom Park, they had begun to collect quite a lot of music equipment. He had a small piano, and everything was set up in my living room. The young people from our church, Broadview, loved to come over, and frequently did, to sing and play music with us. Paulette and Bill enjoyed this too, and we'd take pictures and make tapes. Sometimes we wrote songs. I did pretty well with the lyrics, and Bill was wonderful with writing the tunes, but we did it all. Paulette was great too, and loved to sing the songs we wrote. Bill got copyrights, but they never went anywhere, but we still have them. Paulette and Jeff married in 1991. Bill had married Becca a couple of years before.

Castleberry, where all three of my children went to High School, was well known for the great Broadway plays they did each year. Paulette was in Flower Drum Song and Mame; a star in Mame, and a co-star in Flower Drum Song. Thom's daughter, Amy was also in Mame later, and reminded me so of Paulette—she even looked like Paulette. She would select fabric for dresses to wear in these plays, and I had to make them. But she would help, and learned to make whatever she needed. I had to learn a lot, to keep up with the things she wanted us to make. Thom had been in the choir and sextets too, but was now in the Army. Phil was the only trombone player in "Seventy-Six Trombones". He did a great job! Thom was in several shows before he graduated in 1966. Sometimes he played piano in the programs.

Chapter 19

"Pauline, schoolmasters don't cut the students' hair."

We have certainly changed our daily habits since I grew up, in the years right after World War II. When I was young and in love with Sherman, one of the things I loved about him was the smell of cigarettes; he smoked constantly, and the strong tobacco smell of the leather jacket he wore was somehow attractive to me. Sherman was a handsome man, in spite of a prominent underbite, of which he was very conscious. This may have been the cause of the sensitivity of his gums and teeth, and interfered with his brushing his teeth. Of course, I'm sure now that the smoking wasn't helping that either. I have felt very stupid to love that tobacco smell back then. Later, it was repulsive. But I'm sure I wasn't the only one who felt that way.

He was only 36 when he learned he needed all his teeth pulled and new dentures installed. Altogether, he had 3 or 4 sets of dentures, and was always working on them; it was hard to get them to fit. But he wore them anyway. At this time, he began to show signs of a deep depression. I can't remember if we ever asked a doctor about the depression, as it wasn't a common ailment at the time. But he and I learned that it isn't something you can "shake off" or get rid of on your own. We know that now, but it's been a hard lesson to learn. Occasionally, he could get OK from it, but would get back in the same rut later. It was not easy, as I have never been bothered with depression, and didn't know how to handle it.

Eventually, I started to get irritated with the cigarettes. Sherman had wanted me to start smoking to keep him company, but I didn't like the taste, the expense, or the hassle of having to empty ash trays, etc. And when we had company who smoked, I'd have to go outside to get a fresh breath of air. So I refused to do it, and it was ok with him.

Sherman was a sociable man at times. After he started going to church with me, he enjoyed himself, was active in church life, and made friends easily. He was always loved by the kids, who always teased him and felt great coming to our house for any kind of social activities.

I stayed pretty busy at home, at church, and wherever I was needed in the community. I tried to be helpful to relatives and friends. Sherman's mother had been an inspiration to me. She was a valuable person in our community back home, helping sick folks—she had stayed several days at our house when my grandma, who lived with us, took sick, finally dying of uremic poisoning. Mrs. Ruffin delivered twins for her daughter, Sherman's sister, Bea. She acted as midwife many times. When she and Mr. Ruffin were visiting us, and I asked if she wanted to go to the store with me, she said, "Sure. Just let me put on a clean apron." She always wore an apron. So different from my own mother, who, asked the same question, would need hours to get ready to go anywhere. But Mrs. Ruffin was a dear, and I loved her.

Sherman began coughing early, and after a long time, he coughed up blood. That was scary, and was a source of worry to him. He went and got x-rays of his lungs and didn't tell me until later. But meanwhile, he was thinking seriously about the smoking. When he had one cigarette left from the carton he'd been smoking, he threw it away, and then he got the x-ray results, which they said showed no damage to his lungs. But he'd already quit, and it was a great victory for the whole family. He and I felt that he'd have been dead long before he was 81, his age when he died. And then he was said to have emphysema and heart trouble.

Sherman told me that when he was in the Army, he got 3 free cigarettes a day with his lunch, compliments of Uncle Sam. In those days, kids would start smoking early, and nobody thought about them being harmful. But there weren't so many cigarettes ready to light up. People had to roll their own cigarettes, and probably didn't smoke nearly so many. My Daddy grew his own tobacco, and smoked a pipe.

Another thing he picked up in the Army was the drinking. Now, I can't say that was the whole cause of his alcoholism, but it was partly. This was harder to quit than the cigarettes; but then, he was older, and I guess it's just different. However, he did quit, and I think he had completely forgotten the booze he had been drinking; he never seemed to remember it. One thing he did remember, and maybe this is a memory always remembered by men, was that he was his own boss, and nobody could tell him what to do. When we moved here, I had to go somewhere frequently, and I asked him to please not go up the ladder to the attic.

He went up to the attic as soon as I left, and fell on the concrete floor, hitting his head. A while later, I went to the Johnnie High show with my neighbor who had a friend singing there, and I asked him to stay in his chair unless he needed to go to the bathroom or the kitchen. When we got home, he was bleeding from his head. He had fallen in the garage, and suffered from a subdural hematoma. He never really recovered from that, although he was taken as quickly as possible to the ER at Harris Hospital. When he came home from there, hospice took over the care of him the rest of the time, which was only a few days. I was still getting little pieces of glass off the carpet in my bathroom. He'd gone in there to use the shower because he liked the glass shower doors, and we'd had to take the ones in his bathroom out so he wouldn't fall against them. So he fell in mine, against the glass doors, breaking them into zillions of pieces. They were made of safety glass, which caused them to break into harmless little pieces that wouldn't cut if stepped on. But I picked them up for a long time.

I guess I was in a state of shock after Sherman was gone. I couldn't force myself to do much work around the house. There wasn't much to do at that time. He hadn't been able to work in quite a while, and he'd always kept things done around the house. I had already realized how much would have gone undone without his vast knowledge. I wondered sometimes if there was anything he didn't know how to do or fix. But he hadn't been able to do anything for some time. He hated being waited on, and had taken care of himself as much as possible, which I was thankful for.

We had communicated very little in the last few months with each other, but now I missed him and didn't make many calls or visits to anybody. I sat in Sherman's recliner, wondering a lot about the past few years, and thinking about myself and how I could have treated him better. I decided there were a lot of things I might could have done to improve our relationship, but I realized that the attitude I had then was not helping the situation, nor would it help to make things better. Now I had to improve myself, and I would need to help others as the need arose.

It wasn't long, a few weeks, until Johnnie Hooper called. I had been friends with Johnnie for some time now, and we began to see each other. I've written about this before. I appreciated him and the way he helped me get my mind straight, and to get my life back together.

We were together for some time. We never talked about it much, but thought about marriage. It was out of the question for both of us. After a while, he was hurt in that accident with the truck and trailer, and was home for short periods of time, and then he couldn't even come home. My life changed drastically.

As I read some of the journal I've been keeping, I don't even know myself how I kept up with everybody the way I did. I try to stay busy now, but am not physically able to keep going the way I did. But we have to do whatever we can, just to keep going. I have thought so many times how good the Lord has been to me. I've re-lived the unusual meeting, after so long, of Ken Elliott and me. I've never had a better friend. We met again in such an unusual way that day at Manor Care, and I've been so thankful that after 31 years we met, and then we started singing together. Nothing could have been planned any better without the Lord.

We are still singing together in the nursing homes. It is a great time for both of us to do what we can to try to bring some pleasure to these dear people by singing old songs they remember, and loving them. We talk to them as much as possible, and sometimes take requests for the songs they like. I love the time he and I spend together. I have always been a sociable person, and that doesn't change as I get older. I'm sure Ken feels the same way. I feel that we found each other at exactly the right time. Ken had been widowed a little less than 2 years, and was still grieving for his wife. I had lost Johnnie about 5 months before.

When my son, Thom was about 16 years old and falling in love with music all over again, he had girlfriends, and realized they loved the music, too, and the musicians as well. He capitalized on this, and played a lot at school when the opportunity arose, as well as at church where we can always use a musician.

And he was good. He and I arranged for a meeting one Sunday afternoon at Broadview for anyone who was interested in a youth choir. What a group we had. There were about 20 people, including Thom, Phil, and others I can't remember for sure, so I won't try.

However, I can remember all who eventually joined our choir. We enjoyed singing together, learning some new songs, and working with some who loved to sing solos, duets, etc. I loved them all, and planned several programs, sometimes singing at other churches. I can recall so many young people who led good lives, had great parents, and loved to visit others and invite them to church functions, including the choir. We made trips, one to Buckner Orphans Home in Dallas. Our Pastor, Bro. Moseley, went with us there and to other places. We were invited to sing at a church in Granbury, where our good friend, Bro. Eldon Pritchard was now Pastor.

I wrote a play that our youth choir performed at Broadview. I was not trained to do things like this, I just felt the need for certain things, was encouraged by others, and did my best. I never had any opposition to speak of, and I always loved working with whatever group I was with. I planned, and we performed a play at Azle Avenue, and afterward, had an award show. There I presented Acatamy (my word) awards, which were tall aristocatic (also my word) cats with a tag around their necks, telling what role the award was for. My good friend Tommy, who was the star of the show, kept his award for a long time afterward, and was very proud of it. This was a take-off of Gunsmoke thatI directed. I have to admit after all these years: the awards were kind of rigged. I am the guilty rigger. But each actor received a certificate.

It is so great to hear from these dear friends later. Most of the ones I hear from are from Broadview; as I have said, there was a lack of young people at Azle

Avenue, and so many are gone now. I still am in touch with Dorothy Adams (now Glover), but except for a couple of couples, those good people from Azle Avenue are all gone. I am hearing from many friends who are sending me notes for the last chapter of this book. These are friends from my past: Broadview, Azle Avenue, and some from First Baptist, where I am now. I will always treasure these kind words, and each one brings tears to my eyes and thankfulness to my heart, and to God, who sent these to me—or the other way around. Of course, there are those who are gone. A girl Thom's age, Corky, was beautiful, with a wonderful soprano voice. She lived close to us, was in Thom's grade at school, in our youth choir, and was at our house frequently. She developed melanoma, and died a short time later. And there were others, many becoming lifelong friends.

Castleberry School had a super music program led by Charles Duke, a wonderful accomplished musician. The a cappella choir and double sextet had great performances.

Many of the star actors and actresses went on to California and New York, and other places, and became well-known in their own right. Paulette was popular in some places, including here. Phil gave up playing trombone, but is a great soloist. He doesn't perform much, because he has a sinus problem. Thom has a grand piano and plays a lot, but mostly just at home. I also battle a constant sinus problem. I have never been a great singer, but I have a love of music and a voice that couldn't overcome the sinus and sang anyway. But Paulette's talent became her career, as a singer.

It was a very cold day in December of 1949. The Joneses lived next to our place on the left, facing Biway Street. Dale and Rose had two daughters: Linda and Barbara. Later, their son Jimmy was born. Dale had quite a few chickens, a couple of geese, and some other fowl fenced in their back yard, which was pretty large. Daddy had taken the job of digging postholes for him to put up a sturdier fence. About 11 am, he came in, slowly dragging one foot. He had had a stroke, a bad one; a fatal one, it turned out. He laid down on the sofa in the living room, but soon was in bed in the back bedroom where they were staying. He was unable to get out of bed, and we began sitting up with him at night.

A few days later, it fell my turn to sit up with him. His pastor, Charles Russell was visiting him that afternoon, and he offered to stay and sit up with me. I was glad—I felt I needed someone with me, and I liked Charles anyway. It's strange how the Lord works these things out. Daddy had become a member of the church, and had already been baptized a Baptist long before. But I had not decided yet what to do about my earlier baptism in another denomination. I had heard Charles preach, and we all loved him and his family. I was just confused about different beliefs, etc. But Charles started talking to me about my beliefs. We talked all night.

The conversations we had that night convinced me; I didn't know what to believe. I didn't even know what "my" church stood for until much later. I began to study my bible, and everything I could find about the Baptists. And then, the last of the month, Daddy died. We took him to the church in Moran, back home, and Charles went with us and preached the funeral. I may have mentioned this before.

Soon after we came home, Charles asked me what I had decided. Nothing, I told him, but I was still praying about it. And then, the morning came, and it was like a large drapery opened up and let me see my own heart, and how I hadn't really trusted God for an answer. I gave my whole heart to Him that Sunday morning, and realized what I'd been thinking had been my own devising. I was ready to let God lead me from now on. Not easy for a person who has practiced being stubborn so long. And definitely not easy to make it a lifelong habit, but I finally learned to depend on Him.

I am so thankful for Charles. They, he and Ora, his dear wife, live in Mineral Wells, Texas. He is retired now and no longer able to preach, but still a great man of God and my dear friend. I love you, Charles, in spite of the weird dogs you always have that hated me. I've never figured out how those dogs know I'm the one they are to dislike so much!

One loved for me to come, but tried to bite me when I left! Go figure! But they never kept me away. I come to see you anyway, whenever I can.

I have just learned that Charles and Ora have gone to an assisted living facility in Mineral Wells, and I plan to go and see them in a few days.

Many years later, after Paulette's death, the Jones boy, Jimmie, was flying—s was the love of his young life. He flew into a mountain, and was killed. Rose, his mother, started to work in the school cafeteria. Later, she worked with the activities at Manor Care Nursing Home for more than 20 years. She died the day I went to Virginia in 2010.

She and her family were some of our closest friends, about 50 years.

Love Aviation Training Center was probably the most unconventional school that ever lived. It was my school, and I made the rules, not that I was a strict "schoolmaster."

I charged the students about half what the other schools did, with no interest, because their training was not financed. They paid once a month, and were responsible for paying about $250 per month until the total was paid. If they were late, they might get a notice from me. If a government agency was paying, like Texas Rehab or another state agency, I just waited for the check to come. I never had any trouble with my full-time students. But these things never interfered with the courses we taught. I made sure, and especially with Bill's help, that the students had all the hours required in each class, and that we kept all the rules set down in the FARs for schools.

I tried giving defensive drivers training, but always lost money on that, or rather, never made any money. My students were normally students who wanted to "pay me later," and I gave it up quickly when I found that the TEA was taking it over. Anyway, I was tired of working every Saturday, which was the day that had to be done.

I used to have parties at the school every Christmas, and at other times. We had dinners and all kinds of celebrations which the students all enjoyed and appreciated, but stopped the moment Dalfort took it over. I made sure the contract with Dalfort stated that the cost of the course was to stay the same for the students already enrolled, and they honored that. Also in the contract was if the school closed in the future, they were to keep teaching the students enrolled. That was a rule followed by Dalfort, but not by others who closed about that time. We had a great school, great students, and great teachers.

I guess someone told me, and I believed them, that anyone could do anything they wanted if they wanted to do it bad enough. I don't really believe that, except in some cases, but maybe to an extent. I have cut a lot of hair; not for money, just to help friends. I did my children's and even Sherman's, and he was hard to please. But one day, a student who was being financed was short of money and looking a little shaggy came in, and apologized for needing a haircut. I said, "I can cut your hair. Wash it this evening or in the morning, and I'll bring my clippers and neck cloth." So he did, and I brought my stuff, and never even hesitated. When we took our noon break, he and I went out in the shop, and I started cutting his hair. In the middle of this procedure, Bill, my then son-in-law who was big on formalities, came out of the office. He stood stock still nearby, a shocked expression on his face.

"Pauline," he said.
I continued, and asked him, "What?"
"What are you doing?"
"I'm cutting this student's hair" I answered, being cool.
He said "Pauline, schoolmasters don't cut the students' hair. I've never heard of such a thing."
Bill was a lot more knowledgeable than I about such things, but I told him later about the student's financial situation. I guess he understood, but we never talked about it after that. At one time, I had gone after this same student when he was put in jail for the night. He paid the $10 they charged him, but I just picked him up.

I know I shocked Bill a lot with my unconventional methods of running a school, but he was such a great help to me and the school. I appreciated him and Paulette, who was used to me and my strange ways.

We always had Christmas parties, sometimes at the club room of a motel, sometimes at the school. Once we rented a margarita machine, which was a big hit, if rather expensive, and once we rented a jukebox. The jukebox was delivered in the morning, and someone was playing it all day. It was a holiday. I danced with some of the guys, and so did the other 2 girls. I danced with Carl Maas, the man who did the practicals, and was impressed with his dancing. He was really good! I seem to remember a barbecue lunch once that was outstanding. The students loved these parties, and so did the rest of us. Not long after our school was started, they began to give drinking at parties a bad time. One year, we served all non-alcoholic drinks, such as Virgin Marys, non-alcoholic wine, and some kind of Margaritas with no alcohol. It was pretty good. I'm sure something was missing for those who liked the alcohol, but the music was always good. Bill and Paulette played for these parties, until the marriage dissolved and we made other arrangements.

Very soon after I left Dalfort in 1989, I learned that my good friend Carl Maas had passed away. He wasn't an old man—probably in his 60's. I was so sorry; he was a favorite of mine. I'd met him years before when he came to school at Stephen's Aircraft School.

I'd had him go and get his DME so he could do the practical exams for my school. I never knew a more honest, and great man in everything. In the words of Bobby Moore, another great friend of mine, "May his tribe increase!"

A man who worked for Dalfort after we had the school in Dallas at Love Field was Gene Eubanks. He finished his course, and got a school of his own close to McKinney.

Sherman and I visited him and his wife there. They were living in a trailer home, and he wasn't having much luck with his school. Later, he moved the school to Idabel, Oklahoma, within sight of Highway 70 where Robert and Omia lived. He had a small facility, and I was not excited about the school. It was small and inadequate. Gene was a great guy, but had a really explosive temper, which is not good when you're dealing with students in a school atmosphere. Or maybe any other time. He got his DME license, which meant he could give practical exams, and it opened doors for him. This was after Carl Maas' death. Another former instructor and DME was Fred Shannon.

Gene was a likable fellow. He was a large man and friendly, usually nice and congenial, but when stirred up could become testy, to say the least. He cursed all the time, and I cringed when he did. I've always hated to hear cursing when God's name is used, but I liked Gene and tried not to hear it. I had been teaching a class at night at a facility in Arlington, and had a class of about 6 or 7, including twins Mike and Larry who became my good friends. Mike did love the aviation program, but Larry, not so much. They were taking the short course. Mike had a little more experience than Larry, so I knew him better. He was a young man, married, and a little later became the father of a beautiful little boy. He brought him to my house once, and I fixed lunch for them, and Phil and Sherry, and helped Mike get a letter for Larry to get his approval to take the test.

Sherman and I went to Idabel for two reasons: one was to take a headstone for my sister Addie's grave. She had been buried beside Daddy a few months before that. I'd gotten a small headstone for her, but Sherman wasn't able to lift much anymore, and Mike needed to go to Idabel to take his practical. We went in my Toyota, and Mike and Larry followed in Mike's truck. We went straight to the cemetery, and they put the headstone at her head. There was no cement yet; someone did that later. But the two put the headstone there, and it was set in concrete later. Mike, Larry, Sherman and I got rooms at the motel for the night.

I checked on them in the morning at Gene's school, and Mike was doing well. We had visited with Gene the night we got there. Mike passed his practical, but Larry wasn't eligible yet; he hadn't passed all his tests. Gene tried to help him, but didn't think he showed much ability or skill. Gene took us to lunch, and we had pizza. Sherman preferred to stay with Robert and Omia, and we drove home that evening.

Mike went to work in aviation, but I don't think Larry ever finished getting his license, although I would have taught him here at my house. I guess he lost interest. I haven't heard anything about the two brothers lately. The last word

I had from Mike was that he was a volunteer fireman for a city close by, and loved doing that. His wife was a nurse. What a good student and a nice guy!

I guess my retirement has finally been sure. I don't get students any more, except the IA renewals. But a little competition has come along, and the ones who need this course have retired, themselves, and a number of them have not been able to work at their jobs any more. Some of them have gone into other trades where the work is not so demanding.

But I am still interested and willing to help any of them who come to me. Aviation will always play a large part of my life, and so will my students. I don't see many of them any more, but my heart will always be in the schools where I've been teaching and the industry that has been so much a large part of my life. Also, the ones who worked with me, including Gary, Raymond, Reuben, Charlie, and of course, Bill and Paulette. There are others without whom I could not have accomplished what we accomplished together. I appreciate certain people in the FAA—you know who you are.

For the final chapter of this book, there are several friends, relatives, and ex-students who have written notes to me. Some of these people are in my church, some from my former churches, and friends who stand by me. God has been so good to let me share their love through the years. I can't do the work I used to do, as an old lady, but one thing can never be taken away from us. That is the love for others, as we know the Bible says, "Love one another, for love is of God."

Sometimes, I guess a person spends their whole life looking forward to a particular event or accomplishment. I was raised on a farm with no definite training or ambition in mind to prepare for. People just seemed to fall into something or other. Ambition wasn't aimed at a goal out there somewhere. I think all little girls dream of being a nurse, a singer, or a famous actress; sometimes a wife and mother, having a family and children, and I'm sure I wasn't the only one with all these dreams at different times. I planned to be a famous singer, maybe an actress, and a business executive, accomplishing much, being rich. And, yes, I would be a writer of songs and novels. But I married early, one week after I was 17. I happily raised a family, and had a husband who was a marble mason. He gained the admiration of people who enjoyed his work, and they appreciated his long hours of labor. He always took pride in the buildings he worked on, despite the heavy lifting, but saw that his artistic ability showed in every piece of the beautiful marble he carefully installed.

Shortly after the 3 children started to school, I began to get just a little restless. I started to think about doing some work close to home during school hours. I never thought much about making money, although we needed an extra income. I wasn't trained for anything, and didn't think I'd make more than a very few dollars per week. I could always sew, and loved to keep children, but didn't try to find anything. I'd never hunted a job before, and wouldn't have had any confidence to do so. I hadn't finished high school, but had gotten my GED. I did pretty well on that. Later on, I got through tests for Junior Federal Assistant, which I knew would help me if I ever wanted to be a guard at a federal institution. It was completely unattractive to me.

I started working at James Clardy's cleaners, close to home, just while the kiddos were in school. I did alterations and some of everything else, so when he got sick, I could carry on and do everything. He hired a girl in my place. I worked at a few other cleaners, but didn't feel like I was satisfied. I was very happy when our good friend, Alton Stephens, asked me to go to work with him, starting an A&P school.

I was sorry Dot, his wife, didn't like my going to work for him, but he helped me to get going on a real career. I made very little money, but learned so much, and was happy to learn so I could eventually start teaching.

Aviation was wonderful to me. I was so glad to get into it, although a little fearful at first.

To be expected to explain a process to people who have already worked on aircraft and who are waiting to have it demonstrated is a little daunting.

So I studied.
And studied.
And researched.
And asked Steve.
He knew a lot, but sometimes couldn't answer. He waited, sometimes for me to find the answer and explain it to him. The books we sometimes used hadn't been available when he'd studied for his own tests. And Steve was one of those guys who knew enough about the subjects to talk his way through without a definite answer.

An ex-student told me this recently: "Pauline you were a good teacher because you explained things to us. You learned to teach us what we needed, and didn't try to be smart, but to stay on our level enough that we could understand you and the subject. That's why you were a great teacher."

This is what I appreciated. Who could ever hear sweeter words from an ex-student? I'm so thankful to so many. Lord, thank You for helping me, and for having a plan for me, and for the wonderful people who continued to come and seek help, to make their own lives a little fuller, and to help me to be led by Your Holy Spirit to do the teaching You wanted me to do. And in the process, to send me some of the most wonderful friends I could ever have.

I had a few lady students. One who made quite an impression on me was Shirley, who owned her own business. It was a dope and fabric operation. There were several of these businesses, normally run by men. So hers was unusual. She'd named it "Mudflap Aviation" for whatever reason; she didn't know why. She obviously did quite well. Later, her husband was sent to Germany for the company he worked for, and she moved her company there too. I hear from her by e-mail, and she is still working for herself in "Mudflap Aviation," currently re-covering a tri-pacer. She and her husband have three nearly grown children, and are doing fine. I just had a long letter from her, but didn't find a paragraph to include with the messages that follow in the last chapter.

After I'd started receiving these messages, I called and talked to my former pastor and good friend, Bro. Charles Russell. He can talk fine, despite the fact that he is 86 and can't hear well. I called him again this morning, and found out they are in an assisted living place, he and his wife. I was surprised, but he said they'd been there for some time. I have a call in to someone who can help me to find them, and I'll visit them. When I told him I wanted to put a message from him in my book, he reminded me that we have been close friends for many years. And we have; 65 years since he baptized me. We expressed our love for each other, and I'm planning to visit them. I'm praying for them, and love them dearly.

Chapter 20

Letters

The following is a collection of messages I received from friends, relatives, and ex-students, and also some people who have gone to church with me through the years. I have been very close to these dear people, and am glad to put their messages in this last chapter of "The Other One". These messages are in this chapter as I received them.

Ken Elliott is my great friend, from 1980. We found each other after 31 years! We sing together frequently.

> God issues time to us. We may use it as we choose. He would like for us to praise Him with that time. As we get older, we would like to save, or hold that time. Those with much wisdom write poems, lyrics, or books, to grasp time forever: Pauline Ruffin has succeeded.

C L Shelton and his wife Clara are good friends, and he is director of our Sweet Spirit Singers.

> I have known Pauline for a few years, and I have enjoyed being around her. I admire her Christian walk with the Lord Jesus Christ. I like her "What you see is what you get" attitude. Thank you Pauline for asking me to share these words in this book. Your friend in Christ.

Laurine Graves is my brother Louis's daughter, sweet niece.

Pauline, when I think of you, I smile. Your sense of humor is always there. Even in hard times and sad, your faith shows through. You have been a blessing to me all my life. I treasure our times together and can't wait for more. I love you very much.

Tim Farmer's family went to Broadview. He and Pam are now at First Baptist, Watauga.

Hello, m'lady!

Some of the most memorable times in my life were when I was a member at Broadview Baptist, during the late '50's, through the early '60's. I met my best friends there, Ronnie Deviney, Tony Clark, and the Partains, Dennis and Curtis. We were the adventurous. types, always into something, most of which I would never dare to try again; however, I'm extremely proud to say that we never did anything illegal, malicious, hurtful or harmful to anyone. We always sat together in church, knowing that, if we were irreverent in any manner, during worship service, our ever watchful and strict disciplinarian parents were within seeing and hearing distance.

One of our bunch sometimes pushed the envelope a little; his name I won't mention right now, but one time, during a prayer, eyes closed, I felt something brush by my foot, so I cracked one eye, to see what it was. The culprit was lying on the floor, rolling back and forth beneath the pews like a log. Another time, the same person, during collection of tithes and offerings, when the collection plate was passed to him, he held a large coin, high above the plate, and dropped it in on its edge, into the wooden plate. There was a loud "Clunk" sound, and for some silly reason, it cracked all of us up. That was probably the most effort I ever put into trying to not make a sound, when I laughed.

It was during this era, circa 1963, that I met a girl, on the other side of town, who lived on the same block, as 4 other girls. She and I began to date, and I introduced my 43 buddies to her 4 girl friends. The 5 of us, and the 5 of them dated and cross dated. I ended up with the same girls I'd met in 1963, and 50 years later, she and I are still together. We were the only two of the group that married, but there were some endearing relationships. During those years, among the 2 groups. God has blest these relationships with family and good health. Unfortunately, things didn't always turn out so well for my friends. My best friend, Ronnie Diviney died tragically in a freak dune buggy accident in 2008.Whoever would have thought, after surviving Vietnam and all the dumb, dangerous things we did as teenagers, and survived with only scratches, a few scars and broken bones, that Ronnie would die when he was only 60 years old?

I thank God every day, for my life, and that I've survived this long, by the great sacrifice of His Son, His Grace and His love for me, Dennis and Curtis survived Vietnam: Curtis was wounded, and Dennis has Multiple Sclerosis. Tony Clark was doing well the last I heard from him. Three of the girls have been called Home, and one is retired, and living in Ireland. I am blessed to be with the one I started with. I can honestly say that my success and happiness are deeply rooted in one of the most critical years of a young person's life, during formative years at Broadview Baptist Church. Oh, I could go on for pages and pages in your book, about the life and times of Tim Farmer, Ronnie Diviney, Tony Clark, Dennis and Curtis Partain.

I remember fellowships so many times at your house, Pauline, and in retrospect, I hope that whatever shenanigans we were up to didn't happen at those times. I also remember the many other friends, that I made during that period, and remember that my folks made friends there and we enjoyed many fellowships there at the church and homes of others.

That part of town, Sansom Park, along the infamous stretch of Jacksboro Highway, was an opportunity just waiting to happen to take a wrong turn that could've led to a different life, but in the midst of those opportunities, God had a tighter rein on us, and it led to where we are now, which I'm humbled by, and eternally grateful to our Lord God for. When we left the North side/Sansom Park area, to live in Southlake, we were members of First Baptist Church in Keller for years. Circumstances changed, and the Good Lord led us back to the Saginaw area, and FBC, Watauga. You can't imagine my excitement when you and I met again after all these years. I am truly blessed. Many memories from fun times at Broadview Baptist, and the people associated with those times, continue to flow through my mind, and you are probably one of the top memories for me, all good! Have a blessed day!

Tim Farmer

Terry Thompson (dba The Sign Post) is my good friend from Broadview.

Pauline Ruffin has been many things to me in my life. She was a wonderful teacher who taught me about God. As a Choir

Director, she taught me about music. She was a wonderful confidant, secretary, and friend to my Dad, Bob Thompson.

She has been a great customer and a great friend to me throughout my career. I will always love and respect her as a wonderful example of a fine Christian lady.

Jann Harris is my nephew Dan's step-daughter, my hairdresser.

Pauline, an aunt by marriage. We like to claim each other, and confuse people all we can. I've had so much fun with her in the time I've known her. God bless you, "Aunt Pauline"

Donny Crites is a deacon at First Baptist, Watauga and a good friend.

Pauline,

You are part of the reason that makes life enjoyable. Your stories, your wit and your sense of humor can put a smile on anyone's face. Your caring heart is as warm and sweet as a Ginger Brown cinnamon roll. Judy and I wish you much success with your book, and we look forward to reading it.

Betty Scala is Activities Director at Manor Care.

I am so thankful to be able to call Pauline a fantastic volunteer, and also a fantastic friend. She brings a ray of sunshine to all. Pauline, I want to thank you for all you do, and for bringing joy to everyone you meet.

Brenda Rash is a member of First Baptist, and a good friend.

> Pauline is a powerhouse in a little body. I've loved her sweetness ever since we met, years ago. Don't be fooled, however, she has a wickedly sharp sense of humor. Yes, my dear, you may quote me. I love you.

> Good Friends,

Richard and Chere Bradford are good friends. He's a deacon at First Baptist, Watauga.

> Hey, lady! We are so proud of you for hanging in there and getting your book completed. We are so blessed to know you, and can't wait to read it! You have to include something about your one-liners. I've always said you have more jokes that come out at any given moment than a standup comedian. You have an incredible sense of humor, and everyone loves you! Especially us!

June Tyndall Woodall was a fellow member of the youth at Broadview, and sang in the youth choir.

> In the 1960's Broadview Baptist Church began forming something that time would never be able to erase. The Church is no longer in existence; many members have passed on to their Heavenly reward. Many more of us have moved away from our former home of that time period. But what began then still continues today in the hearts of each of us that were a part of that fantastic happening. The "Youth" of that church, and adult leaders formed a relationship that still continues to this very day. I have no real explanation as to why this link among all of us became so strong, except to say

that it truly was a special gift of love from our Lord. I'm so very thankful I was allowed to be a part of an ever giving blessing. I love each and every one of you as much today as I did back then. May God continue to bless us all.

Sandra Evans edits the church paper. She and her husband, Jay (a deacon) are good friends.

> My husband Jay and I love our sweet and spunky Ms. Pauline! What a hoot she is! Always the comedian. I told her she reminds me of Phyllis Diller, because she is so quick witted!
>
> I remember when I first met Ms. Pauline. We were working a sign up sheet together at Church, and got to know each other a little bit, and she told me that she taught Airline Mechanics. I was floored and totally impressed! How cool is that? I also found out how much fun she was, and how active and out-going she was to be "older", (and I say that with much respect)
>
> From what I've seen, she is such a servant to the Lord, too, with all her visits to nursing homes to sing and visit. In a nutshell, Ms. Pauline is a pure joy to know, and we love her very much.

Carol Tyndall Childress was a fellow member of the youth at Broadview, and sang in the youth choir.

> Pauline, I will never forget all the times you and Sherman invited us into your home. Being a teacher to a group of teenagers in the '70's couldn't have been easy. My life will never be the same, thanks to you and the rest of our youth

group and leaders who grew up together as members of Broadview!

Kenneth Shiro is my brother, Robert's son, a super nephew.

If I had to describe my favorite aunt in a word, I think it would be "genuine". By that, I mean she's always the same warm, funny human being, regardless of who she is with. It is a very endearing and rare quality that makes me very proud to call her my aunt!

Tim Ballog is my good friend and deacon at First Baptist, Watauga.

Pauline has a genuine love and zeal for life. If you are having a 'down' day, it won't last long if you are around Pauline. Her smiles are so contagious, that you can't resist smiling. I haven't even had a chance to read her book, but I don't have to, because I know the warmth and wit of Pauline that she already shares with us. Whether by reading her book, or meeting her in person, you will know how special Pauline is.

Linda Jones Baker was my next door neighbor and a good friend at Broadview.

Pauline, you are a woman who made a HUGE difference in my life and helped me obtain eternal life. It was you who prayed for my salvation, and led me to Christ. You made sure that I had a ride to and from church and all the related activities. You were always there when I needed to talk to someone. Your house was always open to me, and I spent many happy childhood hours there playing with your kids. I always felt like our two families were as close as any relatives could possibly be. Our famous fence meeting place between our houses where Thom and I would come to visit holds a lot of good memories. I remember how patient you were when you guys got a TV before we did, and always invited us over, for "Howdy Doody Time". You were always a very important part of my life, growing up, and the best neighbor anyone could have.

Elbert DK Mitchell (We called him Pete) was a good friend and neighbor. We grew up together and had desks next to each other at school.

The first time I knew of the Fagan's I was with my Dad, and we came by your place in a wagon. You all were living in a tent. Your Dad had a pair of mules, one gray, and one brown. I was about 5 years old. Your Dad built a two story house. Some time later, it burned down. Then your Dad built a log house. I don't know the years this happened. I was helping your Dad put mud in the spaces between the logs, when he was building the log house; you made me some ginger bread cookies. Sure were good.

A few years later, Mr. and Mrs. Fagan would give a party for the kids in the neighborhood, and sometimes, your Mother would play the mandolin and you and Margaret would sing, and we would play games.

People would give dances and parties in the neighborhood. We had to make our own entertainment. I feel like I am a better person being raised around the Fagan's. Harrell's Rice's, Colliers, and Lands. They were all good honest hard working people, and helped each other, including my Dad and Mother.

Paul Michael Vacca is a good friend and associate pastor at First Baptist, Watauga.

> Pauline is high on life! She approaches life with a sense of humor that gives a much needed perspective to any situation. One word of advice.........Just don't believe anything she says!

Cindy Suffka is a member of First Baptist, Watauga and a good friend.

> Pauline, you are such a joy to be with and talk to. Thank you for always having a bright, humorous outlook on life, and enjoying every moment. You are a true inspiration! Love your spirit!

Janet Steppick is Johnnie Hooper's daughter, a dear friend, and my neighbor.

> Pauline Ruffin is a woman who was at the front of the line when challenged to tackle something new and exciting. After all, deciding to be an aircraft mechanic is not normally what the woman of today would have chosen. Her dedication through the years to so many calls for her time and talents have enriched the lives of so many people, it's hard to recollect the details. She has always put others before herself, and served the Lord, and others in so many ways. When my Mom passed away, I know Dad was so lost and miserable (after 61 years of marriage) and there was a big hole in his heart that needed to be filled. And then came

Pauline! Hooray! Pauline made him light up like a Christmas tree when she entered the room. The family watched as Dad broadened his interests, and pursued activities that he would never have enjoyed otherwise', due to Pauline's desire to live life to the fullest.

They enjoyed attending church together, and it's activities, including music programs, took road trips, and charming places to eat---Not that they needed to go out to eat, Pauline is an excellent cook. When Dad's health began to fail, Pauline was always a loving companion, and he always looked forward to seeing her. His many falls resulted in his needing to reside in an assisted living facility, and you could see Pauline there, most days. She also made visits to those who had no family or friends, and volunteered to help with activities. She, and some of her Church members came to sing and uplift the spirits of all, especially on holidays. She has always been very active at Church sometimes teaching a class, or singing in the choir.

Dad lived to be 94 years old, and I have been so thankful for the many years Pauline has been his faithful companion. Over the years, I have grown to love Pauline, and we still try to keep in touch and spend time together. I can only hope that I will have the same stamina and perseverance as she has shown through the years.

By the way, Dad's sister, Irene, lived by Pauline when they were young, and my aunt took me to Pauline's when I was too young to remember. So we have had a long connection during our lives.

May the Lord continue to bless Pauline as she has blessed so many during her lifetime.

Lesley Cook, my sweet granddaughter, lives in Williamsburg, VA.

> I have so many wonderful memories of you, Grandmother. My favorites are as a little girl, spending the night at your house, on Saturday nights. We would sew, play Hi Ho Cheerio, or dominoes, or watch Hee-Haw. I would go shopping with you and GrandDaddy to get the food for our family meal served at your house after Church every Sunday afternoon. Those meals were the best. Baked ham and Ritz crackers chicken were my favorites. After the meal, we would bake bread or pies. You always made me feel so special when you made me an "uncoconut Pie" because I can't stand coconut. As an adult I have enjoyed many visits at your house and mine, and have tried to figure out and write down the "exact" recipe for your wonderful rolls, but somehow, we never have seemed to figure that out. That's OK, because it just gives us another opportunity to try again! Nevertheless, my kids have also grown to love your pies, cinnamon rolls, rolls, and pie crust sticks! You are a wonderful Grandmother and Great Grandmother. Congratulations on your book! I am so proud of you and I love you so much!

Donna Bolton is a great friend who used to live across the street, but moved to Keller.

> What a special friend you are to me! I couldn't have a better neighbor to feed me pie, and other homemade goodies over coffee! You were always trying to feed me something yummy. Hard to be on a diet around you!

I think your profession surprised me as much as anyone I know! Who would have believed that a cute little lady over 75 years would be an airplane mechanic instructor! At least that's what you told me about the men that came in and out of your house during the day.........continuing education????

You were ready to go at any time, to eat at a fun place, or go anywhere, especially to Johnny High's theater. We both love music! You truly are an amazing woman----for any age!

Thank you for being my special friend. I always knew I could ask you for any kind of help and you would be there for me! Blessings to you in all you do! Can't wait to read your book and find out more about the incredible woman across the street! Love you!

Kenneth C. Bino is a good friend who lives down the street.

After knowing Pauline for several years, I can say that there is a great deal of shared wisdom in her heart. It has truly been a blessing to visit for hours, and listen to the most amazing stories of her life. The greatest joy in being young is to listen to those that experienced the life we missed, and the wisdom included in it. Pauline is just such a person, full of life, love, and joy.

Adam Ruffin is my first Grandson! Great guy, now pilot and diver!

I love you Grandmother! You were my introduction and inspiration to work with, and fly aircraft.

Sharon Thatcher Simpson is a sweet girl and friend of my family from Sansom Park.

> Pauline, love that you are publishing a book. I have great memories of Paulette, Phil, and the fun times we had together. Love your family.

Mildred Morris is a dear friend from First Baptist, Watauga.

> PAULINE WROTE A BOOK!

> Well, why not? She is quite a character. The first time I saw Pauline, I thought she was a very attractive lady. It did not take long for me to realize that she was a very interesting person who loved the Lord, music, and people and is always ready to share a kind word, a hug, or a bit of wit.

> I count myself blessed to be one of her many friends and look forward to reading her book.

Nicole and Matt Sherrick are dear friends and neighbors.

> It was early spring of 2008, and I was out walking, with my oldest daughter, Lily, when I came upon a sweet, sweet woman, sitting in her car. Concerned that she needed help, I stopped to check on her only to find that she was just fine, and waiting on a friend. After a brief conversation about politics, and finding we had so much in common, we swapped names and I informed her that I lived nearby, and would come and visit her. I could say "the rest is history", but her friendship is too important to leave out the details. My daughter, Lily and I began visiting her on a regular basis. We

baked pies, sticky buns, and rolls together. Over Christmas holidays, we made her famous and fabulous candy, which, by the way, has the most unusual name you'll ever hear; "Chocolate Candy"!

In 2009, she shared in our excitement and joy as I expected our second baby, Larissa. While pregnant, she taught me how to make ponchos; of course, I think she did most of the work! Over the past few years, we've shared many laughs and meals together. Then, when I was expecting baby #3, and finding out it was a boy, Levi, she was happy for us again. Due to the business of motherhood, I don't get to visit as often as I like, or should, but I'm still so very thankful for the gift God has given me in her dear friendship!

Bro. Ray and Joyce Simpson now live in Mississippi. He served as music and youth director, and she was pianist at Broadview.

While at school (SW Seminary) in Fort Worth, our best part was when we moved to Sansom Park, where Ray began serving in the Broadview Baptist Church; there, we met the Ruffin's, Pauline and her family immediately took to our family. Our youngest son, Steve called her "Paulie". She always wanted to take him home with her. Her whole family was so special to us. We still have a wonderful friendship, after 53 years, all the jokes and funny things she says, and does. Steve is 56 yrs. old and still calls her "Paulie". We all love that girl!

LaVerne Lebow Griggs is my sister Ruby's daughter, a sweet niece. She heard me talk to her dad, Vernon, about the Lord when she was a child, and listened to me.

> The part of Pauline's life that I always remember, and am thankful for, is her love for the Lord, and the way she has always won other people to Him. She witnessed to my Dad, and in the process, caused me to give my life to Jesus.

Janice, LaVerne's sister, says:

> The same goes for me too. Pauline. I love you.

I love you too, girls!-

Jimmie Youree is a great Sunday school teacher at FBC. He and Patti Ann are in our adult class.

> Pauline is a wonderful Christian woman, and it is a pleasure having you in our Sunday School Class the past few years. "The Young at heart" attitude and the wit you bring to life sets an example for all of us. Thank you so much for being my friend and sharing your life history with us from time to time. The Youree's love you.

Kevin Skinner is pastor of the children's ministry at FBC. He is a super bass singer.

> I have had the pleasure of knowing Pauline through First Baptist Church of Watauga. In the time that I have known her, I have learned that joy, beauty, and a young Spirit know no

age. Pauline is an inspiration with her continued enthusiasm for Aviation, as well as music. One of my favorite things to do is to sing with Pauline. I am not able to sing with the Sweet Spirit Singers as often as I would like, because of conflicting meetings, but I can be sure that anytime I join them, I will be met with a great big smile, and a hug from Pauline. We sit together, sing together, and worship our Savior together.

Many people might say the older generation is outdated, and might not even give them the time of day, but, in my experience with Pauline, the older generation has wisdom to spare, and through the passing of their knowledge, we will stay grounded in our future, and, most importantly, in our Faith.

Alan Cook has been my good friend since 1974.

I met Pauline in the fall of 1974. I had been in Vietnam, and came to Fort Worth to get my Airframe and Powerplant License. A gentleman I worked with in Vietnam, had attended Pauline's School, and highly recommended it. It was an interesting class, because I learned a lot of stuff that I would have absolutely no use for in my area of expertise. Never-the-less, I graduated with honors, so much that Pauline invited me to teach some of her classes after I got my license.

Of course, life got in the way, and we lost touch with each other for several years. In 1989, I had a bone marrow transplant at Baylor, Dallas. Afterward, I began volunteering to talk to family members and patients that were undergoing treatment. One evening Nov. '93, I introduced myself to a lady, having no idea it was Pauline sitting with her. I told her my name, and Pauline looked at me and said, "Are you MY Alan Cook?" This was one of those moments in life that you never forget. Paulette was undergoing a transplant for breast cancer and I had had the opportunity to sing high harmony with Paulette, when we listened to tapes. This was particularly touching, since I didn't know I could sing when we first knew each other. Paulette was an amazing woman, with a gorgeous voice, and a great witness to her faith.

Since then, Pauline and I have kept in touch. She always comes to my Super Bowl and Christmas parties, and, on occasion, we get together at the Country Music Show, in Arlington. Through God's Grace, we were able to re-unite again, and it has been a joy to have her in my life.

Boni Fraustro was my business partner, 1994-95.

I found, in Pauline, a very dear friend, who loves her Lord, her Church, her children and grand children and all her family, also her students, who have meant so much to her. She is a very good business woman.

Charles Ray Stephens has been my good friend from his childhood. He and his family have been my neighbors, co-workers, and fellow church members.

I'm 67 years old, I have known Pauline since I was very young. She has been my Sunday School teacher, Training Union Leader, and neighbor. I worked with Pauline for many years. Pauline is the most unforgettable character I have ever known. No one who ever met her has forgotten her. Her kindness, thoughtfulness, and teaching through my growing up years have been remarkable. I love her. I think the world of her. She was an active part of my life from age 6 to age 23.

Karen Griggs is the wife of my great-nephew, Jeff Griggs. Great singer.

Our dear Aunt Pauline, always the one to find the third part harmony & did it with such grace and accuracy!

Jim and Donna Foote are good friends from church.

My husband, Jim, and I met Pauline and Johnny Hooper at church. We liked them both immediately. Pauline & I walked and talked at North Hills Mall. Afterward we would have a cup of tea together.

She has a beautiful singing voice and loves to sing to the Lord to make life brighter. She has had many adventures and always has a funny story to tell. She loves to make people laugh.
We love you.

Lea York is a very good friend of mine who works in Dr. Kallal's office:

There are no words to describe Ms. Pauline Ruffin. She was one of the first patients I came in contact with after starting with Dr. Kallal, and very soon became one of my favorites. It doesn't matter how bad she feels or what is going on in her life, she always comes to see us with a smile, make-up on, and hair done. Ms. Ruffin is so fun to listen to, she has done so many things in her life and I have gotten myself in trouble a few times for talking with her too long. No matter how bad the day, as soon as she comes in it makes all the bad things go away. She is a ray of sunshine, and my favorite patient.

Lea York
Medical Assistant

Lea York is a very good friend of mine who works in Dr. Kallal's office:

All who read this life story will meet one of the most inspiring, uplifting ladies around. Ms. Pauline Ruffin spent years training airline personnel when women just didn't have those positions. Oh, the stories she can share. She continues to minister to others. I had the wonderful opportunity to witness her love for others as she sang for a local nursing home. She has spent a lifetime helping others all the while with a contagious smile on her face. You are going to love her as much as I do.

Sharon
Dr. Kallal's office